A CENTURY OF TRAN

STUDIES OF WORLD MIGRATIONS

Donna R. Gabaccia and Leslie Page Moch, editors

A list of books in the series appears at the end of the book.

A CENTURY OF TRANSNATIONALISM

Immigrants and Their Homeland Connections

EDITED BY
NANCY L. GREEN
AND ROGER WALDINGER

UNIVERSITY OF ILLINOIS PRESS

Urbana, Chicago, and Springfield

Library of Congress Cataloging-in-Publication Data
Names: Green, Nancy L., editor. | Waldinger, Roger David, editor.
Title: A century of transnationalism : immigrants and their homeland
    connections / edited by Nancy L. Green and Roger Waldinger.
Description: Urbana : University of Illinois Press, 2016. | Series: Studies of
    world migrations | Includes bibliographical references and index.
Identifiers: LCCN 2016004958 (print) | LCCN 2016016926 (ebook) | ISBN
    9780252040443 (cloth : alk. paper) | ISBN 9780252081903 (pbk. : alk.
    paper) | ISBN 9780252098864 (E-Book)
Subjects: LCSH: Transnationalism—History—20th century. | Emigration and
    immigration—Social aspects. | Immigrants—Cultural assimilation.
Classification: LCC JV6035 .C46 2016 (print) | LCC JV6035 (ebook) |
    DDC 305.9/06912—dc23
LC record available at https://lccn.loc.gov/2016004958

CONTENTS

ACKNOWLEDGMENTS

This book on transnationalism in historical perspective is a truly transnational effort, prompted and supported by funders, friends, and colleagues on both sides of the Atlantic. The project was launched by a conversation with Michel Wieviorka, who pointed us in the direction of a collaborative project on immigrant cross-border activity over the *longue durée* and promised that the Fondation de la Maison des Sciences de l'Homme (FMSH), of which he is the director, would provide support. As a historian based in Paris and a sociologist based in Los Angeles we thought that the recipe for success would lie in combining trans-Atlantic and transdisciplinary perspectives. We convened an initial such group for a conference held in Paris in May 2012, followed by a second similar event in Los Angeles in April 2013. Greatly revised versions of some of the papers presented in those two conferences appear in this book. A number of other colleagues participated in these gatherings, as either paper writers or commentators. We are especially grateful to César Ayala, Catherine Collomp, David Cook-Martin, Cecilia D'Ercole, David Gerber, Rubén Hernandez-Leon, Tobias Higbie, Rebecca Kobrin, Dan Lainer-Vos, Emmanuel Ma Mung, Ewa Morawska, José Moya, Constance Pâris de Bollardière, Hector Perla, Paul-André Rosental, Guido Tintori, Andreas Wimmer, Florence Vychytil-Baudoux, Min Zhou, and Jean-Paul Zuñiga, whose contributions greatly enriched our discussions. Donna Gabaccia and Leslie Page Moch, coeditors of the University of Illinois Press series Studies of World Migrations, early saw merit in this project; their confidence and that of the Press's editors provided much needed support from early stages right through the end.

We are also grateful to the colleagues who assisted with the practical aspects of this project, as well as the funders who made it possible. At the FMSH, Jean-Pierre Dozon provided guidance and helped mobilize resources.

Dana Diminescu, the director of the FMSH program on Migration and In-formation Technology and Communication, also provided the opportunity and resources for an invaluable collaboration. She suggested organizing a joint event on "Homeland Connections," which resulted in stimulating parallel sessions on the E-Diaspora Atlas that she coordinated and pre-sented to the public at this conference, and our own sessions on A Century of Transnationalism. Thanks also to Luc Gruson, Marianne Amar, and the Cité Nationale de l'Histoire de l'Immigration, Paris, which hosted our May 2012 conference. In addition, invaluable material support was provided during 2012–2013 by the FMSH and the Consulat général de France à Los Angeles as well as a variety of entities at our own institutions: at the École des Hautes Études en Sciences Sociales, the Centre de Recherches Histo-riques, and the Division of Research Development; and at the University of California, Los Angeles, the International Institute, the UCLA Program on International Migration, the Burkle Center for International Relations, the Center for European and Eurasian Studies, the Centre Pluridisciplinaire, and the Department of History.

Last, we thank one another!—for the many years of enjoyable and stimu-lating conversation leading up to this volume and for the collegiality and friendship that made this particular endeavor a pleasure from beginning to end.

A CENTURY OF TRANSNATIONALISM

Introduction

Roger Waldinger and Nancy L. Green

Immigrants were once known as "uprooted." Later, they became seen as "transplanted," reflecting a new scholarly appreciation of the ways in which social networks facilitated migration.[1] Today, the "discovery" of "transnationalism" has transformed migration studies again. Ubiquitously invoked to describe mobility present and past, the term has been used to show how international migration generates ideas, goods, and civil and political engagements spilling across national boundaries.

Though immensely influential, the transnational perspective has also generated great controversy, with questions related to change consistently yielding dispute. Initially, scholars asserted that the home country connections of contemporary international migrants were unprecedented, with many contending that transnationalism was a late-twentieth-century phenomenon fueled by new modes of communication and transportation. Historians instantly countered: the last age of mass migration entailed a similar transoceanic ebb and flow of people, goods, and ideas; likewise, many nationalist movements were born in exile, which is why a contemporary immigrant preoccupation with homeland politics represents nothing new. While that response elicited general agreement, debate over the novelty of transnationalism continued, without, however, fully meeting the challenge of thinking through long-term patterns. In many assessments of the historical record, the starting point entails an opposition between "now" and "then," yet that contrast takes for granted what needs to be explained: we need to know when and why "now" began and "then" ended—crucial questions that have not seriously been posed. Moreover, the many migration experiences seem too great to fit into any one scheme: period boundaries are likely to take a variety of forms, depending on the precise connection between place of origin and place of destination. How then to describe and analyze change over time?

The nature of the core claims and the underlying theoretical framework have also triggered debate. To some extent, the very term "transnational" is unfortunate: it collapses state and nation, one referring to a political unit, the other to a social collectivity. The crossing of state boundaries fundamentally differentiates international from internal migrations: in the latter, migrants change places *within* a state; in the former, the migrants go *between* states. Moreover, while migrants' cross-state connections sometimes extend "beyond the nation" (as implied by the Latin prefix *trans*), they usually do not. Instead, those ties often tend to take highly particularistic form, linking up a particular category of people "here" to some specific set of people "there." The "home" to which the migrants prove attached is as likely—if not more so—to involve the village, region, or even ethnic minority of origin, as opposed to the sending state or the imagined nation to whom that state is presumed to belong. And for that reason, local memories of the place left behind may be more salient to the migrant than patriotic or sentimental attachments to the abstract entity of the nation never personally experienced.

Furthermore, the "transnational" concept conflates history and historiography, mixing the behavior of a panoply of actors—in our case, migrants, states of emigration and immigration, and nationals on both sides of the chain—with the interpretations and concepts offered by social scientists in their efforts to understand those activities.[2] As *history*, we understand "transnational" as referring to the cross-border feedbacks produced by international migrations, encompassing the circulation of ideas, information, resources, political and communal engagements, as well as the sending and receiving state responses that these patterns of circulation trigger. As *historiography*, the concept refers to a sensibility to this myriad of cross-border phenomena. The transnational literature is a way of seeing, one that enlarges the boundaries of inquiry to include both sending *and* receiving states and thus goes beyond the historiography and sociology of *immigration* with its single-minded focus on the state and society of reception.

As so defined, this book adopts a transnational optic; however, *transnational* does not necessarily imply *transnationalism*, as the latter entails a claim about the nature of the phenomena extending across borders and the ties between places of origin and destination. As articulated by Linda Basch, Nina Glick Schiller, and Cristina Szanton Blanc in their pathbreaking book, *Nations Unbound*, one particularly influential view sees the transnational as yielding and constituting transnationalism, with immigrants

> developing and elaborating transnational practices that allow them to remain incorporated in their country of origin while simultaneously becoming incorporated in the United States.[3]

But whether the transnational leads to transnationalism—and if so, when and under what conditions—is precisely the question at issue. Some migrants may behave just as described in *Nations Unbound*, but not all do. In general, migrants vary in their effective capacity to retain cross-border ties across space as well as time. While international migrations yield subsequent chains of circulation between communities of destination and origin, those patterns of circulation also trigger reactions from both sending and receiving states; as states and emigrants respond to different motivations, opportunities, and constraints, the study of the transnational needs to extend beyond the activities of the migrants themselves. Moreover, emigrants' spatial cross-border activities, whether those involving everyday activities such as travel and communication or more concerted efforts, such as those associated with homeland-oriented, emigrant politics, can be held back by states. Hence, migrants may be constrained from pursuing or implementing transnational activities, let alone transnational*ism* as defined above.

Migration is a transformative experience, in turn affecting the phenomena circulating after borders have first been crossed. Migration changes the migrants, giving them resources not previously possessed; consequently, their efforts to engage across borders have the potential to turn the broad range of cross-border interactions—whether involving homeland kin, communities, or states—into arenas of conflict; those strains sometimes yield splits, whether taking the form of divisions among co-ethnics "abroad" or cleavages between emigrants, on the one hand, and sending states and stay-behinds, on the other. And change over time, possibly resulting from specific events such as wars or more general shifts in international relations, can render transnational activities sensitive to short-, as well as long-term, fluctuations. Hence, the stability, intensity, and meaning of migrants' cross-border activities cannot be taken for granted but rather belong at the heart of the analysis.

This book seeks to build on both the contributions and critiques of the transnational perspective in order to shed new light on the cross-border activities of migrants and states over the past century and more, emphasizing changing circumstances and changing practices over the *longue durée*. By bringing together a group of historically minded sociologists and sociologically minded historians, we look at migrants' transnational practices under an expanded temporal framework—easily showing that they are not a turn-of-the-twenty-first-century phenomenon. In so doing, we also demonstrate that the pattern of historical change is far more complicated than the now-then contrasts that have thus far preoccupied scholarly discussions. The essays present ample evidence of both continuity and change; they also show that change does not take a single linear form. Connections depend on immigrant practices, on home state policies, on settlement society conditions, on geopolitics and power relations between homeland and hostland. Consequently, the underlying influences may follow a variety of temporal sequences, with technology, the guiding "new" for many transnational theorists, possibly changing in a linear fashion but macro-political factors shifting in a more contingent, unpredictable way. Moreover, the phenomenon takes a dual form, involving, on the one hand, the extension of states across borders to connect with "their" emigrants and, on the other, the extension of emigrants across borders to connect with their place of origin.

Transnationalism in Historical Perspective

Transnationalism entered migration scholarship with a manifesto insisting that "our earlier conceptions of immigrant and migrant no longer suffice."[4] With these words, anthropologists Nina Glick Schiller, Linda Basch, and Cristina Blanc-Szanton simultaneously introduced a new intellectual perspective and identified the salient characteristic that distinguished contemporary migrations from those gone by. Though forcefully stated, the insistence on the novelty of the phenomenon actually got short shrift in their founding document. As the authors saw it, the source of the migrants' continuing dual orientation toward both home *and* host society stemmed from the ways in which the global restructuring of capitalism was producing dislocations on both ends of the chain, thus triggering emigration from the state of origin while impeding settlement in the state of destination. "Hence this vulnerability increased the likelihood that migrants would construct a transnational existence."[5] In this early text, the authors then quickly moved on to other matters, doing likewise in *Nations Unbound* (1994), their book-length effort to develop and then apply the transnational perspective.[6]

If the assertion about historical novelty was made in passing, historians immediately detected the argument that "in crucial respects . . . the present is not a replay of the past,"[7] which in turn became a mantra as a variety of prominent immigration scholars quickly took up the cry. In a 1997 article on "Immigration Theory for a New Century," sociologist Alejandro Portes, for example, contended that transnational activities "become a novel path of adaptation quite different from those found among immigrants at the turn of the century," a "path reinforced by technologies that facilitate rapid displacement across long distances and instant communication" as well as by the impact of globalization.[8] Other researchers associated with the transnational perspective, such as Peggy Levitt or Robert Smith, echoed that contention, likewise arguing that the transnational connections of the turn of the twenty-first century took an altogether distinctive form.[9] That view then became self-reinforcing as, for Alejandro Portes and his coauthors, the conviction that "the high intensity of exchanges, the new modes of transacting, and the multiplication of activities that require cross-border travel and contacts on a sustained basis" were "truly original phenomena" that made transnationalism "a justifiable new topic of investigation."[10]

Historians reacted in a variety of ways. Most frequently, they contended that the discipline had always been attentive to transnational phenomena, although not necessarily with the same terminology deployed by the anthropologists and sociologists. After all, the manifesto of modern immigration historiography, Frank Thistlethwaite's celebrated 1960 address, had insisted that the migrations of the turn of the *last* century entailed transoceanic, back-and-forth traffic of such amplitude that only some portion of the phenomenon fell into the standard categories of settlement and acculturation.[11] And just as the sociologists and anthropologists were "discovering" transnationalism, a trio of books, published in the early 1990s by historians Dino Cinel, Bruno Ramirez, and Mark Wyman, focusing on immigrant associational life, long-distance nationalism, and return migration at the turn of the twentieth century, underlined the many commonalities between "now" and "then."[12] Nonetheless, the very same historians of immigration who reacted skeptically to the *historical* proposition advanced by the scholars insisting on the novelty of transnationalism admitted that immigration *historiography* had not given the phenomenon the attention it deserved. Thus, historian David Gerber noted that the literature produced by such scholars as Cinel, Ramirez, and Wyman "has been compartmentalized to the extent that it has not influenced the larger narrative of immigration history."[13] As independently noted by the authors of two of the chapters to this book (David FitzGerald and Victor Pereira), as well as the historian coeditor,[14] the historians of immigration had long been talking about the transnational, albeit unknowingly, just like Monsieur Jourdain in Molière's *Le Bourgeois Gentilhomme*, who learned to his surprise that he had always been speaking in prose.

In pointing to continuities in historical transnational activities, Gerber also tweaked the writings of the transnationalists for "missing the opportunity to see the continuities over long historical time of the unfolding of mobility and opportunity across the world stage" and thereby failing "to assert their influence over immigration historiography."[15] Whereas Gerber principally looked backward, essays by anthropologist Nancy Foner and sociologist Ewa Morawska looked across periods to directly question the contention that transnationalism distinguished the mass migrations of the turn of the twenty-first century from those of the turn of the twentieth century. Both scholars sounded themes similar to the historians' critique. They underlined the many cross-border connections established by the earlier migrants from Europe, whether involving engagement with homeland politics, attention by homeland states, the sending of remittances, involvement in hometown associations, and return migration. Yet, each also insisted that "much is new about transnationalism,"[16] similarly emphasizing the greater acceptance of multiple allegiances, the spread of dual nationality, and the greater socio-economic diversity of the immigrant population, to which Morawska added the presence of "a growing army of marginalized 'illegal' migrants."[17]

Yet for all their subtlety and attention to historical detail, all of these efforts took the temporal boundaries between transnationalism "now and then" for granted. Much of the contemporary literature continues to emphasize the ways in which the instantaneity of contemporary communications technologies brings here and there together in ways that could not have been true during the last era of mass migration. But if, indeed, technology is the key factor, one would need to define the critical technological shift, then identify when it struck, and then show that the timing triggered a decisive shift in either emigrants' mode of interacting with kin and communities at home or emigration states' engagements with nationals abroad.

Contemporary researchers emphasize the transformative effect of the web and the innovations, like Skype, that it has sprung.[18] However, the first web browser was not invented until 1991, that is, *after* the transnational program was launched by Nina Glick Schiller and her collaborators in 1990, and all of their empirical material was based on research conducted in the 1970s and 1980s. Large numbers of migrants did not begin using the internet until well after that period, and widespread adoption of the mobile phone came later still. It seems unlikely that the fax, which became widely used in the 1980s, did much to tie together migrants in U.S. or European cities with their relatives at home in rural Mexico or North Africa. While one cannot find a clear correlation between a specific technological change and some aspect of transnational connectedness in the contemporary period, it is also the case that the technology of long-distance communication and travel has been in constant change throughout the migrations of the past two hundred years. In the early nineteenth century, it took months to cross the Atlantic; by 1910, it took only ten days. In the early nineteenth century, a letter sent from the United States to Europe could arrive months if not a year later; by 1910, receipt was almost certain and in a time interval not that different from today's mail. As migration is itself one of the drivers compressing time and space, it seems unlikely that some technological change generated a fundamental divide distinguishing "now" from "then."

In looking across the entire time spectrum connecting the two ages of mass migration, this book reminds the reader that the period *in-between* the conventional divides of "now" and "then" was one of ongoing population movements across boundaries, during which time migrants kept up connections with kin and communities left behind while emigration states sought both to maintain and shape those linkages. Rates of international migration changed at varying tempos across the Americas. In the United States, mass European immigration came to a halt in the 1920s, just when emigration from Mexico rapidly accelerated; indeed, as a share of the Mexican population living in Mexico, the immigrants in the United States hit a peak in the late 1920s that was not reached again until the late 1980s. Though the Great Depression stopped immigration from Mexico, that flow resumed with the *Bracero* program, beginning in 1942 and continuing until 1964. As described below by David FitzGerald, the interwar period was in many ways the high point of Mexico's interaction with its emigrants, with the postwar Bracero program also providing an ongoing framework for interaction between Mexican officials and migrants in the United States. Unlike the situation south of the 49th parallel, international migration to Canada approached a full stop only during the depression, continuing on at a high rate during the 1920s and then building up rapidly in the immediate aftermath of World War II, as Canada continued to search for population to fill up its huge landmass. In Brazil, as Mônica Raisa Schpun shows, 174,098 Japanese migrated to Brazil during the first half of the twentieth century, of whom 81 percent arrived during an eleven-year period between the mid-1920s and the mid-1930s.

On the other side of the Atlantic, a French economy depleted by the huge losses in World War I attracted labor migrants from Italy and Eastern and Central Europe during the 1920s. Building on a tradition of bilateral treaties that had been established in the early 1900s, "guestworker" agreements were signed between France and various sending states: Italy, Poland, and Czechoslovakia. Labor migration resumed and even increased after World War II. Indeed, no sooner was a new regime installed in Rome than it began searching for employment outlets for the millions of Italians displaced by the war's destruction. As the doors to the United States remained firmly shut (notwithstanding the efforts among Italian Americans to reopen them),[19] Italy's only option was the negotiation of guestworker agreements elsewhere, of which the very first was signed with Belgium in 1946. Agreements with additional countries soon followed, with other sending (Spain, Portugal, Greece, and Yugoslavia, among others) and receiving (Germany, the Netherlands, Switzerland) countries following suit as the post–World War II recovery bred a demand for low-skilled labor in Europe that could not be supplied by domestic sources. For those European countries that were still imperial powers, migration from their colonies provided an important source of labor. The arrival of the *Empire Windrush* at the port of Tilbury in 1948, with almost 500 Jamaican passengers, marked the beginning of a colonial migration to England from the West Indies but also from India and Pakistan that soon expanded to impressive proportions. Whereas Algerian migrants had already established a sizable presence in France prior to World War II, that flow also quickly burgeoned in the postwar period, notwithstanding the French state's simultaneous encouragement of Spanish and Portuguese immigrants. To a large extent, the source of much of Europe's late-twentieth-century foreign-origin population originated in these postwar, guestworker migrations.

Like the mass migrations at the turns of the twentieth and twenty-first centuries, the intermediary migration waves—Mexican migration of the 1920s, interwar intra-European labor migrations, and the guestworker migrations of the post–World War II period—did not inevitably lead to severed ties with people and communities at home. *Au contraire*. Migrants continued to send back remittances, to keep in touch (via the mail, but also via intermediaries), and to use their savings to build "dream houses" in home communities, to which they often never returned.[20] When formal agreements were signed between sending and receiving states, they gave the former privileged access to their nationals abroad, which the sending states exploited with varying degrees of success.[21] On the one hand, the costs of servicing nationals abroad meant the expenditure of resources in higher-priced locales.[22] On the other hand, as the migrants gained freedoms not always available at home, leading in many cases to the burgeoning of opposition parties abroad, this, in turn, often stimulated sending states to intensify efforts at monitoring and control.[23] For displaced colonials, migration indeed provided an environment more conducive to agitating for liberation at home, though in doing so they exposed themselves to surveillance and repression by the metropolitan police.

Finally, although contemporary analysts rightly point to the importance of high-skilled migration—a development motivating emigration states to find ways in which competencies, innovations, and relationships can be channeled back home, thus turning "brain drain" into "brain gain"—this too is a phenomenon for which significant historical precedents, though not necessarily parallels, can be found. In the early years of the new millennium, the increase in international student mobility far outpaced overall global international migration.[24] And yet at the turn of the twentieth century, a significant flow brought students from southern and eastern Europe to French and German universities.[25] And while these intra-European movements largely involved circulation of elites, whose sojourns abroad were subsidized by family funds, imperial China, as discussed in Madeline Hsu's chapter in this book, contemporaneously launched a program of student migration designed to send Chinese students to the United States so that they would come home with the skills that China wanted.

In recounting this history, we do *not* seek to say that the more things change, the more they stay the same. On the contrary, in responding to the assumption that everything has changed and that "now" can be sharply distinguished from "then," we are simply noting that *some* things have remained the same while others have not. Moreover, the close reader will note how many of the influential factors that may structure transnational ties have been in flux over the last century. The southern European dictatorial regimes from which refugees and guestworkers found sanctuary in northern and western Europe are no more; neither are the colonies, for which some of the colonial migrants sought liberation. And other sources of long-term temporal variation—most notably, the degree of international stability or conflict between origin and destination countries—have altered in unpredictable ways, leaving the capacity to maintain homeland connections as well as the types of ties possible unsettled. Moreover, time is but one of the relevant variables, as the particularities of the migrations and the places from which the migrants come and to which they arrive vary significantly even when the time period in question is more or less the same. The nature, duration, and acceptability of the homeland connections established by migrants heading from colonies to the metropole turn out to be very different from those whose displacements took them from an already independent national state. Likewise, the characteristics of the homeland—whether empire or nation-state, whether multiethnic or largely monoethnic—also have had a significant impact on transnational ties. Hence, in examining the relatively *longue durée* with which this book is concerned, we seek to go beyond the polarized debate triggered by the advent of the transnational perspective and instead identify both sources of continuity *and* variation.

Homeland and Hostland:
Lessons from a Long-term Approach

While nothing stays the same and no migration proves identical with another, similarities abound. For our concerns the most important resemblances involve the recurring ties linking migrants to people and places in the societies of origin and the ways in which sending states repeatedly seek to reinforce and shape those connections.

The prevalence of cross-border ties stems from the duality at the heart of the migratory phenomenon: the people moving across borders are both immigrants *and* emigrants, retaining ties to the people and places left behind even while putting down roots in the place where they live.[26] Migrants from poor societies and their relatives at home typically pursue entwined survival strategies: the migrants move to rich countries to secure resources that can be found only there and channel them home; in turn, the relatives still in place take care of the children, elderly parents, and properties that the migrants have left behind and to which the latter often want to return. The newcomers are likewise entwined in the place of destination, turning to one another for help in order to solve the everyday problems of migration: how to move from old home to new, how to find a job and settle down, and how to pick up the skills needed to manage in their new world. In the process, the migrants extend and embed their networks, creating a new community where the density of familiar faces, tongues, and institutions serves to reproduce the world left behind. As the home country society gets transplanted onto receiving states, *alien* territory gets turned into a *familiar* environment, while at the same time putting in place the infrastructure needed to keep up "here-there" connections and providing the means by which migrants can sustain identities as home state *nationals*, even while living on *foreign* soil. However, as *immigrants* searching for a better life, the new arrivals also adapt to the new environment and adopt the skills it demands. While over the long term these changes complicate their capacity to maintain cross-border connections, in the short to medium term they increase the emigrants' capacity to help out their significant others still living in the home society. Migrants' decisions to depart one country for another paradoxically implant an infrastructure that knits those two countries together. Individual migrants typically cross international borders while leaving many, if not most members of the core, familial network behind. Obligations to aging parents at home can keep remittances, letters, phone calls, and visits flowing well after roots in the host country have become deeply established.

This emphasis on the social processes of migration and the cross-border links that they forge nonetheless leaves out an important dimension, which has been under-theorized in the transnationalism literature but clearly emerges from many of the articles in this book: the political dimension. As we know, the inherently political character of population movements across boundaries[27] deeply affects both sending and receiving societies. The emigrants' cross-border involvements are mainly social and highly particularistic, directed primarily at their kin; nonetheless, their private actions undertaken from *abroad* have produced profoundly public consequences *at home*. The flow of migrant remittances traveling from rich to poor countries, now as in previous eras of mass migration, is not simply an individual, economic act but also ultimately a collective and political one.[28] Even more explicitly, having relocated to a different state, migrants gain the potential to exercise *home* country political influence never previously experienced; some then try to exercise that influence, doing so with varying levels of success. The receiving state's borders thus do more than help create wealth for immigrants; they also keep *out* the tentacles of the sending state, providing the migrants with political protection against home state interests that might seek to control them as emigrants.[29] Moreover, those who acquire citizenship in the new country can gain additional political entitlements facilitating their capacity for political action to produce change at home. Hence, the new political environment often gives rise to social movements built in the place where the migrants *live* but designed to effect change in the place that they have *left*.[30]

In turn, the movement of nationals to foreign soil generates sending state responses, an aspect of transnationalism that much of the transnational literature has ignored. To the extent that migration studies have long focused principally on the ways in which *receiving* states have reacted to *immigrants*, the attitudes and policies of *sending* states toward *emigrants* has often been neglected, although recent work has begun to explore the stances that states of emigration have taken toward citizens who leave.[31] Since the nineteenth century, states have reached out across their borders to cultivate loyalty, foster the maintenance of cultural traditions, promote instruction in the homeland tongue, and keep the corrosive effects of settlement and acculturation abroad at bay. Early on, sending states realized the importance of making sure that human and financial resources generated by the emigrants could flow back to home soil. Facilitating the successful transmission of remittances from the country of immigration back to the country of emigration while discouraging the flow of subversive ideas in the same direction has indeed been a particularly persistent objective of the sending country. In pursuit of these cultural and economic goals, emigration states have repeatedly established an infrastructure—usually, through the consular network—designed to engage with the diaspora. That consular infrastructure has consistently provided a means for responding to the migrants' repeated vulnerability to exploitation but also, as we will see, to the challenges posed by politically oriented emigrants, who can no longer be coerced but possibly influenced.

Thus, ties across borders, whether established by migrants or by sending states, recur wherever and whenever international migrations occur, a pattern evident over the past 150 years, as the articles in this book show. But as those movements link particular sending places with specific sending states and take place under distinctive, ever-changing circumstances, these connections assume myriad forms. Moreover, maintaining these ties is not for either migrants or sending states to decide on their own. No less important are the views and behavior of receiving states and receiving state nationals, who prove sometimes more accepting, sometimes less accepting, of these linkages traversing boundaries. Thus, continuity is just one side of the phenomenon. Now turning to variation, we identify several domains in which transnational ties are particularly dependent upon changing circumstances, notably in the realm of political activity.

Emigrant Politics

The cross-border migrations discussed in this book have taken place in a particular context, that of populations moving into developed, democratic states. Too little attention has been given to the ways in which the combination of economic and political resources found in receiving states of this sort has given many migrants capacities never previously possessed. Once in the receiving state, migrants obtain newfound leverage, benefiting from both the wealth of the economic environment and from the freedom of a polity no longer controlled by the home government. For the politically oriented, the new home can thus provide the space for autonomous migrant social action, unfolding in the place of *destination* but oriented toward the place of *origin*.

More will be said about the nature of emigrant political activities in a moment, but we first need to remember that home country politics are rarely important for the mass of rank-and-file migrants. Almost all migrations are implicitly political: the migrants are voting with their feet, *against* the state of origin and *for* the state of destination—its economy, its institutional infrastructure (which makes its economy successful), and the public goods and public security it provides. Nonetheless, most have had little political experience before migration; after settling down in a new country, their lives unfold largely independent of political matters back home. Moreover, migrants who have left in search of material betterment may be less disposed from the outset to look to politics to provide a solution for their needs.

The experience of labor migrants discussed in this book—whether from Algeria, India, Italy, Portugal, or Mexico—exemplifies this pattern. Emanating largely from rural areas, these labor migrants were in turn typically oriented back toward a homeland understood in local, not national, terms. Thus, as we see in Victor Pereira's chapter, Portuguese emigrants have fierce attachments to the particular communities from which they stem, but less interest in the broader Portuguese nation. Only under certain conditions do they lay claim to membership in that national community, most notably by invoking long-gone Portuguese greatness—e.g., Vasco da Gama—to foment loyalties toward an utterly nonpolitical pursuit: a football (soccer) team. Local attachments have been all the more important when the home state was a multiethnic polity dominated by a group from which the migrants were excluded. Thus, the migrants from Algeria settling in the Parisian industrial suburb of Nanterre discussed by Marie-Claude Blanc-Chaléard were Berbers from Kabylia, a minority in a home population dominated numerically and politically by Arabs. Though nonetheless engaged in the Algerian struggle for decolonization, their crucial ties were those linking Nanterre to the Souf, their area of origin in Algeria. For migrants of this sort, the firmest loyalties, reinforced by overlapping ties of neighboring and kinship, were to the home region, which functioned as a little homeland.

As shown in many of the cases discussed in this book, the motivation to come together in the country of immigration stemmed precisely from the intensity of the attachments to the people who stayed home in the local place left behind. Whether Mexicans in the United States or Indians in the UK—Thomas Lacroix speaks of "translocal" religious and caste ties—otherwise depoliticized migrants have proved recurrently willing to dip into their pockets in order to aid their families and finance development in the communities from which they have fled. Of course, success in bringing together migrants sharing a common hometown origin means putting aside other differences, whether those separating right from left, believers from secularists, proletarians from entrepreneurs. The need to keep those sources of dissonance to a minimum explains why hometown associations so often adhere to an *a*-political stance.[32]

For the politicized minority, however, bilocalism comprises only one of the many different options of diaspora mobilization and often one of very limited appeal. Those emigrants for whom politics matter dearly can be classified into different types. On the one hand, a distinction may be made between political exiles and politicized exiles, the former carrying their politics and contestation with them, as with the Jewish revolutionaries from Russia discussed in Tony Michels's chapter, the latter gaining politicization abroad, as demonstrated by Houda Asal in her examination of the way in which an "Arab" political identity was constructed in Canada.

Yet another axis of variation concerns the political stance taken toward the country left behind. For emigrant activists, the outcome of migration may be the *exo-polity*, a political space formed by emigrants "refusing to recognize the legitimacy of the regime in place in their country of origin or considering that their country or state of origin is under foreign occupation."[33] Yet, even this antagonistic relationship opposing emigrants to emigration states may take different forms. A vocal minority of emigrants may engage in "state-seeking nationalism," striving to build a new state at home. Depending on circumstances, some may be like the Sikh nationalists, discussed by Thomas Lacroix, wanting to carve a new state (in this case, an independent Khalistan) out of a multiethnic polity (in this case, India). Under other conditions—such as the Algerians described by Marie-Claude Blanc-Chaléard—the goal may entail severing a new state from a colonial empire. In still other cases, emigrant activists pursue "regime-changing nationalism," trying to replace the government in place, whether from right to left, as among the Jewish revolutionaries from Russia *prior* to 1917, discussed in Tony Michels's chapter, or from Communism to some other type of state *after* 1917. Yet another option entails "nationalizing nationalism," to borrow the term coined by Rogers Brubaker,[34] where the objective is instead that of gaining ownership over an existing multiethnic state, either extruding the minority or compelling it to undergo forced assimilation, precisely the course of action pursued by the radical Hindu nationalists, whose activities are described in the chapter by Thomas Lacroix.

Other emigrants have more pacific political goals, most notably regaining home country membership, as in the many late-twentieth-century campaigns for expatriate voting rights. With the vote in hand, many expatriates then engage in campaigning, encouraging visits by homeland leaders and contributing funds to homeland parties. In some cases, as with the Portuguese discussed by Victor Pereira, special parliamentary seats have been created for legislators elected by the emigrants. Expatriate voting has elicited great interest from migration scholars, and often great enthusiasm; however, the rank and file often proves uninterested. As David FitzGerald recounts in his chapter, pressure from emigrants in the United States led the Mexican government to grant expatriate voting rights as of the 2006 presidential election. However, of the roughly 3 million eligible Mexican voters in the United States, only 33,000 cast a vote.

Emigrant Factionalism and Conflict

That migrants may choose among a variety of political paths reflects the new-found freedoms resulting from arrival in a receiving state that offer more scope for such activities than the often more repressive home states. Yet at the same time, the politicization of emigrants can also result in internal conflicts within the immigrant communities, thereby belying the notion that migration brings "the emergence of veritable 'transnational communities' suspended, in effect, between two countries."[35] Instead, entry into the new political jurisdiction of the receiving state can create the means whereby migrants mobilize in favor of diverging views of the homeland community they wish to support, transform, or create. Mônica Raisa Schpun's chapter on the Japanese in Brazil describes the most dramatic such example appearing in the pages to follow. In the aftermath of World War II, having undergone years of intense repression, the Japanese Brazilians found themselves split into two factions, one insisting on the impossible—that Japan had won, not lost, the war—the other accepting Japan's defeat. The former, which had engaged in sabotage during the war, turned its fury inward, assassinating members of the so-called "defeatist groups" and injuring scores of others. The wounds of this schism did heal however, and the majority of Japanese Brazilians followed a path of upward mobility during much of the postwar era, until the conjuncture of Brazil's economic crisis and Japan's economic boom produced yet another divergence, in the course of which some immigrant descendants stayed in Brazil and others returned to Japan, where they ironically learned how Brazilian they had become.

The World War II–era split in Brazil was a cleavage born in the receiving society. In some of the other cases discussed in this book, conflict instead diffuses *from* the home *to* the host context. A case in point is that of the Jewish radicals in the United States, recounted by Michels. Especially in the period before 1905, radical ideas and literature migrated from west to east. Jewish immigrants in the United States, able to express themselves more freely there, furnished their revolutionary counterparts still in Russia with a steady source of material support. Books and newspapers suppressed by the czarist police were printed in New York and sent to underground activists in Russia; dollars mainly flowed from west to east, supplemented by efforts to lobby U.S. officials in order to get them to intervene in defense of the Jewish victims of Russian persecution and pogroms. After 1905, however, ideas and literature also flowed from east to west. Then, with the consolidation of Bolshevik rule in the early 1920s, the question of whether to support or oppose the new regime provoked a virtual Jewish civil war *within* the Jewish American left. As with other fratricidal conflicts, the many things shared by the pro- and the anticommunist Jewish radicals produced intracommunal divisions of an especially deep and long-lasting nature.

Like the Jewish revolutionaries, Algerian immigrants found that the freedoms enjoyed by living in metropolitan France—no matter how tightly policed—provided resources and options that could be put to good use by the liberation movement at home. But that movement, too, was badly divided. The internecine conflict between the first established movement (the *Mouvement national algérien*, MNA), led by Messali Hadj, and its ultimately successful rival, the *Front de Libération Nationale*, spilled over into deadly violence in Paris, as Blanc-Chaléard explains. The FLN's ability to invisibly control the community, combined with hostility to and from French authorities, left many immigrants vulnerable to intracommunal violence.

Somewhat similar events appear in Lacroix's chapter on Indian organizations in the UK. Though dominated by a Sikh leadership, the left-leaning *Indian* Workers' Association (IWA) initially acted as the dominant influence within the broader, post–World War II immigrant population originating in India. Downplaying internal ethnic differences, the IWA instead emphasized issues related to the common class origin of the immigrants from India in ways that converged with the conventional organization of British politics. Nonetheless, as the number of highly skilled Indians grew and the migrant population diversified away from its original, largely working-class base, new political cleavages emerged. From the 1980s on, many of the more skilled Indians residing abroad flocked to radical Hindu nationalist (Hinduvta) organizations. Simultaneously, the echoes of ethnic conflict in the Punjab led to radicalization and heightened nationalism among Sikhs abroad, seriously diminishing the Indian Workers' Association's influence.

Both Michels's and Lacroix's chapters point to another form of emigrant politics, one organized around a very different imagined community than that of the ethnically defined nation itself imagined in much of the transnational literature: the world of international proletarian fellowship. We should not forget that from the mid–nineteenth century through the third quarter of the twentieth century, a significant proportion of the international movers understood themselves to be "workers of the world." And they were also understood as such—as shown by the role of migrants in transmitting laborist, socialist, or anarchist ideas from one national setting to another, not to speak of their simultaneous or successive participation in several national movements.[36] As the solidarities generated by the migration process often provided the underpinning for labor movements of various kinds, labor internationalism and home-country allegiances continued to prove compatible well through the first part of the twentieth century. Of course, some immigrant radicals—notably the anarchists—abhorred nationalism and renounced any home-country allegiance. But for a broad variety of reasons, having to do with the commonalities and barriers of language, as well as the ways in which migrant social networks enveloped the radicals along with the rank and file, the labor internationalists were not rootless cosmopolitans. Rather, to borrow the felicitous phrase of Sidney Tarrow, they comprised "embedded cosmopolitans," oriented toward a larger humanity yet part and parcel of immigrant populations delimited by language, national, and sometimes religious origins.[37]

An appreciation of immigrant proletarian internationalism underscores an aspect of change over time that most students of transnationalism and cross-border immigrant politics have ignored: namely, the decline, indeed demise of this once vital current. Its last embers seem to appear in Lacroix's recounting of the history of the Indian Workers' Association, which reigned hegemonic during the years of labor migration but lost influence in the 1980s under the twin impact of home country nationalism and the emergence of a sizable second generation middle class. Nationalism seems to have largely replaced internationalism as the ideal informing emigrants' imagined community as community has trumped class as an organizing principle.

International Relations and the Question of Dual Loyalty

From the standpoint of receiving states, international migration produces the arrival of alien peoples from alien lands whose alien connections and attachments render them suspect. By contrast, sending states experience not just *emigration*, but the displacement of citizens to whom home governments retain obligations, regardless of residence abroad. However, as *immigrants*, the newcomers enjoy the option of gaining formal citizenship in the state on which they have converged. Consequently, international migration invariably generates issues of loyalty and formal membership on both sides of the chain. Reflecting the inherent duality of their situation, the people who are simultaneously immigrants *and* emigrants often prefer to have it both ways, as opposed to choosing either place of destination *or* place of origin. Eager to retain emigrant loyalty and access to the emigrants' resources, sending states have become more and more willing to go along, which is why they have increasingly found dual citizenship acceptable. Yet persistent foreign attachments can nonetheless render receiving state citizens suspicious of their new co-nationals; peering in from the other side, home country nationals likewise look skeptically at the new commitments of their compatriots abroad. As formal membership in the receiving state yields no guarantee of perceived loyalty to that state, migrants' persisting international connections prove vulnerable to broader events in the international arena.

Devotees of the social science literature are apt to learn that acceptance of dual citizenship provides at once evidence of the novelty of transnational connections as well as today's greater acceptance of persisting loyalties to home and host countries. But, as shown by Caroline Douki in her chapter on Italy, a de facto "dual citizenship" is of much older vintage. As Italy concluded in the early twentieth century, it was far better to remain in close contact with citizens who took U.S. nationality in order to be able to facilitate if not encourage their return—and to allow them, in the meantime, to act on behalf of Italy. Indeed, one could argue that prohibition of dual citizenship has the potential for yielding two contrary effects, neither consistent with sending state goals. On the one hand, it can reinforce the *emigrants'* tendency to reject acquisition of receiving state citizenship, viewing it as a repudiation of the country of birth and the *national* family to which they still feel tied. However, as that decision entails retention of alien status, it also makes ongoing residence and thus continued remittance-sending capacity uncertain.[38] On the other hand, if forced to decide, the *immigrant* orientation may prevail, leading to the acquisition of receiving state citizenship at the expense of continued home country formal membership. By contrast, allowing dual citizenship can both retain the loyalty of settlers and turn them into ethnic lobbyists, benefits that many countries have discovered over the past quarter-century, as the enactment of dual citizenship laws in home countries has encouraged emigrants to the United States to obtain American citizenship without forgoing home membership. This has in turn often boosted the earnings of the newly naturalized, which, in turn, might increase their ability to send money home.[39]

Of course, dual citizenship becomes a practical option only when both receiving *and* sending countries agree to relent on exclusivity; as of this writing, that pattern characterizes traditional settler states like Canada and the United States, as well as some of the European recipients of post–World War II migration, such as France. Yet such immigrant-receiving countries as Austria, Denmark, and Germany remain bulwarks for more exclusive citizenship practices.[40] Moreover, sending states can liberalize the rules concerning formal membership without necessarily extending *all* citizenship rights to nationals residing in foreign lands. Retaining emigrant loyalty is one thing, expanding opportunities for emigrant influence from abroad is another.

From the perspective of the receiving states, the international dimension is also a source of constraint. While hostland states may tolerate, even support migrant engagement with homelands abroad, acceptance is contingent on the degree of stability and tranquility of the broader international order. When international troubles arise—as they inevitably do—hostland states are apt to act in ways that restrain and possibly punish migrants insisting on maintaining a cross-border political connection. Schpun's chapter on the Brazilian Japanese, for example, provides a powerful illustration of the oscillations of acceptance and the potentially devastating impact of international conflict on transnational ties. Working in concert, Japan and Brazil had stimulated a migration that built up a large Japanese population in Brazil. And the Japanese Brazilians' connections to Japan remained strong—thanks to schools and other structures established by the Japanese government with Brazil's approval. Yet, beginning in the 1930s, a wave of extreme Brazilian nationalism put that thriving Japanese Brazilian community on the defensive. The advent of hostilities due to the war quickly made things worse, cutting off ties with the home country and prohibiting the public use of Japanese and virtually all Japanese language or culturally oriented activities. Yet after the war ended and international tranquility returned, cross-border ties eventually resumed.

The experience of the Syro-Lebanese in Canada discussed by Houda Asal also demonstrates how tensions abroad affected activities in the new home. For most of the twentieth century, Arab emigrants in Canada interacted intermittently with their home countries while militating for greater rights in Canada itself. After 1948, however, in agitating for an independent Palestine, many Arab-Canadians went against the grain of Canadian foreign policy, thus falling under the government's suspicion and making them subject to close monitoring as well as attacks from the press. While solidarity with the Palestinian cause resonated powerfully with some Canadians—most notably Québécois nationalists—as seen from Ottawa, associations of this sort were grounds for viewing the immigrants from the Middle East with even greater doubt. Changing international and national politics both at "home" and abroad created the powerful backdrop for the ebb and flow of Arab mobilization in Canada.

Likewise, loyalties extending across borders created problems for Jewish radicals in the United States as U.S. policy toward Russia changed. As Michels points out, in early-twentieth-century America, opponents of czarist Russia were looked on favorably; the U.S. turned a blind eye to the revolutionaries' gun-running and indeed joined in on their efforts to pressure the czar. But the tables turned drastically once some of the Jewish revolutionaries in the United States embraced the Soviet Union, at which point their association with a foreign, hostile power brought them under suspicion. Over time, those associations left the immigrant radicals increasingly vulnerable, a risk that culminated in a rash of ideologically motivated, Cold War deportations in the late 1940s and early 1950s.[41]

Emigration Policy

While host country attitudes to immigrants' political activities merit further exploration, we turn also in this book to the sending states and their encouragement or discouragement of transnationalism, be it politically oriented or not. As we have noted, the earlier debate over transnationalism in historical perspective focused, for the most part, on (the consistency of) the activities undertaken by the immigrants themselves; very little attention was paid to the role of sending states. The essays in this book show how, although certain continuities may be seen in the way in which home states have been interested in their emigrants, the mechanisms and modalities by which they connect with their citizens abroad have taken on distinctive form over time. As early as the mid- to late nineteenth century, mounting levels of emigration left sending states increasingly concerned about the loss of their departing citizens and the consequences that might ensue.[42] Responses took the form of new understandings of nationhood: as opposed to the then prevailing conception, linking territory and nation such that the latter fills up and governs the former,[43] emigration gave rise to a new, deterritorialized conception, in which the nation is present wherever the nationals live, whether within "their" state or elsewhere.

Of the cases discussed in this book, the Italians were first to take this "deterritorialized" turn, not surprisingly, since those residing in the newly created state hardly thought of themselves as Italian, and the southerners who comprised the mass of the emigrants could rarely understand the official, Tuscan-derived "Italian." Hence, securing the emigrants' allegiance ranked high among Italy's goals. Like others, Caroline Douki shows how Italy's quest for emigrant loyalty involved an effort to inculcate Italian-ness—*italianità*—via activities oriented toward a deterritorialized vision of the nation understood as *italiani del mundo*.[44] Though unaware of the Italian example, Mexican state officials followed a similar course in the 1920s, dubbing the emigrants as the Mexico outside of Mexico (*México de afuera*), a theme reprised by the country's leaders in the 1990s. Portuguese officials, aware of Italy's emigrant-oriented initiatives, similarly incorporated emigration into the prevailing national narrative by the 1930s, insisting that Portugal existed wherever any Portuguese citizen was to be found. As Victor Pereira shows, that rhetoric made a virtue out of necessity—obscuring the migrants' need to flee abroad in order to escape misery at home. Thus, well before the advent of "now," a variety of emigration states found attractions in conceptions of a "deterritorialized nation" as a means of symbolically including nationals who had traversed state boundaries, but whose loyalty and resources they wanted to retain.

In her chapter, Douki makes the case that Italy had perhaps the most developed emigration policy of the late nineteenth/early twentieth century, and that incitement to return was virtually a cornerstone of a sending-state–sponsored transnationalism. Emigration confronted turn-of-the-twentieth-century Italy with a variety of challenges—all of which will be familiar to today's sending states. Consequently, Italy went far beyond symbolism, developing mechanisms to retain its nationals' loyalties (in part, so that, as naturalized citizens, they could then act as effective ethnic lobbyists) and to facilitate the secure transfer of money back across the Atlantic while putting into place policies that both aided vulnerable immigrants in the ports of embarkation and brought them back home for free if they became sick or injured. This panoply of policies amounted to a full-blown policy of "diaspora engagement," to use the contemporary parlance.[45] Many of the initiatives begun by Italy at the turn of the twentieth century were put in place by other states in subsequent years. Shortly after Italy developed a large-scale consular infrastructure to connect to emigrants in North and South America, the Japanese government implemented an ambitious program of assistance to Japanese emigrants in Brazil; as Mônica Raisa Schpun explains, Japan's emigration policy facilitated emigrant upward mobility. In the 1920s, Mexico took similar measures designed to assist, but also to retain influence over the emigrant population in the United States whose numbers had grown greatly after World War I (David FitzGerald). Like Italy, Portugal found that movement abroad left migrants exposed to the arbitrary exercise of receiving state power and to depredation from the profit-seeking migration industry;[46] hence, as Pereira shows, Portugal followed the Italian example detailed by Douki in implementing a variety of practices aimed at controlling ship conditions during the trans-Atlantic passage.

State efforts to connect with emigrants—from cultural policies to banking structures (to encourage remittances)—have been subject to ebb and flow, but the consular infrastructure—an understudied hub for transnational connections—has persistently been key. As part of its buildup of a contemporary consular infrastructure, Italy developed many cultural programs through its consulates designed to retain the allegiance of emigrants. The Mexican consulate too comprised a key institution in the transnational ties cultivated by the home state. However, consulates are resource-consuming operations, requiring poorer *emigration* countries to spend scarce resources in the high-cost locations of richer *immigration* states, where the ability to effectively engage with nationals abroad is often constrained by the yawning social gap between immigrants and diplomats.[47]

Though recurrent, investment in consular services is not necessarily constant; nor does it grow in linear proportion to the expanding size of the emigrant population. Although Mexico developed an extensive infrastructure to deal with emigration in the 1920s and 1930s, it withdrew from consular engagement in the United States in the years after World War II. Even when

Mexican emigration began skyrocketing in the 1960s, reconnection with emigrants came only slowly, not taking full form until the late 1980s. Today, Mexico maintains a vast consular infrastructure, including 56 consulates scattered throughout the United States and Canada, following Mexican emigrants as they have dispersed, even to Alaska.

Yet, the consular connection has historically been a two-edged phenomenon, one entailing both protection and surveillance of nationals. The creation of an extraterritorial presence allows home states to better monitor and possibly control unwanted activities abroad. Thus, though living on American soil, Mexican immigrants were still subject to the coercive power of the Mexican state, which chose to cooperate with U.S. authorities in organizing the massive deportations of the early 1930s. Similarly, in the interwar period, Italy's priorities included monitoring nationals abroad, in addition to protecting them, particularly insofar as migration to France also provided sanctuary for opposition to the fascist regime, which led to further efforts to deepen the consular infrastructure with new mandates for overseeing emigrant welfare, mutual aid, and cultural and sports associations.[48] In some cases, the two sides can reach a quid pro quo, as Marie-Claude Blanc-Chaléard explains, with France and Algeria finding a common path to the restriction of migration; the first cutting down on numbers, the second gaining the authority to monitor departures. The new Algerian state also kept close tabs on its emigrants through the *Amicale des Algériens en Europe*, in principle a migrants' organization, in practice an extension of the Algerian state. Something similar transpired in Canada, where, as Houda Asal mentions, beyond having its diplomats attend ceremonies, banquets, and social meetings, the new Lebanese state, hesitant to do much for its nationals there, was wary of the emigrants' activism in support of the Palestinian cause. The consulate even at times used its privileged access to the migrants to act as an informer on behalf of the Canadian government. As Lacroix explains, India, trying to crack down on Sikh diaspora groups mobilizing for an independent Khalistan, convinced host states in the west to classify those groups as terrorist organizations and to restrict the entry of Sikhs seeking to immigrate as refugees fleeing violence in the Punjab.

Last, state emigration policy can take a variety of forms. In the mid- to late-nineteenth century, states did not simply neglect emigrants and their needs; they opposed emigration and tried to halt it, a position influenced by a persistent mercantilist understanding that viewed population as a resource that a country could not afford to lose. Restrictions on emigration globally faded in Europe during the late nineteenth century,[49] although not all countries followed the Italian example, described by Douki, in shifting from constraint to engagement. A contrasting case is described by Pereira, in which the Portuguese state long used a variety of tools to impede emigration, often under the grounds that the would-be emigrants were being tricked into leaving and needed protection. Though the "exit revolution" of the late nineteenth century marks the long-term tendency, the mid–twentieth century saw a swing back in the other direction, as first the Soviet Union, and then the eastern bloc and other communist countries, sought to impede emigration, doing so with considerable success. While only North Korea still seeks to bottle up its people, the back and forth shifts in policies toward emigration yet again show that change has occurred in nonlinear ways.

In the Italian, Portuguese, and also Mexican cases, state policy toward emigrants evolved, shifting from a constraining to a reactive stance. For the most part, the cases discussed in this book highlight the reactive mode: first, the migrants act on their own; only later do states respond. While the migrants often leave against the preferences of both sending *and* receiving states, citizens' exit is both an expression of discontent and a blow to national self-image, and therefore an unpleasant reality that emigration states—like the postindependent India discussed by Lacroix—simply prefer to ignore. Furthermore, diaspora engagement policy is resource-consuming, but emigration state capacity is low. Eventually, however, as the number of emigrants grows, their impacts—whether ongoing (due to remittance-sending or political involvement) or future (due to possible detachment or possible engagement as ethnic lobbyists)—gain in importance and prove compelling, leading to engagement with nationals abroad.

Yet the essays in this book also offer testimony to an alternative, proactive option, one in which states organize the emigration itself *and* seek to maintain ties to emigrants after they have gone abroad, as illustrated by Mônica Raisa Schpun's chapter on Brazil and Madeline Hsu's chapter on the *Liuxuesheng*—educated emigrants from China. As Schpun explains, a confluence of factors—Japan's search to export populations displaced by its agrarian crisis; restriction on immigration to the United States; the ceasing of immigration from Europe, under the impact of World War I; and Brazil's preference for nonblack workers—led Japan and Brazil to mutually agree to a policy that would bring over 140,000 Japanese immigrants to Brazil in the space of a mere eleven years. Not only did Japan incentivize the migration; it provided the migrants with technical assistance designed to facilitate and hasten their economic adjustment as well as the funding, curricular material, and teachers needed to establish a parallel schooling system. As both a process of population movement and population settlement, this experience stands out for the degree to which it was structured by emigration state policy from the outset. On the other hand, the Japanese migration to Brazil—like that of Italians to the Americas, Indians to the UK, Algerians and Portuguese to France—involved the transplantation of displaced peasants, starting out in the country of immigration at the very bottom of the ladder.

Labor migration may be the more common modality, but Hsu's chapter reminds us that emigration policy can also be focused at the high end. Like the guestworkers, the students sent abroad by China from the 1870s on through the Chinese revolution, were intended to go as sojourners, though in this case emigration was not motivated by a search for an escape valve or a source of remittances, but rather as a means of gaining knowledge and acquiring skills. If the Italian returns were largely self-motivated after years of successful savings or, on the contrary, the failure of establishment, the Chinese students were seen as obliged to return. Worries about brain drain could undercut the hopes of the sending country's aims, but the initial impetus came from the state itself. As Hsu shows, reaping the dividends of student migration was a difficult end to pursue, as it required the right mixture of acceptance and rejection in the receiving society. On the one hand, too much *acceptance* undermined China's highly instrumental goal of exposing students to just those skills that China wanted and no more: when they were embraced in the United States, Chinese students were likely either to remain there or to return to China excessively Americanized (and Christianized to boot). On the other hand, *rejection* was more common than acceptance, making it difficult for students to obtain the skills they needed and leaving China loath to pursue student emigration, given the ways in which anti-Chinese reactions in the United States generated hostility toward the United States in China. If China's own expectations of student migration provide the standard of success, then the experience can only be judged a failure. But, as Hsu points out, the influence exercised by returned foreign students may provide the more realistic criterion, in which case this early episode underlines the potential dividends of high-skilled emigration policy.

Looking backward, historicizing its very emergence, it is hard not to reflect on the fact that the transnational perspective was launched in a different period than today's. It is not simply that this once new approach gained currency before the dawning of the internet age. More importantly, it emerged at the end of what Eric Hobsbawm called the short twentieth century,[50] that fin-de-siècle period when the tensions that had split the globe seemed resolved, with a "new world order," as proclaimed by a U.S. president. In that context, with former foes appearing to becoming friends, it seemed entirely reasonable to assume that the immigrant and the emigrant orientation could peacefully and stably coexist. In a more pacific, cooperative world, neither nationals "here" (the country of *immigration*) nor nationals "there" (the country of *emigration*) had much to fear from immigrants/emigrants maintaining ties in both places. In that light, the hypothesis that immigrants can gain incorporation in the countries where they reside and "at the very same time . . . build institutions, conduct transactions, and influence local and national events in the countries from which they emigrated" seemed utterly compelling.[51]

But that was then. The "new world order" has since metamorphosed into a new world disorder, indeed so disorderly that one might wax nostalgic for the stability of the second half of Hobsbawm's short twentieth century. Not only has the distance traveled since the early 1990s turned what was then "new" into something "old"; it has shown how the very nature of the phenomenon recurrently but contingently changes the environment in which connections between home- and hostlands can be pursued and maintained.

As those connections are international, the very different levels of political stability found in the poorer, weaker states of emigration and the richer, stronger states of immigration predictably yield unpredictable feedbacks, producing period effects but also yielding cross-country variations in the nature of homeland-hostland connections at any given time.

Over the long term, as shown by the U.S-Mexico case profiled by David FitzGerald, a shift from conflictual to stable, cooperative relations between sending and receiving countries can alter the conditions under which emigrants and emigration states interact, encouraging a variety of activities, whether emanating from a home state wanting to engage with emigrants or emigrants seeking involvement in the place left behind. At any given time, as shown by the contrast of the Portuguese and the Algerian cases profiled, respectively, by Victor Pereira and Marie-Claude Blanc-Chaléard, disparities in relationships between sending and receiving states can make for variations in the nature of cross-border connections. Algerians and Portuguese both moved to France as labor migrants, enduring similar conditions, at least at the earlier stages of the migrations. But tensions infused by Algeria's struggle for independence and later postcolonial strains with France fundamentally distinguished the context of reception and the relationship between Algeria and Algerians in France from that of the simultaneously arriving Portuguese, who comprised an "invisible" migration. Moreover, with continentwide cooperation having replaced strife, the Portuguese could move from one European Union country to another at will. By contrast, as Blanc-Chaléard's chapter shows, polarization on the two sides of the Mediterranean condemned the Algerians to a "poor man's transnationalism," with options for back-and-forth movement constantly constrained, whether during colonial or postcolonial periods. A shift from cooperative to conflictual relationships between home and host states can prove disastrous, as shown by Mônica Raisa Schpun's chapter; but when conflict can be replaced by cooperation, as shown by Brazil and Japan in the years following World War II, the rupture in cross-border relations caused by international conflict can be repaired. Not all international issues can be so easily mended, of which the conflict over Israel/Palestine is a prime example. As Houda Asal's chapter shows, that conflict shadowed Arab Canadians from even before the formation of the state of Israel, consistently constraining the immigrants' efforts to engage in their place of residence on behalf of a (real or symbolic) place of origin. While Asal's chapter ends in the 1970s, it seems safe to say that the shadow cast by conflict in this part of the world has since only darkened, continuing to shape the conditions under which Arab Canadians pursue ties to this troubled part of the globe. One only need think of the population movements triggered by the troubles of today's times—Syrians, Iraqis, Somalis, Ukrainians, Rwandans, Tamils—let alone the repercussions of international conflicts on long-settled populations of immigrant origin—to realize that the inherently unsettled relations among states will consistently bear down on immigrant cross-border connections—albeit in ways that are hard to forecast with any degree of certainty.

Not only was the emergence of the transnational perspective specific to a time. It was also specific to a place, namely the United States, whose location and history led many researchers to focus mainly on intrahemispheric migrations. While those migrations are surely not of a piece, the broader geographical scope of this book nonetheless shows how they differ from migrations found elsewhere. Neocolonialism may characterize the relationship between the United States and Latin America; Puerto Rico aside, there are no U.S. colonies found in the western hemisphere. Hence, the strains and difficulties experienced by the Algerians discussed in Blanc-Chaléard's chapter—first as colonial migrants engaged in the liberation struggle from the metropole and later as residents of the former colonial power looked on suspiciously by the new ex-colonial state—made for a relationship between emigrants, hostland, and homeland of a type infused with colonial history. Furthermore, interethnic conflicts at home may yield fallout among emigrants abroad, as in the case of the Indian emigrants in the UK profiled by Thomas Lacroix. While the notion of state-seeking nationalism may link up the activities of contemporary emigrants to the Irish emigrants of the nineteenth century or the eastern European immigrants of the turn of the twentieth, it points to an axis of variation that can only be understood by looking beyond the western hemisphere boundaries that have often constrained the focus of U.S. migration scholars. Hence, we end with a plea, not just for more research, but for a wider frame of research vision, one extending to a broader range of migration temporalities as well as a more encompassing, indeed possibly global, set of sending and receiving places.

States and Groups

We have organized the book around two foci: that of the states' attitudes toward their citizens abroad and that of immigrants' transnational practices over time, although the two are linked as all of the papers show.

Part One explores the ways in which home states themselves have had an impact on facilitating or impeding connections. Italy, Portugal, Japan, Mexico, and China have over time elaborated different emigration policies, some of which are destined to keeping citizens who live abroad within the national sphere. Caroline Douki focuses on returns as an understudied manifestation of transnationalism, postulating in particular that the Italian state's early "return policy" was a way of favoring such movement, actively encouraging its citizens abroad to remain connected transnational subjects. Victor Pereira reminds us of Portugal's particularly long history of emigration and how the Portuguese state at times discouraged and at others encouraged emigration; at the same time he notes that the Portuguese abroad have often clung less to the home state per se than to local or cultural symbols that become their "transnational" identity. The case of the Japanese in Brazil (Mônica Raisa Schpun) serves to show how foreign relations between the countries of origin and settlement can have dramatic consequences on the possible continuities but also ruptures in the transnational activities of immigrants. In taking a long view of political engagement of Mexicans in the United States, David FitzGerald shows the ways in which the Mexican state has, especially recently, sought to harness that energy; he argues that the long history of engagement on both sides of the Rio Grande in itself disproves the technologically driven theories of contemporary transnationalism. In the case of China, Madeline Hsu provides an example of an explicit policy encouraging student emigration followed by return migration in order to bring back transnational skills.

Part Two looks at how emigrants have mobilized socially, politically, and economically over the last century to keep in touch with their countries of origin. The figures of the Irish nationalist or the Italian republican in America mobilizing for their homeland are by now fairly well known. But here we examine the processes in which a variety of other communities have organized, from the political mobilization of Arabs in Canada (Houda Asal) to Jewish radical immigrants in the United States (Tony Michels) to Sikhs in Britain (Thomas Lacroix). From the informal activities of early settlers to the growth of voluntary associations as communities grow, forms of mobilization change due to changing cohorts and growing numbers but also due to political events at home. Lacroix, Asal, and Michels thus argue that temporalities matter in understanding the oscillations of homeland-directed political activity over time. Transformations in home countries, international relations between home and place of settlement and changing policies in the country of settlement thus all help explain periods of quiescence and periods of more intense transnational political activities. Finally, Marie-Claude Blanc-Chaléard inquires into the impact of decolonization and its aftermath on the transnational practices of Algerian immigrants to France since the 1950s, from the continuity of yearly visits to the political and cultural ruptures of war or changing cultural norms.

By bringing together historians, sociologists, and a geographer from both sides of the Atlantic, and by focusing on the United States and Europe as sites of immigration and countries from China to India as places of origin, we make no pretense to a "total" history of transnational connections. However, we believe that the study of homeland connections over this long historical period is necessary both to bridge the disciplines and to deepen our understanding of the continuities *and* the changes that have characterized the international movements of people over the past century.

NOTES

1. Oscar Handlin, *The Uprooted: The Epic Story of the Great Migrations that Made the American People* (Philadelphia: University of Pennsylvania Press, 2002); John Bodnar, *The Transplanted: A History of Immigrants in Urban America* (Bloomington: Indiana University Press, 1985).

2. For further elaboration, see Nancy L. Green, "French History and the Transnational Turn," *French Historical Studies* 5 (2014): 551–564.

3. Linda Basch, Nina Glick Schiller, and Cristina Szanton Blanc, *Nations Unbound: Transnational Projects, Postcolonial Predicaments, and Deterritorialized Nation States* (New York: Gordon and Breach, 1994) 1, 286.

4. Nina Glick Schiller, Linda Basch, and Cristina Blanc-Szanton, "Transnationalism: A New Analytic Framework for Understanding Migration," *Annals of the New York Academy of Sciences* 645 (1992): 1.

5. Ibid., 9.

6. Basch, Glick Schiller, and Szanton Blanc, *Nations Unbound*.

7. Barry Goldberg, "Historical Reflections on Transnationalism, Race, and the American Immigrant Saga," *Annals of the New York Academy of Sciences* 645 (1992): 201–215.

8. Alejandro Portes, "Immigration Theory for a New Century," *International Migration Review* 31 (1997): 799–825, 873.

9. Peggy Levitt, *The Transnational Villagers* (Berkeley: University of California Press, 2001); Robert C. Smith, *Mexican New York* (Berkeley: University of California Press, 2006).

10. Alejandro Portes, Luis E. Guarnizo, and Patricia Landolt, "The Study of Transnationalism: Pitfalls and Promise of an Emergent Research Field," *Ethnic and Racial Studies* 22 (1999): 220.

11. Frank Thistlethwaite, "Migration from Europe Overseas during the 19th and 20th Centuries," in *Population Movements in Modern European History*, ed. H. Moller (New York: Macmillan, 1964), 73–92.

12. Dino Cinel, *The National Integration of Italian Return Migration, 1870–1929* (New York: Cambridge University Press, 1991); Bruno Ramirez, *On the Move: French Canadian and Italian Migrants in the North Atlantic Economy, 1860–1914* (Toronto: McClellan and Stewart, 1991); Mark Wyman, *Round-Trip to America* (Ithaca: Cornell University Press, 1992).

13. David A. Gerber, "Forming a Transnational Narrative: New Perspectives on European Migrations to the United States," *History Teacher* (2001): 66.

14. Green, "French History and the Transnational Turn," 552.

15. David A. Gerber, "Theories and Lives: Transnationalism and the Conceptualization of International Migrations to the United States," *IMIS-Beiträge: Transnationalismus und Kulturvergleich* 15 (2000): 37.

16. Nancy Foner, "Transnationalism Old and New," chapter 3, in Foner, ed., *In a New Land: A Comparative View of Immigration* (New York: New York University Press, 2005), 85.

17. Ewa Morawska, "Immigrants, Transnationalism, and Ethnicization: A Comparison of This Great Wave and the Last," in *E Pluribus Unum? Contemporary and Historical Perspectives on Immigrant Political Incorporation*, ed. Gary Gerstle and John H. Mollenkopf (New York: Russell Sage, 2001), 190.

18. Anastasia N. Panagakos and Heather A. Horst, "Return to Cyberia: Technology and the Social Worlds of Transnational Migrants," *Global Networks* 6 (2006): 109–124; for a more nuanced statement, see Dana Diminescu, "The Connected Migrant: An Epistemological Manifesto," *Social Science Information* 47 (2008): 565.

19. Danielle Battisti, "The American Committee on Italian Migration, Anti-Communism, and Immigration Reform," *Journal of American Ethnic History* 31 (2012): 11–40.

20. George Gmelch, "Return Migration," *Annual Review of Anthropology* (1980): 135–159; Robert E. Rhoades, "From Caves to Main Street: Return Migration and the Transformation of a Spanish Village," *Papers in Anthropology* 20 (1979): 57–74; Roselyne De Villanova, Carolina Leite, and Isabel Raposo, *Maisons de rêve au Portugal* (Paris: Créaphis éditions, 1994).

21. Virginie Escafré-Dublet, *Culture et Immigration: De la question sociale à l'enjeu politique, 1958–2007* (Rennes: Presses Universitaires de Rennes, 2014).

22. Victor Pereira, *La dictature de Salazar face à l'émigration: l'État portugais et ses migrants en France (1957–1974)* (Paris: Presses de Sciences Po, 2012).

23. Mark Miller, *Foreign Workers in Western Europe: An Emerging Political Force* (New York: Praeger, 1981).

24. From 2010 on, however, the massive increase in the number of refugees—up from 10.5 million in 2010 to 15.1 million in mid-2015—outpaced any gains in student migration. United Nations High Commission on Refugees, *Mid-Year Report, 2015.* www.unhcr.org/56701b969.html (accessed Dec. 24, 2015).

25. Victor Karady, "La migration internationale d'étudiants en Europe, 1890–1940," *Actes de la recherche en sciences sociales,* 145 (2002): 47–60.

26. This section draws on material developed at greater length in Roger Waldinger, *The Cross-Border Connection: Immigrants, Emigrants, and Their Homelands* (Cambridge: Harvard University Press, 2015).

27. Aristide Zolberg, "Matters of State: Theorizing Immigration Policy," *The Handbook of International Migration: The American Experience,* ed. Charles Hirschman, Philip Kasinitz, and Josh DeWind (New York: Russell Sage, 1999), 71–92; James F. Hollifield, "The Emerging Migration State," *International Migration Review* 38 (2004): 885–912.

28. Dilip Ratha, "Workers' Remittances: An Important and Stable Source of External Development Finance," in *Remittances: Development Impact and Future Prospects,* ed. S. M. Maimbo and D. Ratha (Washington, D.C.: The World Bank, 2005), 19–52; Susan Eckstein and Adil Najam, eds., *How Immigrants Impact Their Homelands* (Durham: Duke University Press, 2013).

29. Fiona Adamson, "Displacement, Diaspora Mobilization, and Transnational Cycles of Political Violence," in *Maze of Fear: Security and Migration after September 11th,* ed. J. Tirman (New York: New Press, 2004), 45–58.

30. Some of the best known historical examples of political transnationalism and disaporic nationalism are those of nineteenth-century Italian nationalists abroad and Irish Fenians. See, e.g., Donna Gabaccia, *Italy's Many Diasporas* (London: UCL Press, 2000); and Michael Hanagan, "Irish Transnational Social Movements, Deterritorialized Immigrants and the State System: The Last One Hundred and Forty Years," *Mobilization: An International Journal* 3 (1999): 107–126.

31. Nancy L. Green and Francois Weil, *Citizenship and Those Who Leave* (Urbana: University of Illinois Press, 2007); Nancy L. Green, "The Politics of Exit: Reversing the Immigration Paradigm," *Journal of Modern History* 77 (2005): 263–289; Stéphane Dufoix, *Diasporas* (Berkeley: University of California Press, 2008); Mark Choate, *Emigrant Nation: The Making of Italy Abroad* (Cambridge: Harvard University Press, 2009).

32. As argued in Roger Waldinger, Eric Popkin, and Hector Aquiles Magana, "Conflict and Contestation in the Cross-Border Community: Hometown Associations Re-assessed," *Ethnic and Racial Studies* 31 (2007): 1–28.

33. Dufoix, *Les Diasporas,* 73.

34. Rogers Brubaker, "National Minorities, Nationalizing States, and External National Homelands in the New Europe," *Daedalus* (1995): 107–132.

35. Alejandro Portes and Ruben Rumbaut, *Immigrant America* (Berkeley: University of California Press, 2006, 3rd edition).

36. See Gabaccia, *Italy's Many Diasporas*; Eric J. Hobsbawm, "Working-class Internationalism," in *Internationalism in the Labour Movement*, ed. Frits van Holthoon and Marcel van der Linden (Leiden: E. J. Brill, 1988), I:1–18.

37. Sidney Tarrow, *The New Transnational Activism* (New York: Cambridge University Press, 2005).

38. As Blanc-Chaléard points out in her chapter, Algerians were deeply reluctant to acquire French citizenship until the Algerian civil war of the mid-1990s and the violence it engendered forced them to realize that they were in France for good.

39. Francesca Mazzolari, "Dual Citizenship Rights: Do They Make More and Richer Citizens?" *Demography* 46 (2009): 169–191.

40. Based on scores from the 2010 Migration Integration Policy Index; downloaded from www.mipex.eu/ (accessed Feb. 16, 2015).

41. Daniel Kanstroom, *Deportation Nation: Outsiders in American History* (Cambridge: Harvard University Press, 2007).

42. See Green and Weil, *Citizenship and Those Who Leave*.

43. Rogers Brubaker, *Nationalism Reframed* (Cambridge: Cambridge University Press, 1996).

44. See also Gabaccia, *Italy's Many Diasporas*; Choate, *Emigrant Nation*; and Guido Tintori, "L'Italie et ses expatriés: Une perspective historique," in "*Loin des yeux, près du cœur*," *Les États et leurs expatriés*, ed. Stéphane Dufoix, Carine Guerassimoff, and Anne de Tinguy (Paris: Presses de Sciences Po, 2010), 79–104.

45. Alan Gamlen, "The Emigration State and the Modern Geographical Imagination," *Political Geography* 27 (2008): 840–856.

46. For further details on the migration industry, see Rubén Hernández-León, *Metropolitan Migrants: The Migration of Urban Mexicans to the United States* (Berkeley: University of California Press, 2008).

47. Pereira, *La dictature de Salazar face à l'émigration*.

48. Pierre Guillen, "L'antifascisme: Facteur d'intégration des Italiens en France entre les deux guerres," in *L'emigrazione Socialista nella lotta contro il Fascismo* (Milan: Sansoni, 1982), 209–220; Clifford Rosenberg, *Policing Paris: The Origins of Modern Immigration Control between the Wars* (Ithaca: Cornell University Press, 2006).

49. Aristide Zolberg, "The Exit Revolution," in Green and Weil, *Citizenship and Those Who Leave*, 33–62. For treatment of another, southern European state's effort to impede emigration eventuating in gradual acceptance, see José Moya, *Cousins and Strangers: Spanish Immigrants in Buenos Aires* (Berkeley: University of California Press, 1998).

50. Eric J. Hobsbawm, *The Age of Extremes: A History of the World, 1914–1991* (New York: Pantheon, 1994).

51. Glick Schiller et al., "*Transnationalism*," 1.

PART I

THE STATE AND

TRANSNATIONALISM

CHAPTER I

THE "RETURN POLITICS" OF A SENDING COUNTRY

The Italian Case, 1880s–1914

Caroline Douki
Translated from the French by William Bishop

Return migration stands out as one of the distinguishing features of Italian migration at the turn of the twentieth century. Even at the time, Italian statistics already demonstrated the strength of a veritable back-and-forth movement, sometimes lasting for several generations, a singular pattern of migratory behavior that continued until at least the First World War.[1] The first attempts to quantify repatriation from the Americas, done by the Italian Commissariato Generale dell'Emigrazione (CGE) in 1905–1910, already showed the importance of a back-and-forth movement in that they calculated that stays in the United States lasted an average of five years, and those in Latin America ranged from two to five years.[2] In the mid-1920s, the CGE estimated a more general rate of return from the Americas of 63 percent for the years 1902–1923 (including the numerous repatriations that occurred due to World War I).[3] Later, using a wider variety of Italian statistics, the Italian historian Francesco Paolo Cerase showed the regional variations for returns from America for 1905–1906: the return rate among North Italians was 75 percent, but it was 45 percent among Central Italians and 42 percent among South Italians.[4] Using different methods, the U.S. immigration services came up with different estimates (which, by definition, did not have information on the totality of returns from all of the Americas): 60 percent among South Italians and 30 percent among North Italians, for the period 1908–1923.[5] The international and scientific institutions at the time themselves emphasized how statistical categorizations were still in their infancy and how this multiplied divergent results; this made it all the more urgent to cross-check information and find more uniform methods of classification in order to count flows in both directions.[6] Thus, the return statistics assembled by Marc Wyman for different nationalities can be considered indicative of only a range of estimated returns: between 33 and 40 percent for 1900–1914 for Croatians, 46 percent for 1908–1913 for Greeks (but according to U.S. statistics only), between 24.3 and 46.5 percent for Hungarians, 20 percent for Lithuanians from 1898 to 1914, between 30 and 40 percent for Poles before 1923, between 20 and 36.5 percent for Slovaks, and so forth.[7] This article proposes neither a new evaluation nor a new typology of Italy's return migration (distinguishing between economic failure or success, expulsion or nostalgia), as these issues have already been treated in several studies in demography and social history.[8] Here, rather, we will seek to consider explanations for this form of migratory behavior.

The explanations most frequently advanced in the historiography have long privileged the role of individual actors. On the one hand, historians have emphasized the modest price charged for crossing the Atlantic, attributing it mainly to technical progress and the pitiless competition between maritime companies.[9] On the other hand, scholars have also stressed the role of migratory networks formed in the place of origin, based on micro-social, familial, professional, or village solidarities. These connections have been presented both as the fundamental causes and the means that facilitated these returns: by constantly reinvigorating the affective, social, and economic ties that migrants maintained with their place of origin, these bonds stimulated frequent return migrations; at the same time, regulated by the migrants themselves and based on mutual aid, they furnished the financial assistance needed to make the multiple journeys.

In this essay, I do not seek to question the role of migratory networks, as they are fundamental in configuring the transnational territories of the migratory economy, in terms both of the back-and-forth movement of people and of its financing. Yet subscribing to an explanatory model centered uniquely on the actions of individuals is difficult, as it uses the paradigm of a free economic market resulting in a virtuous circle that combines all interests, making the commercial strategies of one party (the shipping companies that, pursuing unbridled competition, are thought to have brought down the price of transportation) to serve the strategies of another (the migrants who, for their part, are thought to have helped one another). But in this period, in fact, self-regulation alone did not govern the overall market for migratory traffic, and in particular not that involving the Italians.

First of all, the market for transatlantic transportation was not one of laissez-faire. Starting in the 1890s, it was structured by strongly organized firms that sought to maximize profits from the exponential swelling of the migrant clientele; fairly quickly, the price of transatlantic transportation stopped decreasing and even increased.[10] Secondly, the role of familial or private networks in the financing of journeys, often presented as naturally positive, must be nuanced: many exchanges of services within groups of the same national or local origin, including those of the same family, were in fact based on paying intermediaries or high-interest loans that trapped migrants in an inextricable web of debt, which did not necessarily make the payment for journeys any easier and sometimes raised their final cost.[11]

Undoubtedly, up until the Great War, the reasons that explain why such high proportions of Italians continued to remain attached to their original regions and frequently returned there need to be linked to the socioeconomic strategies of migrants and their networks, to the ups and downs of their professional and social lives abroad, as well as to the cyclical vicissitudes of the American labor market.[12] Yet these many return migrations cannot be explained entirely through the actions of private individuals, who could also impede these movements. Rather, that so many people returned home—and did so continuously—reflected the ways in which Italy's public policy deliberately facilitated return movement.

Given its determination to protect migrant nationals in all phases of their travels and turn the international mobility of its rural population into a genuine resource for economic development, starting in the 1900s, the Italian state launched a global policy that went beyond a mere "exit policy."[13] Toward this end, it took measures to encourage the repatriation of remittances, to consolidate—beyond distance and borders—lasting political, social, and affective ties between migrants and Italy as a nation, and to alleviate obstacles to emigrants' returns as much as possible. This policy was grounded in a wide variety of cultural and ideological as well as economic and legal instruments. Promoted through the combined action of the state (through the CGE), various associations that represented members of the Italian elite, and even the Italian Catholic church, this policy thus involved both private (collective) organizations and state support.

The Construction of *italianità* across Borders: What Effect on Return Migration?

Once we take into account just how much, starting in the 1880s, the Italian state itself redoubled its efforts to consolidate migrants' sentimental and political attachments to their country of origin, our understanding of the maintenance of migrants' connection to home cannot be limited to private emotions and the functioning of micro-localized connections. An abundant scholarship has shown how this policy aimed at strengthening the sense of belonging to the Italian national community among migrants across borders.[14] But what we need to understand here is the importance of this policy, not simply with regard to the search for stabilizing and strengthening the Italian *colonie* abroad, but in relation to return migration to the peninsula.

The cultural and ideological initiatives undertaken by the Italian elite and the state are the most well known. At the end of the nineteenth century, efforts at national pedagogy deployed within the peninsula itself were complemented by an identical effort under way aimed at emigrants. Under the guise of struggling against the "denationalization" of the emigrants, the Italian elite sought to inculcate in them a collective identity, a sense of belonging to a national community, forging what at the time was called *italianità* beyond borders, independent of diverse regional origins. This notion referred to a shared culture that considered Italian language, history, and certain social practices as tied to a common origin. With historical hindsight, one can easily see that this *italianità* resembled a genuine "imagined community,"[15] constructed ad hoc and diffused through the unceasing efforts of the Italian elite and the state as a way to "nationalize" emigrants' ties with the "motherland," as it was henceforth called. Emigrants were offered assistance and recreational organizations that were nationally, rather than locally based, which worked in close connection with the Italian consulates and Chambers of Commerce abroad. Meetings, banquets, conferences, or entertainment shows provided multiple occasions for mixing. Despite their frequent rivalries, these institutions created much broader forms of sociability, allowing emigrants to participate in the major events of national life by celebrating patriotic holidays or the birthdays of the royal family. Just as a politics of language favoring a standard Italian over regional dialects was becoming a central element of national pedagogy within Italy itself, simultaneous efforts were made to diffuse or sustain the practice of the Italian language among emigrants through the construction of a network of Italian schools abroad or the committees of the Dante Alighieri Society.

Even if they did not always live up to official expectations, and varied considerably from one country of residence to another, the results were real, notably among Italian communities living in large North and South American metropolises, in some Mediterranean cities,[16] and among certain categories of migrants (artisans and shopkeepers). While not diminishing the sense of belonging to local or regional networks, the new national reference points gradually took hold.[17] At the same time, references to a much wider circle of Italian belonging, of both national and transnational scope, progressed. The idea of a "Greater Italy"[18]—which the elites interested in the fate of the emigrants hoped to see spread—claimed to link all Italians scattered throughout the world in a broad political and cultural community.

Historians have emphasized that the main goal of these initiatives was to maintain ties from afar: the objective was to consolidate Italian communities established abroad so that they might serve as leverage, from afar, for Italian commercial, economic, and geopolitical power. Consequently, in the 1910s, and even more so in the interwar period, the Italian governments and political elite reflected on how they could transform the immigrant communities in America into a lobbying instrument to affect those countries' decisions in terms of foreign policy in relation to Italy.[19]

At the beginning of the twentieth century, this policy of maintaining ties also sought to ensure that the Italian communities abroad would produce a continuous flow of remittances toward Italy.[20] Social and economic private and familial logics had long worked in this direction, but the state now sought to maximize the flow of emigrant labor earnings back toward the peninsula. As early as 1901, a banking and financial strategy was put into place to better channel funds. Entailing new means for transferring money and presented to families as safer and more practical, this strategy sought to encourage the repatriation of savings from abroad as quickly and in as continuous a way as possible. The stakes were high for Italy, at a moment when the development of banking structures for small savers in the countries of immigration were starting to nibble at the market of Italian immigrants who prolonged their stay or who decided to settle there for good. This was the case, for example, of a network of popular savings banks in France[21] or certain private banking networks in the United States. The configuration of Italy's banking mechanisms oriented toward migrants thus placed great importance on the return of money independent of the return of people. For that reason one might think that the Italian state's policies of maintaining social, cultural, and economic ties with emigrants indeed sought to create a community of interest with a population abroad that it seriously thought would not return. However, because these policies also revived the social, ideological, economic, and affective ties with Italy as a nation, they also encouraged frequent return trips of emigrants, without however comprising an explicit policy of return. Such policies involved an extremely diversified range of strategies to which we now turn.

The Codification of Italian Nationality and Repatriation

At the beginning of the twentieth century, the conditions for the transmission or attribution of Italian nationality were reformed in ways that aimed at maintaining the nation's ties with its emigrants. The 1865 civil code, which recognized *jus sanguinis*, was furthered with three legislative texts: articles 35–36 of the January 31, 1901, law on the protection of migrants; the

1906 law; and the 1912 law on nationality. These laws allowed emigrants residing or born abroad to retain Italian nationality for as long as possible. In a context of increasingly massive emigration, this was a way for Italy to respond to the new challenges introduced by the assimilating aims of the main receiving countries (Latin America, France, United States), which were also engaged in the task of reforming their own nationality codes.

In the new codification of Italian nationality, various arrangements could affect emigrants who chose to return. To ensure that legal ties would be maintained in lasting fashion, the law established that children of Italian immigrants, even if born and residing in foreign countries where they were considered as nationals by birth, would nonetheless automatically retain Italian nationality unless, upon reaching majority, they explicitly refused it through a written administrative procedure.[22] While this law could lead to situations of de facto "dual citizenship" that were sometimes problematic, in practice it facilitated the situation both of emigrants who periodically returned to Italy and those who came back to the peninsula after a long absence, sometimes accompanied by children born abroad. Even more specific measures were put in place for emigrants who had changed nationality and abandoned Italian citizenship. As long as these emigrants or their children came back to reside on the peninsula, diverse legal procedures allowed them to easily be reincorporated into the Italian nationality. They could recover the Italian citizenship they had lost abroad simply by renouncing the foreign nationality acquired elsewhere and establishing residency in the peninsula during the year of the renunciation.[23] An alternative involved naturalization, which was readily accorded to the descendants of emigrants born abroad who, in the second or third generation, wanted to return to reside in Italy.[24] In addition, for repatriated persons who, once they were reestablished, were not concerned with quickly recovering their original nationality, measures of de facto "renationalization" were set into place after two years of continuous residence in the kingdom.[25]

On the basis of this legal apparatus, how can we explain the Italian policy of nationality as applied to repatriation? We need to remember that this right to nationality and citizenship was the product of negotiations among different milieus, each with their own preoccupations: jurists, Italian reformers who sought to protect migrants and who expressed themselves through different consultative institutions (such as the Chamber of Deputies, the Senate, and the Superior Council of Emigration). And there was the logic of sovereignty of the Italian state.

First of all, we can observe that, in text after text, the Italian lawmakers sought to open avenues for the recovery of citizenship that were sufficiently varied to be adapted to the great diversity of cases. Over the years, it became clear that distinctive migratory paths and international experiences were crucial factors. Legal situations varied as a function of the countries frequented by migrants (each one having its own more or less assimilating legal regime of nationality, with the Latin American[26] and perhaps French cases worrying the Italian elite the most) and as a function of the moment within the lifecycle chosen for return to Italy.

One then sees that this right to nationality exerted its usual function of maintaining national homogenization, as an intangible good decreed from on high. By allowing emigrants who had lost Italian nationality to recover it shortly after they had reestablished a somewhat durable residence in Italy, the legislature clearly expressed the logic of a sending state that refused to submit to the paradoxical effect of finding "foreign" groups on its own territory whose presence did not result from immigration but rather from the propensity of its own emigrants for repatriation.[27] But at the same time, because it quickly brought the repatriated back into Italian nationality, this provision also allowed these return migrants to recover the totality of rights conferred by the nationality of the country in which they now lived. These entitlements were far from negligible thanks to the political and social reforms of the Giolittian Era, which extended social and political rights to disadvantaged groups. Thus, up until the early 1920s, emigrants or their children who had been away for a more or less long time were in no way treated as second-class citizens once they had again become residents of the peninsula.[28]

The regime of Italian nationality in the era of mass emigration thus responded to a double dynamic: a logic of legal inclusion of emigrants that sought to maintain as tightly woven a net of nationality as possible by giving the state the means to sew up any holes that migration might have created; and, at the same time, a pragmatic adaptation to the transnational situations of Italian migrants who returned in large numbers, even after long absences, all the while having had to conform to foreign juridical regimes that varied from one country to the next, but were increasingly assimilationist.

This necessary pragmatism was often underscored by jurists and the politically reformist elites during the debates that accompanied the reform of Italian nationality law: they repeated that it was necessary to adapt this sector of law to the major changes of the modern world, including the burgeoning of emigration and the transformations of international relations that allowed individuals to change nationality much more often than before, and sometimes several different times over.[29] These adaptations coincided with the recommendations developed in the same period by the Institute of International Law and one of its key figures, the jurist Augusto Pierantoni.

Thus, these legal adaptations of citizenship law, reflecting the flexibility of the reformist Italian governments of the time, provided additional grounding for an Italian policy of return.

Modulating Military Duties for the Repatriated

The obligation to serve in the military produced contradictory effects on the dynamics of return. Military service, mandatory since 1875 and linked to the possession of Italian nationality, affected young men, who were the largest category of migrants. Requirements for military service could simultaneously encourage but paradoxically also discourage their return migration. Some returned to Italy to do their military service on time, but others were more likely to postpone their return or even stay abroad. Because conscription for two or three years of service in Italy occurred at the precise moment in the migrants' lifecycle when they were the most productive workwise, and since many came from Italy's southern countryside where conscientious objection to military service was widespread, the number of draft evaders (*renitenti*) increased.[30]

Needing both military manpower *and* migration, the Italian state had contradictory objectives. On the one hand, the logic of sovereignty, the need for a strong army, and concern for the credibility of the country's strength in the eyes of neighboring states pushed the balance toward extending conscription to the entirety of Italy's male population, wherever they lived. On the other hand, there was the realization that seeking too strict an imposition of the obligation to return (with no consideration for the young emigrants' remoteness and consigning them to the category of *renitenti* for lateness or absence, leading to subsequent exposure to prosecution if they later returned to the peninsula) could precipitate a definitive rupture with Italy, undoing all the other efforts to create national ties from afar. Yet still another logic, tied to the interests of the national economy, which benefited from the remittances of the most active cohorts abroad, discouraged policies that would hinder the mechanisms of those emigrants' work cycles abroad.

Starting in the 1880s, Italian military authorities conceded certain accommodations that accepted the induction of late-arriving return male migrants without any penalty.[31] At the beginning of the twentieth century, a compromise between these different logics and the different concerned state sectors (military, CGE, and diplomatic and police authorities) was reached so that a whole group of young men living or born abroad legally benefited from certain accommodations concerning the military and civic obligations attached to citizenship. The 1901 law on emigration distinguished two subgroups on the basis of distance from Italy. For the Italians in America, men of Italian nationality who were born abroad or who had arrived there before age 17 were exempted from having to return in order to fulfill military service; if they did return to the peninsula before the age of 32, they remained obliged to perform military service, but not if they returned after age 32. For Italians born or living in Europe or the Mediterranean countries, accommodation was granted only for timeliness: they could defer their return until the age of 25,[32] and more often than not, even if they returned after this legal limit, they were merely inducted into the troops without sanction.[33]

On the eve of World War I, the legal and actual situation can be summarized as follows: emigrants, obligated in theory like all other Italians to military service, were allowed to return at their own rhythm. When they came back, they were inducted into the military without sanction for any delay due to time abroad and were exempted from service if they returned during later adulthood. To be in good standing, emigrants were asked to sign up for military lists in consular offices, thus allowing for the updating of statistics on potential military reserves without forcing the emigrants to return solely for that purpose, something that would have been economically or socially problematic for many. In return for these accommodations, the Italian elite nonetheless counted on the fact that emigrants would indeed remain committed to their birth country and that they would respond to its appeal in the case of urgent need and a general mobilization.

This policy reflected the situation of a sending country that had to juggle with a plurality of possible interpretations of its interests (civic, national, and economic) with regard to migratory matters and that in particular had to take into account its real means of influence over the migrants. Coercion, even in military matters, was not considered an option. Thus, at the beginning of the twentieth century, a flexible way of regulating migration was being put into place: state action struggled to play an increasingly important role in the lives of citizens abroad through attempts to institute national ties that could be reconciled with a free emigration that could be assisted, and even controlled, but never coerced, whether at the point of exit or return.

At first glance, the legislative solution modulating conscription requirements for emigrants and the repatriated may seem to offer little incentive to return among those who should have the obligation to do so. Nonetheless, in two ways these policies comprise a part of the politics of regulating returns. First, by affording real autonomy to the logics of private individuals concerning the possibility or the moment of return they gave deliberate priority to work rhythms over the strict civic calendar of conscription dictated by national belonging. Second, the Italian authorities explicitly saw their solution as a way of facilitating return migration in the medium term: demanding neither punctuality nor forced return at around 20 years of age also meant avoiding obstructing return at a later point in life, when the rhythms of work would be more permissive or when the migrants would want to spend the last part of their life in the peninsula, at which point they would bring their savings with them.

Assisted Repatriations, Facilitated Mobility, Secure Transfer Payments: The Social Protection of Migrants

At the turn of the twentieth century, Italy's policy toward emigrants reflected an understanding that the most vulnerable migrants, those who returned because of an accident or economic failure, required protection. Orphans, widows, the indigent, and the sick were housed at ports and repatriated, for free, thanks to provisions that closely linked the diverse means of public action available at the time: peripheral state structures (consular assistance), Italian philanthropic associations in American ports that provided shelter to migrants before reboarding to return to Italy, and private businesses. In effect, one of the main solutions for the repatriation of these indigent emigrants was to have the costs of the crossing supported by the maritime companies. Ever since the 1901 law,[34] in exchange for the accreditation they needed to participate in the lucrative transatlantic transportation market, companies transporting migrants who boarded and landed in Italian ports had to provide to the state, for free, a number of third-class seats, in proportion to the ships' capacities.[35]

This form of state intervention was not specific to Italy, as most states did as much for their citizens in trouble abroad. In the second half of the nineteenth century, protecting the most vulnerable emigrants became a humanitarian obligation, reflecting not simply the duty of national protection but the influence of international agreements on reciprocal responsibility for indigent populations.[36]

While some repatriations came about because of personal failure, many other returns crowned a successful professional career. Still others reflected temporary forms of mobility. At the beginning of the twentieth century, state policy sought to facilitate this rotation of persons, particularly as it was accompanied by sizable and rapid transfers of money. Toward this end, the state could use a specific instrument tied to economic regulation and social protection: the organization of maritime transport of migrants as a public service, by regulating the price of the crossing.[37] To understand the importance of Italian public policy in this matter, one must remember that, after the phase of lowered prices that marked transatlantic crossings in the years between 1880 and 1898, the trend reversed during the years between 1900–1914, precisely when the circulation of Italian emigrants intensified. These increased costs came about as the result of a variety of factors: an improved international economic situation; an expansion of the market for passengers as people from the peripheral countryside of Central, Eastern, and Mediterranean Europe emigrated in even greater numbers; and the new market structure set into place by the most powerful maritime companies, which organized themselves into cartels dividing market sectors and maritime paths in ways that precluded competition, all the while diversifying their service to an increasingly numerous and solvent clientele of emigrants.[38] Also at play were the regulations of states implicated in the transatlantic circulation of migrants (as sending, receiving, or transit countries) that compelled the companies to make improvements in the material and sanitary conditions of transport.

In the case of the market for Italian migration, state regulations that obliged accredited companies to operate within a system of set prices did not reverse the trend toward rising prices but were careful to contain it, particularly by stipulating that the rise in price must correspond to an equivalent amelioration in the conditions of transport, in the manner of a "fair price" policy. In the Italian perspective, which considered the emigrants no longer as uprooted but as workers across borders, the goal was not only to give everyone the possibility of crossing at nonprohibitive costs, but also to accelerate the improvement of conditions by authorizing transportation companies to set prices that corresponded to their investments. Thus, the prices for a trip between American and Italian ports had a tendency to rise between 1900 and 1914; a third-class trip on good ships between New York and Italy, for example, cost around 150–220 liras (or 30–45 dollars).[39] Prices were even higher for the second-class passages that better-off migrants, Italians included, increasingly preferred.[40] The amount spent for transshipment is thus not the only criterion to take into account for understanding the practice of frequent crossings that characterized Italian emigration.

Even though these prices did increase, they were nonetheless within the migrants' means, although the first trip still frequently entailed recourse to a loan from the close circle of kith or kin or from the credit networks spread throughout the rural world. But once the migrants had established residence in America, prices could be managed much more readily for coming and going, particularly because their financial means increased in proportion to the nature or regularity of their salaried work abroad. Yet an accounting exercise comparing the increase in the price of transportation with the increase in income of immigrant workers does not suffice since state regulation also must be taken into account. Though companies were constantly attempting to profit from the clientele's growing income by attempting to sell return journeys at a higher rate or by seeking to modulate prices according to the fluctuations of employment and salaries that were very common in the United States, the relation between the migrant workers' salaries and the price of transport remained advantageous for the workers because Italian state regulations and its "fair price" policy stopped companies from charging excessively exorbitant prices. Similarly, the Italian administration vigorously opposed the idea that the cost of a return trip might exceed the cost of the outward-bound trip on the same line. This principle was imposed by the CGE from the outset and constantly defended—even by the Council of State to which appeal was made by recalcitrant shipowners—against the strategies of companies that sought to take advantage of the greater resources, or greater impatience, of emigrants who had amassed savings abroad.[41]

Furthermore, one cannot accurately estimate the costs of a transatlantic crossing based solely on the nominal prices advertised by companies and billed to buyers. These costs must be considered globally, in a way that also takes all the other costs of the transatlantic trip into account: access to information, possible lateness, or different dangers over the course of the trip (sickness, accidents, theft, loss of luggage). State regulation struggled to act on the entirety of these costs, not just those charged by the shipping companies. But if ticket prices properly speaking were on the increase, these global costs were strongly decreasing. It became easier to undertake a crossing because it was less costly in terms of time—risks of exhaustion, accident, late departure or arrival decreased—while the uncertainty of the price to pay was limited by the obligation henceforth imposed on companies to use fixed and set prices. The reduction in uncertainty on all levels thus truly caused a general decrease in the global cost of a crossing, even when the nominal price of the crossing itself never decreased. And this evolution was neither the sole effect of maritime companies' business strategies nor of self-organized networks or kith and kin solidarities: all these factors certainly entered into play, but the greater security was also largely the effect of the Italian state's normative regulation and deliberate policy.

The new regulations devoted to attracting remittances, set in place in 1901 and mentioned earlier, included several measures designed to repatriate the money of those who returned to Italy in person. One objective entailed dissuading the emigrants from bringing their savings back by carrying cash at the risk of its being lost or stolen during the journey. Instead, using information and advice given out by philanthropic associations and consulates and notices published in the emigrant press—and even through a printed notice placed on passport back covers—migrants were encouraged to expedite their savings by postal mandate or bank transfer before returning to Italy. The same objective motivated Luigi Luzzati, a recognized international expert on popular savings and social insurance and the negotiator of the Franco-Italian agreement on the social rights of migrant workers, to ensure that the agreement included provisions that would allow returning migrants to transfer their accounts from a French popular savings bank to an Italian *Cassa di Risparmio* without fees.[42] That identical goal was reflected in the huge effort undertaken in the negotiation of bilateral treaties to protect Italian migrants by ensuring that those who had contributed to social insurance funds abroad (against workplace accidents or old age) could receive their benefits not only in the country of immigration, but also in Italy, if they chose to return there.[43]

Statistics, An Instrument in the Politics of Return Migration

The Italian administration's creation of a statistical measure of returns was both a product of and witness to its policies of assisting repatriation. From their beginning in 1876, statistics on emigration took the phenomenon of return migration into account, though initially not with the goal of studying return migration in and of itself. Rather, the statistics recorded only emigrants' expressed intentions of return at the moment of departure. Responding to political priorities, these statistics both showed that emigration was often temporary—quieting worries about its rapid growth—and simultaneously gave emigrants a place in the official representation of the national population. Later, at the beginning of the twentieth century, the question of return migration became the object of a specific statistical construction whose goal went beyond that of merely representing the nation-state but included the formalized data needed for thinking about and administering a social question. This turning point was part of a much wider effort to perfect statistics on emigration (which were reorganized in 1904–1905),[44] which was part of a willful decision on the part of the state to better oversee emigration, perceived as a social and economic reality that should be accompanied, and no longer merely seen as a question of public order.

The precocious and highly technical nature of Italian statistics on return migration conflict with the claims of some historians, who, having discovered the magnitude of return migration contend that, at the time, efforts to record return migration were insufficient and incoherent.[45] In the case of Italy, it is hard to agree with this analysis.[46] Not only did Italy continue to perfect the methods designed to illuminate these complex movements of return, but as of the first decade of the twentieth century, it already sought to turn these statistics into an instrument of the government by providing a framework for acting on return migration and, at the same time, to forge the means for evaluating the effects of these policies.

Toward this end, responsibility for the first major project for gathering data according to the improved procedures resulting from the 1904–1905 reform was entrusted to the most brilliant of all statistical experts available to the CGE at the time, Alberto Beneduce.[47] Beneduce undertook the first systematic presentation of the demographic characteristics of return migration,[48] to which he added a numerical and cartographic presentation of its spatial distribution (showing the Italian arrival port and ultimate destination of the returnees). This in turn allowed for a consideration of the potential economic impact of the phenomenon. Beneduce also launched the first efforts designed not simply to count the number of returnees, but also to calculate the average length of stay and rotation. The statistical work on return migration was constantly improved between 1900 and 1914 with the goals of finding better observation points; improving, unifying, or systematizing survey and classification methods; and combining the numbers on the movement of people with sanitary or financial statistics. Other experts—statisticians, demographers, and economists—who, independent of the entities charged with the administration of migration, shared a conviction about the need to elaborate a policy on return migration, added to the studies undertaken in the official framework of the CGE.[49] Hence, the question was not simply one of quantifying return movements, but also of attempting to predict them and encourage them—in other words, to govern them and highlight their value.

These objectives can be seen in the publications concerning return migration which, already in the 1910s and 1920s, multiplied attempts to forge statistical tools that would allow for the observation of tendencies, constants, and correlations, while consistently proposing typologies capable of making sense of the many forms and significance of return migration. Faced with a phenomenon characterized by great situational variability, the statisticians sought to enlighten public action through a quest for regularities, reasoning through tendencies, and through the comparison of different situations. And they sought to take things further by combining demographic, economic, or social factors and by connecting Italian data to other sources of information linked to the international economic situation.

Many different combinations were used for constructing detailed tables of the currents of returns, varying by family type or composition: heads of family, bachelor workers, married or unmarried women, and children. In addition, calculations of the length of stay and the rhythms of rotation from different countries in the Americas were done with ever-increased precision.[50] Like statisticians and economists in other countries,[51] Italian experts began to identify migration cycles as a major subject of study: attempts were made to find a model that could correlate rates of exit and rates of return, with the idea that one could distinguish within the same year cycles where there were more departures and others where there were more returns.[52] Efforts were also made to define correlations among the cycles of rotation of emigrants revealed by these studies and the variations in the economic or financial situation in the Americas. At the beginning of the 1920s, the CGE even thought it would be able to establish the laws of return under "normal conditions" and those that would pertain to times of crisis.[53]

All of this statistical work led to the enrichment of an administrative science and an economic science of returns. These forms of knowledge were employed in several ways. First, they were used to evaluate and highlight the economic effects of emigration. Thus, this so-called science of returns carefully combined the data on population returns with those concerning the financial effects of emigration, due to remittances, that the ministry of the Treasury and the Central Bank of Italy were including in public accounts.[54] In particular, attempts were made to identify how return migration affected the patterns of transferring money to Italy.

The attention given to all forms of return to the peninsula did not simply reflect an accounting perspective, solely oriented toward maximizing remittances. More profoundly, it accompanied a global rereading of the place and significance of emigration in Italian society. A typology of returns was quickly drawn up from the effort to elaborate statistical data; this typology diverged from the dichotomies that continued to obscure the political and economic understanding of emigration at the end of the nineteenth century. At the time, definitive emigration and temporary emigration were understood as opposed in principle; consequently, those who were for and those who were against emigration had diametrically opposite perceptions of the role of emigration in Italian life.[55] Afterward, the public and scientific publication of the magnitude of return migration demonstrated the circulatory nature of emigration, invalidating the equation between long distance and definitive exile. With the exception of the deforming and aggressive discourse of nationalist circles, emigration could no longer be presented as a demographic or economic loss. Thanks to the force of the presentation of the statistical data, the representation of return migration as simply either failure or success was shown to be an ideological construct.

In the end, statistics allowed for a formal presentation of the coming and going of migrants as a circulation of workers across borders through a vast yet functional space. This new perception of emigration as a form of international mobility, linked to work and not simply as a question of public order, was already underway at the turn of the century as evidenced in the 1901 law. But the statistical proof of returns allowed this understanding to be deepened considerably. The evolution was confirmed by the new 1913 law on the protection of migrants that explicitly and fundamentally linked emigration to the motivation of work, and no longer to poverty or to a problem of public order.[56] The emigrant was no longer a poor person running away in an emergency or driven by vain illusions, but a person who went abroad to work,[57] perhaps coming back more or less often.

*   *   *

The mass of returns and of comings-and-goings that characterized Italian migration at the beginning of the twentieth century remind us that migratory practices and social identities were related at several different levels. While return migration effectively displayed and sustained a local or national attachment to the sending country, it also represented the development of forms of transnational practices.

We may draw a conclusion about the historiographic importance of understanding return migration as a form of transnationalism. By examining the plurality and diversity of private, collective, and state dynamics that favored the massive practice of migrant Italians' returns in this period, we can see the limitations of certain analytical schema that have long remained prevalent in the historiography of migration: models that seek out push and pull factors, for example, or analyses that frontally oppose the private logics of migrant solidarity to state logics that are seen as only being constraining. On the contrary, what needs to be explained is how, after the turn of the twentieth century, transatlantic or transmediterranean migratory movements, even as they became increasingly normalized and organized, remained massive, and genuinely circulatory. As argued in this paper, that pattern did not result from frontal opposition, but rather an interaction between private dynamics, national logics (much less homogeneous than what has long been held to be true), and economic, commercial, and legal movements of a truly transnational nature.

NOTES

1. We will not be addressing the question of returns tied to the Great War, evaluations of which in fact vary substantially in the historiography.

2. Commissariato Generale dell'Emigrazione, *Bollettino dell'Emigrazione*, no. 11.

3. *L'emigrazione italiana dal 1910 al 1923. Relazione presentata a S. E. il Ministro degli Affari Esteri dal Commissario Generale dell'Emigrazione* (Rome: CGE, 1926), vol. 1, 208ff.

4. Francesco Paolo Cerase, "Sviluppo, sottosviluppo ed emigrazione: Riflessioni e ricerche intorno all'emigrazione di ritorno," in *Il movimento migratorio italiano dall'Unità nazionale ai giorni nostri*, ed. Franca Assante (Geneva: Droz, 1978), vol. 1, 73ff.

5. U.S. Secretary of Labor, *Eleventh Annual Report, 1923* (Washington, D.C., 1923), quoted in Mark Wyman, *Round-Trip to America. The Immigrants Return to Europe, 1880–1930* (Ithaca: Cornell University Press, 1993), 11.

6. See *Methods of Compiling Emigration and Immigration Statistics* (Geneva: International Labour Organisation, 1922) and the methodological discussions tirelessly conducted between ILO experts during the 1920s–1930s, with input from U.S. scientific foundations such as the Social Science Research Council and the National Bureau of Economic Research; Imre Ferenczi, Walter F. Willcox, eds., *International Migrations*, vol. 2: *Interpretations* (New York: National Bureau of Economic Research, 1931).

7. Wyman, *Round-Trip to America*, 10–12.

8. Massimo Livi Bacci, *L'immigrazione e l'assimilazione degli italiani negli Stati Uniti, secondo le statistiche demografiche americane* (Milan: Giuffrè, 1961); Francesco Paolo Cerase, *L'emigrazione di ritorno: Innovazione o reazione? Esperienza dell'emigrazione di ritorno dagli Stati Uniti d'America* (Rome: Bulzoni, 1971); John D. Gould, "European Inter-Continental Emigration. The Road Home: Return Migration from the U.S.A.," *Journal of European Economic History* 9 (Spring 1980): 41–111; Dino Cinel, *The National Integration of Italian Return Migration 1870–1929* (Cambridge: Cambridge University Press, 1991); Wyman, *Round-Trip to America*; Francesco Paolo Cerase, "L'onda di ritorno: I rimpatri," in *Storia dell'emigrazione italiana. Partenze*, eds. P. Bevilacqua, A. De Clementi and E. Franzina (Turin: Donzelli, 2001), vol. 1, 113–126.

9. Wyman, *Round-Trip to America*.

10. Drew Keeling, "International Networks, Corporate Strategy, and the Improvement of Travel Conditions for Migrants Crossing the North Atlantic, 1890–1914," paper for European Business History Association Annual Conference, Sept. 2007, Geneva.

11. *Bollettino dell'Emigrazione* [BE], 1908–1909, 60–66; BE, 1909–1912, 95–99, 114.

12. Michael J. Piore, *Birds of Passage. Migrant Labor and Industrial Societies* (Cambridge: Cambridge University Press, 1979).

13. Nancy Green and François Weil, eds., *Citizenship and Those Who Leave. The Politics of Emigration and Expatriation* (Urbana: University of Illinois Press, 2007).

14. For example, Daniel J. Grange, *L'Italie et la Méditerranée (1896–1911). Les fondements d'une politique étrangère* (Rome: Ecole Française de Rome, 1994) vol. 1, 615–702; Patricia Salvetti, *Immagine nazionale ed emigrazione nella Società Dante Alighieri* (Rome: Bonacci, 1995); Matteo Sanfilippo, "Nationalisme, *italianité* et émigration aux Amériques (1830–1990)," *Revue européenne d'histoire* (1995): 177–191; Mark I. Choate, *Emigrant Nation. The Making of Italy Abroad* (Cambridge: Harvard University Press, 2008).

15. Benedict Anderson, *Imagined Communities. Reflections on the Origin and Spread of Nationalism* (London: Verso, 1991).

16. Dino Cinel, *From Italy to San Francisco. The Immigrant Experience* (Stanford: Stanford University Press, 1982); Stefano Luconi, *From Paesani to White Ethnics. The Italian Experience in Philadelphia* (Albany: State University of New York Press, 2001); Sanfilippo,"Nationalisme, *italianité*"; Anouchka Lazarev, "La colonia italiana: Una identità ambigua," in *L'Italia e l'Egitto (1882–1922)*, ed. R. Rainero (Milan: Marzorati, 1991), 175–186; Choate, *Emigrant Nation*.

17. For a more detailed demonstration, see C. Douki, "Lucquois au travail ou émigrés italiens? Les identités à l'épreuve de la mobilité transnationale, 1850–1914," *Le Mouvement social* 188 (1999): 17–41.

18. Andrea Cantalupi, "La federazione dell'italianità," *Nuova Antologia* (Nov. 1908): 138–145.

19. The usefulness of the possible participation of emigrants in the political life of countries in South America, through the vote of those who had been naturalized, is mentioned in the 1909 parliamentary debates (*Atti parlamentari*, cam. dep., leg. XXIII, 1a sessione 1909, Discussioni, 2833), or in the 1908 Congresso degli Italiani all'estero. On the strategies of influence proper to fascism, see Stefano Luconi, *La "diplomazia parallela." Il regime fascista e la mobilitazione politica degli italo-americani* (Milano: Angeli, 2000). See also Donna R. Gabaccia, *Foreign Relations: American Immigration in Global Perspective* (Princeton: Princeton University Press, 2012).

20. Luigi De Rosa, *Emigranti, capitali, banche 1896–1906* (Napoli: Banco di Napoli, 1980); Luigi Mittone, "Le rimesse degli emigrati sino al 1914," *Affari sociali internazionali* 4 (1984): 125–160; Caroline Douki, "Les retombées financières de l'émigration et le développement régional en Italie entre XIXe et XXe siècle," in *Crise espagnole et nouveau siècle en Méditerranée. Politiques publiques et mutations structurelles des économies dans l'Europe méditerranéenne (fin XIXe-début XXe siècle)*, ed. G. Chastagnaret (Madrid-Aix-en-Provence: Casa de Velasquez-Publications de l'Université de Provence, 2000), 131–145; Gino Massulo, "Economia delle rimesse," in *Storia dell'emigrazione italiana. Partenze*, 161–183.

21. Istituto Veneto di Scienze, Lettere ed Arti [Venice], *Archivio Luzzatti*, Atti, b. 307.

22. 1912 law, article 7.

23. 1912 law, article 9.

24. Article 36 of the January 31, 1901, law on emigration, confirmed by the 1912 law on nationality.

25. 1912 law, article 9, § 3.

26. The question is discussed in the Chamber of deputies and the Senate in 1900–1901 and 1909–1910 and at the 1908 Congresso degli Italiani all'estero (*Atti parlamentari*, Cam. Dep., *Discussioni*, 27/1/1900; Senato, *Discussioni*, dic.1900–Jan. 1901; Cam. Dep., XXIII leg., *Discussioni*, vol. 3, 22/6/1909).

27. This provision also allowed for a rapid legal integration of the "Italian" populations from the *unredeemed Italian territories*.

28. It is true that they could become the object of police surveillance if they were suspected of being politically radicalized, but this was also true for all Italian citizens.

29. This mode of argumentation is mentioned when the Senate, in its January 29, 1901, session, invites the government to quickly present a general project for a law on nationality. It figures among the interventions of the jurist Emilio Pagliano in Italian or international legal networks, *Revue du Droit international* (1907): 306–312; it is taken up again in the explanation of motivations that accompanied the submission of the governmental law project on nationality by the Italian minister of Justice in February 1910.

30. Piero Del Negro, *Esercito, Stato e società* (Bologne: Capelli, 1979), 183–243.

31. For example, Archivio di Stato di Lucca [Lucca], Prefettura, Gabinetto, b. 24 (relazione pel 2 semestre 1884).

32. Art. 33 of the July 17, 1910, law, art. 94 of the 1911 military law.

33. Archivio Centrale dello Stato [Rome], PCM, 1914, fasc.3/2.

34. Caroline Douki, "Protection sociale et mobilité transatlantique: Les migrants italiens au début du XXe siècle," *Annales. Histoire et sciences sociales* 66 (Apr. 2011): 375–410.

35. Art. 25 of the January 31, 1901, Emigration law. This can be negotiated, but there are always at least two seats per ship traveling to the peninsula at the disposition of consular services. The navigation companies receive from the Italian State an indemnity of 2 lira per day per adult seat, 1 lira for children between 3 and 12 years of age; the service is entirely free for children under 3.

36. Paul-André Rosental, "Migrations, souveraineté, droits sociaux. Protéger et expulser les étrangers en Europe du XIXe siècle à nos jours," *Annales. Histoire et sciences sociales* 66 (Apr. 2011): 335–373.

37. Douki, "Protection sociale et mobilité transatlantique."

38. Keeling, "International Networks, Corporate Strategy."

39. CGE, *L'emigrazione italiana dal 1910 al 1923* (Rome: CGE, 1926), 431, 437.

40. Keeling, "International Networks, Corporate Strategy." For Italian migrants: Archivio Storico Diplomatico, Ministero Affari Esteri [Rome], CGE, Affari Generali, b. 41.

41. Douki, "Protection sociale et mobilité transatlantique," 403.

42. The question is addressed in the 1904 framework for the agreement between the two countries. A complementary agreement deals with this precise point in 1906.

43. Before the Great War, this was acquired in the framework of the treaties signed with France (1904–1906), Luxemburg (1909), and Germany (1912). See also C. Douki, D. Feldman, and P. A. Rosental, "Pour une histoire relationnelle du ministère du Travail en France, en Italie et au Royaume-Uni dans l'entre-deux-guerres: Le transnational, le bilatéral et l'interministériel en matière de politique migratoire," in *Les politiques du travail, 1906–2006. Acteurs, institutions, réseaux*, ed. A. Chatriot, O. Join-Lambert, and V. Viet (Rennes: Presses Universitaires de Rennes, 2006), 143, 152–156.

44. *Annuario statistico della emigrazione italiana dal 1876 al 1925* (Rome: CGE, 1926), XVII–XXI. For a historical perspective, see Dora Marucco, "Le statistiche dell'emigrazione italiana," in *Storia dell'emigrazione italiana, Partenze*, 61–76.

45. See, for example, Wyman, *Round-Trip to America*, 7–9.

46. For a more detailed demonstration, see C. Douki, "Compter les 'retours' d'émigrants dans l'Italie du début du XXe siècle: Conventions statistiques, libéralisme économique et politique publique," *Revue Européenne des Migrations Internationales* 29 (Nov.-Déc. 2013): 11–32.

47. Before becoming a famous statesman at the head of structures for public social and economic policies created before and during fascism, Beneduce (1877–1944) began his career as an expert in mathematics appreciated for his ability to apply statistics to the fields of demography, economy, and social insurance. See Franco Bonelli, "Alberto Beneduce" in *I protagonisti dell'intervento pubblico in Italia*, ed. Alberto Mortara (Milan: Angeli, 1984), 329–356.

48. Alberto Beneduce, "Saggio di statistica dei rimpatriati dalle Americhe," in *BE*, 1911/11. Earlier, in 1904, 1905, and 1910, he had published articles of economic theory and statistical methodology on how to evaluate the financial consequences of emigration in the *Giornale degli economisti*.

49. For example, the statistician and economist Francesco Coletti, *Dell'emigrazione italiana. Cinquant'anni di storia italianna 1860–1910* (Milan: Hoepli, 1911), 71–79.

50. According to the estimations coordinated by the CGE, at the time, stays lasted 5 years on average in the United States and from 2 to 5 years in Latin America (*BE*, 1911/11). F. Coletti estimated that emigrants' returns represent about 30 percent of all departures during the period from 1905–1909, with a higher rate of return for the United States (60 percent of the departures to the United States) than for Argentina (44 percent of departures for Argentina) (*Dell'emigrazione*, 71–79).

51. On the different models of cycles and statistical or graphical tools that emerged in the 1910s–1920s, see Christian Deblock, "Le cycle des affaires et la prévision économique: Les instituts de conjoncture et la méthode des 'baromètres' dans l'entre-deux-guerres," in *L'ère du chiffre. Systèmes statistiques et traditions nationales*, ed. Jean-Pierre Beaud and Jean-Guy Prévost (Sainte-Foy, Québec: Presses de l'Université du Québec, 2000), 357–410.

52. CGE, *L'emigrazione italiana dal 1910 al 1923*, vol. 1, 36–37.

53. Ibid., 35.

54. See, for example, the essay published by the general director of the Bank of Italy, Bonaldo Stringher, "Sur la balance des paiements entre l'Italie et l'étranger," *Bulletin de l'Institut international de Statistique* 19/3 (1912): 93–126.

55. Fernando Manzotti, *La polemica sull'emigrazione nell'Italia unita* (Città di Castello: Ed. Dante Alighieri, 1969).

56. August 2, 1913, law 1073 on emigration.

57. Carlo Furno, *L'evoluzione sociale delle leggi italiane sull'emigrazione* (Varese: Tip. Multa paucis, 1958), 35; Manzotti, *La polemica sull'emigrazione*; Géraldine Rieucau, *Emigrants et salariés. Deux catégories nouvelles en Italie et en Espagne (1861–1975)* (Paris: La Documentation française, 1997), 41–49.

CHAPTER 2

PORTUGUESE MIGRANTS AND PORTUGAL

Elite Discourse and Transnational Practices

Victor Pereira
Translated from the French by Miguel Cardoso

Histories of Portuguese emigration often begin with a reference to a famous 1978 article by Vitorino Magalhães Godinho that characterized emigration as a "structural constant"[1] of Portuguese society. Working within a Braudelian perspective, Magalhães Godinho endeavored to pinpoint the deep structures of Portuguese society, perceiving emigration within the *longue durée*. However, this structuralist point of view, taken up by many authors since, has often foreclosed discerning the singularities of each historical period, and of each migratory flow. Moreover, as critiques of structuralist history have highlighted, the search for structures and permanencies virtually shuts out agents, their capacity for initiative and their strategies. Hence, in many works migrants are depicted as marionettes whose strings are pulled by the invisible forces of international capitalism.

During the 1970s and 1980s, a quantitative approach to migratory flows took center stage, and the handful of global syntheses on Portuguese emigration privileged figures and maps while overlooking the lived experience of migrants themselves.[2] Studies addressing migrants' strategies; migratory chains; cultural, religious or sporting practices; dwellings—both in France and Portugal; their insertion into the different labor environments; and the relations they maintained with Portugal—as a nation and as a state, since the two terms do not fully coincide—and with their villages of origin first arose from within sociology, geography, and anthropology.[3] Only later would these fields and the conceptual tools that they use be appropriated by historians. Yet disciplinary boundaries should not be exaggerated, since migration research is often interdisciplinary.[4]

Unlike studies on migration in most host countries, research on transnationalism—often conducted in the manner of Monsieur Jourdain, whether scholars have realized it or not—was relatively precocious in Portugal. This was the case because emigration was not perceived as definitive departure. Temporary or definitive returns and various types of relations that migrants cultivated with their society of origin have drawn the attention of political, intellectual, economic, and religious elites. Migrants represent a capital that is worth retaining and cultivating. Migratory experience has marked territory within Portugal, even in some remote areas: houses belonging to "Brazilians," "Americans," or "French" are scattered across the country's villages. These residences are often recognizable since migrants project their migratory trajectories onto them: building materials, forms, and ornaments, in an exercise in hybridization that betrays and displays the country where the money that enabled the construction of that "dream house"[5] was earned.

However, the study of the bonds created between Portuguese migrants and their society of origin bears many risks. The main one consists in not studying anything beyond the discourses of Portuguese rulers (political and/or intellectual) and elites. Indeed, migrants and their ties to the Portuguese nation, the direction and "sense" of their mobility, have been widely discussed. But we have very few documents produced by the migrants themselves. "Spokespersons," sometimes mobilizing an "indigenous militant capital,"[6] seek to represent the migrants, but doing so often results in distorting discourses which do not give voice to migrants' ways of seeing in their social and/or gender variations. Moreover, these discourses are prone to essentializing a Portuguese "identity" passed along from generation to generation, thus omitting the processes of integration in host societies and the dilution of ties with the society of origin. They privilege identification with the Portuguese nation when in fact many migrants are tied, first and foremost, to their villages of origin. In short, more often than not, these discourses say more about those who produce them than about migrants themselves.[7]

The other danger is that of not retaining anything but the set of practices deemed legitimate by Portuguese leaders, by emigration elites (leaders of migrants' associations, "community" press) and social science researchers. Hence, particular attention has been paid to a so-called "Portuguese culture" (the diffusion of Camões's work, for example), at times to a "Portugueseness," running the risk of registering only legitimate cultural practices,[8] of essentializing a "Portuguese identity," of reifying Portuguese populations and their descendants and of rendering the processes of hybridization invisible. This focus on cultural practices related to literature, poetry, cinema, or the history of the Great Discoveries further runs the risk of reproducing the "symbolic violence" exerted by Portuguese elites on migrants, the majority of whom possess a meager cultural capital.

Discourse on migrants and their relations with Portugal must, in short, be handled with care, as they produce social effects, impose categories and mental maps, and constrain social practices. As pointed out by Stéphane Dufoix, drawing inspiration from the work of Pierre Bourdieu, language is formative: certain agents have translated transnational practices of migrants into words and have assigned meanings to them.[9] These words and categories have social effects. When reappropriated, they induce ways of thinking and ways of doing. The same holds true, as we will see, in the case of Portuguese emigration. Political and media elites in Portugal have been employing terms such as "diaspora" and "communities" for decades and often inscribe migrations of the 1960s and 1970s in a continuous line with the great discoveries of the fifteenth and sixteenth centuries. These terms and this noble filiation are sometimes appropriated by migrants themselves, namely by those self-appointed as their spokespersons, all the while hiding some of the causes producing emigration. Furthermore, these terms tend to reify the Portuguese or Luso-descendant population living abroad, a population that is much less homogeneous than the term *community* implies.

One must also avoid another risk: that of reducing transnationalism either to migrants' practices (a "transnationalism from below," which, as widely perceived in the United States, often postulates that migration, particularly illegal migration, is a sign of the decline of the state[10]) or to state practices (an approach privileged in France, where the state is deemed a pivotal and inescapable agent). The articulation of these two approaches is more fruitful as it allows us to capture migrants' strategies with greater subtlety, to grasp how they adapt to, or circumvent, state constraints that are brought to bear on them and how states, in turn, adapt to mobilities that cannot be reduced to a challenge to the Westphalian international system. As argued by Nancy Green, a "post-structural structuralism" that combines the study of state constraints and migrants' practices is a heuristically rewarding practice.[11]

With these various pitfalls in mind, we will first study the discourse produced about these transnational practices and policies by the Portuguese state, used to maintain its ties with its citizens living abroad. Second, we will focus on transnational practices "from below." In this case, it is a matter of seizing the discourse and practices over the long term, from the independence of Brazil, in 1822, to the present, and of teasing out continuities without papering over the breaks.

Before we begin, it is nonetheless useful to characterize the key Portuguese migratory flows throughout the course of this period. Up until the 1950s, the majority of Portuguese migrants had crossed the Atlantic with Brazil as the main place of destination. One estimate puts the number of Portuguese who emigrated between 1820 and 1930 at two million. For the most part, migrants left from the rural regions of the Center and North of the country, where small landholding peasants, who toiled their own land within the framework of the family unit, were prevalent. The archipelagos of the Azores and Madeira also saw high levels of departure. A new migratory cycle opened toward the end of the 1950s and from then onward turned toward Europe and, more specifically, France. Between 1957 and 1974, nearly 1.4 million Portuguese emigrated, France alone receiving 900,000 migrants. After 1974, the volume of emigration decreased but the migratory flow did not dry up. From that point onward, migratory flows were more diversified and, in the wake of Portugal's entry into the CEE (1986) and later the Schengen space (1995), took place within the framework of the European labor market. Since the beginning of the 2000s, with the rise in unemployment in Portugal, departures gained further momentum, toward Western Europe but also to the former colonies (Brazil and Angola in particular), even if it is impossible to quantify them accurately.

Transnationalism from Above

Between 1822 and 1974, discourses on emigration and transnational practices of the Portuguese abroad—drawn from legislative and regulatory texts, parliamentary or political speeches, the writings of politicians or intellectuals—are marked by the permanence of four topoi. The first deplores departures. The second foregrounds the necessary protection of migrants, depicted as victims. The third inscribes migrants within the "imagined nation." Last, the fourth ties mobility to the Empire. Other themes can be found, to be sure, yet the constancy of these topoi, spanning two centuries, is striking. Still, one must highlight a major break in Portugal's history: the emergence of democracy in 1974–1975.

Discourse did change after the Carnation Revolution in 1974. (The discourse on emigration had already been shifting from the 1960s, and there are indeed continuities—paradoxically at times, as we shall see—between discourse produced prior to 1974 and after this key date.) For the first time in history, all adult Portuguese citizens could vote, and democracy was consolidated. Be that as it may, discourse on migrants and their transnational practices were marked by a profound ambivalence. On the one hand, the emigrants were heroized (municipalities have erected statues devoted to emigrants) and courted (by banks and by politicians, since migrants now had parliamentary representatives). On the other hand, however, they were denigrated: their houses were described as crimes against landscape heritage; they were associated with the most illegitimate brand of popular culture (their taste for the popular music style called "pimba," for instance); and they were represented as the most conservative elements of Portuguese society, which, by contrast, was continuously evolving. Some people have depicted migrants as frozen in time, unsightly relics of a past that must be left behind: that period when Portugal was poor and exported its labor force to other European countries.

Finally, emigrants were, in the 1990s and for a period in the 2000s, partially hidden in political discourse. The financial impact of remittances was often omitted, as Portuguese leaders were reluctant to admit that public finances still depended on money sent by migrants, a segment of the population seen as a relic of the country's backwardness. Throughout the process of convergence between the Portuguese economy and the central European economies, a process by and large unsuccessful—and, one could argue, in regression since 2001—emigration was largely silenced, while still taking place. Attention was instead turned toward immigration. Many researchers who had previously worked on emigration now focused on immigration (a subject that received public funding, whereas emigration was no longer deemed a pertinent topic). Immigration emerged as a sign of Portugal's modernity. With immigrants from Africa, Eastern Europe, Asia, and Latin America, Portugal rose to the level of developed countries that drew in workers. Immigrants transformed Portugal into a core European country.[12] As a sign of its modernity, Portugal no longer exported workers but rather imported them. Yet, this discourse, occluding the persistence of emigration, which in fact never abated (toward Switzerland, Spain, or the United Kingdom, for instance), suffered a jolt after 2000. From 2001 on, the country stagnated economically, and the financial crisis of 2008 aggravated a situation that was already hardly comfortable. Departures have risen since 2000, and an Emigration Observatory was created by the government in 2008, several years after the Immigration Observatory. Yet, unlike in the years prior to 1974, emigration, while muffled, is free and even encouraged. In 2010, in the face of the profound economic crisis and the substantial rise in unemployment (from 4 percent in 2001 to nearly 18 percent in 2013) various political leaders, in particular the Prime Minister, openly encouraged the Portuguese to seek employment abroad.

Having underlined the singularity of the democratic period, we will now focus on three topics: the continuity of a discourse on the protection of migrants, the place of emigration in the national imaginary, and the close ties between emigration and empire.

Protecting Migrants

Portuguese leaders have consistently vowed to protect Portuguese emigrants, both in Portugal and abroad. The discourse of protection is omnipresent, with most legislation, administrative regulations, and practices justified in the name of "the protection of emigrants." Promulgated in 1933, the Constitution of the Estado Novo—the longest standing right-wing dictatorship in twentieth-century Western Europe, lasting from 1933 to 1974 and dominated by the figure of António de Oliveira Salazar, Council President between 1932 and 1968—stipulated that the state must "protect emigrants."[13] In the name of such protection, it was a matter of determining how the Portuguese could leave the country legally, of punishing those who aided them in leaving illegally, of regulating transatlantic crossings, and of intervening in the country of immigration. The most restrictive laws on emigration were legitimized in the name of the protection of migrants, under the guise of protecting migrants from themselves and from all those that would wish to exploit them: travel agencies, traffickers, smugglers, ship captains, and their employers abroad. Women were even more "protected" than men since feminine emigration was often reduced to "human trafficking of whites."[14] One should not deduce from this discourse on emigration that Portuguese rulers were magnanimous or concerned with the fate of the population. This discourse was often a smoke screen for authoritarian and draconian practices that curtailed the right to emigration.[15]

This discourse of protection had a number of goals. On the one hand, it sought to legitimize government initiatives that restrict emigration, all the while hiding the interests of the state and labor force employers, who more often than not were adamantly opposed to emigration.[16] On the other hand, by depicting migrants' future employers as potential exploiters, by denouncing the "human trafficking of whites" as victimizing the Portuguese in Brazil throughout the nineteenth century, and by describing the insalubrious dwellings in which migrants lived (namely in 1960s France), Portuguese leaders hid the misery, social inequality, employer exploitation, and authoritarianism within the country.

In short, the discourse on protection was part and parcel of the leaders' paternalist stance. They legitimated their power—authoritarian and undemocratic—by construing the Portuguese as children, unable to govern themselves and hence incapable of participating in the affairs of the polis, or of voting. Until 1974, the Portuguese were not citizens, but rather subjects in need of guidance.[17] Migrants were always represented as gullible, devoid of critical sense, ready to chase after the false promises of traffickers, emigration agents, or unscrupulous smugglers who, motivated by profit alone, artificially spawned emigration. These middlemen—operating either legally or illegally—were turned into convenient scapegoats. They were to blame for emigration: surely none of the various abhorrent features of Portuguese society (misery, social inequality, lack of freedom, rigid social hierarchies) could explain the massive levels of departure.

While the discourse on protection must be deconstructed and relativized, one should nonetheless not forget that the Portuguese state, as many other emigration states, did at times make genuine efforts to protect migrants. Anchored in the work of the "international network of social reformers and international associations,"[18] which set out guidelines for international migrations, and drawing particular inspiration from the 1901 Italian legislation,[19] Portuguese authorities established numerous laws and regulations in order to protect migrants, with special attention to the trans-Atlantic crossing. Authorities tried to control the actions of maritime companies and different agents in "emigration affairs"[20] (maritime companies, emigration agents, travel agencies). Still, the Portuguese state did not always have the "infrastructural power,"[21] the agents and the means necessary for enforcing its laws, namely toward maritime companies, and there was often a large chasm between laws and their enforcement.

The passport was the touchstone of Portuguese emigration policy and the instrument supposed to protect migrants. In the late nineteenth and early twentieth centuries, at a time when many European states had ceased to demand an emigration passport for their citizens,[22] the Portuguese government persisted in forcing emigrants—those who traveled in third class on boats—to possess this administrative document. (Wealthier travelers, those who moved to the colonies or toward the European continent by land could leave the country without it.) Rulers claimed this document would protect emigrants abroad when in fact it was mostly a matter of restricting legal migratory flows and ensuring the means for financial compensation of the administrative agents of the prefectures that collected taxes from the granting of passports.

After the First World War, the passport was once again required of any individual leaving the country, regardless of social standing or destination. Under the dictatorship, in 1947, an institution was created with the express purpose of managing emigration and was placed under the responsibility of the Ministry of the Interior.[23] This institution, the Junta da Emigração, inspected ships, placed doctors on boats to care for the sick, regulated food, and issued emigration passports.

The protection of migrants also took the shape of labor force and social welfare agreements signed with various countries of immigration.[24] The first of these agreements was signed with France in 1957, so that Portuguese workers in France could enjoy the same social rights as French nationals and retain some of these rights (pensions, medical assistance) upon their return to Portugal.[25] To further protect its migrants, the Portuguese state "transstaticized"[26] itself. For a long period, the state was present abroad solely through its diplomats. This presence was both quantitatively and qualitatively limited, and the social distance separating diplomats from emigrants often prevented a real engagement on the part of the former. Diplomats did not always consider the protection of migrants as a worthy task, and their powers were often limited by international law and the laws of the country in which they resided. Their presence and actions could be construed as unwarranted interference. Nonetheless, certain diplomats informed the Portuguese authorities of abuses suffered by emigrant Portuguese nationals due to stringent contracts that were practically forms of indentured labor. Throughout the nineteenth century, Portuguese consuls in Brazil warned Lisbon, occasionally doing so in hyperbolic terms, that Portuguese migrants were sometimes reduced to slaves by "service contracts"[27] that stipulated that they had to work a certain number of years to pay back their trip. The Portuguese consul in Honolulu in the 1880s sought to ensure compliance with the terms of emigrants' work contracts and reported eventual breaches affecting his compatriots (trips not reimbursed, poor working or housing conditions).

With a very limited direct presence abroad until the 1970s, for a long time the Portuguese state depended on other institutions to protect its citizens: voluntary associations and the Catholic Church. Making up for the state's shortcomings, these organizations were also often seen as more efficient and better adapted than the state for deployment outside national borders. The Catholic Church, for instance, had acquired significant know-how in the management of mobile populations. It could more easily accompany its flock outside of the metropolitan territory.[28] Both the hierarchy of the Portuguese Catholic Church and the parish priests sought to reaffirm ties between migrants and their country of origin. In 1962, the Portuguese Episcopal Council created the Portuguese Catholic Organization for Migrations in order to provide a framework for its missionaries abroad.

From the nineteenth century onward, numerous Portuguese associations were created in Brazil. Among other things, they enabled mutual assistance and provided relief for the afflicted. The mobilization of an ethnic capital was indispensable to offset the lack of social policies. In this context, migrants who had become rich played the role of patrons, which often enabled them to become ethnic leaders[29] or to become notables in the local "Portuguese colony." Largely dependent on these notables, who substituted for diplomats in organizing social and cultural activities, the Portuguese state offered them symbolical rewards such as the status of "comendador" (commander).

After 1947 and the creation of the Junta da Emigração, agents from the Ministry of the Interior occasionally traveled to countries of immigration to pay a visit to emigrants and verify whether the clauses on their work contracts were being met. Then, from the 1970s, even prior to the Carnation Revolution, the Portuguese state put forward a trans-statist action, reinforcing its presence near its citizens residing abroad. Social services were created in France and Germany, including social workers and social counselors who provided assistance to workers, offered them counsel and defended their rights. Information bulletins were regularly issued and announced through the press; brochures that explained the various rights of workers and their beneficiaries were distributed. The Portuguese state also gave further support to associative movements by channeling subsidies, offering books, or financing entertainment shows.

Finally, from the 1960s, the teaching of the Portuguese language to children of migrants gradually developed. This was, in fact, the key demand that Portuguese abroad had been placing on the Portuguese state since the 1960s.[30] For many Portuguese parents, learning Portuguese was essential if their children were to retain a bond with their country of origin, especially with any relatives (grandparents, uncles, and aunts) still residing there. Some parents also saw the Portuguese language as a heritage that they wished to pass on to their children.

An Imagined Nation

In *Le Creuset français*,[31] Gérard Noiriel put forward a set of reasons explaining why France had long been "an unwitting country of immigration."[32] The key elements in the representation of the French nation dated back to the French Revolution and the construction of the "national narrative" (by historians such as Augustin Thierry and Jules Michelet[33]) and could be traced back to the first decades of the nineteenth century, before the massive arrival of foreigners in France, which began in the last quarter of that century. The latter's arrival was thus largely left out of public and even scientific discourses and their demographic, economic, and cultural contributions to French society were long overlooked. More often than not, immigrants were perceived as a problem,[34] a threat against a supposed "national identity."[35]

On the contrary, the Portuguese outside of the metropolitan territory were not excluded from the "national imaginary"[36] as emigration preceded its formation in the nineteenth century.[37] As we have seen at the start of this essay, it is frequently remarked that emigration has existed in Portugal since the fifteenth century. The conquest of Ceuta in 1415 and the colonization of the Atlantic isles (Madeira from 1419 and the Azores archipelago from 1432) marked the beginning of a long migratory tradition. Some go even further: the reconquest from the eleventh century onward, for instance, is sometimes represented as emigration.[38] Mobility is thus inscribed at the heart of the discourse on Portuguese national identity. In numerous public discourses, emigration is seen as springing from the will to discover new spaces, to "give new worlds to the world," and to establish contact with other peoples. Expansion and emigration are therefore closely linked. This reading of mobility tends to fold it into the epic of the Great Discoveries, magnified by the Portuguese elites, and to dissimulate the political and economic dimension of departures. To construe Portuguese emigrants as heirs to Vasco de Gama allows the elite to hide the extent to which emigration springs from misery and social inequality.

While national identities are often founded on a territory, emphasizing deep roots in the soil,[39] Portuguese elites have perceived the Portuguese nation as a deterritorialized one.[40] The 1933 constitution of Estado Novo states the following: "Are deemed part of the Nation any Portuguese citizens residing within or outside its territory who are considered dependent on the Portuguese state and its laws, within the boundaries set by the rules of international law."[41] Public discourse often stressed that wherever there is a Portuguese citizen, Portugal is present. A profound ambivalence traverses the discourse on emigration: while it is deplored and several governments have attempted to curb it, the emigration that has already taken place—even illegally—is accepted and folded within the "national narrative."

However, between this discourse that places individuals first, at the expense of territory, and actual practice, there is an important hiatus. Portugal was at no point a deterritorialized nation, unconcerned with its borders, as presented by its elites. The Portuguese abroad (leaving aside civil servants and diplomats, which are a separate case) were not able to vote until 1975 and were only represented in parliament on that year. Furthermore, only four members of Parliament—out of more than two hundred—are currently deemed to represent the alleged 5 million Portuguese living abroad. An important gap has thus remained between the discourse, which claims to include all the Portuguese in the Portuguese nation and the practices that exclude them from a broad participation in the life of the polis, signaling a vast distance between the Portuguese within and those without. The fact that public discourse on emigration is often tinged with lyricism and poetic evocations—Luis de Camões or Fernando Pessoa are recurrently mobilized to speak of the "diaspora" or of "communities" abroad—may be interpreted as an attempt to bridge the gap between discourse on the "deterritorialized Portuguese nation" and the actual practices of Portuguese authorities.

Emigration and Empire

Emigration is closely intertwined with colonization.[42] One cannot understand the discourse on emigration and the ties between the Portuguese and their society of origin without referring to the Portuguese Empire. Until 1822, the lines between emigration and colonization were blurred. The independence of Brazil did not cut off the migratory flow linking the metropolis and its ex-colony. Portuguese emigration, up until the 1950s, was mostly turned toward Brazil, with networks linking the Portuguese countryside, particularly in the north of the country, and the former colony. The Portuguese Minister of Foreign Affairs acknowledged as much in 1843: "this emigration is natural since almost all [Minho inhabitants] have a relative down there [in Brazil], which springs from the fact that certain parents employ some of their offspring in agriculture while others go to Brazil . . ., therefore, anything that would be done to prevent emigration in this province [Minho], would do it great harm."[43] Still, this positive stance toward this migratory flow was not shared by all. On the one hand, employers—large and medium-sized agricultural landowners—and a segment of the political leadership deplored the departures and believed that an adequate labor force was lacking in Portugal itself.[44] On the other hand, after the independence of Brazil, Portuguese governments entertained the project of creating "new Brazils" in Africa. Thus, wherever labor force excess existed, people should head toward Angola and Mozambique rather than Brazil. To support this thesis, numerous—and often hyperbolic—statements suggested that the Portuguese in Brazil were nothing but a replacement of African slaves, reduced to the status of "white slaves," thus "disgracing"[45] the home country. Hence, there emerged the notion that emigration to countries outside of the Empire undermined it, diverting settlers from colonizing Portuguese territories, developing their economies, civilizing the indigenous, and defending national sovereignty. This type of statement recurred over and over between the 1830s and 1974. From 1836 onward, Sá da Bandeira, one of the key promoters of the expansion of Portuguese possessions in Africa (which until 1880–1890 were limited to trading posts and a fairly modest hinterland), called on the

Portuguese to go to Africa rather than Brazil. Various colonization projects were carried out until 1974.

These projects, however, proved illusory. Angola and Mozambique did not possess the riches foretold and were not the "new Brazils" that had been prophesied. For a long time the Portuguese could not settle into these territories because of deplorable sanitary conditions and climatic difficulties. Subsequently, the sending of colonists to Africa brought about numerous perverse effects. The Portuguese peasants were more often than not illiterate and lacked the skills or experience needed to work the land profitably. They were in direct competition with African workers who were exploited in the framework of a system of forced labor. Governments in Lisbon limited the departure of settlers because they feared that the latter, in the case of economic difficulties, would rebel against the metropolis and seek independence, as Portuguese colonists in Brazil had done previously. Wary of white nationalism, the sending of colonists was conditioned by the elasticity of the white labor market in those territories. All of these reasons meant that, despite their discourse and various projects, Portuguese rulers could not achieve their dream: to form small peasant colonies abroad.[46] To give one illustration of such failure: in 1974, after less than twenty years of emigration, there were more Portuguese in France than in the overseas provinces after 450 years of colonization! In a single year—1970—departures to France were of the same order as those heading toward Angola and Mozambique between 1957 and 1974. And this took place while departures to France were officially restricted and considered inconvenient, whereas departures to the overseas provinces were consistently encouraged and praised by the elite of the dictatorship.

The discourse on the deterritorialized nation was equally instrumentalized in defense of "the last Empire"[47] in Europe. In fact, in the 1960s, a part of the ruling elites, which sought to justify the Portuguese refusal to decolonize, forged a rationale and a string of arguments in which emigration was given pride of place. Portuguese rulers then utilized the work of Brazilian sociologist Gilberto Freyre, who had defended the nonracist character of Portuguese colonization in Brazil and the miscegenation carried out by the Portuguese in the tropics. This "Lusotropicalist vulgate" was then applied to emigration. Emigration was inserted within the framework of a colonization motivated only by a will to know other peoples and to mix with them. Portuguese imperialism was not at all "materialist," that is to say grounded in economic purpose. Instead, the Portuguese were said to have spread out throughout the world, adapting to whatever circumstances they had met, all the while holding on to their ties to Portugal and to a feeling of belonging to a Portuguese community spread across the four corners of the earth.

Paradoxically, Lusotropicalist discourse and its application to the transnational practices of the Portuguese throughout the world, despite its intentions and its essentialization of "Portuguese culture," survived the Carnation Revolution and the fall of the Empire. Ever since, one of the common ties with Portuguese living abroad and their descendants consists in affirming that they are perfectly adapted to the societies where they are established and are appreciated by local populations because they display their hardworking qualities and their orderliness. Yet while "integrated," they remain Portuguese and proudly so, attached to their country of origin, suffering from *saudade* (melancholic nostalgia). This representation—far from the truth—allows Portuguese elites to flatter migrants that they are simultaneously a material and symbolic resource. They are a material resource because the serious financial difficulties (commercial trade deficit, inflation, IMF intervention, and so forth) undergone since 1975 make emigrant remittances indispensable. Banks (nationalized in 1975) offer attractive rates to emigrants, and specific accounts are created for them. Political leaders often visit "communities" abroad. The migrants are a symbolic resource because "Portuguese communities" abroad replace the recently lost Empire. Unwilling to accept Portugal's reduction to a small country on the periphery of Europe, migrants allow Portuguese leaders to continue articulating a universalist discourse, offering Portugal both a singularity and a worldwide dimension. The translation of Empire into "communities" is perceptible in the fact that, for a number of years, the logo of the administration responsible for the Portuguese abroad was a caravel.

In this context, the term *diaspora* is often used as a synonym for "Portuguese communities." These terms are nonetheless problematic because they reify the Portuguese and their descendants abroad; paper over the social, sexual, regional, and other divisions within the "population"; and classify as Portuguese even those individuals who do not represent or identify themselves as such. Yet, it is true that a segment of emigrants and their spokespersons appropriated this discourse, transforming proletarians in industrialized societies into heirs to fifteenth- and sixteenth-century navigators.[48] For example, the main association of Luso-descendants in France, founded in 1991, is called Cap Magellan.[49] In Brazil, the main soccer club supported by the Portuguese and Luso-descendants was called Vasco da Gama, created in 1898, four centuries after the navigator's arrival in India. The story of the Great Discoveries offers the Portuguese throughout the world a repertoire from which they themselves can draw, and which allows them to transform a mobility motivated by misery and the will to pursue a better life into an adventure that takes part in the imperial epic.

In many immigration countries, the uses of a narrative of the heroic history of Portugal distinguish the Portuguese and their descendants from other foreign populations. In France, populations from France's former colonies have a harder time mobilizing the achievements of their country or their "culture" of origin. In fact, these countries are often "colonial inventions" whose borders were drawn by European powers. Furthermore, the colonizers tried hard to efface the history of subjected peoples and disseminated among these populations a feeling of inferiority which legitimized colonial rule. Consequently, migrants and their descendants from the former French colonies not only have access to a limited repertoire of historical narratives but the use of that history (namely resistance to colonization) is problematic in France since it can be perceived by public authorities, political parties, and part of the media as a challenge—indeed a repudiation—of "integration," an act of "communitarianism." To reclaim a "history" or a "culture" thus becomes a risk that many migrants originating from the former colonies avoid taking. Such is not at all the case for Portuguese migrants, who can draw upon the history of Portugal without appearing disloyal to France. Since the Napoleonic wars, no conflict has divided the two countries and both were colonial powers. The appropriation of Magellan is thus inscribed within an ethnocentric European discourse shared by France and Portugal alike.

The co-optation of this discourse of the Portuguese political and media elites by certain migrants, and namely by the "ethnic leaders," shows how it had an impact on the practices of migrants abroad. Yet, transnationalism must not be reduced to discourse, and we need to look more closely at migrants' actual transnationalist practices.

Transnationalism from Below

Transnationalism, a process by which "immigrants establish and maintain multiple social relations which connect societies of origin and host societies,"[50] is not a recent process, tied to current globalization, as some scholars sometimes argue.[51] From the nineteenth century onward Portuguese migrants in Brazil have bridged the two sides of the Atlantic by regularly sending money to their families, corresponding, and returning occasionally or definitively to their country of origin. Migratory chains connected certain Portuguese villages to Brazilian, Argentinian, or U.S. localities. Marcelo Borges, for instance, has described connections dating back to the 1920s between villages in the south of Portugal, in the Algarve, and Villa Elisa, situated in the vast outskirts of Buenos Aires, where many Portuguese devoted themselves to horticulture.[52] These flows fed on information that circulated continuously, namely by means of mail correspondence, which, prior to the "dissociation of time and space,"[53] linked migrants and their families. By means of these letters, migrants could incite (or discourage) their close ones to join them, and thus continued to play a role within their family. In certain letters, men who had left their wives in Portugal continued to manage their properties from a distance.[54] The exercise of a "double presence" did not wait for modern means of communication and the decrease in travel time.[55]

As shown by numerous sociological and anthropological studies, emigration in the decades between 1950 and 1970 is likewise a part of migratory chains founded on the solidarities or "mutual aid society"[56] in the Portuguese countryside, on a "village culture of mobility."[57] Individuals migrate because they generally know that acquaintances (families and friends) will be able to accommodate them, temporarily house them, point them in the direction of a job, or enable them to regularize their legal situation. Since the end of the 1950s, Portuguese migrants in Europe—who form different "strata" that we cannot always simply amalgamate, as the social traits of those who departed between 1960 and 1970 are not always identical with those of migrants from the 2000s—have circulated regularly between their place of departure and their places of residence abroad. Certain Portuguese repeatedly return to visit their families. Pensioners divide their time between their residence in France and the one in Portugal, depending on the school holidays of their children and grandchildren or medical appointments. The substantial improvement of roads in the Iberian Peninsula and the expansion of transportation options (more bus routes, railroads and later, airlines, especially low-cost ones) facilitate a regular "to-and-fro."[58] For certain authors, many Portuguese who emigrated to Europe in the 1960–1970s and have since retired, live in a "bipolar"[59] situation, dividing their time between the two spaces, between their village of origin in which they invested (in the construction of a "dream house") and their place of residence abroad (where they have likewise invested in real estate) where their children and grandchildren live.

From within the framework of this intense circulation of people, goods, capital, and representations that configures transnationalism from below, we shall retain three elements: the role of religious practices; the role of soccer; and, finally, the return trips. Still, these three elements do not sum up transnationalism from below: the study of culinary, folklore, or musical practices would be entirely pertinent to the subject at hand.

A Religious Transnationalism

The practice of Catholicism holds a key position in transnational practices of Portuguese migrants across the world, particularly for women. Religious practice was prevalent in Portugal until the 1970s,[60] particularly in the center and northern regions of the country, where emigration was particularly pronounced. Up until the 1970s, village parish priests were not only spiritual figures but quite often the key intermediaries between the inhabitants, the majority of whom were illiterate or barely literate, and the state. Clerics established themselves as representatives of the rural populations to the state and the surrounding society.[61]

Abroad, Portuguese migrants living in countries where Catholicism is predominant (Brazil and France in particular), hold on to their own rites and beliefs, just as Polish and Italian immigrants did in interwar France.[62] These specific religious practices transform the territories in which they live into places of belonging.[63] Religious practices enable migrants to appropriate the places in which they live and connect the territories of the society of origin and those of the host society. In fact, in many churches they attend abroad, Portuguese parishioners are offered masses celebrated entirely or partially in Portuguese, as well as catechism classes in Portuguese. They have also found a way for statues of Our Lady of Fátima—whose cult constitutes the main distinctive trait of Portuguese migrants and one of their key links with Portugal—to be positioned in their new places of worship. On August 12th and 13th, during the summer holiday period, many migrants make a pilgrimage to Fátima, and this date is now specifically dedicated to migrants by the Portuguese ecclesiastical authorities. There are churches abroad devoted to Portuguese believers, such as that of Notre-Dame de Fátima in the nineteenth Paris district or the parish of Notre-Dame de Fátima in Edmonton (Alberta, Canada). The migrants from the Azores stand out through their organization of Holy Ghost festivals in Canada, the United States and Brazil.[64]

If migrants form communities of believers in the places where they live, appropriating religious and even public spaces for processions (which often take place near May 13th, the anniversary of the supposed first apparition of the Virgin Mary to three young shepherds in 1917) and festivities (such as that of the Holy Ghost), they nonetheless continue to be a part of their parish of origin. Such sacraments of the Catholic religion as baptism, communion, and marriage[65] are often conducted in the two parishes. Migrants' children are frequently baptized and receive their first communion in Portugal, symbol of their link to their parents' parish of origin.

Parishioners abroad follow local life closely by way of local newspapers to which they subscribe and which allow them to stay informed about "important" events at home: deaths, marriages, births, and construction work on the church or the cemetery. Migrants are regularly solicited to partake in the funding of the village's religious festivities (which are often concentrated in the month of August so that migrants can take part and all parishioners may participate) and in renovation projects in churches, chapels, or other places of worship.

The death of migrants abroad raises the problem of deciding where the body is to be buried. Burial in the country of immigration allows the body to remain close to their children, a key factor for Portuguese migrants who often emigrated to offer a better life for their offspring and a large majority of whom believe parents should "sacrifice themselves for the sake of their children."[66] Burial in the village of origin, however, allows migrants to lie in rest near their ancestors and to signal their attachment to their community of origin, in its religious and social dimensions. It allows them to fully complete the migratory project, which is consummated by a "post-mortem return."[67] A 2003 survey on the place of burial of migrants living in France indicates that 34 percent of Portuguese migrants wished to be buried in Portugal (the highest percentage among migrants of European origin), near their ancestors, while 31 percent wished their bodies to remain in France.[68] An "entrepreneurial chain of migrants' deaths"[69] was established between the host countries, mostly in Europe and Portugal, to allow for the "final return."[70]

The bonds between the migrants' parish of origin and those they come to frequent in the host society are also maintained thanks to the circulation of clerics. The parish priests from Portuguese villages often make their way to where their flock resides abroad, celebrating mass there and thus perpetuating their belonging to their parish of origin. "Pastoral power" knows no borders.[71] Likewise, certain parish priests from the host societies, if a portion of their parishioners are Portuguese, sometimes travel to Portugal. More generally, contemporary Portuguese migration has led to hundreds of town-twinning schemes between Portuguese and foreign villages, particularly French ones. (More than a hundred town-twinning arrangements existed in 2012.)

The Portuguese ecclesiastical hierarchy also takes a close interest in Portuguese migrants, devoting specific organizations and ceremonies to them (the Portuguese Catholic Organization for Migrations, migrants' pilgrimage on August 13th, and so forth). Through agreements with the churches in the host countries,[72] Portuguese missionaries have been sent to where migrants live to celebrate mass in Portuguese and provide spiritual support to Portuguese believers. As we have seen, the Portuguese state relied on this action on the part of the Church to preserve ties with its citizens abroad.

A Sporting Transnationalism

While the "transnational way of life" bears an obvious religious dimension, it also expresses itself in a profane activity that does not fit *stricto sensu* into the "Portuguese identity": soccer, the near-universal sport.[73] It may seem inappropriate in a study on transnationalism to give such weight to a sport that is not particular to Portuguese migrants. Yet, the consumption and practice of soccer holds a "profound meaning" for Portuguese migrants, being at one and the same time a vector of affirmation in host societies, a constantly renewed bond with the Portuguese "imagined community," and a transmission medium for Portuguese "identity" between generations, particularly among males. The study of soccer is essential to understanding the processes of identification of the Portuguese and their descendants as well as the ties they establish with Portugal. And yet the importance of soccer is routinely overlooked in works that prefer to focus on objects deemed nobler: literature, art, or cinema.[74] This disregard springs partly from the social background of most researchers (particularly in Portugal, where access to higher education and academic careers is partly circumscribed to the higher social strata) and from the position, marginal until recently, of studies on sport. Yet soccer—both its practice within the scope of teams playing in amateur championships and its "consumption" through the reading of Portuguese sports newspapers or following television broadcasts of the Portuguese championship matches or of the Portuguese national team[75]—is seldom evoked when in fact it is often the key activity of the Portuguese associations.[76] In the case of France, in the 1980s, one estimate put the number of Portuguese teams in France at over 1,000, and in 2009 there were still 205 soccer clubs of Portuguese origin.[77] In the French context of the 1960s and 1970s, for a migrant population originating from a poor country, relegated to the least skilled and toughest jobs, and at times stigmatized, the creation of soccer clubs was a means of ensuring a shared space, occupying leisure time and—through competitions—measuring up against non-Portuguese teams. From the 1960s onward, seizing on the good sporting results of the Portuguese national teams and clubs, Portuguese migrants brought to the fore their soccer know-how and transformed this popular sport among the French popular classes into a cultural commodity enabling them to raise their profile in their places of residence and to facilitate their social insertion.

This appropriation of soccer is not simply a phenomenon of the last few decades, as the case of Portuguese migration to Brazil proves. And yet, there, too, studies on the Portuguese in Brazil have given very little weight to this practice. For example, Heloïsa Paulo's book on the propaganda of Salazar's regime directed at Portuguese emigrants in Brazil between 1930 and 1960 describes the bonds created between the Portuguese in Brazil and their country of origin, listing Portuguese associations in Brazil and cultural practices that developed there.[78] She argues that the Portuguese population in Brazil, generally speaking, supported the dictatorship. Hence, numerous pages are devoted to the Real Gabinete de leitura in Rio de Janeiro, to newspapers published in the "colony," and to Portuguese schools. Yet the author does not address anything outside of legitimate cultural activities. She devotes no more than twenty words to one of the institutions in Brazil, which throughout the twentieth century was among the most important for Portuguese and their descendants in the country, the one that had most strongly materialized the ties between that population and their country of origin, Club de Regatas Vasco da Gama, more widely known as Vasco da Gama. A large part of the Portuguese and their descendants identified with this soccer club created in 1898 in Rio de Janeiro. In massively asserting their support for Vasco[79] and in playing with stereotypes (from the 1940s, the club's mascot was a fat and moustachioed shopkeeper, the very same figure used to denigrate the Portuguese), Portuguese and Luso-descendants, particularly those living in Rio de Janeiro, the main residential concentration of Portuguese in Brazil, fought against the stigmatization directed at them for decades on end and affirmed themselves collectively. Indeed, after independence, a part of the Brazilian elite rejected the political and cultural heritage of the former metropolis. Furthermore, throughout the nineteenth century and early twentieth century, several social movements, at times violent in nature, by black or mixed race urban wage workers, namely in Rio de Janeiro, were directed against the Portuguese because the latter were their direct competitors in the unskilled job market or, if they were small businessmen, they were accused of growing rich at their expense.[80] In the 1920s, Vasco da Gama was deemed by the country's white elites as the team of "cashiers, blacks and the illiterate."[81]

Yet, in the case of Portuguese emigration, since the early twentieth century, transnational practices have harmonized with soccer, particularly for men.[82] Most Portuguese men support a soccer club, often as a result of a family tradition and/or territorial ties, and they remain steadfast to their club over the course of their entire lives.[83] With the internet, Portuguese men living abroad can now follow the Portuguese championship on a daily basis and are often better informed about sports results than about Portuguese political or cultural life. Some of them go to Portugal, sometimes from as far away as the United States, for the sole purpose of watching their team play.[84] For the Portuguese abroad, namely teenagers who dote on Portuguese celebrities like Cristiano Ronaldo and a number of whom support the Portuguese national team, soccer plays a pivotal role in identification processes in everyday social interactions and in their workplaces or schools.[85] Soccer is also a central element in intergenerational relations between parents born in Portugal and sons socialized abroad.[86] This shared passion for soccer—both its practice and the identification with a Portuguese club—is all the more important since, in the migratory situation, parents and offspring are often divided by linguistic barriers and by the latter's social mobility. Soccer is what brings together that which migration tends to pull apart. By practicing soccer, namely in a Portuguese club, and/or supporting a Portuguese club or the Seleção, immigrants' children show their fidelity to parental origins, a fidelity that does not exclude other identifications tied to the society in which they live.[87]

The Country to Which One Doesn't Return

For many Portuguese migrants, both in the nineteenth and twentieth centuries, migration often represented a "maintenance migration."[88] It was a matter of going abroad to save the necessary financial capital to better reintegrate Portuguese society. One left one's village so that one could return to it on better terms: it was leaving without leaving behind.[89] Return was thus for many migrants the consummation of the migratory project. Likewise, Portuguese elites have always underscored the will to return of the Portuguese living abroad. The "myth of return"[90] they had forged was thought to facilitate the continuity of the ties between migrants and their families back in Portugal, ties which materialized in the sending of money (essential to the equilibrium of the Portuguese trade balance) and donations. Portuguese banks, some of which were created in the nineteenth century to drain money from migrants in Brazil, participated widely in spreading this representation, namely by way of advertising in various media (community press, TV channels devoted to Portuguese abroad, and so forth). This myth of return nonetheless occludes the fact that many migrants definitively established themselves abroad, and ties with Portugal have weakened over the generations.

To estimate the proportion of return migrants is, however, a difficult, not to say impossible, task. On the one hand, it is difficult to assess the volume of returns, in the nineteenth century in particular, due to the lack of reliable statistics. Documentation from Portuguese ports from which migrants departed may permit certain calculations, but it does not enable us to account for the temporary returns and does not take into account returns by way of Spanish ports (namely Vigo). In his thesis on emigration from the Porto region in the nineteenth century, Jorge Fernandes Alves suggests that somewhere between 40 percent to 60 percent of the migrants returned.[91] This view goes against the grain of the notion of a nineteenth-century emigration in which returns were totally nonexistent or limited to a handful of individuals who became rich and who went on to build large manors back home. Beyond these newly rich migrants, who left their trace in the landscape and literature of the time, numerous other migrants, having acquired a little or some capital, returned to their village of origin. Be that as it may, it is difficult to fine-tune estimates of the magnitude of this phenomenon.

On the other hand, the concept of return is hardly adequate, particularly in the case of contemporary migrations. As we have seen, many Portuguese who emigrated to Europe in the second half of the twentieth century live in a bipolar situation, circulating between the place they left behind and the one in which they settled, between their village of origin and the society of their children and grandchildren, who more often than not possess the nationality of the country in which they were born. Others, who thought about returning definitively (relying on assisted return schemes, such as the one put in place in France in 1977[92]) have re-emigrated toward the place they thought they had left behind for good, or toward another destination. In fact, in the nineteenth and twentieth centuries, cases of re-emigration were far from exceptional. Among migrants arriving in France in the 1960s and 1970s, some had been born in Brazil and had come to Portugal with their parents when they were young. Return is thus an elusive process and it is preferable to frame the question in terms of circulation.

*   *   *

The transnational practices of Portuguese migrants have been intense for the past two hundred years, not only within the framework of the trans-Atlantic space during the nineteenth and the first half of the twentieth centuries but also within the framework of European space since the end of the 1950s. These practices have adapted to existing means of communication and transportation and have evolved in line with more global social processes. Hence, the emergence of mass sports at the end of the nineteenth century had a strong bearing on transnational practices: sport allowed for the expression of a sense of ethnic belonging and fidelity to the society of origin all the while favoring insertion into the host societies. Other factors have played a role in the intensity of these transnational practices and their persistence across the generations. The configuration of host societies and the actions of the state in the processes of social integration have played a pivotal role. French "integration policy" and its application of jus solis have favored the dilution of the identification with Portugal among numerous Portuguese descendants, whereas in Germany that identification has lasted down the generations because—until the 1990s—it was difficult for the children and grandchildren of migrants to acquire German citizenship.[93] A detailed comparison of the various national and local contexts in which Portuguese migrants were inserted would be necessary in order to understand variations that may have existed between different transnational practices. This comparison would enable us to avoid any essentialization of a supposed Portuguese "culture" and "identity" and would allow us to grasp processes of hybridization and fusion. A focus on these transnational practices should also not obfuscate the processes of insertion into host societies, processes that in certain cases take the form of a radical break with the country of origin.

The fact remains that the intensity of these transnational practices, in various configurations, has retained a certain degree of invisibility in the media and political landscape. That is the case in France, a country where the Portuguese population (the Portuguese and their descendants, whether French or binational) is estimated at 1.2 million persons. In France, immigration is often perceived through the prism of "integration" or "assimilation," producing either regrets over the lack of integration—this concept being employed then as an instrument of stigmatization of certain populations, as underlined by Abdelmalek Sayad[94]—or a showcasing of the "successful cases" of "integration." In any case, immigration is perceived in terms of a unilateral and irreversible displacement, thus hiding the migratory circulations that the "transnational" focus brings out. Despite the recurrent statements on the part of French and Portuguese leaders on the "admirable integration" of the Portuguese in France, many return to Portugal or, in most cases, live in a bipolar situation.[95] Transnational practices of Portuguese migrants are never perceived as a breach of loyalty toward France, or as a weakening of the state. The process of invisibilization and tolerance in the face of these transnational practices, which is not the case for other immigrant populations in France, namely those originating from Africa, would also unquestionably deserve to be analyzed from a comparative perspective.

78   VICTOR PEREIRA

NOTES

1. Vitorino Magalhães Godinho, "Émigration Portugaise (XV–XXe siècle): Une constante structurale et les réponses au changement du monde," *Revista de História Económica e Social* 1 (1978): 5–32.

2. Jorge Carvalho Arroteia, *A emigração portuguesa. Suas origens e distribuição* (Lisbon: Biblioteca breve, 1983).

3. Maria Beatriz Rocha Trindade, "Emigração portuguesa: As políticas de trajecto de ida e de ciclo fechado," *Revista de História Económica e Social* 1 (1978): 71–90; Elizabeth Leeds, "Labor Export, Development, and the State. The Political Economy of Portuguese Emigration," doctoral thesis, Massachusetts Institute of Technology, 1984; Mária Engrácia Leandro, *Au-delà des apparences: Les Portugais face à l'insertion sociale* (Paris: CIEMI/L'Harmattan, 1995); Yves Charbit, Marie-Antoinette Hily, and Michel Poinard, *Le va-et-vient identitaire* (Paris: PUF-INED, 1997); Albano Cordeiro and Marie-Antoinette Hily, "La fête des Portugais: Héritage et invention," *Revue Internationale des Migrations Internationales* 16 (2000): 59–76; José Portela and Sílvia Nobre, "Entre Pinela e Paris: Emigração e regressos," *Análise Social*, 37 (2001): 1105–1146.

4. Dulce Freire and Victor Pereira, "Introdução. Interdisciplinaridade em acção. Experiências de pesquisa em contexto rural," *Ler História*, 62 (2012): 125–128.

5. Roselyne de Villanova, Carolina Leite, and Isabel Raposo, *Maisons de rêve au Portugal* (Paris: Créaphis, 1994); Isabel Cardoso Lopes, "Imaginário e história das casas dos 'Portugueses de França,'" doctoral thesis, New University of Lisbon, 2008.

6. Choukri Hmed, "Contester une institution dans le cas d'une mobilisation improbable: La 'grève des loyers' dans les foyers Sonacotra dans les années 1970," *Sociétés Contemporaines*, 65 (2007): 55–81.

7. Albertino Gonçalves, *Imagens e clivagens. Os residentes face aos emigrantes* (Porto: Afrontemento, 1996).

8. Bernard Lahire, *La culture des individus: Dissonances culturelles et distinction de soi* (Paris: La Découverte, 2004).

9. Stéphane Dufoix, "Un pont par-dessus la porte: Extraterritorialisation et transétatisation des identifications nationales," in *Loin des yeux, près du cœur: Les États et leurs expatriés*, ed. Stéphane Dufoix, Carine Guerassimoff, and Anne de Tinguy (Paris: Presses de Sciences Po, 2010), 15–57, 51. See also Nancy L. Green and François Weil, eds., *Citizenship and Those Who Leave* (Urbana: University of Illinois Press, 2007).

10. Béatrice Hibou, "Retrait ou redéploiement de l'Etat?" *Critique Internationale* 1 (1998): 151–168; Jean-François Bayart, *Le gouvernement du monde: Une critique politique de la globalisation* (Paris: Fayard, 2004).

11. Nancy L. Green, *Repenser les migrations* (Paris: PUF, 2002).

12. Maria Ioannis Baganha and Pedro Góis, "Migrações internacionais de e para Portugal: O que sabemos e para onde vamos?" *Revista Crítica de Ciências Sociais*, 52–53 (1998–1999): 229–280; Nuno Dias and Bruno Peixe Dias, eds., *Imigração e racismo em Portugal* (Lisbon: Edições 70, 2012).

13. Jorge Miranda, *As constituições portuguesas. 1822–1826–1838–1911–1933–1976* (Lisbon: Livraria Petrony, 1976), 230–231.

14. Paul-André Rosental, "Géopolitique et État-providence: Le BIT et la politique mondiale des migrations dans l'entre-deux-guerres," *Annales HSS* 61 (2006): 99–134, 114.

15. Alan Dowty, *Closed Borders: The Contemporary Assault on Freedom of Movement* (New Haven: Yale University Press, 1987).

16. Victor Pereira, "La construction du problème de l'émigration: L'élite politique et l'émigration portugaise vers la France (1957–1974)," *Agone*, 40 (2008): 61–80.

17. Rui Ramos, "Portuguese, But Not Citizens: Restricted Citizenship in Contemporary Portugal," in *Lineages of European Citizenship: Rights, Belonging and Participation in Eleven Nation-States*, ed. Richard Bellamy, Dario Castiglione, and Emilio Santoro (New York: Palgrave Macmillan, 2004), 92–112.

18. Caroline Douki, David Feldman, and Paul-André Rosental, "Pour une histoire relationnelle du ministère du travail en France, en Italie et au Royaume-Uni dans l'entre-deux-guerres: le transnational, le bilatéral et l'interministériel en matière de politique migratoire," in *Les politiques du travail (1906–2006): Acteurs, institutions, réseaux*, ed. Alain Chatriot, Odile Join-Lambert, and Vincent Viet (Rennes: Presses Universitaires de Rennes, 2006), 143–159, 144.

19. Caroline Douki, "Protection sociale et mobilité transatlantique: les migrants italiens au début du XXe siècle," *Annales HSS* 66 (2011): 375–410.

20. Joaquim da Costa Leite, "Os negócios da emigração (1870–1914)," *Análise Social* 31 (1996): 381–396.

21. Michael Mann, "The Autonomous Power of the State: Its Origins, Mechanisms and Results," *Archives Européennes de Sociologie* 25 (1984): 185–213.

22. John Torpey, *The Invention of the Passport. Surveillance, Citizenship and the State* (Cambridge: Cambridge University Press, 2000).

23. Victor Pereira, *La dictature de Salazar face à l'émigration. L'État Portugais et ses migrants en France (1957–1974)* (Paris: Presses de Sciences Po, 2012).

24. Paul-André Rosental, "Migrations, souveraineté, droits sociaux: Protéger et expulser les étrangers en Europe du 19e siècle à nos jours," *Annales HSS*, 66 (2011): 335–373.

25. Victor Pereira, "Emigração e desenvolvimento da previdência social em Portugal," *Análise Social*, 44 (2009): 471–510.

26. Dufoix, "Un pont par-dessus la porte."

27. Jorge Fernandes Alves, "Os Brasileiros: Emigração e retorno no Portugal oitocentista," doctoral thesis, Universidade of Porto, 1993, 147ff.

28. David FitzGerald, *A Nation of Emigrants: How Mexico Manages Its Migration* (Berkeley: University of California Press, 2008), 70ff.

29. Marco Martiniello, *Leadership et pouvoir dans les communautés d'origine immigrée* (Paris: CIEMI/L'Harmattan, 1992).

30. Pereira, *La dictature de Salazar*, 346ff.

31. Gérard Noiriel, *Le creuset français: Histoire de l'immigration en France XIXe-XXe siècle* (Paris: Seuil, 1988).

32. Dominique Schnapper, *La France de l'intégration* (Paris: Gallimard, 1991), 10–11.

33. Christian Delacroix, François Dosse, and Patrick Garcia, *Les courants historiques en France, 19e-20e siècle* (Paris: Gallimard, 2007).

34. Gérard Noiriel, "L'immigration: naissance d'un 'problème' (1881–1883)," *Agone* 40 (2008): 15–40.

35. Gérard Noiriel, *A quoi sert "l'identité nationale"?* (Marseille: Agone, 2007).

36. Benedict Anderson, *L'imaginaire national: Réflexions sur l'origine et l'essor du nationalisme* (Paris: La Découverte, 1996).

37. Rui Ramos, "A segunda fundação (1890–1926)," in José Mattoso, *História de Portugal*, vol. 6 (Lisbon: Estampa, 2001); José Manuel Sobral, *Portugal, Portugueses: Uma identidade nacional* (Lisbon: Fundação Manuel dos Santos, 2012).

38. António do Amaral Pyrrait, "Raisons et possibilités de l'émigration portugaise," in Institut National d'Études Démographiques, *Études européennes de population: Main-d'œuvre-emploi-migrations: Situation et perspectives* (Paris: INED, 1953), 233–243.

39. See, e.g., Anne-Marie Thiesse, *La création des identités nationales: Europe XVIIIe-XXe siècle* (Paris: Seuil, 1999).

40. Bela Feldman-Bianco, "Multiple Layers of Time and Space: The Construction of Class, Ethnicity, and Nationalism among Portuguese Immigrants," in *Towards a Transnational Perspective on Migration: Race, Class, Ethnicity, and Nationalism Reconsidered*, ed. Nina Glick Schiller, Linda Basch, and Cristina Blanc-Szanton (New York: Annals of the New York Academy of Science, 1992), 145–174.

41. Miranda, *As constituições*, 220.

42. Nancy L. Green, "The Politics of Exit: Reversing the Immigration Paradigm," *Journal of Modern History* 77 (2005): 263–289: 283ff.

43. Speech of the Foreign Minister at the Chamber of Peers, Session of April 26, 1843, 353.

44. Miriam Halpern Pereira, *A política portuguesa da emigração 1850–1930* (Lisbon: A regra do jogo, 1981).

45. Speech of the Lavradio Count at the Chamber of Peers, Session of April 26, 1843, 353.

46. Cláudia Castelo, *Passagens para Africa. O povoamento de Angola e Moçambique com naturais da métropole (1920–1974)* (Porto: Afrontamento, 2007).

47. Steward Lloyd-Jones and António Costa Pinto, eds., *The Last Empire: Thirty Years of Portuguese Decolonization* (Bristol/Portland: Intellect Books, 2003).

48. Michel Oriol, "Du navigateur au prolétaire. L'histoire comme ressource identitaire dans la diaspora portugaise," *Peuples Méditerranéens* 31–32 (1985): 203–215.

49. Jean-Baptiste Pingault, "Jeunes issus de l'immigration portugaise: affirmations identitaires dans les espaces politiques nationaux," *Le Mouvement Social* 209 (2004): 71–89.

50. Linda Basch, Nina Glick Schiller, and Cristina Szanton Blanc, *Nations Unbound: Transnational Projects, Postcolonial Predicaments, and Deterritorialized Nation-States* (New York: Gordon and Beach, 1994), 6.

51. Roger Waldinger, "'Transnationalisme' des immigrants et présence du passé," *Revue Européenne des Migrations Internationales* 22 (2006): 23–41.

52. Marcelo Borges, *Chains of Gold: Portuguese Migration to Argentina in Transatlantic Perspective* (Leiden: Brill, 2009).

53. Anthony Giddens, *Les conséquences sociales de la modernité* [1990] (Paris: L'Harmattan, 1994), 25.

54. Paulo Filipe Monteiro, *Terra que já foi terra: Análise sociológica de nove lugares agro-pastoris da Serra da Lousã* (Lisbon: Salamandra, 1985).

55. Dufoix, "Un pont par-dessus la porte."

56. Boaventura de Sousa Santos, "O Estado, as relações salarias e o bem-estar social na semiperiferia: o caso portugués," in Santos, *Portugal um retrato singular* (Porto: Afrontamento, 1993), 46.

57. Laurence Fontaine, "Solidarités familiales et logiques migratoires en pays de montagne à l'époque moderne," *Annales ESC* 6 (1990): 1433–1450, 1434.

58. Charbit, Hily, and Poinard, *Le va-et-vient*.

59. Maria Beatriz Rocha-Trindade, "Réseaux de transnationalité: Le cas portugais," *Ethnologie française* (1999): 255–262.

60. Teresa Líbano Monteiro, "Fés, crédos e religiõe," in *História da vida privada em Portugal*, vol. 4, *Os nossos dias*, ed. José Mattoso (Lisbon: Temas e Debates/Círculo de Leitores, 2011), 278–307.

61. See, for instance, João de Pina Cabral, *Filhos de Adão, Filhas de Eva: A visão do mundo camponesa do Alto Minho* (Lisbon: Dom Quixote, 1989); Colette Callier-Boisvert, *Soajo entre migrations et mémoire: Études sur une société agro-pastorale à l'identité rénovée* (Paris: Fundação Calouste Gulbenkian, 1999).

62. Nancy L. Green, "Religion et ethnicité: De la comparaison spatiale et temporelle," in *Les codes de la différence: Race-origine-religion. France-Allemagne-États-Unis*, ed. Riva Kastoryano (Paris: Presses de Sciences Po, 2005), 67–88.

63. On religion and transnationalism, see José Mapril, *Islão e transnacionalismo: Uma etnografia entre Portugal e Bangladeche* (Lisbon: Imprensa de Ciências Sociais, 2012); Guillaume Etienne, "Religion, ethnicité et patrimoine: un pélerinage berrichon approprié par les migrations," doctoral thesis, University of Tours, 2013.

64. João Leal, *Açores, EUA, Brasil: imigração e Etnicidade* (Ponta Delgada: Direcção Regional das Comunidades, 2007).

65. Irène Strijdhorst dos Santos, "Being a Part of Several 'Worlds': Sense of Belonging and Wedding Rites among Franco-Portuguese Youth," *Croatian Journal of Ethnology Folklore Research* 42 (2005): 25–45.

66. Claudine Attias-Donfut and François-Charles Wolff, *Le destin des enfants d'immigrés: Un désenchaînement des générations* (Paris: Stock, 2009), 193.

67. Françoise Lestage, "Editorial: La mort en migration," *Revue Européenne des Migrations Internationales* 28 (2012): 7–12.

68. Twenty-eight percent of the migrants surveyed were indifferent regarding their preferred location of burial. Claudine Attias-Donfut and François-Charles Wolff, "Le lieu d'enterrement des personnes nées hors de France," *Population* 60 (2005)1 813–836, 828.

69. Françoise Lestage, "Entre Mexique et États-Unis: La chaine entrepreneuriale de la mort des migrants," *Revue Européenne des Migrations Internationales* 28 (2012): 71–88.

70. António Branquinho Pequeno, "Les morts voyagent aussi . . . Le 'dernier retour' de l'immigré portugais," *Esprit* 83 (1983): 153–156.

71. Michel Foucault, *Sécurité, territoire, population* (Paris: Gallimard/Seuil, 2004), 135.

72. Marie-Christine Volovitch-Tavares, "L'Église de France et l'accueil des immigrés portugais (1960–1975)," *Le Mouvement social* 188 (1999): 89–100.

73. Paul Dietschy, *Histoire du football* (Paris: Perrin, 2010).

74. Ana Paula Coutinho Mendes, *Lentes bifocais: Representações da diaspora portuguesa do Século XX* (Porto: Afrontamento, 2009); Teresa Cid, Teresa Alves, Irene Blayer, and Francisco Fagundes, eds., *Portugal pelo mundo disperso* (Lisbon: Tinta da China, 2013).

75. Manuel Antunes da Cunha, *Les Portugais de France face à leur télévision. Médias, migrations et enjeux identitaires* (Rennes: Presses Universitaires de Rennes, 2009).

76. Victor Pereira, "Le football parmi les migrants portugais en France, 1958–1974," *Migrance*, 22 (2003): 28–38.

77. Victor Pereira, "Une passion portugaise," in *Allez la France! Football et immigration, histoires croisées*, ed. Claude Boli, Yvan Gastaut, and Fabrice Grognet (Paris: Gallimard/Cité Nationale de l'Histoire de l'Immigration/Musée National du Sport, 2010), 50–53.

78. Heloisa Paulo, *Aqui também é Portugal: A colónia portuguesa do Brasil e o salazarismo* (Coimbra: Quarteto, 2000).

79. Mário Rodrigues Filho, *O negro no futebol brasileiro* [1947] (Rio de Janeiro: Civilização editora, 1964), 122.

80. Gladys Sabina Ribeiro, "'Por que você veio encher o pandulho aqui?' Os portugueses, o antilusitanismo e a exploração das moradias populares no Rio de Janeiro da República Velha," *Análise Social* 29 (1994): 631–654.

81. Fernando da Costa Ferreira, "As múltiplas identidades do Club de Regatas Vasco da Gama," *Revista Geo-Paisagem* 6 (2004).

82. Victor Pereira, "O desporto além-fronteiras: Portugueses e desporto nos contextos migratórios," in José Neves and Nuno Domingos, eds., *A história do desporto em Portugal*, vol. II, *Nação, Império e Globalização* (Vila do Conde: Quid Novi, 2011), 93–135.

83. Emmanuel Salesse, "'De quel club êtes-vous?' Identité footballistique au Portugal," in Jean-Michel Waele and Alexandre Husting, eds., *Football et identités* (Brussels: Éditions de l'Université de Bruxelles, 2008), 65–82.

84. Miguel Moniz, "Identidade transnacional adaptativa e a venda do soccer: O New England Revolution e as populações immigrantes lusófonas," *Análise Social* 41 (2006): 371–393, 381.

85. Victor Pereira, "Os futebolistas invisíveis: os portugueses em França e o futebol," *Etnográfica* 16 (2012): 97–115.

86. Gérard Noiriel and Stéphane Beaud, "L'immigration dans le football," *Vingtième siècle. Revue d'Histoire* 26 (1990): 83–96.

87. Evelyne Ribert, "A la recherche du 'sentiment identitaire' des Français issus de l'immigration," *Revue Française de Science Politique* 59 (2009): 569–592.

88. The subtitle to this section is inspired by José Vieira's documentary, "Le pays où l'on ne revient jamais," *La Huit Production, 2005*. Paul-André Rosental, "Maintien/ rupture: un nouveau couple pour l'analyse des migrations." *Annales HSS* (1990): 1403–1431.

89. Fariba Adelkhah, "Partir sans quitter, quitter sans partir," *Critique Internationale* 19 (2003): 141–155.

90. Paulo Filipe Monteiro, *Emigração: o eterno mito do retorno* (Lisbon: Celta, 1994).

91. Alves, *Os Brasileiros*, 301.

92. Michel Poinard, *Le retour des travailleurs portugais* (Paris: La documentation française, 1979); Sylvain Laurens, *Une politisation feutrée: Les hauts fonctionnaires et l'immigration en France* (Paris: Belin, 2009).

93. Andrea Klimt, "Autenticidade em debate: Folclore e representações dos portugueses em Hamburgo," in *Vozes do povo: A folclorização em Portugal*, ed. Salwa El-Shawan Castelo Branco and Jorge Freitas Branco (Oeiras: Celta, 2003), 521–530.

94. Abdelmalek Sayad, *La double absence: Des illusions de l'émigré aux souffrances de l'immigré* (Paris: Seuil, 1999), 396.

95. Rocha-Trindade, "Réseaux de transnationalité."

CHAPTER 3

JAPANESE BRAZILIANS (1908–2013)

Transnationalism amid Violence, Social Mobility, and Crisis

Mônica Raisa Schpun
Translation from Portuguese (Brazil) by Sarah Abel

On June 18, 1908, the steamer *Kasato Maru*, arriving from the Japanese port of Kobe, approached the Brazilian port of Santos, bringing with it the first 781 Japanese immigrants destined for the coffee plantations of the state of São Paulo. In Brazil, a long period of debate and vacillation had preceded this arrival. The process was marked by conflicts of interests between elite factions, but also by different visions of the ideal composition of the Brazilian population and the role of immigration. From the 1870s onward, debates regarding the substitution of slaves by free laborers occupied the Brazilian political scene, as the abolition of slavery, which was to take place in 1888, already loomed on the horizon. The burning question, which concerned the very construction of the nation, was whether or not future free workers would be recruited from within the population already present in the country, thus including ex-slaves, and largely comprised of blacks and mestizos. A large number of the rural elites rejected this idea, instead expressing the desire that new workers—and future citizens—be foreigners and white. Nevertheless, "the solution" to "the problem" attracting immigrants was at odds with the issue of the costs of attracting free laborers. It was precisely in this context, that the possibility of importing Asian workers was discussed, presented as an alternative (and provisional) measure, marking the transition between enslaved and free (preferably European) workers. This was a double compromise: besides being less costly than Europeans in the eyes of the Brazilian elites, Asians were also considered to be "intermediate" between blacks and whites in the racial hierarchy, not representing the ideal solution for the much desired "whitening" of the population, but also not black.[1] Yet among the coffee planters themselves, who wielded considerable power over decisions about the guidance of the country, Asians, while viewed as "submissive" were also considered to be of "unscrupulous character." Not only might they lead the country's Europeans astray; they could even contaminate the Brazilian population. Their presence was seen as degrading for the nation, contrary to the aim of constructing a "civilized future" upon a "vigorous and conquering race." Thus, for some sectors of the economic elites, these cultural concerns outweighed more immediate economic objectives linked to the costs of a free work force.

The same fears were expressed by other sectors of the political elite that also participated in the debates. For example, Joaquim Nabuco, a prominent leader of the abolitionist movement, revealed his belief in the superiority of the "white race" in relation to the inferior "black and yellow races." Despite the trepidation regarding the threat of an overwhelmingly black population in the country, Nabuco believed that the importation of Asians would contribute to the "mongolization" of the nation, degrading the country's existing "races." Thus, he opposed Asian immigration, as well as any other spontaneous immigration, supporting instead a control on migratory flows in the hope of guaranteeing the "whitening" of the population.[2]

A specific debate focused on the Japanese. On the one hand, the defenders of this immigration praised Japanese workers for their docility, discipline, and virtue; on the other, its opponents never ceased to attack the "unassimilable" character of the "yellow race."[3] In 1879, Brazil charged an official envoy to the United States with the task of observing the situation of the Japanese immigrants in that country. In the impressions that he wrote at the time, Salvador de Mendonça proved favorable to this immigration, on the condition that it be temporary and regulated by multiyear contracts, thus keeping the immigrants from setting down roots in the country and mixing with the local population. Once these precautions were put in place, the presence of the Japanese would become, in his eyes, not only inoffensive, but useful, as it would pave the way for the arrival of Europeans, and avoid the greater and more pressing danger of the country's "Africanization." Other accounts confirmed this belief in the utility of Asian workers, stressing their low cost.

Although Japanese immigration continued to be prohibited by law and the Brazilian government was in no hurry to annul or circumvent this restriction, Japanese representatives visited Brazilian coffee plantations in 1894. In the following year, Brazil signed a treaty of friendship with Japan, establishing trade and shipping between the two countries.

In truth, reservations existed on both sides: the Japanese turned down a Brazilian proposal in 1900 to bring in a first contingent of Japanese migrants

for experimental purposes, perhaps on the basis of their impressions garnered from visiting the plantations six years earlier. Furthermore, by 1900,
the Japanese were immigrating to the United States and Hawaii: the Brazilian
route was not crucial for them. The situation altered with the restriction
of Japanese entries into the United States and Hawaii in 1907–1908. With
Japan then in the throes of an agrarian crisis and undergoing significant
demographic pressure, to which mass emigration might serve as a reliable
antidote, Japanese emigration companies began desperately searching for
other countries that were prepared to receive new groups.

However, European immigration to Brazil remained at high levels until
the First World War. In addition, the measures adopted by the United States
offered a supplementary argument to the opponents of Japanese immigration in Brazil: why should the country open its borders to this immigration
at the very moment when other countries were closing them? Yet Brazilian
immigration policy of the time proved dominated by coffee-growing interests, which sought to maintain a permanent reserve army of labor in order
to guarantee its low cost. In this context, the readiness of Japan to provide
extra "pairs of hands for coffee" did not go unnoticed. In 1907, Brazil promulgated a new law, eliminating restrictions linked to the national origin
of immigration candidates, which thus paved the way for the immigration
agreement signed with Japan the following year.

It was thus, amid the different, but not always divergent, interests of the
two countries that Japanese immigration to Brazil began. Traditionally,
the periodization of this migratory flow is broken up into three phases:
1908–1925, 1926–1941, and the postwar period from 1953 onward, when
immigration recommenced.[4] From 1923 until 1941, the Japanese government provided subsidies to immigration candidates, which the state of São
Paulo had ceased to provide since 1921. With this decision, Japan effectively
and efficiently incentivized immigration to Brazil, which became a privileged
destination after the closure of Peruvian and American borders to the Japanese, in 1923 and 1924 respectively. This second phase saw the majority of
entries to Brazil: 67.1 percent of the total, compared to 13.4 percent in the
preceding period, and 19.5 percent after the war, from 1953 to 1963.[5] In
1934, just when Japanese immigration reached its peak, Brazil adopted an
extremely restrictive Quota Law, which particularly affected the Japanese,
as they were the only group entering the country in significant numbers at
the time. Even though the quotas only came into force in 1938, deceleration
was immediate, beginning the year after the new law was passed. For this
reason, the majority of Japanese immigrants actually entered Brazil between

1924 and 1935: 141,732 arrivals, as compared to 32,366 in the preceding period, 1908–1923.[6]

The adoption of the Quota Law marked the beginning of the most difficult period for Brazil's Japanese community, which found itself divided between Japanese and Brazilian interests and two strong nationalist ideologies. Indeed, an intense nationalism marked the entire Vargas Era (1930–1945), becoming ever more evident during the *Estado Novo* ("New State") era (1937–1945).

However, first-generation immigrants, who had been schooled in Japan, were heirs to a Japanese nationalism no less strong than the nationalism that they encountered in Brazil. With the onset of modernization in Japan, in the Meiji Era (1868–1912), organizational models were imported that permitted a better functioning and greater centralization of the nation (banking system, army, schools, police, justice, postal, and telegraph services).[7] This process brought the issue of national identity and of Japanese singularity—in the midst of "imitations" from other countries—to the fore, with a movement calling for a return to tradition in response to Japan's perceived "occidentalization." School became the key to this return to so-called Japanese roots. After various attempts to implement a schooling model, the Education Edict was finally promulgated in 1890. School textbooks, reflecting the new educational policy, conveyed values of loyalty, patriotism, and courage, impregnated with Confucianism and the imperial cult. The process of "Japanization" was constructed, therefore, through the selection of whatever elements were deemed worth taking, both from abroad, and from local traditions, for the purpose of constructing modernity. In both of these cases, the centralization of the state operated as a filter "capable of giving meaning to the 'digestion' of 'imported' elements, and of reformulating the heritage bequeathed by history."[8]

It was with this baggage that the Japanese of Brazil first faced the heightened nationalism during the presidency of Getúlio Vargas and the more extreme situation of opposition between the two enemy nations in the theater of war. As we will see later in this article, this confrontation had profound consequences for the Japanese Brazilian community, yielding a continued legacy in the immediate postwar period.

In spite of everything, migration from Japan to Brazil resumed after the occupying American forces left Japan. Although discrimination against Japanese Brazilians during the Vargas period had been considerable, the Japanese community in Brazil never underwent internment, as it did in the United States. And the return to migration after the war was in the economic

interests of both Japan and Brazil. Thus, the renewal of immigration upon
new bases, in 1953, benefited from a fairly diverse international context,
in which the new interests that had come into play, both in Brazil and in
Japan, helped to pacify tensions little by little. This new migratory wave
ended in the 1970s. It was less numerous and marked by a new profile,
that of a skilled labor force that was no longer solely agricultural and that
was largely made up of single men, in contrast to the family migration of
the earlier period. However, the ending of emigration from Japan was not
enough to put a stop to the flow of migrants between the two countries. In
the following decade, Brazil became, for the first time in its history, a country of emigration, and a significant number of Japanese Brazilians began
to emigrate to the country of their ancestors. Today, Brazilians in Japan,
numbering roughly 300,000 individuals in 2007, comprise the third largest
foreign-born population, after the Chinese and Korean communities.[9] This
Brazilian presence in Japan has contributed to keeping the links between
the two countries alive, bringing young generations of Japanese Brazilian
descendants closer to Japan while reaffirming but also questioning an ethnic
identity that is in a constant process of negotiation.

For more than a century, innumerable tensions have marked the immigration and the presence of ever more numerous contingents of Japanese and
their descendants in Brazil, home today to the largest Japanese community
outside of Japan, with around 1.5 million individuals spread over six generations. In the following pages, I show how such tensions are linked to the
international dimension of this migratory process, which bears the marks
both of the relations between Brazil and Japan but also of each country's
relations with the immigrants and their descendants. Throughout this period,
both Brazil and Japan have acted and reacted in different and even conflicting ways toward the immigrants, with consequences that have affected not
only the migratory experiences of various generations of Japanese Brazilians,
but also their links with Japan. Diverging from the three-phase periodization indicated above, the article unfolds in seven parts, following the theme
of international relations and of the converging, diverging, conflicting, and
coinciding interests between Brazil and Japan with regards to the history
of this migratory flow. The transnational ties that took the form of a particularly strong attachment to their language and culture were facilitated
or impeded depending on the period, as we shall see later. Depending on
the time frame and the international stakes, there was more or less tension
obliging immigrants to abandon cultural practices that were dear to them
or to practice them clandestinely, which led only to reinforcing their attachment to their homeland.

The First Years (1908–1934): Setting Down Roots

As we have seen, at the time when the first Japanese immigrants arrived in Brazil, Japan considered emigration to be a safety valve for the agrarian crisis and the great demographic pressure the country was experiencing. But this solution would be truly effective only if the emigrants did not return, instead setting down roots in their country of destination. For this reason, the government, along with private Japanese colonizing firms, furnished the immigrants with a greatly varied range of assistance as a means of guaranteeing their economic success as agricultural laborers. Agronomists traveled around the countryside providing advice about agricultural techniques, soil quality, seeds, and products; various financial aids were also offered to assist settlement and the purchase of tools, utensils, and land. The choice of land was also made on the basis of recommendations that were to guide strategies regarding the group's geographic mobility—a well-informed and by no means random process. For example, in the 1930s, Japanese agricultural laborers began to develop cotton cultivation on Brazilian lands, having been helped in this endeavor by technicians sent from Japan. At the same time, Japanese firms were setting up processing factories for yarn that was then exported to Japan, meeting a strong demand from the local internal market and furthermore contributing to the development of the Japanese merchant navy. The Japanese also helped develop a vibrant commercial mixed farming sector—nonexistent up until that point—which helped provide the needed food supplies for the expanding Brazilian cities.[10]

Thanks to such investments, Japanese immigrants during this period displayed an extremely high rate of permanence: in the State of São Paulo, for example, where the vast majority of Japanese cohorts were concentrated, 93 percent settled for good.[11] Moreover, the immigrants' process of social ascension was particularly rapid: they left the coffee plantations (where they had first been employed) more rapidly than other workers (half of them moved on in less than five years, and a significant number in less than two years);[12] they also had easier and more prompt access to land ownership.

A key element of Brazilian migratory policy in those years also played a part in this success. In contrast to those who went to the other target destinations of this migration flow—Hawaii, the continental United States, and Peru—Japanese immigrants to Brazil were not mainly young men, but rather families, thus responding to a specific request by the Brazilian agrarian elites, which was codified in signed agreements. The coffee plantations organized labor by a system known as *colonato*, in which each family of laborers was entrusted with a certain number of coffee plants and allowed to plant foodstuffs for family consumption or commercial use in the interstices between those plants. In this way, the very basis of the system relied on family units: the more hands, the better the productivity, and the greater the benefits in kind. Thus, family immigration was a first step toward setting down roots—an outcome sought both by the Japanese state and Brazilian interests.

In an apparent paradox, the immigrants' stabilization, guaranteed by their economic success, was only possible thanks to their strong and continuous links, not so much to the Japanese territory that they left behind but to the Japanese state and the Japanese colonizing firms that were deployed in Brazil. Furthermore, in that initial period, Japan was able to intervene on Brazilian soil alongside the immigrants without problems and without provoking adverse reactions. This was, therefore, a system of "supervised immigration."[13]

The Quotas Act (1934): Xenophobia

Just as the group was experiencing a situation of full ongoing expansion, due to both the increase in new arrivals and the constant improvement in the socioeconomic conditions of families in the countryside, the Brazilian context changed radically. Anti-Japanese sentiment, although not completely absent before, rose to a new peak.

In 1933, Getúlio Vargas, who had been in power since 1930, called for nationwide elections of a National Constituent Assembly, which was charged with adopting a new Brazilian constitution. Propelled by deputies representing the coffee elites but also by eugenicist physicians, a genuine campaign against the "yellow peril" emerged amid the Assembly's heated debates.[14] As we have seen, even when the arguments had been favorable to the entry of the Japanese, racism had suffused the debates that preceded the arrival of the first Japanese immigrants: the defenders of Japanese immigration viewed them not simply as less costly than Europeans but also more submissive and, from a racial point of view, "intermediates" between whites and blacks. In any case, it was hoped that immigration from Japan would be a temporary and strictly controlled measure.

By the beginning of the 1930s, the context had changed considerably, and not only in Brazil. The local elites followed with concern the closure of all other borders to the Japanese and the subsequent increase in entries into Brazil. The constituent deputies thereby used and abused arguments such as the theory of "social cysts," which referred to the incapacity and refusal of the Japanese to integrate themselves into the nation, or, to quote

Oliveira Vianna, an intellectual who was held in particular esteem by the political elites of the era: "The Japanese are like sulphur: insoluble."[15] It is worth remembering here that since the 1920s Brazilian identity had been constructed according to a model—not of segregation but rather miscegenation—which had already become hegemonic and amply recognized by the national population as of the 1930s. As understood at the time, miscegenation had a dual, biological and cultural, character. Consequently, for those who had wagered on the "whitening" of the population, so yearned-for by the elites, the solution lay precisely in the biological miscegenation between blacks and whites, since the progeny of mixed couples had paler skin than the darkest spouse, and so on progressively. From a cultural point of view, the Brazilian "synthesis" comprised the heritage of the three principal groups that had populated the country since its colonial origins: Indians, blacks, and (Portuguese) whites; this mixture constituted the originality of *brasilidade* ("Brazilianness"). Added to this cultural synthesis were the immigrants who had arrived later, with their extremely varied baggage. All of these, therefore, were expected to demonstrate a desire and a predisposition to integrate themselves into, and to incorporate, *brasilidade*. During the Constituent Assembly debates, anti-Japanese sentiment took the form of an accusation: viewed as foreign to the national body, Japanese immigrants were held to blame for this foreignness, which was thought to stem from their refusal to blend in with local society and instead to maintain a predatory relationship with the latter.

Another issue that appeared during the debates was the decreasing power of the São Paulo coffee interests. Externally, the Great Depression of 1929 generated severe consequences for the landowners of the state of São Paulo as the crisis dealt coffee exports a strong blow. Internally, with regard to domestic politics, the seizing of power by Vargas in 1930 led to transformations that distanced the coffee growers and their allies from the center of the national political scene, where they had been hegemonic throughout the whole First Republic (1889–1930). The Constituent Assembly was, therefore, a fundamental arena in the struggle for coffee interests, which the landowners of the state of São Paulo represented.

In this context, the landowners were forced to confront the consequences of the immigration and settlement of the Japanese. With the crisis, they brusquely realized that over a short period, a large proportion of Japanese agricultural laborers had left the coffee plantations. As leaseholders or small property-holders, the Japanese had turned to the intensive polyculture of fruit and vegetables, and also to cotton. True social actors, they were now able to insert themselves into the gaps left by the coffee expansion, while also creating their own economic niches, thanks to the support and incentives offered by the Japanese government and with the help of Japanese firms. By extending their agricultural holdings and transforming part of the coffee-growing region's playing board into small and midsized estate properties, the Japanese had modified the agrarian structure of the area and became a subject of concern, above all in this moment of crisis. A xenophobic and racist reaction rapidly took off, expanding upon the preexisting biases we have seen above.

By 1934, this successful anti-Japanese campaign resulted in the adoption of an extremely restrictive Quotas Act, of which the main objective was curbing Japanese immigration. The Japanese diplomatic mission did what it could not only to prevent the law from being adopted, but also to avoid having the Japanese explicitly mentioned in the new text. While it failed to halt the law, the latter demand was met, and the law's targets were identified in general terms. Both the Japanese Ambassador to Brazil and the Minister of Foreign Affairs in Japan handed in their resignations after the law was adopted.[16]

Although migration from Japan had already gone into sharp decline, as we have seen, the adoption of the Quotas Act, with its xenophobic repercussions and the interruption of the migration flow, landed the first blow to Brazil's Japanese community, above all affecting new candidates for admission to the country. Further blows came with subsequent assimilationist measures, which, bearing the badge of the strong nationalism of the Vargas Era, intensely and directly affected the Japanese already living in the country.

"Nationalizing" Measures (1938): Combatting "Cysts"

The November 1937 coup d'état brought about by Getúlio Vargas launched the *Estado Novo*, making the regime's nationalism and mistrust of immigrants—particularly of those who appeared most distant from the local culture, starting with the Japanese—all the more marked.

Accordingly, from the first months of the *Estado Novo*, a series of decrees hindered the operation of foreign language schools and the publication of foreign language books and periodicals. These measures were especially harmful to the Japanese community, which had only been established in the country for a short time and whose members had yet to master the local language and culture, instead retaining extremely close ties to the Japanese institutions that continued to aid them in various ways. As for the schools, since Brazilian support for education, especially in the countryside, was severely deficient, the Japanese had founded their own institutions. In doing

so, they received aid from the Japanese authorities, reflecting Japan's overall policy, which aimed to stabilize the settlement of immigrants in Brazil,
reducing their dissatisfaction as far as possible and, thus, diminishing the
rate at which they would return.

The first school, Taisho, was founded in the city of São Paulo in 1915,
seven years after immigration commenced; many others opened their doors
thereafter: by 1938, 476 Japanese primary schools were already in operation in the state of São Paulo.[17] In organizing this network of schools, the
consulate relied on associations that had been specifically created to build
and administer these establishments and provide them with teaching staff.
While the textbooks came from Japan, the curricula were adapted to suit
the lives of the immigrants, as perceived by the Japanese government and
its diplomatic representatives, who thought it necessary to concentrate their
efforts on ethnic maintenance to facilitate community cohesion. Language
teaching was designed primarily to evoke and nourish a taste for literature, rather than knowledge of grammar, as the endeavor focused on the
maintenance of the "Japanese spirit," which the Japanese authorities feared
might be lost in the migratory context. With this aim in mind, through the
practice of kendo, dramatic arts, and the telling of traditional Japanese
tales and legends, as well as through the commemoration of important
dates in the Japanese calendar, the immigrants hoped to pass their values
and behavior—filial respect, the cult of ancestors, and a strong community
conscience—on to their children.

Exerting an extremely important influence on community bonding and
cultural transmission, these schools were in active operation until the start
of the *Estado Novo*. By prohibiting any foreign funding for educational,
cultural, charitable, or aid organizations, articles 3 and 4 of Decree Law
no. 383, promulgated on April 18, 1938—a few months after the coup
d'état—represented the first obstacle to the functioning of these schools.
The difficulties then piled up: the following month, another decree required
that all textbooks adopted by primary schools be written in Portuguese.[18]
Finally, some months later, a new law decreed that teachers working in
agricultural settlements, where many Japanese people resided, must be native Brazilians.[19] These repressive measures quickly made the functioning
of the Japanese schools network impossible. In December 1939, practically
all the remaining schools in the state of São Paulo were closed. In order to
assure that the language teaching that they so highly valued was not totally
abandoned, the Japanese began to turn to clandestine methods. Classes
were given on a rotating basis in family homes and in small groups. In this
way, Japanese nationalism—the strong awareness of belonging to a unique

and exceptional nation and culture—continued to be transmitted through language and the study of literary texts, as had formerly been the case in Japan for the first generation and in the schools network set up in Brazil before the restrictions of the Vargas Era.

As for the prohibition imposed upon the foreign-language press, only one of the existing Japanese language newspapers opted to translate its editions into Portuguese. Moreover, those that continued in circulation during the *Estado Novo* were closed down in 1941, after the onset of the war in the Pacific; book and magazine imports were simultaneously suspended. This does not mean that reading in Japanese was completely brought to a halt by these measures: Mario Yendo, who owned a business importing books and magazines from Japan, reverted to buying and selling used books and magazines. As he recalled later, the idea was successful (and profitable) despite the decrease in prices: Yendo's fellow migrants did not lose interest in his shop, and the secondhand magazines were sold without any trouble.

The isolation imposed by the new legislation added to the geographical isolation of the Japanese, who still mainly lived in the countryside and among whom the cultural and linguistic gap, relative to the rest of Brazilian society was extremely pronounced. This brutal rupture further prevented a good part of the community from accessing journalistic reportage, since many were incapable of reading in Portuguese, as a 1939 survey on the situation of the community of the northwest region of the state of São Paulo (the area with the greatest concentration of Japanese people in the country) showed. Of the nearly 12,000 interviewees who had lived in Brazil for an average of eleven years, 88 percent subscribed to Japanese-language newspapers. None of the families referred to any magazine in Portuguese; the nearly one hundred Brazilian newspapers that were mentioned were read mainly by intellectuals living in cities in the region.[20] The immigrants' attachment to their language and culture of origin confirmed to Brazilian political leaders that the Japanese were unassimilable and unwilling to become integrated into the idea of *brasilidade*.

The "nationalizing" methods that characterized the treatment reserved for immigrants by Vargas during the *Estado Novo* are generally considered by specialists to have been effective, forcing the diverse groups, and notably those that had spent less time in the country, to break ties with their country of origin. In the case of the Japanese, this assessment deserves to be reevaluated as the effects of the measures implemented by the Vargas regime often ran contrary to their desired aims. For example, some responses obtained by the survey mentioned above clearly indicated the effects of the atmosphere of growing xenophobia that marked the period beginning in 1933 (with the debates of the National Constituent Assembly), until the first years of the *Estado Novo* (1937–1941), when the "nationalizing" measures were decided upon and applied: 85 percent of the 12,000 persons interviewed said that they would like to return to Japan, as opposed to a mere 10 percent who would opt to remain definitively in the country and 5 percent who were undecided.[21]

The survey revealed the conflict in which the Japanese were caught. Humiliated by the policy adopted by the Brazilian state and by the public image attributed to them, they turned back to their Japanese roots as the source of a more positive self-image. While the great majority said they wanted to return to Japan, those statements contradicted the reality of the extremely high rate—93 percent, as previously mentioned—of Japanese settlement in Brazil as well as the socioeconomic context that was particularly favorable to the Japanese, whose agricultural activities were booming. In effect, the group found itself trapped between two types of nationalism: on the one hand, that which had nurtured and raised members of the first generation back in Japan and which continued to be transmitted to their descendants via official or "mobile" schools (clandestine, itinerant schools that moved from house to house as needed in order not to be discovered); and, on the other hand, the nationalism that they were experiencing in Brazil, which sought to violently crush the Japanese ethnic values that had been learned and passed on with pride.

Nevertheless, the hopes of return expressed by that mass of immigrants in 1939 had to be abandoned, at least for the time being, as war broke out.

The War on the Side of the Allies (1942–1945): Isolation

After a long period of hesitation and negotiations, Brazil broke diplomatic relations with the Axis nations in February 1942, before entering the war alongside the Allies in August of the same year. From the beginning of that year, Brazil began to put in place repressive measures targeting Italian, German, and Japanese immigrants in particular. Yet these measures were not evenly applied to the three groups. For the Japanese, the new regulations represented an addition to the already existing burden of anti-Japanese sentiment, already shared by fractions of the country's political and intellectual elite since well before the start of the war. In aligning with the Allies, Brazil brought this anti-Japanese sentiment once more to the surface as the climate of war strengthened the already existing antipathy. In addition to the restrictions imposed upon all Axis citizens, a racist tone permeated those texts and police reports specifically relating to Japanese immigrants, who were collectively considered to be a threat to the country. Toward this end, certain "character" stereotypes were mobilized: the Japanese were seen not only as "unassimilable," but also as "undecipherable," "treacherous," "disloyal," and "fifth-columnists"—unlike the Germans, and above all the Italians, who, having lived longer in the country, did not seem as strange as the Japanese in the eyes of those responsible for applying the new rules. Those distinctions among the immigrants originating in the Axis countries were not exclusively due to greater cultural distance, but also to a difference envisioned as "racial," since the Germans and Italians were "white," while the Japanese were "yellow," and perceived, as we have seen, as a threat to the "whitening" of the population. Moreover, they were also criticized for their presumed unwillingness to take an integral part in Brazilian society.[22]

With the declaration of war, the Japanese and their descendants, already deprived of their local community press and of books and newspapers imported from Japan, found themselves cut off from all links with their country of origin. Their diplomatic representatives left the country; the agricultural workers' financial aid and technical guidance were suspended. New measures now prohibited the use of foreign languages in public spaces and meetings; and their clandestine, "mobile" school teaching also continued to be strongly repressed.

In São Paulo, police officers patrolling the Japanese quarter—Liberdade—detained many Japanese people overheard talking or even just greeting someone in Japanese. Avoiding such repressive measures was extremely difficult for those who did not know any other language. Yet many took the utmost care to do precisely that. An example is Mariko Kawamura, an inhabitant of the neighborhood, living with her husband, her father-in-law, and her two brothers-in-law and the only one of these five to have been born in Brazil; due to the jus soli citizenship system operating in the country, she was therefore Brazilian by birth. Following an unexplained visit to her house by police officers who claimed to be looking for "suspicious" documents and objects but who ended up taking away her husband and keeping him imprisoned and out of contact for more than a month, Mariko became the only person to leave the house for shopping and other chores. Made wary by her experience, she never again spoke Japanese in the street, in the Japanese shops she frequented, or elsewhere in the neighborhood. In a less dramatic example, when the father of painter Flavio Shiró was arrested by a police officer as he spoke Japanese in the street with an acquaintance, he began singing the Brazilian national anthem. Highly amused at the memory of this incident, Shiró emphasized his father's intelligence: not only had he grasped what was expected of him and what would free him from this quandary, but he knew the entire lyrics to the anthem, which was probably more than could be said for the police officer, according to my interviewee. In any case, his father was left alone: his attitude was enough to convince the police officer of his love for Brazil.[23]

Repression was enacted in a way that was completely disproportionate to the daily lives of immigrants, being based on far-fetched ideas of a "fifth column," working undercover throughout the territory. Thus, many immigrants were detained in the streets of their ethnic quarter for speaking Japanese with someone who did not speak Portuguese, or for simply making a habitual gesture of respect to an elder. Many were also detained erroneously for "looking Japanese," as police officers and representatives claimed, although they were actually Japanese descendants born in Brazil and, therefore, Brazilian, and thus protected from the prevailing regulations against foreigners and especially citizens of enemy nations.

At home and far from the eyes of repression, Japanese continued, in those years, to be the common tongue for young and old for Japanese and "born Brazilians" alike. Nonetheless, in due course the difficulties—and the eventual impossibility—of schooling the second generation in Japanese resulted in the transformation of this reality.

The Fall of Japan (1945–1947): *Shindo Renmei*

Japan's defeat in the war provoked a veritable split in the Japanese community, placing the *kachigumi* ("victory groups")—largely members of the *Shindo Renmei* organization ("League of the Subjects' Path"), which was formed sometime between 1944 and 1945—in direct opposition to the *makegumi* ("defeatist groups"). The former believed in the invincibility of the Emperor; the latter accepted the fall of the country. The *Shindo Renmei* organization appears to have been created with the initial aim of cultivating the "Japanese spirit" and became progressively more radical during the war, when some of its members were embroiled in acts of sabotage and imprisoned for destroying peppermint plantations and silkworm farms. They believed that these products, to be exported to the United States, would be used in the war effort against Japan (that the silk threads, for example, would be used to sew parachutes) and therefore considered their fellow countrymen—the cultivators *par excellence* of these products in Brazil—to be traitors to the fatherland.[24] Intracommunity conflict continued after the war's end; between 1946 and 1947, the *Shindo Renmei* committed a score of assassinations of members of the community and left a much greater number wounded. Throughout those years, the organization amassed around

30,000 official members and enjoyed support from roughly four times that number—all of them Japanese immigrants and their descendants located in the interior of the state of São Paulo.[25]

Various authors have written on this topic in an attempt to explain this phenomenon, which did not occur in any of the other countries that received Japanese immigration. Some scholars have emphasized the importance of intracommunity resentment, hypothesizing a connection to differences in economic success among fractions of the community or to unequal access to the management of community associations or even to generational differences.[26] None of these explanations seem to truly take into account the situation of the singular violence that had affected the Brazilian Japanese community. Above all, the intracommunity violence was due to the repression brought about by the Vargas regime, which did not succeed in breaking the links between the Japanese community and Japan, but instead provoked an even more intense and radicalized nationalist reaction. The lack of direct access, in Japanese, to information about the war's progress made for an extreme level of confusion at the very heart of the community. The declaration of Japan's surrender was conveyed in a very indirect way: the Emperor's pronouncement, which was thoroughly unanticipated by the community, was communicated in a very formal format that was incomprehensible to the immigrants and via very poor quality radio transmissions. The formerly held conviction that the Emperor was invincible, and the commonly shared loyal pride in an expansionist and militaristic Japan not only permitted the rise of the "victory groups" but also the acceptance by many others of the arguments presented by these groups, who dismissed news of the defeat as American war propaganda. Many went so far as to sell their land, buying Japanese currency and traveling to the port of Santos, 80 km from São Paulo, to wait for a Japanese ship to come and pick them up to return to the victorious fatherland. Such a ship, of course, never even set sail. Even if only a minority dedicated themselves to violent and extreme attitudes, a considerable mass supported the principles that guided them.

The Postwar Period (1950–1980): New Immigration

After the liberation, in 1949, of the *Shindo Renmei* members condemned in 1946–1947, new protests from militants of the organization took place from 1950 onward, giving rise to new condemnations in 1953, the year in which immigration recommenced. The renewal of immigration occurred after the peace treaty, signed by Japan with her 48 enemy countries, came into effect in April 1952.

In the first postwar years, the prejudice and xenophobia of the prewar and wartime period largely continued to contaminate the public image of the Japanese and their descendants—as inassimilable fanatics. Moreover, the Shindo Renmei court case only served to feed into this viewpoint. Although neither the international context nor the socioeconomic situation of the two countries involved was the same as before the war, restrictive Brazilian legislation also continued to operate. However, this phase saw a somewhat positive change in mentalities leading, in 1958, to commemorations of the fiftieth anniversary of Japanese immigration to Brazil that garnered the support of both countries' governments.

One of the principle side effects of these commemorations involved a large-scale inquiry into the situation of the Japanese community carried out by the Japanese government. This study uncovered a wealth of details concerning the lives of Japanese Brazilians, well beyond the amount of information available for any of the other immigrant groups living in Bra-zil.[27] The survey revealed, among other things, that Japanese Brazilians had experienced significant social ascension, doing so more quickly than other groups.

Aside from the arrival of new immigrants, the years following the war were marked by the mass urbanization of Japanese Brazilians: with no possibility of returning to Japan, devastated by the war, and in the absence of better prospects in the countryside, they had largely begun to move to Brazilian cities, then in the midst of rapid expansion, where better living conditions existed. In 1958, 49 percent of Japanese Brazilians in the state of São Paulo lived in cities.[28] This new reality afforded Japanese Brazilians a greater visibility in the public sphere. The opening of new institutions such as the Brazilian Society of Japanese Culture or the Brazil-Japan Cultural Alliance also contributed to this end, consecrating both the presence of the Japanese community in Brazil and their recognition by local society, a significant shift indeed since the Vargas Era repression that had seen the successive closure of community associations and the subsequent extremely difficult wartime years.

In the 1950s and 1960s, Brazil experienced a "developmentalist" phase, with a strong industrializing thrust. Meanwhile, though Japan was in the midst of a period of economic growth, it still suffered from a surplus of population; consequently, it once again mobilized its institutions to manage departures and to aid and accompany emigrants.[29] "Supervised" emigration was reconfirmed as the approved model, and Brazil closed its eyes to the dreaded "ethnic cysts," instead embracing the image of efficient laborers, which was also associated with the Japanese.

The profile of the new immigrants, known as "new Japan," also changed. This time, they consisted of young and for the most part single men, selected for their technical qualifications. The migration flow was still mainly directed toward agriculture, focusing on settlement projects of agricultural frontiers in the theretofore sparsely inhabited and little developed spaces of the north, northeast, and center-west of the country. Yet urban immigration also existed, primarily accompanying the establishment of multinational companies.

Brazil was in need of skilled labor and technology, both of which were available in Japan. At the same time, Japan hoped to compete with the world's capitalist powers by exporting industries that were considered to be outmoded, such as the textile industry, alongside others associated with cutting-edge technology. It was upon these industries that Brazil constructed its new image of Japan and its professionals: productive, specialized, and highly qualified. Ultimately, the fact that Brazil was prioritized by Japan as a target destination for emigrants and industries was also due to the presence of a large Japanese community in the country. This was considered to be a foundation of significant support, conducive to the success of the new emigration projects and, once more, to the effort to promote immigrant permanence, thus easing Japanese demographic pressure.

The Reversal of the Migration Flow (1980–2000): The *dekasegi* Phenomenon

Japanese continued arriving in Brazil, albeit in smaller numbers, until the 1970s. Then, from the middle of the next decade onward, the migration flow reversed. The grave Brazilian crisis of the 1980s and 1990s turned Brazil into an emigration country, resulting in a new flow, that of Japanese descendants leaving for Japan. As economic immigrants, they found work at the bottom of the social ladder, especially in automobile and electronics factories.

The so-called *dekasegi* caused a revival of discussions about Japanese Brazilians' relations with their ancestral country. Many were of the opinion that, since their phenotype caused them to be seen as Japanese in Brazil, even when they were third- or fourth-generation immigrants, it would be worthwhile "returning" to Japan to feel once more among equals. The same idea also existed in Japan: a law in 1990 guaranteed Brazilians the right to reside and work in Japan. For the Japanese government, return migration from Brazil provided an opportunity to preserve the country's supposed homogeneity, favoring Japanese descendants over other immigrants.

Overall, the migratory experience proved that the Japanese Brazilians, who had been treated as Japanese in their country of birth, instead found themselves treated as Brazilians in Japan. Those who thought that they spoke Japanese, having learnt the language at home, soon realized that their language was old-fashioned, out of step with the current vernacular. Many perceived that their phenotype did not render them identical to the Japanese of Japan; the new awareness of their bodies and their corporeality brought to light a previously unrevealed *brasilidade*.[30]

Moreover, the connection between these immigrants and Brazilian society was extremely strong. Underlining the situational character of identity formation, Daniela de Carvalho argues that this attachment to Brazil was in response to the expectations of Japanese society. In fact, despite their heritage and their phenotype, the *dekasegi* were seen by the Japanese as "Brazilian."[31] In any case, in a few years, a very significant proliferation of "ethnic" stores (specializing in food, clothes, and so forth) sprang up: Brazilian schools, publishing houses, newspapers and other media, bars and restaurants, and bank branches seeking to channel remittances. Their presence can now be felt and seen in the Japanese cities and neighborhoods that are most densely populated by Brazilians. Nevertheless, the same cannot be said of the relationship with the Brazilian state: despite the existence of some sporadic measures, this can by no means be considered a case of "supervised immigration."

More recently, the Japanese economic crisis coincided with a period of growth in Brazil, reversing the migration flow of the 1990s. From the middle of the 2000s, many *dekasegi* began returning to Brazil. Migration is not solely linked to economic cycles, and it is difficult to know whether a flow of Japanese Brazilians to Japan will resume and whether the Japanese-Brazilian community in Japan is a long-term phenomenon. In their quantitative survey, McKenzie and Salcedo believe that the *dekasegi* migration is ending, both due to the changing demographic structure of the Japanese-Brazilian population and due to the economic situation unfavorable to new migration.[32]

Meanwhile, in Brazil, young people of Japanese descent attach great importance to Japan and to Japanese pop culture.[33] Many of them regularly attend ethnic associations linked to their ancestors' regions of origin and take part in the activities they offer—learning Japanese or participating in events linked to manga and anime culture—allowing them to feel close to Japan, just like nondescendants the world over who adhere to Japanese pop culture. However, there is a difference: these are the descendants of immigrants, disposing of familial reference points that, if brought into play, can create a convenient "cultural" familiarity, which is not shared by non-descendants. This being the case, are we in fact dealing with a phenomenon that is linked to transnationalism or to globalization?

*   *   *

With this chapter, I question the validity of the notion of transnationalism as it is commonly accepted in migratory studies, that is to say, the dual capacity of immigrants to settle—and even set down roots—in a country of immigration, and to maintain, at the same time, strong and enduring links with their country of origin. In some cases, such as that of the Japanese in Brazil, another variable can be shown to be as powerful or even more powerful than transnationalism. Such is the case, here, with regards to the nationalist and international policies implemented by the two countries in question, Brazil and Japan, each following its own interests in diverse moments and contexts.

In following the various stages of the history of migratory flows between Japan and Brazil, I want to emphasize this interplay of conflicting interests and the effects of the centripetal forces of nationalism upon the immigrants' experience. Divided between, on the one hand, the demands of the Vargas Era's exacerbated nationalism, and, on the other, loyalty to their country of origin, Japanese immigrants in Brazil suffered the consequences of mistrust and racism, of which they were the target. Yet they also suffered the consequences of an intracommunity violence provoked by the extreme situation of opposition between the two countries in the ambit of war, which left them highly isolated. Separation had the further effect of reinforcing and even radicalizing the identification of significant sectors of the group with their country of origin—tautologically confirming the racist arguments employed by the leading Brazilian elites.

Yet migratory temporality does its work, silently, and it is best studied over the long term. The Japanese descendants who, having lived in Brazil during the "lost decade" of the 1980s, emigrated to Japan, the land of their ancestors, in search of better material conditions and also in quest of those whom they considered to be their "equals," discovered, to their surprise, that they were "Brazilians" after all. Indeed, the "Japanese of Japan" perceived them as such. The "Brazilianization" of the "Japanese of Brazil" was imperceptible for many decades, concealed by the expression of racism and the barrier of phenotype. Yet it proves that, in the interstices of the often brutal demands of the two nationalisms in play, the immigrants constructed their own path over the course of generations, finding a margin of freedom that was often limited, but never nonexistent.

NOTES

1. Concerning the debate preceding the adoption of the immigration policy and the question of "whitening," with regards to Japanese immigration, see R. Dezem, *Matizes do "amarelo": A gênese dos discursos sobre os orientais no Brasil (1878–1908)* (São Paulo: Humanitas, 2005); and A. R. Nogueira, *A imigração japonesa para a lavoura cafeeira paulista (1908–1922)* (São Paulo: IEB-USP, 1973), chap. 5, 51–69. The following observations were taken, for the most part, from these works.

2. Decree no. 528, of June 28, 1890, was the first legal text of the Republic (founded in November of the previous year) to regulate immigration. Article 1 established that entry via the "ports of the Republic" (a sign of the expectation of immigration via the Atlantic and not via land borders) was "entirely free" to "individuals who are legally acceptable and fit for the work, who are not subject to criminal action in their country, excepting natives of Asia or Africa, who only through authorization by the National Congress may be admitted in concordance with the conditions thereby stipulated." L. Demoro, *Coordenação de leis de imigração e colonização* (Rio de Janeiro: Instituto Nacional de Imigração e Colonização, 1960), 90–91. Note that the law left open a loophole for the government to circumvent the prohibition: to do so required only the approbation of the Legislative Power.

3. Among these are to be found positivists, fervent abolitionists, who saw the introduction of Asians into the country as a disguised attempt to reintroduce slavery.

4. This periodization was established by Hiroshi Saito in *O Japonês no Brasil: Estudo de mobilidade e fixação* (São Paulo: Ed. Sociologia e política, 1961). Cf. Matheus Gato de Jesus and Gustavo Takeshy Taniguti, "Sociologie de l'immigrant: Hiroshi Saito et l'institutionnalisation des études sur les Japonais du Brésil (1940–1960)," in *Brésil(s). Sciences humaines et sociales* 2 (Nov. 2012): 218.

5. Cited in Saito, *O Japonês no Brasil*. Ruth Corrêa Leite Cardoso, *Estrutura familiar e mobilidade social: Estudo sobre os japoneses no estado de São Paulo* (São Paulo: Kaleidos-Primus Consultoria e comunicação integrada S/C Ltda., 1998, trilingual ed. Portuguese, English, Japanese), 34.

6. Kaori Kodama and Célia Sakurai, "Episódios da imigração: Um balanço de 100 anos," in *Resistência & integração: 100 anos de imigração japonesa no Brasil*, ed. Célia Sakurai (Rio de Janeiro: IBGE, 2008), 21 (also published in English: *Resistance & Integration: 100 Years of Japanese Immigration in Brazil*).

7. This section was taken from R. Ortiz, *O próximo e o distante: Japão e modernidade—mundo* (São Paulo: Brasiliense, 2000), 54–57.

8. Ibid., 57.

9. Based on figures collected by the Japanese Ministry of Justice. Cf. Yumi Garcia dos Santos, "Les familles étrangères au Japon: Une étude comparative sous le prisme du genre," in "1908–2008. Le centenaire de l'immigration japonaise au Brésil: L'heure des bilans." *Cahiers du Brésil contemporain* 71/72, ed. Mônica Raisa Schpun (CRBC-EHESS/MSH, 2008), 260. www.revues.msh-paris.fr/vernumpub/15-Y.Garcia%20dos%20Santos.pdf (accessed Aug. 19, 2013).

10. Comissão de Elaboração da História dos 80 anos da Imigração Japonesa no Brasil, *Uma epopéia moderna: 80 anos da imigração japonesa no Brasil* (SãoPaulo: Comissão de elaboração da história dos 80 anos da imigração japonesa no Brasil/ HUCITEC/Sociedade brasileira de cultura japonesa, 1992), 198–201, 229.

11. According to data from 1940, of the approximately 210,000 Japanese who were living in Brazil in that year, 193,000—more than 90 percent—were concentrated in the State of São Paulo. *Uma epopéia moderna*, 205.

12. Comissão de recenseamento da colônia japonesa, *The Japanese Immigrants in Brazil* (Tokyo: University of Tokyo Press, 1964), table 377, 731. Cited in Cardoso, *Estrutura familiar e mobilidade social*, 57.

13. Célia Sakurai, "Imigração tutelada—Os japoneses no Brasil," PhD dissertation, University of Campinas (Brazil), 2000.

14. On this subject, see: Flávio Venâncio Luizetto, "Os Constituintes em face da imigração. Estudo sobre o preconceito e a discriminação racial e étnica na Constituinte de 1934," master's thesis, University of São Paulo, 1975; and Sakurai "Imigração tutelada," chap. 3, 48–75.

15. F. de Oliveira Vianna, *Raça e assimilação* (São Paulo: Cia. Editora Nacional, 1934), 209.

16. Sakurai, "Imigração tutelada," 67.

17. This detail, on Japanese schools, was taken from Hiromi Shibata, "Les écoles des immigrants japonais: Organisation de l'enseignement et orientation japonisante," in *1908–2008. Le centenaire de l'immigration japonaise au Brésil*, 85–122. www .revues.msh-paris.fr/vernumpub/09-H.Shibata.pdf (accessed Aug. 19, 2013).

18. Decree-law 406 of May 4, 1938, art. 93, § 3d.

19. Decree 3010 of August 20, 1938, art. 168.

20. *Uma epopéia moderna*, 256, n. 5.

21. Ibid., 248.

22. Artur Ramos, "Aculturação negra no Brasil," *Boletim do Ministério do Trabalho, Indústria e Comércio* 106 (June 1943). Cited in R. Cytrynowicz, *Guerra sem guerra: A mobilização e o cotidiano em São Paulo durante a Segunda Guerra Mundial* (São Paulo: Geração Editorial/Edusp, 2000), 154.

23. Interview, Feb. 12, 2013.

24. Rosangela Kimura, "Shindô Renmei: Défaite de 1945 et conflits intra-communautaires chez les Japonais du Brésil," in *1908–2008. Le centenaire de l'immigration japonaise au Brésil*, 123–124. www.revues.msh-paris.fr/vernumpub/10-R.Kimura.pdf (accessed Aug. 19, 2013).

25. R. Dezem, *Shindô Renmei: Terrorismo e repressão*, collection "Inventário Deops," módulo III—japoneses (São Paulo: Arquivo do Estado/Imprensa Oficial, 2000), 75.

26. Ibid., 139–141.

27. Comissão de recenseamento da colônia japonesa.

28. Ibid., table 1, 6. Cited in Cardoso, *Estrutura familiar e mobilidade social*, 21.

29. The information provided in this section was taken from Célia Sakurai, "A imigração dos japoneses para o Brasil no pós-guerra (1950–1980)," in *Cem anos da*

imigração japonesa: História, memória e arte, ed. Francisco Hashimoto, Janete Leiko Tanno, and Monica Setuyo Okamoto (São Paulo: Editora Unesp, 2008), 189–239. Also published in French: "L'immigration des Japonais au Brésil dans l'après-guerre (1950–1980)," in *1908–2008. Le centenaire de l'immigration japonaise au Brésil,* 151–174. www.revues.msh-paris.fr/vernumpub/11-C.Sakurai.pdf (accessed Aug. 19, 2013).

30. On the relationship between ethnic identity and the body among Japanese Brazilians, see Mônica Raisa Schpun, "Les descendants d'immigrés japonais au Brésil et les chirurgies d'occidentalisation des yeux," in *Images et représentations du genre en migration (mondes atlantiques XIXe-XXe siècles). Actes de l'Histoire de l'Immigration,* ed. Natacha Lillo and Philippe Rygiel, 7 (2007): 105–122, and "História de uma invenção identitária: A estética nipo-brasileira dos descendentes de imigrantes (temporalidade migratória, etnia e gênero)," *Nuevo Mundo Mundos Nuevos* 7 (2007). nuevomundo.revues.org/3685 (accessed Aug. 19, 2013).

31. These immigrants "consent strategically to the social definitions that are imposed upon their identities, selectively accepting or rejecting these controlling images in an attempt to make sense of themselves and of their place in the dominant order." Daniela de Carvalho, *Migrants and Identity in Japan and Brazil: The Nikkeijin* (London: Routledge Curzon, 2003), xv. For an analysis of the impact of the transformation of the *dekasegis,* from being members of a "positive minority" in Brazil to that of a "negative minority," marginalized, in Japan, see Takeyuki Tsuda, *Strangers in the Ethnic Homeland: Japanese Brazilian Return Migration in Transnational Perspective* (New York: Columbia University Press, 2003).

32. David McKenzie and Alejandrina Salcedo, "Japanese-Brazilians and the Future of Brazilian Migration to Japan," in *International Migration* 52, 2 (2014): 66–83.

33. This contradicts certain assertions of McKenzie and Salcedo, who consider, too quickly in my opinion, that there will be a lessening of ties between Japanese Brazilians and Japan, over the generations. Ibid., 80–81.

CHAPTER 4

150 Years of Transborder Politics
Mexico and Mexicans Abroad

David FitzGerald

Migration from Mexico to the United States is the largest sustained flow between any two countries in the world. The 11.7 million people of Mexican birth living north of the border in 2011 represented more than the total number of immigrants in any other country. An additional 21.9 million people of Mexican origin were born in the United States.[1] Studies of this massive migration have played a leading role in conceptualizations of "transnational migration circuits," "transnational communities," and "transnationalism from below."[2] Studies in the 1990s making only the most cursory historical references insisted that a new phenomenon of cross-border ties had been uncovered.[3] Later work sought to ascertain what was novel by comparing different migration systems at different historical periods, such as Robert Smith's comparison of Mexican hometown associations in New York (1940s–1990s) with Swedes in the American Midwest (1860s–1920s). Few studies have attempted to assess systematically just what is new in the Mexican case by taking the historical long view of transborder political engagement.[4]

Many of the most important forms of transborder politics and their implication in transformational events in Mexican history have been forgotten in contemporary accounts of transnationalism because of four different kinds of blinders. Removing the blinders of when, who, how, and why reveals what is new about transborder politics, what has caused historical change, and the consequences of those changes.

The "when" blinder obscures the historical record with presentist assumptions that practices today are somehow different in the context of Mexico-U.S. migration, without actually investigating the form and content of earlier practices. Most accounts of Mexican transborder politics begin their discussion in the 1990s and ignore the previous 140 years of migration history. The "who" blinder obscures the broad range of political actors that have been involved in transborder politics. The ongoing romanticization of "transnationalism from below" focuses on labor migrants, thus obscuring the activities of Mexican political elites living in the United States, from nine-teenth- and early-twentieth-century political reformers and revolutionary leaders such as Benito Juárez and Francisco Madero, to the five presidents beginning with Miguel de la Madrid (1982–1988) who studied in U.S. universities and then returned to steer the ship of state on a new course of neoliberalism. The transborder actors that have most transformed Mexican politics have been drawn from the ranks of political exiles and elite techno-crats. The "how" blinder is the failure to see the full range of transborder political acts, such as violent insurrection, because of an unstated norma-tive preference to focus on peaceful forms of politics such as voting from abroad.[5] The "how" blinder also hides the involvement of labor migrants in older projects of cross-border violence led by exiles. The "why" blinder is a technological determinism that becomes so focused on the effects of various forms of electronic communication and high-speed travel on jet aircraft that it obscures the more consequential causes of changing patterns of cross-border politics—the contours of the U.S.-Mexico relationship and institutions in Mexico that shape the boundaries of political contestation. Together, these blinders of when, who, how, and why obscure the most seri-ous consequences that transborder actions have had on Mexican politics.

The alternative approach here considers the broad range of Mexican transborder politics to uncover lapsed practices, continuities, and novelties with an eye to explaining those patterns. Transborder political activities of Mexicans in the United States have included projects that ignore U.S. politics, such as agitation for the right to vote in Mexican elections by absentee ballot, as well as activities that engage U.S. politics as a means to accomplish an end in Mexico, such as lobbying in Washington. I argue that emigrants and exiles have been involved in every major violent conflict and political transformation in Mexico since the 1860s. The changes since the 1920s are the new institutions and pacific goals of transborder politics. At the elite level, technocrats returning from the United States have played an underappreciated role in transforming Mexico since the 1980s. At the level of mass politics, the major shift in the 1990s and 2000s was to institutional-ize the promotion of dual loyalty and long-distance engagement through a dual nationality law, extending suffrage abroad, and establishing multiple government agencies to forge ties with migrants sharing a town of origin. Technology has not played a consequential role in these changes, which are mostly caused by the unintended consequences of U.S. immigration policies

that have created hometown satellite communities in the United States, the
pacific integration of North America in a way that upholds the sovereignty
of Mexico, and the revival of competitive yet peaceful partisan politics in
Mexico.

A Rebel Sanctuary

Mexicans have been engaged in cross-border politics as long as there has
been a border. An estimated 75,000 to 100,000 Mexicans lived in the territory seized by the United States in the 1848 *Treaty of Guadalupe Hidalgo*.
Most residents stayed on the U.S. side of the border and became U.S. citizens.
Their numbers swelled in the late nineteenth century as labor migrants arrived to work on U.S. railroads and agriculture. The Mexican-origin population became a critical source of political support for exiled Mexican reformist and revolutionary leaders crossing back and forth across the border
through the 1930s.[6] While border studies specialists and students of Mexican
political history are familiar with these early aspects of transborder politics,
they have fallen out of almost all accounts of "migrant transnationalism"
despite their critical importance in shaping modern Mexico.

Benito Juárez is one of Mexico's most revered presidents. He was also the
first of many major Mexican leaders to plot his revolt from the safety of U.S.
territory. In 1853, Liberal leaders opposed to the dictatorship of General
Antonio López de Santa Anna fled to New Orleans to conspire against the
general. Benito Juárez spent two years in exile working at a cigar factory
and building a coalition with Melchor Ocampo and other revolutionaries.
They published a series of political pamphlets and drafted their 1854 *Plan
de Ayutla* that set the overthrow of Santa Anna in motion. Juárez then
returned to Mexico, where he became president in 1858 during the War of
Reform (1857–1861) between Liberals and Conservatives. Throughout the
mid-1860s, Liberals sought political support, weapons, and soldiers from
the United States to fight the Conservatives and their French allies who
had landed an expeditionary force in 1861. Liberal generals in the United
States organized solidarity groups known as "Juárez Clubs," "Mexican
Clubs," and "Monroe Doctrine Societies" to raise money, recruit soldiers,
and generate propaganda against the Conservatives and their French allies. General Plácido Vega spent two and one-half years and US$600,000
organizing the Liberal cause in California. In what must have been one of
the earliest attempts to form a "Mexican lobby," General Vega sent a letter
to the presidents of all of the clubs during the 1864 U.S. presidential election urging them "for the salvation of the American Continent . . . to use

all the influence possible . . . with the Hispanic Americans so that in the coming election of November 8 they will give their vote in support of the candidates of the Republican party, for President Abraham Lincoln and Vice-President Andrew Johnson."[7] At least fifteen Juárez clubs operated in California alone. Liberal agents paid Spanish-language newspapers in cities such as San Francisco to support the movement. Californians of Spanish or Mexican descent played a prominent role in the Liberal project. An armed expedition of 400 volunteers, many of whom claimed Spanish or Mexican descent, attempted to sail for Mexico from San Francisco in 1865, but U.S. authorities tipped off by the French consul turned them back. Still, the successful influx of weapons and munitions for the Liberal cause was critical to their victory. Historian Robert Miller concludes that "the militant resurgence of the [Liberal] Mexican republicans would have been impossible without the aid secured by secret agents in the United States."[8]

After Juárez died in 1872 and was succeeded by Sebastián Lerdo de Tejada, Liberal general Porfirio Díaz fled to New Orleans to organize an attack on the new regime. In 1876, Díaz attacked Mexico from several towns in South Texas with an estimated force of 500 to 1,000 men, including some who had been living on the U.S. side of the border. When Díaz overran the garrison in the Mexican border town of Reynosa, the losing soldiers then fled to Texas themselves.[9] Díaz went on to become president of Mexico and its longest-serving ruler.

Intensive cross-border political activity continued in the early twentieth century when President Díaz forced Ricardo Flores Magón into exile in 1903. Flores Magón founded the anarchist Mexican Liberal Party (PLM) sworn to the overthrow of the Mexican government. He released the *Programa del Partido Liberal* in St. Louis, Missouri, in 1906 and organized an extensive propaganda campaign and local chapters in Arizona, Texas, Illinois, and California. The Mexican consulates responded with physical assaults and campaigns of intimidation against the anarchists. Street fighting broke out in Los Angeles and San Diego between pro- and anti-PLM forces. After U.S. authorities arrested Flores Magón for his revolutionary activities, his deputy organized Mexicans living in Texas to attack border towns on the southern side of the river in 1908. Flores Magón was released in 1910 and moved the party's headquarters to Los Angeles, where its weekly newspaper, *Regeneración*, enjoyed a circulation of over 10,000. The party allied with the International Workers of the World to organize labor on both sides of the border.[10]

When the Mexican Revolution erupted in 1910, cross-border raids from anti-Díaz forces in Texas already had a twenty-year history. General Torres of the Mexican army observed that "[t]he problem would be resolved very quickly if it were not for the help the rebels receive in Texas."[11] Throughout the revolution, thousands of exiles from various factions fled north and used U.S. territory as a rebel sanctuary. They organized sympathizers, raised money, manufactured counterfeit Mexican pesos, smuggled arms, recruited soldiers, and unleashed raids across the border. The Mexican Secret Service monitored insurgent organizations and attempted to disrupt their operations.[12]

Francisco Madero, the losing contender against Porfirio Díaz in the fraudulent 1910 election, fled to Texas after his defeat. While in San Antonio, Madero issued his manifesto, the *Plan de San Luis Potosí*, and prepared for the fight against Díaz. Sympathizers from California to Texas raised money, recruited men, and bought guns. Madero invaded the state of Chihuahua in February 1911 and fought a successful campaign with weaponry smuggled across the border from the United States. By June, he had deposed Díaz and became president.[13]

Madero's presidency lasted less than two years. The commander of his armed forces, Victoriano Huerta, conspired with U.S. ambassador Henry Lane Wilson to launch a coup and have Madero shot. Huerta assumed the presidency until 1914, when Venustiano Carranza and other revolutionary generals forced him into exile. Huerta arrived in New York the following year, where he met with an estimated 400 exiled Mexican army officers. American officials bugged Huerta's conversation with a German naval officer about the possibility of using German financing and arms to launch another coup in Mexico and then detained Huerta near El Paso on June 27, 1915, as he apparently headed for the border to attempt a crossing. Huerta died of natural causes in U.S. custody seven months later.[14]

The Carranza regime that had seized power in 1914 also looked north for support among Mexicans in the United States. His government recruited men in Laredo, El Paso, Los Angeles, San Antonio, San Diego, and Calexico and formed "Constitutionalist Clubs" of his supporters.[15] Following the lobby model initiated by the Benito Juárez clubs in the 1860s, a newspaper financed by the Mexican consul in San Diego urged Constitutionalist Clubs to petition President Woodrow Wilson to acknowledge Carranza as Mexico's legitimate president. The U.S. government finally offered Carranza de facto recognition in October 1915. The following year, the Mexican government asked Mexicans in the United States to register at the consulates. A San Antonio newspaper explained that "the principal reason for the register is to see on which side lie the sympathies of Mexicans living in the United States, in case there is an uprising."[16]

The end of the Mexican Revolution did not end political intrigue across the border. President Plutarco Elías Calles launched a secularizing crusade against the Catholic Church in 1926 and fought armed Catholic rebels known as *cristeros* with particular intensity in the central-west plateau that was the origin of most Mexican emigrants. Calles exiled half of Mexico's bishops by May 1927. San Antonio, Texas, became the headquarters of the Church-in-exile, where Mexican bishops worked with the U.S. Church leadership to lobby Washington to apply pressure on Calles to ease the anticlerical restrictions. In Los Angeles's Mexican neighborhoods, street processions to celebrate the Day of the Virgin of Guadalupe turned into public rallies in support of the cristeros. The U.S. ambassador finally brokered an agreement between the Mexican clergy and the new president, Emilio Portes Gil, which ended the first Cristero War in 1929. However, the United States once again became a center of exile when a brief, second Cristero War erupted in 1932 over President Lázaro Cárdenas's socialist and secular education campaign. Archbishop Leopoldo Ruíz y Flores, the apostolic delegate in Mexico, fled to the United States with other Church leaders.[17]

As the victorious generals pacified Mexico in the 1920s, Mexican politicians and leaders in the Mexican community in the United States dubbed the population *México de afuera*, the Mexico outside of the country's territory. According to Douglas Monroy's study of Los Angeles during the 1920s and 1930s, "Mexican politics fired the passions of mexicanos de afuera much more than, say, the election of 1924, which pitted Calvin Coolidge against another americano."[18] In 1928, Mexican presidential candidate José Vasconcelos campaigned in the Southwest and in Chicago against the "official" candidate, Pascual Ortiz Rubio. During the first Cristero War, Vasconcelos had exiled himself to Los Angeles, from which he supported cristero rebels in Mexico. On his return to Los Angeles as a presidential candidate, his supporters formed *Clubes Vasconcelistas*. The major Spanish-language daily, *La Opinión*, supported Vasconcelos and organized a presidential straw poll, which he won. The Revolutionary National Party (PNR), precursor to the Institutional Revolutionary Party (PRI) that ruled Mexico until 2000, countered by organizing *Clubes Reforma Pro-Ortiz-Rubio* in California. When Ortiz Rubio won the election, *vasconcelistas* in the United States publicly charged the Mexican government with fraud and protested to the U.S. State Department.[19]

Mexican consulates organized unions and social assistance among the Mexican population during the 1920s and 1930s,[20] but historian Gilbert González argues that "no other activity occupied as much time and effort as that of fomenting and orchestrating loyalty to the Mexican government and adherence to its politics."[21] Prominent people of Mexican origin were given honorific commissions (*comisiones honoríficas*) to organize patriotic activities. Mexican organizations in Los Angeles were organized into the *Confederación de Sociedades Mexicanas*.[22] Until the 1940s, the consulates made little distinction between Mexican citizens (including children born abroad to Mexican parents) and U.S. citizens of Mexican origin. Because most of the Mexican-origin population consisted of first- or second-generation immigrants, the consulates assumed they were all Mexican nationals.[23]

Unlike the Mexican organizations that emerged decades later to focus on hometowns of origin in Mexico, early organizations sponsored by the government focused on maintaining migrants' broader national ties to Mexico, avoiding seditious transborder activities, and promoting better labor conditions in the United States. The lack of hometown-based organizing reflected settlement patterns of Mexicans in the United States. Ties between the descendants of the pre-1848 population and their places of origin in the Mexican interior were attenuated by time and the imposition of the international border. Recent immigrants were recruited by railroad companies and other U.S. employers targeting Mexican men. The strong social networks creating satellite communities in the United States formed by migrants from the same locality in Mexico did not emerge fully until permanent family settlement migration took hold in the 1970s—a process that the 1986 Immigration Reform and Control Act accelerated.[24]

One of the consulates' main projects during the Great Depression of the 1930s was to support U.S. authorities in the repatriation of an estimated 400,000 Mexicans between 1929 and 1939.[25] Officials hoped that migrants would return with valuable skills that were lacking in Mexico and settle the sparsely populated northern states. The government did not anticipate the political consequences of mass repatriation. Returnees led miners' strikes in Sonora and were accused throughout the country of being agents of Bolshevism.[26] In conducting oral histories among *ejidatarios* in the Los Altos de Jalisco region, Ann Craig found that "the single most distinctive characteristic shared by the majority of the first *agraristas* is that they had worked in the United States before becoming *ejidatarios*, usually even before joining the agrarian reform."[27] Similar concentrations of former migrants among the first *agraristas* formed in various sending communities in the state of Michoacán.[28]

From the 1850s to the 1920s, people of Mexican origin living on the U.S. side of the border and exiles fleeing Mexico used the United States as a base for fomenting revolution and political change in Mexico. Every one of the major developments in Mexican political history during that period—including the War of Reform, the expulsion of the French expeditionary force, the establishment of the dictatorship of Porfirio Díaz, the early voice of dissent among anarchists, the revolutions of Madero and Huerta, U.S. recognition of the victorious Carranza regime, the Cristero War, and the agrarian reform of Cárdenas—involved transborder political action. The weight of emigrants and exiles in defining the outcomes of these sagas varied, from a minimal role in the agrarian reform to critical importance in the wars of the Reform and the Revolution.

Ignoring Mexico de Afuera

The 1940s through 1960s were the nadir of cross-border politics. George Sánchez argues that the 1930s repatriations fundamentally shifted the orientation of the remaining Mexican-origin population in Los Angeles away from Mexico and toward life in the United States. Those who stayed were much more likely to have been born in the United States and see their futures there.[29] While the break in orientation may not have been quite so dramatic in Texas, given its greater proximity to population centers in Mexico, cross-border political action declined throughout the Southwest. In the short run, the Bracero program from 1942 to 1964 created large numbers of circular labor migrants, not settlers who could create networks of clubs. In Mexico, the Institutional Revolutionary Party (PRI) consolidated power in the 1930s and ruled virtually unopposed until the late 1980s. The party pacified Mexico and eliminated the possibility of armed insurgency based in the United States. The last president to be deported to the United States, Plutarco Elías Calles, lived quietly in Los Angeles when he was exiled with his aides in 1936. President Ávila Camacho allowed Calles to return to a peaceful Mexico in 1941.

There was little political contact between U.S.-resident Mexicans and the Mexican government in the 1950s and early 1960s.[30] Major Latino organizations such as the League of United Latin American Citizens (founded in 1929), the United Farm Workers of America (1962), and the Mexican-American Legal Defense and Educational Fund (MALDEF, 1968) focused on U.S.-based issues rather than Mexican politics.[31] Interactions increased in the early 1970s when some Chicano activists began seeking the support of the Mexican government to promote Chicano socioeconomic and political advancement within the United States.[32] President Luis Echeverría (1970–1976) saw Chicanos as a potential ethnic lobby in the United States and met with Chicano leaders while excluding critics of the PRI.[33] The administration of José López Portillo (1976–1982) also met with leaders of organizations such as MALDEF and formed a Hispanic Commission comprised of Mexican-American and Mexico-based elites and officials.[34]

Notwithstanding these contacts, transborder politics from the 1940s through the early 1980s was restricted to a handful of activists in the United States whose primary orientation was plainly toward U.S. politics. Their activities did not affect Mexican politics in any appreciable way. The principal reason for this lack of impact was the near-absence of competitive politics in Mexico, given the PRI's hegemonic grip on power that used everyday cooptation and episodic coercion to control the political process. Military campaigns against scattered leftist guerrillas in the 1970s were based in the south of the country. Geography and the potential U.S. military reaction kept guerrillas from attempting to use the United States as a base. The days of cross-border raids definitively ended with the Mexican government's pacification of the country in the 1920s and '30s.

Institutionalizing Pacific Ties

The return of competitive party politics in the late 1980s was the primary reason for the reengagement between emigrants and the Mexican state, but it was accompanied by background demographic, economic, and political factors that complement this explanation. The percentage of the Mexican population living abroad skyrocketed from 2 percent in 1970 to 10 percent in 2000.[35] The Mexican population in the United States became more important to the Mexican government and opposition political parties by virtue of its size. A tendency for whole families to settle permanently rather than for men to migrate seasonally meant that extraordinary efforts were needed to maintain ties that would otherwise attenuate over time.[36] As a consequence of demographic growth and settlement, the volume of remittances rose dramatically as well, from US$1 billion in 1980 to US$3 billion in 1990 and US$22 billion in 2010.[37] The Mexican government sought not only to increase the volume of remittances by supporting migrants' ties with Mexico, but also to channel the money into job-creating investments.[38] Finally, the growing links between the U.S. and Mexican governments, expressed most dramatically through the North American Free Trade Agreement (NAFTA) that went into effect in 1994, made it possible for a Mexican political establishment that historically had been very suspicious of the United States to allow and promote dual ties. Such a policy of *acercamiento* (rapprochement) would have been unthinkable during the nineteenth and early twentieth centuries, when U.S. settlers seized Texas (1836), U.S. forces conquered half of northern Mexico (1846–1848), the U.S. Navy seized Mexico's principal port of Veracruz (1914), and General Pershing's expeditionary force invaded Chihuahua in search of Pancho Villa (1916–1917).

Technology was largely irrelevant in the transition toward renewed cross-border ties. To be sure, improved communications, transportation, and infrastructure make transborder engagement faster and easier for hometown clubs in particular. Migrants communicate using cell phones, Skype, email, Facebook, and web pages, and fly back and forth between the United States and Mexico, to maintain club projects in ways that would be more difficult in the absence of such technologies.[39] Yet, technology has improved consistently over the past 150 years, while the pattern of engagement is a U-shape over the course of the twentieth century. The scholarly fascination with technology threatens to miss the far more important institutional context that shapes transborder politics.

Relations between Mexican political actors and the Mexican-origin population in the United States changed significantly in the aftermath of the 1988 Mexican presidential election. Cuauhtémoc Cárdenas, the center-left opposition candidate for president in 1988, drew large crowds of Mexican migrants while campaigning in California and Chicago. Cárdenas appealed to Mexicans in the United States to influence the vote of their family members in Mexico and promised emigrants dual nationality and the right to vote from abroad if he won.[40] Although Cárdenas lost the election, which was marred by widespread irregularities, he remained active in politics and helped found the Party of the Democratic Revolution (PRD). His supporters formed U.S.-based organizations such as the Mexican Unity Group and the Organization of Mexicans for Democracy (OMD). At the PRD's first national congress in Mexico City in 1990, the leader of the OMD and two Southern California *cardenistas* were appointed as California delegates to the PRD's national assembly.[41] PRD supporters in California helped raise money for campaign events in California, sent pro-PRD pamphlets to Mexico, and—according to the PRI—raised money for PRD candidates in Mexico in violation of Mexican law.[42] Local PRD committees in California also raised funds, which they claimed to send to their home communities for nonelection expenses.[43] Whatever the legal controversies were in Mexico over raising funds abroad, it is uncommon in practice. In the 2006 National Latino Survey, fewer than 1 percent of Mexicans in the United States reported contributing to a Mexican political campaign after they migrated to the United States.[44]

A former Mexican consul in Los Angeles acknowledged that the 1988 Cárdenas campaign in the United States and subsequent protests against electoral fraud in the presidential race demonstrated migrants' transborder influence and encouraged the Mexican government to reformulate its policy toward Mexicans abroad. Prior to 1988, the network of Mexican consulates controlled most government programs directed at emigrants. In the early 1990s, the PRI created a separate system of Compatriot Aid Committees in U.S. cities to support the party in open ways that consular agents could not. The new policies aimed to circumvent the opposition's organizations among emigrants.[45] Echoing the old discourse of "México de afuera" in his 1995–2000 National Development Plan, President Ernesto Zedillo declared that "the Mexican nation extends beyond the territory contained within its borders."[46]

The government and migrants demanding reform negotiated a series of institutional reforms over the next decade that strengthened cross-border ties. The novelty in these programs lay in their promotion of dual ties to both the United States and Mexico, rather than simply calling for Mexicans to return home or at least maintain their affections from afar. Whereas the programs of the 1920s were based almost exclusively on the *long-distance nationalism* of identification with a nation despite physical absence from the homeland, the programs of the 1990s and beyond were based to a much greater degree on the *dual nationalism* of political identification with two distinct nations.[47] The promotion of dual ties was promoted through a dual nationality law and efforts to encourage a Mexico lobby in Washington, D.C. Long-distance nationalism was promoted through the extension of the voting franchise to Mexicans abroad and government programs promoting ties to the Mexican federal government, particular states, and particular migrant communities of origin. Migrant activists were critical actors in shaping these institutions.

Dual Nationality

One of the principal novelties in the relationship between the Mexican government and its emigrants is the government's promotion of dual nationality. Naturalizing abroad has been grounds for losing Mexican citizenship or nationality since 1857. Since the adoption in 1886 of a mixed system of attributing nationality based both on descent (jus sanguinis) and birth in the territory (jus soli), many children born to Mexican nationals in jus soli countries like the United States or born in Mexico to foreigners from jus sanguinis countries were de facto dual nationals. "Voluntary" foreign naturalization was grounds for denationalization beginning in 1934, but the interpretation of "voluntary" narrowed between 1939 and 1993, so that emigrants who adopted a foreign nationality as a requirement of employment were considered to have involuntarily naturalized and thus were able to maintain their Mexican nationality. They became de facto dual nationals as well. Although the 1993 nationality law adopted the principle that nationality should be singular and required de facto dual nationals to choose a single nationality at the age of majority, just five years later, the "nonforfeiture" (*no pérdida*) of nationality law that took effect in 1998 protected native Mexicans from mandatory denationalization, though they may still voluntarily expatriate. In effect, the nonforfeiture legislation was a dual nationality law. The term "dual nationality" was likely not adopted in official documents to avoid raising the hackles of those who discursively associate dual nationality with "dual loyalty" and to maintain a semblance of continuity in Mexican law.[48]

In Mexico, dual nationality has been considered a potential way that foreign-born or "gringoized" Mexicans could intervene in Mexican affairs, buy land and economic concessions in strategic border and coastal areas, and call on the backing of foreign governments in disputes with Mexican authorities. Yet the vote in favor of dual nationality carried 405 to 1 in the Chamber of Deputies because such arguments were simply no longer as salient given that nationalism directed against the United States had faded. Unlike the nineteenth and early twentieth centuries, the Mexican state was now secure from invasions by a foreign power.

The substantive prerogatives of dual nationals remain contested and ambiguous, however. The Mexican constitution appears to prohibit dual nationals from holding the offices of federal deputy, federal senator, president, or state governor. The 1917 Constitution still in effect specifies that these positions are reserved for "Mexicans by birth," and Article 32 specifies that positions for which one is required to be Mexican by birth "are reserved for those who have this quality and do not acquire another nationality." The question of whether dual nationals can serve as federal deputies has not been resolved conclusively, however. Manuel de la Cruz, a dual U.S. and Mexican national and longtime California resident was believed to have won election to the Mexican Congress's Chamber of Deputies based on his position on the PRD's party list in 2003. Despite the controversy over whether a dual national was legally eligible for the office, none of the Mexican political parties formally challenged de la Cruz's election with election authorities, likely because they wanted to avoid antagonizing emigrants. At the last moment, after de la Cruz had already been issued a key to his new congressional office, the Federal Electoral Tribunal ruled that to rectify a technical miscalculation, it would reapportion to another party the PRD's seat that de la Cruz thought he had won. De la Cruz never took federal office, but the question of the political rights of dual nationals will likely resurface as more Mexicans residing in the United States run for office in Mexico.

The Elusive Lobby

The Mexican government has hoped that Mexicans in the United States will become a lobby for its interests, but that hope has largely remained unfulfilled. The creation of a Mexican lobby in the United States became one of Mexico's serious foreign policy goals in the 1990s, beginning with the campaign to negotiate and pass NAFTA in the U.S. Congress. The Mexican government advertised heavily in U.S. Spanish-language media urging Mexican Americans to contact their U.S. congressional representatives to approve fast-track negotiating authority. It spent at least US$30 million promoting NAFTA in Washington, D.C.—an effort that catapulted Mexico from a conspicuous absence among foreign powers lobbying on Capitol Hill to one of the most prominent. The Mexican NAFTA lobby worked with Latino organizations like the National Council of La Raza and the National Hispanic Chamber of Commerce to hire former administration officials and pay for U.S. policymakers' trips to Mexico. In 1993, all but one of the Mexican American members of Congress voted to approve NAFTA. Yet most studies of Mexico's NAFTA lobbying agree that the ethnic factor was not a decisive factor in NAFTA's passage. Only five of thirty major lobbyists contracted by the Mexican government were Latino, and only two of the major lobbyists focused on promoting NAFTA among Latino voters. Many Mexican American congressional representatives agreed to vote for NAFTA only at the last minute after funding for a North American Development Bank to cultivate community projects was added to the agreement. As the political scientist Rodolfo de la Garza summarized, "There is no evidence . . . that Mexican American members of Congress voted for NAFTA because of Mexican lobbying or because they supported Mexican interests."[49]

In 1994, Mexican consulates and Mexican American political organizations unsuccessfully worked together to try to defeat Proposition 187, the California ballot measure endorsed by Governor Pete Wilson that would have restricted a wide range of services for unauthorized immigrants had a federal judge not thrown out most of its provisions after it passed. Mexico's dual nationality law that took effect in 1998 was intended in part to encourage Mexican nationals to become U.S. citizens so they would vote against measures like 187 and the politicians who supported them.[50] Mexican consular officials and President Felipe Calderón spoke against state-level laws such as SB 1070 in Arizona and similar legislation in Alabama, Georgia, and

South Carolina that targeted unauthorized immigrants in the early 2010s,[51] but there is no evidence that such efforts drove Mexican American protests against the law. Mexican Americans protested such policies because they sensed that Latinos were being targeted, not because they represented the interests of the Mexican government.[52]

Multilevel Ties

Mexican authorities at the federal, state, and county levels of government are forging ties with migrants abroad. The federal government began institutionalizing ties with emigrants through the Foreign Ministry's Program for Mexican Communities Abroad (PCME). From 1990 to 2003, the PCME sought to promote patriotic events like parades celebrating independence on the 16th of September and the study of Mexican history and the Spanish language. In this sense, the PCME took up the mantle of the *comisiones honoríficas* of the 1920s. More transformationally, the PCME built on existing efforts by migrants and local priests to organize hometown associations (HTAs) based on their places of origin within Mexico.[53] According to Mexican consular registries, the number of Mexican HTAs grew from 263 to 815 between 1995 and 2005. However, Guillaume Lanly and M. Basilia Valenzuela estimate that only about a quarter of Mexican HTAs register with a consulate.[54] HTAs often disintegrate and then form again a few years later, sometimes under a different name. In some communities, ad hoc groups form and disband with each fiesta cycle.[55] A loose definition of associations to include the many ad hoc groups would suggest there are around 3,000 Mexican HTAs in the United States. In a 2004 survey of Mexicans in the United States soliciting a *matrícula consular* identification document, 14 percent reported belonging to an HTA.[56] Fewer than 4 percent of Mexican immigrants claimed to belong to an HTA in the 2006 National Latino Survey.[57] Even if the lower figure is more accurate, that would imply more than 400,000 adult Mexican immigrants are affiliated with an HTA.

The major emigrant initiatives survived the change in administration from the PRI to the PAN in 2000. When Vicente Fox Quesada won the Mexican presidency in July 2000, he pledged to govern on behalf of "118 million Mexicans," including the 18 million people of Mexican origin then living in the United States.[58] One of his first acts as president was to tour Mexico's northern border cities to "monitor" returning migrants, whom he called "heroes."[59] He quickly inaugurated a Presidential Office for Communities Abroad directed by Juan Hernández, a dual national literature professor born in Texas. The cabinet level position was abolished in 2002 after conflicts with Secretary of Foreign Relations Jorge Castañeda over how to manage two cabinet agencies simultaneously conducting foreign policy. In 2003, the PCME and the presidential office were folded into the new Institute for Mexicans Abroad (IME), which includes an advisory council comprised of 105 Mexican community leaders and 10 Latino organizations in the United States, 10 special advisors, and representatives of each of the 32 state governments in Mexico.[60]

The state of Zacatecas, which has the highest international emigration rate in Mexico, is in the vanguard of policies incorporating emigrants into its political and economic life. Ties between provincial governments and emigrants have been a vehicle for spreading Mexican partisan politics to the Mexican population in the United States through visits by gubernatorial candidates and incumbents seeking emigrants' political support. That has prompted the party in control of the federal government to respond with its own programs to avoid being left out of the transborder game. Noting Zacatecano success, the Foreign Ministry encouraged all states to create their own emigrant affairs offices and cooperate with the National Coordinator of State Agencies for Migrant Affairs (CONOFAM).[61]

Hometown associations are the primary vehicle for collective remittances. In 1992, President Salinas created Solidarity International, a small branch of his signature *Solidaridad* antipoverty program, which solicited financial contributions from Mexicans abroad for infrastructure development projects in their places of origin. The PCME also drew on models of matching fund development created by migrants from Zacatecas living in California and the Zacatecan state government in the mid-1980s to formalize ties between the clubs and the Mexican government at the state and county levels. The most successful program involving all three levels of government in Mexico is *Tres por Uno* (3x1), in which migrants and Mexican government agencies jointly develop infrastructure projects in migrants' places of origin. Federal, state, and municipal governments match the funds that migrants contribute. In 2010, the 3x1 program approved 2,488 projects at a total cost of around US$92 million. Sixty percent of the projects involved improving hometown infrastructure, such as paving roads, building potable water systems, and laying electrical line; 14 percent involved education, health, and sports; and 13 percent involved "productive" projects aimed at generating jobs. Approximately 700 HTAs and 574 *municipios* (county governments) in 28 of Mexico's 31 states participated in these projects in 2009.[62]

Matching fund programs can create real improvements in the lives of community members in impoverished rural communities with few government resources, though the extent to which they substitute or complement existing state funding varies by locality.[63] However, collective remittances are a pittance compared to individual remittances, valued at US$22 billion in 2010.[64] The principal economic value of collective remittances is to keep migrants engaged in their towns of origin so the private transfers will keep flowing.

Voting from Abroad

As early as 1929, the *La Opinión* daily in Los Angeles called on the Mexican president to give Mexicans in the United States the right to vote, but the demand lay dormant until the 1988 presidential campaign of Cuauhtémoc Cárdenas.[65] In July 1996, the PRI-dominated Congress amended the Constitution to allow Mexicans to vote for president outside their districts of residence.[66] The amendment hypothetically allowed Mexican citizens to vote from abroad, but it did not include the necessary enabling legislation directing the Federal Electoral Institute (IFE) to organize elections outside Mexico. The opposition-controlled federal Chamber of Deputies passed the implementing law in July 1999, but the PRI-controlled Senate killed the measure.[67] The PRI intended to incorporate emigrants only at a symbolic level to protect itself politically and to create a Mexican ethnic lobby in Washington, D.C., but in doing so, the PRI inadvertently opened the door to a Mexican emigrant lobby in Mexico City. Various emigrant groups expanding from a PRD base to include activists from across the political spectrum formed the Coalition for the Political Rights of Mexicans Abroad, which successfully pushed through a bill in 2005 that enabled Mexicans to vote from abroad by absentee ballot in the 2006 presidential elections. The emigrant lobby achieved a dramatic success that showed the possibilities of binational grassroots mobilization.[68]

Ironically, the migrant vote was not a factor in the closest election in modern Mexican history, decided by only half a percent of the ballots cast. Three million out of ten million Mexicans in the United States were eligible to vote in the 2006 Mexican elections. Only 56,000 citizens, or half a percent of the U.S-resident Mexican population, tried to register to vote, and only 33,000 actually cast a ballot. Fifty-eight percent voted for the candidate of the incumbent PAN party.[69] The reasons for low turnout include the absence of a Mexican voter registration program in the United States, a series of bureaucratic hurdles to obtain absentee ballots, and a new ban on Mexican presidential candidates campaigning in the United States. The ostensible reason for the ban was that the Mexican government could not enforce its electoral regulations in another country's sovereign territory, so it simply prohibited campaigning altogether. The more likely reason was that the PRI and PAN parties in Congress saw migrant voters as wild cards, and deliberately sought to suppress turnout by limiting their exposure to the campaigns and making the process onerous.

In a 2006 representative survey of Mexican-born adults in the United States, the Pew Hispanic Center found that while 78 percent of the sample was aware that Mexicans could vote from abroad, 55 percent did not know there would be elections that year. Only 13 percent of the sample had a positive opinion of the way that Mexican political institutions function, while a third said they had a negative opinion.[70] During the registration period for the 2012 election, the IFE received only 61,687 absentee ballots, about 4,000 more than in 2006.[71] In short, widespread dissatisfaction with Mexican politics among migrants has not generated widespread political action.

At the subnational level, migrants have forced open procedural opportunities to participate in the political process as well. The vote from abroad has been extended to two subnational jurisdictions, beginning with the state of Michoacán in the 2007 gubernatorial elections and the Federal District in 2012. Roughly a million migrants born in Michoacán lived in the United States at the time. In the 2011 gubernatorial elections, only 341 of them voted from abroad, 9 less than in 2007.[72] As at the national level, voting from abroad has not affected any election outcomes in Mexico.

Returnee Participation

While the vote abroad and government programs at the federal, state, and local levels are aimed at promoting the mostly symbolic engagement of migrants living in the United States, returned migrants are potentially a greater source of political change. The effect at the mass level is uncertain. Pérez-Armendáriz and Crowe report, based on their 2006 national survey in Mexico, that returnees were more critical of the Mexican government's rights violations and more likely to claim greater tolerance of different religions, political views, and sexual orientations than peers who had never migrated. Rod Camp's survey found that for Mexicans who have lived in the United States for even brief periods, views of what constitutes democracy are closer to the norm of other Americans than the norm of other Mexicans living in Mexico. These findings are consistent with Yossi Shain's notion of "marketing the American Creed abroad," though the robustness of the evidence and the actual consequences of those attitudes remain to be seen.[73]

Most scholarly attention to returnees and institutional change has focused on migrants from a working or middle-class background. The most spectacular case in the 2000s involved Andrés Bermúdez, the "Tomato King," who had originally crossed the border into California illegally in 1974. After making his fortune as a tomato farmer, Bermúdez returned to his hometown of Jerez, Zacatecas, to run for mayor against two other candidates in 2001. The candidate of the *Convergence for Democracy* coalition, Salvador Espinosa, was himself a wealthy returnee, who vied for the support of voters by hiring a small aircraft to fly over the town and throw U.S. currency and campaign flyers out the window. Bermúdez won the most votes, but his enemies prevented him from taking office because he was not a local resident. In response, Bermúdez's allies in the Zacatecas state assembly passed a law in 2003 that allows binational Zacatecano residents to run for state and local office. The Tomato King was subsequently elected again and served his term. Since 2003, Zacatecanos living abroad may run in Zacatecas congressional and county elections, though they cannot vote in such elections from abroad.[74]

In the state of Michoacán, the PRD in 2005 assigned one of the six seats it won on its party list to Jesús Martínez Saldaña, a California State University, Fresno Chicano Studies professor who had moved to the United States as a child. Martínez served a term as the representative of migrants from the state. Many more returnees serve without claiming to represent migrants in particular. A 2004 survey in Michoacán found that 35 percent of current mayors had U.S. migration experience. Seven of the 113 mayors were U.S. citizens.[75]

The most important effect of returned migrants on Mexico has been forgotten in the migration literature even if it is widely recognized in studies of Mexican politics. Just as the Mexican migration literature has largely ignored political exiles in the late nineteenth and early twentieth centuries, it has ignored elite student migration during the late twentieth century. A generation of Mexican technocratic elites was shaped by their advanced studies at prestigious U.S. universities, including every Mexican president from 1982 to 2012. Not coincidentally, these presidents introduced and consolidated a neoliberal political economy in Mexico based on the Washington Consensus of limited budget deficits, reduced public spending, free trade, privatization, and deregulation. Their policies utterly transformed Mexico in ways that political scientists have shown to be directly attributable to their experiences studying in the United States.[76]

President Miguel de la Madrid (1982–1988) earned a master's degree in public administration from Harvard in 1965.[77] Upon assuming office, he

steered Mexico's economy away from decades of import substitution industrialization and set a neoliberal course by selling state-owned businesses, encouraging foreign investment, reducing social spending, firing large numbers
of government workers, and bringing Mexico into the General Agreement
on Tariffs and Trade. His successor, Carlos Salinas de Gortari (1988–1994)
also attended Harvard, earning master's degrees in public administration in
1973 and political economy in 1976, followed by a doctorate in economics in 1978.[78] Salinas continued to privatize state-owned businesses and
negotiated the NAFTA agreement. His dissertation formed the basis of his
National Solidarity Program. Salinas hoped that a decentralized development program that involved community leaders in the planning process
would be less corrupt and more likely to address local needs, while simultaneously generating support for the federal government.[79] Major figures
on Salinas's economic team held advanced degrees from U.S. universities,
including his Minister of Programming and Budget, Ernesto Zedillo, who
earned his doctorate in economics from Yale in 1981.[80] Zedillo served as
president from 1994 to 2000. He and his Stanford-educated finance minister reacted to Mexico's worst economic crisis since the Great Depression
by negotiating a set of "structural adjustment" austerity measures with the
International Monetary Fund. Vicente Fox (2000–2006) of the center-right
National Action Party broke the PRI's grip on power dating back to 1929,
but economically, he continued the neoliberal vision of his three predecessors. Fox had earned a diploma in Top Management Skills from the Harvard
Business School in 1974 while working as an executive for Coca-Cola.[81]
His successor, President Felipe Calderón (2006–2012), earned a master's
degree in public administration from Harvard's Kennedy School.[82] Calderón
maintained the policy of focusing on exports and foreign investment. While
it is uncertain to what extent working-class and middle-class returnees have
affected Mexican politics, there is no question that a cadre of technocratic
returnees dramatically reshaped the country.

*   *   *

What, then, is new about Mexican migrant political "transnationalism"?
If transnationalism is defined as the quality of acting both in the country
of origin and destination, or acting across the international border, there is
overwhelming evidence of such activity extending back to the 1850s. The
involvement of emigrants and exiles in the wars and struggles that defined
modern Mexico has never been a secret to historians, who, perhaps like
Molière's gentleman who discovered he was speaking in prose, were writing
about transnationalism all the while without knowing it.

The single greatest shift in transborder politics was the transition from violent to peaceful engagement after the 1920s, though important aspects of peaceful engagement, such as the formation of political clubs, lobbies, and patriotic societies, began in the earlier period. At the level of mass politics, the key differences are a shift to the institutionalized promotion of both dual ties and long-distance engagement by promoting dual nationality; extending the right to vote to Mexicans living abroad; and creating agencies to engage migrants in hometown projects. The major shifts in patterns of engagement have practically nothing to do with improved technology but rather derive from the unintended consequences of U.S. immigration policies that have shaped whole family migration and hometown-based settlement patterns in the United States, the greater integration within North America that legitimizes dual ties, and the establishment of peaceful yet competitive politics in Mexico. While symbolically important, the actual effects on Mexico of new institutions of transborder politics and the activities that they channel pale in comparison to the dramatic consequences that U.S. experiences have had on a handful of technocratic elites at the turn of the twenty-first century. Transborder political engagement among Mexicans in the United States has certainly changed over a century and a half, but it is only by removing blinders of when, who, how, and why that the topography of the changing political landscape comes into view.

NOTES

1. Seth Motel and Eileen Patten, "Statistical Portrait of Hispanics in the United States, 2011" (Washington, D.C.: Pew Hispanic Center, 2013).

2. Roger Rouse, "Mexican Migration to the United States: Family Relations in the Development of a Transnational Migrant Circuit," doctoral thesis, Stanford University, 1989; M. Kearney, C. Nagengast, and J. E. Taylor, *Anthropological Perspectives on Transnational Communities in Rural California* (Davis: California Institute for Rural Studies, 1989); Michael P. Smith and Luis E. Guarnizo, eds., *Transnationalism from Below* (New Brunswick, N.J.: Transaction Publishers, 1998).

3. Nina Glick Schiller, Linda G. Basch, and Cristina Blanc-Szanton, *Towards a Transnational Perspective on Migration: Race, Class, Ethnicity, and Nationalism Reconsidered* (New York: New York Academy of Sciences, 1992).

4. Robert C. Smith, "How Durable and New Is Transnational Life? Historical Retrieval through Local Comparison," *Diaspora: A Journal of Transnational Studies* 9 (2000): 203–233. For exceptions that take the long view, see Rachel Sherman, "From State Introversion to State Extension in Mexico: Modes of Emigrant Incorporation, 1900–1997," *Theory and Society* 28 (1999): 835–878; David FitzGerald, *A Nation of Emigrants: How Mexico Manages Its Migration* (Berkeley: University

of California Press, 2009), and Alexandra Délano, *Mexico and Its Diaspora in the United States: Policies of Emigration since 1848* (Cambridge: Cambridge University Press, 2011).

5. Roger Waldinger and David FitzGerald, "Transnationalism in Question," *American Journal of Sociology* 109 (2004): 1177–1195.

6. David Gutiérrez, *Walls and Mirrors: Mexican Americans, Mexican Immigrants, and the Politics of Ethnicity* (Berkeley: University of California Press, 1995).

7. Robert Ryal Miller, "Arms across the Border: United States Aid to Juárez during the French Intervention in Mexico," *Transactions of the American Philosophical Society* 63 (1973): 22.

8. Ibid., 61.

9. Charles C. Cumberland, "Mexican Revolutionary Movements from Texas, 1906–1912," *Southwestern Historical Quarterly* 52 (1949): 301–324; Richard Blaine McCornack, "Porfirio Díaz en la frontera texana, 1875–1877," *Historia Mexicana* 5 (1956): 373–410.

10. Juan Gómez-Quiñones, "Piedras contra la luna, México en Aztlán y Aztlán en México: Chicano-Mexicano relations and the Mexican consulates, 1900–1920, an extended research note," *IV International Congress of Mexican Studies* (1973); Anne Pace, "Mexican Refugees in Arizona 1910–1911," *Arizona and the West* 16 (1974): 5–18; Douglas Monroy, "Anarquismo y Comunismo: Mexican Radicalism and the Communist Party in Los Angeles during the 1930s," *Labor History* 24 (1983): 34; Cumberland, "Mexican Revolutionary Movements"; Claudio Lomnitz, *The Return of Comrade Ricardo Flores Magón* (New York: Zone Books, 2014).

11. Gómez-Quiñones, "Piedras contra la luna."

12. Cumberland, "Mexican Revolutionary Movements"; Arturo Santamaría Gómez, *La política entre México y Aztlán: Relaciones chicano-mexicanas del 68 a Chiapas 94* (Universidad Autónoma de Sinaloa, 1994); Michael M. Smith, "The Mexican Secret Service in the United States, 1910–1920," *The Americas* 59 (2002): 65–85.

13. Gómez-Quiñones, "Piedras contra la luna"; Pace, "Mexican Refugees in Arizona 1910–1911," 5–18.

14. George J. Rausch Jr., "The Exile and Death of Victoriano Huerta," *Hispanic American Historical Review* 42 (1962): 133–151.

15. Gómez-Quiñones, "Piedras contra la luna"; Santamaría Gómez, *La política entre México y Aztlán*; Devra Weber, "Historical Perspectives on Transnational Mexican Workers in California," in John M. Hart, ed., *Border Crossings Mexican and Mexican-American Workers* (Wilmington, Del.: SR Books, 1998).

16. Gómez-Quiñones, "Piedras contra la luna," 40.

17. Richard Gribble, "Roman Catholicism and US Foreign Policy, 1919–1935: A Clash of Policies," *Journal of Church and State* 50 (2008): 73–99; Gilbert G. González, *Mexican Consuls and Labor Organizing: Imperial Politics in the American Southwest* (Austin: University of Texas Press, 1999); George J. Sánchez, *Becoming Mexican American: Ethnicity, Culture, and Identity in Chicano Los Angeles, 1900–1945* (New York: Oxford University Press, 1993).

18. Douglas Monroy, *Rebirth: Mexican Los Angeles from the Great Migration to the Great Depression* (Berkeley: University of California Press, 1999), 232.

19. Carlos H. Zazueta, "Mexican Political Actors in the United States and Mexico: Historical and Political Contexts of a Dialogue Renewed," in Carlos Vásquez and Manuel García y Griego, eds., *Mexican-U.S. Relations: Conflict and Convergence* (Los Angeles: Chicano Studies Research Center, University of California, Los Angeles, 1983); Santamaría Gómez, *La política entre México y Aztlán*; Monroy, *Rebirth*.

20. F. E. Balderrama, *In Defense of la Raza: The Los Angeles Mexican Consulate, and the Mexican Community, 1929 to 1936* (Tucson: University of Arizona Press, 1982).

21. González, *Mexican Consuls and Labor Organizing*, 37.

22. During President Cárdenas's nationalization of the oil industry in 1938, some Mexicans living in California voluntarily sent money to the national treasury to pay for the expropriation. Santamaría Gómez, *La política entre México y Aztlán*.

23. Armando Gutiérrez, "The Chicano Elite in Chicano-Mexicano Relations," in Tatcho Mindiola Jr. and Max Martínez, eds., *Chicano-Mexicano Relations* (Houston: University of Houston, Mexican American Studies Program, 1986), 47; Zazueta, "Mexican Political Actors," 458.

24. David FitzGerald, "Colonies of the Little Motherland: Membership, Space, and Time in Mexican Migrant Hometown Associations," *Comparative Studies in Society and History* 50 (2008): 145–169.

25. Abraham Hoffman, *Unwanted Mexican Americans in the Great Depression: Repatriation Pressures, 1929–1939* (Tucson: University of Arizona Press, 1974).

26. Weber, "Historical Perspectives," 228.

27. Ann L. Craig, *The First Agraristas: An Oral History of a Mexican Agrarian Reform Movement* (Berkeley: University of California Press, 1983), 178. *Ejidatarios* are members of *ejidos*, a collective form of land tenure that was a principal means of distributing land during Mexico's postrevolutionary agrarian reform.

28. Rafael Alarcón, "Los primeros norteños de Chavinda," *Relaciones* 3 (1986): 163–186; Omar Fonseca, "De Jaripo a Stockton, California: Un caso de migración en Michoacán," in *Movimientos de población en el occidente de México*, ed. Thomas Calvo and Gustavo López (Zamora: El Colegio de Michoacán, 1988); John Gledhill, *Casi Nada: Capitalismo, estado y los campesinos de Guaracha* (Zamora, Mexico: El Colegio de Michoacán, 1993); Weber, "Historical Perspectives."

29. Sánchez, *Becoming Mexican American*.

30. Jorge Bustamante, "Chicano-Mexicano Relations from Practice to Theory," in Mindiola and Martinez, *Chicano-Mexicano Relations*.

31. Gutiérrez, *Walls and Mirrors*.

32. Rodolfo O. de la Garza and Claudio Vargas, "The Mexican-Origin Population of the United States as a Political Force in the Borderlands: From Paisanos to Pochos to Potential Political Allies," in *Changing Boundaries in the Americas: New Perspectives on the U.S.-Mexican, Central American, and South American Borders,*

ed. Lawrence A. Herzog (La Jolla: Center for U.S.-Mexican Studies, University of California, San Diego, 1992).

33. Rodolfo O. de la Garza, "Chicanos as an Ethnic Lobby: Limits and Possibilities," in Mindiola and Martinez, *Chicano-Mexicano Relations*; Santamaría Gómez, *La política entre México y Aztlán*.

34. Santamaría Gómez, *La política entre México y Aztlán*.

35. FitzGerald, *A Nation of Emigrants*.

36. For the demographic and policy background of the demographic shifts, see Douglas S. Massey, Jorge Durand, and Nolan J. Malone, *Beyond Smoke and Mirrors: Mexican Immigration in an Era of Free Trade* (New York: Russell Sage Foundation, 2002).

37. World Bank staff estimates based on the *International Monetary Fund's Balance of Payments Statistics Yearbook*, 2011. siteresources.worldbank.org/INTPROSPECTS/Resources/334934-1288990760745/RemittancesData_Inflows_Dec11(Public).xlsx (accessed Dec. 7, 2015).

38. Natasha Iskander, *Creative State: Forty Years of Migration and Development Policy in Morocco and Mexico* (Ithaca: Cornell University Press, 2010).

39. See Robert C. Smith, *Mexican New York: The Transnational Lives of New Immigrants* (Berkeley: University of California Press, 2006); and FitzGerald, "Colonies of the Little Motherland" for empirical examples and Tomas Soehl and Roger Waldinger, "Making the Connection: Latino Immigrants and Their Cross-border Ties," *Ethnic and Racial Studies* 33 (2010): 1489–1510, on the frequency of such contacts.

40. Michael Jones-Correa, "Under Two Flags: Dual Nationality in Latin America and Its Consequences for the United States" (Cambridge: David Rockefeller Center for Latin American Studies, Harvard University, 2000).

41. Jesús Martínez Saldaña, "At the Periphery of Democracy: The Binational Politics of Mexican Immigrants in Silicon Valley," doctoral thesis, University of California, Berkeley, 1993.

42. S. Mara Pérez Godoy, "Social Movements and International Migration: The Mexican Diaspora Seeks Inclusion in Mexico's Political Affairs, 1968–1998," doctoral thesis, University of Chicago, 1998.

43. PRD activists, interview by author, Anaheim, California, June 2000.

44. Soehl and Waldinger, "Making the Connection," 1489–1510.

45. Denise Dresser, "Exporting Conflict: Transboundary Consequences of Mexican Politics," in *The California-Mexico Connection*, ed. Abraham F. Lowenthal and Katrina Burgess (Stanford: Stanford University Press, 1993); María Rosa García-Acevedo, "Politics across Borders: Mexico's Policies toward Mexicans in the United States," *Journal of the Southwest* 45 (2003): 533–556.

46. Carlos González Gutiérrez, "Decentralized Diplomacy: The Role of Consular Offices in Mexico's Relations with its Diaspora," in *Bridging the Border: Transforming Mexico-U.S. Relations*, ed. Rodolfo de la Garza and Jesús Velasco (Lanham, Md.: Rowman and Littlefield, 1997), 49–67.

47. David FitzGerald, "Beyond 'Transnationalism': Mexican Hometown Politics at an American Labor Union," *Ethnic and Racial Studies* 27 (2004): 228–247.

48. The discussion of dual nationality is drawn from David FitzGerald, "Nationality and Migration in Modern Mexico," *Journal of Ethnic and Migration Studies* 31 (2005): 171–191, and David FitzGerald, "Rethinking Emigrant Citizenship," *New York University Law Review* 81 (2006): 90–116.

49. Rodolfo de la Garza, "Foreign Policy Comes Home: The Domestic Consequences of the Program for Mexican Communities Living in Foreign Countries," in Garza and Velasco, *Bridging the Border*, 82; Gómez-Quiñones, "Piedras contra la luna,"; Santamaría Gómez, *La política entre México y Aztlán*; Jesus Martínez Saldaña and Raúl Ross Pineda, "Suffrage for Mexicans Residing Abroad," in *Cross-Border Dialogues: US-Mexico Social Movement Networking*, ed. David Brooks and Jonathan Fox (La Jolla: University of California, San Diego, Center for US-Mexican Studies, 2002).

50. FitzGerald, "Nationality and Migration," 171–191.

51. Brian Knowlton, "Calderón Again Assails Arizona Law on Detention," *New York Times*, May 20, 2010.

52. Pew Hispanic Center, "Illegal Immigration Backlash Worries, Divides Latinos" (Washington, D.C.: The Center, Oct. 28, 2010).

53. FitzGerald, "Colonies of the Little Motherland," 145–169.

54. Guillaume Lanly and M. Basilia Valenzuela V., Introducción, in *Clubes de migrantes oriundos mexicanos en los Estados Unidos*, ed. Guillaume Lanly and M. Basilia Valenzuela V. Guadalajara (Centro Universitario de Ciencias Económico Administrativas, Universidad de Guadalajara, 2004), 11–36; "Mexico: HTAs, Fertility, Labor," *Migration News* 13 (Oct. 16, 2006). Even ascertaining the number of formal HTAs registered is difficult given errors in the IME's database of organizations. It listed many organizations as "*clubes de oriundos*" (HTAs) when they were not (e.g., the *Journal of Latino-Latin American Studies*) and failed to list many HTAs as *clubes de oriundos* when they clearly were (e.g., Club de Migrantes de "Carmen de Sánchez"). www.ime.gob.mx/DirectorioOrganizaciones/ (accessed May 2, 2012).

55. David FitzGerald, *Negotiating Extra-Territorial Citizenship: Mexican Migration and the Transnational Politics of Community* (La Jolla: Center for Comparative Immigration Studies, University of California, San Diego, 2000).

56. Roberto Suro, "Attitudes about Voting in Mexican Elections and Ties to Mexico" (Washington, D.C.: Pew Hispanic Center, 2005).

57. Soehl and Waldinger, "Making the Connection," 1489–1510.

58. James F. Smith, "Fox Embraces Mexicans Living in U.S.," *Los Angeles Times*, Dec. 4, 2000.

59. "Mexican President Praises Migrant 'Heroes,'" *New York Times*, Dec. 13, 2000.

60. Délano, *Mexico and Its Diaspora in the United States*.

61. FitzGerald, *A Nation of Emigrants*; Guillermo Yrizar Barbosa and Rafael Alarcón, "Política de emigración y gobiernos estatales en México," *Migraciones Internacionales* 5 (2010): 165–198.

62. SEDESOL, "Cuarto Informe Timestral 2010 H. Cámara de Diputados. Programas de Subsidios del Ramo Administrativo 20 Desarrollo Social" (Mexico City:

SEDESOL, 2011), CONEVAL, "Informe de la Evaluación Específica de Desempeño 2009–2010," 2011.

63. Lauren Duquette, "Making Democracy Work from Abroad: Remittances, Hometown Associations and Migrant-state Coproduction of Public Goods in Mexico," doctoral thesis, University of Chicago, 2011.

64. Banco de México. www.banxico.org.mx (accessed Dec. 7, 2015).

65. José Manuel Valenzuela Arce, "Diáspora social y doble nacionalidad," in *La identidad nacional mexicana como problema político y cultural*, ed. Raúl Bejar and Héctor Rosales (Mexico City: Siglo Veintiuno, 1999), 283.

66. See Martínez Saldaña and Ross Pineda, "Suffrage for Mexicans Residing Abroad," on the history of changes in constitutional and election law relating to citizens abroad.

67. FitzGerald, "Beyond 'Transnationalism,'" 228–247.

68. Robert C. Smith, "Contradictions of Diasporic Institutionalization in Mexican Politics: The 2006 Migrant Vote and Other Forms of Inclusion and Control," *Ethnic and Racial Studies* 31 (2008): 708–741.

69. Instituto Federal Electoral, "Informe final sobre el voto de los mexicanos residentes en el extranjero" (Mexico City: IFE, 2006).

70. Roberto Suro and Gabriel Escobar, "Survey of Mexicans Living in the U.S. on Absentee Voting in Mexican Elections" (Washington, D.C.: Pew Hispanic Center, 2006); Instituto Federal Electoral. www.ine.mx/documentos/votoextranjero/libro_blanco/pdf/tomoII/tomoII.pdf (accessed Dec. 7, 2015).

71. David Gutiérrez, Jeanne Batalova, and Aaron Terrazas, "The 2012 Mexican Presidential Election and Mexican Immigrants of Voting Age in the United States" (Migration Policy Institute, April 2012).

72. "Finiquita voto de michoacanos en el extranjero," *Cambio de Michoacán* (Nov. 12, 2011); "Viven más michoacanos en Estados Unidos que en el estado," *La Jornada Michoacán* (Mar. 7, 2007); May 1, 2012, = secure.iedf.org.mx/resultados2012/voto-extranjero.php?ve=1 (accessed Dec. 7, 2015).

73. Clarisa Pérez-Armendáriz and David Crowe, "Do Migrants Remit Democracy? International Migration, Political Beliefs, and Behavior in Mexico," *Comparative Political Studies* 43 (2010): 119–148; Roderic A. Camp, "Learning Democracy in Mexico and the United States," *Mexican Studies* 19 (2003): 3–27; Yossi Shain, *Marketing the American Creed Abroad: Diasporas in the U.S. and Their Homelands* (New York: Cambridge University Press, 1999).

74. Michael P. Smith and Matt Bakker, *Citizenship across Borders* (Ithaca: Cornell University Press, 2008); "Los migrantes regresan a votar . . . y ser votados," *La Jornada* (June 24, 2001).

75. Xochitl Bada, "Market Membership without Absentee Suffrage: Civic Participation and Community Development Strategies of Michoacano Hometown Associations," XXV International Congress of the Latin American Studies Association, Oct. 6–8, 2004, Las Vegas, Nev.

76. Miguel Angel Centeno, *Democracy within Reason: Technocratic Revolution in Mexico* (University Park: Pennsylvania State University Press, 2007); Sarah

Babb, *Managing Mexico: Economists from Nationalism to Neoliberalism* (Princeton: Princeton University Press, 2001); Roderic A. Camp, *The Metamorphosis of Leadership in a Democratic Mexico* (Oxford: Oxford University Press, 2010).

77. "Mexico's Harvard Man," *New York Times*, Dec. 2, 1982.

78. Larry Rohter, "Man in the News; A Mexican on the Fast Track: Carlos Salinas de Gortari," *New York Times*, Oct. 5, 1987.

79. Carlos Salinas de Gortari, *Political Participation, Public Investment, and Support for the System: A Comparative Study of Rural Communities in Mexico* (La Jolla: Center for U.S.-Mexican Studies, University of California, San Diego, 1982), 39–42.

80. Anthony DePalma, "Man in the News: Ernesto Zedillo Ponce de Leon; A Tragedy's Stand-In," *New York Times*, Mar. 30, 1994.

81. "Fox Rough and Ready to Toss Out PRI," San Antonio Express-News, June 20, 2000.

82. Marc Lacey, "Felipe Calderón: A Politician at Birth," *New York Times*, Sept. 6, 2005.

CHAPTER 5

TRANSNATIONALISM AND THE EMERGENCE OF THE MODERN CHINESE STATE

National Rejuvenation and the Ascendance of Foreign-Educated Elites (*Liuxuesheng*)

Madeline Y. Hsu

In 1792, the Qianlong Emperor famously rejected British requests to expand relations and increase trade, declaring in an edict to King George III, "We have never valued ingenious articles, nor do we have the slightest need of your country's manufactures."[1] China's precipitous decline in the century and a half following this prideful pronouncement reflects the shortsightedness of its traditional ruling elite immersed in millennia of Confucian-based political, economic, and cultural systems, values, and power in the face of the ascendant nations of the industrializing west. Unlike the many other areas of the world colonized by these imperial powers, however, China retained sufficient sovereignty and domestic control to strategize for national rejuvenation. This article explores how China's turn to the transnational included an ambitious policy of sending students abroad. In its ambivalent and contradictory quest to selectively acquire aspects of western learning and civilization, *liuxuesheng* (Chinese international students) were meant to further the goal of developing a Chinese path to "self-strengthening" (*ziqiang*) and modernity.

For developing states such as China playing catch-up, students—in addition to diplomatic personnel—have arguably been the form of migration most closely associated with enacting government and other nation-oriented objectives. The Qing dynasty (1644–1911) collapsed under the plummeting capacities of traditional Confucian systems of dynastic governance, management, and foreign relations to navigate the increasingly integrated global order dominated by western powers and driven by Westphalian principles and capitalist competition backed by military force. In the face of such challenges, the Qing reluctantly turned to intensifying efforts to acquire western learning for the sake of self-strengthening, a project that is still ongoing and enacted in significant ways through the reform and expansion of educational infrastructures domestically and by promoting study abroad.

As this brief overview of early Chinese student migrations abroad (1872–1955) explores, both homeland and hostland states attribute the highest value to educated migrants. Consequently, the employment, settlement, and citizenship choices made by educated migrants, particularly those who have received government sponsorship and support, exacerbate tensions regarding migration flows as forms of national "losses" and "gains" played out on an international field of competition. After World War II, as technological innovation became a chief determinant of both economic clout and military advantage, and in the context of the Cold War, governments set out ever more explicitly to woo educated migrants, particularly those specializing in the fields most associated with technological, infrastructural, and economic advancement. The global debate over brain drain that flared during the 1960s illustrates these tensions as high percentages of educated elites from developing nations chose to remain and work in the first world economies in which they had been studying. The United States was a chief beneficiary of such flows, to the detriment of countries such as Taiwan, South Korea, and India. Although such "drains" have, since the 1980s, become more circular, integrating both sending and receiving economies, the heated discussions over gains and losses, exploitation and victimization, and the naturalized role of market forces and "unnatural" government restrictions illustrate key disjunctures in attempts to subsume and direct migration flows according to national interests. Through student migration, employment, and settlement, we can observe both the evolution and limits of state efforts to leverage transnational systems of mobility and international relations.

Transnationalism has characterized the emergence of Chinese modernity, a process framed by China's struggles to manage foreign encroachments along with domestic crises in part through the rapid acquisition and adaptation of western science and technology, political philosophies and institutions, military strategies, and cultural forms. Since the 1870s, Chinese government programs for study abroad have aimed to provide such expertise, strategic and institutional practices that expanded and grew in influence during the twentieth century. Through evolving versions of the Chinese Educational Mission, the Ministries of Education and Foreign Affairs, the National Resources Commission, and the China Institute in America, a succession of Chinese regimes have sought to direct the activities of Chinese studying abroad (*liuxuesheng*) as key resources to develop industry and a modern infrastructure for China's economy. As China has modernized by adapting western models across the twentieth century, returned *liuxuesheng* have wielded significant influence as interpreters of western knowledge, technology, institutions, and ideals in application to Chinese agendas and have significantly shaped both the Nationalist and Communist parties and constituted a considerable technocratic elite directing economic and educational developments.[2] This article tracks the early evolution of ideologies and institutions for Chinese study-abroad programs in hopes of expanding contemporary discussions of transnationalism and migration studies.

Study Abroad and Unequal Foreign Relations

As suggested by the Qianlong Emperor's dismissive remarks, Chinese had long assumed the superiority and prestige of their Confucian-based civilization, which limited hospitality and interest in foreign visitors while providing scant cause to travel away from China. The regional dominance of ethnic Han Chinese over their barbarian neighbors infused centuries of political, cultural, and social practices with a staunch aura of nearly invincible dominance against which the growing agitations of British, French, German, and American traders and governments barely registered in the late eighteenth century. Confined to the marginal trading posts of Macau and Shamian Island in Guangzhou, with severe restrictions placed on their inland mobility and access to valuable goods such as tea, silk, and porcelain, westerners found more and more reasons to criticize Chinese as uncivilized heathens requiring more overtly military measures to force their engagement with the civilized Christian West. From the 1790s onward, the trade in opium from British India generated imbalances to China's disadvantage for the first time, compounding worsening domestic pressures stemming from demographic growth, inflationary effects of New World silver, official corruption, and general conditions of underemployment and social unrest. When the western powers attacked China in the first Opium War (1839–1842), they aggravated these already severe problems by challenging the Qing's greatest weakness, its navy, and forcing it to confront and learn about an unmanageable coalition of foreign powers, which for the first time imposed new systems of international relations dominance on China. This abrupt displacement and marginalization forced the Qing to take once unthinkable measures to learn from foreigners once considered barbarian and irrevocably inferior, in part by sponsoring studies overseas.

Christian missionary agendas and institutions laid the foundations for the unequal exchanges that characterized China's early acquisition of western learning. Drawn by the enormous reserves of unsaved souls in China, as well as their relatively high levels of literacy and civilizational attainment, missionaries risked long-distance travel, xenophobia, and disease to proselytize among Chinese. The goal of converting Chinese required the study of languages and systems of philosophy, governance, and knowledge production. Understandably, schools and education were key components in missionary efforts. The earliest Chinese students to journey to Europe did so under missionary sponsorship, which also established the first western-style schools in China. As early as 1650, the Polish Jesuit priest Michael Boym (1612–1659) brought a Chinese convert with him to Rome to aid with translation projects. Such travels remained occasional until the nineteenth century when growing numbers of missionary schools trained greater numbers of Chinese students in the languages and curriculum that would allow them to study abroad. A scant resource through the turn of the twentieth century, the first generations of western-trained Chinese played significant roles as translators and bridges in Sino-western interactions. Among the earliest were five boys who attended the Foreign Mission School in Cornwall, Connecticut, run by the American Board of Commissioners for Foreign Missions during the 1820s. One, Alum, returned home and translated for the leading Qing official Lin Zexu (1785–1850) on the cusp of the first Opium War (1839–1842).[3]

This first open confrontation demonstrated conclusively China's weakness in the face of western gunboats. The Treaty of Nanjing (1842) set the terms for China's defeat and imposed the earliest of an expanding array of debilitating terms set by the victorious powers for rights of inland travel and residency, preferential trade conditions, extraterritorial legal status, and other treaty port advantages. Protected by these impositions, missionary numbers and institutional investments grew into the 1930s. For example, just a year after arriving in 1844, the first American Presbyterian missionary established the Ningbo Boys' Academy that eventually expanded to become Hangzhou Christian University. Within a couple of decades, about seventy mission schools were in operation in a dozen cities, primarily treaty ports.[4] The succession of military conflicts engulfing China, such as the Taiping Rebellion (1851–1864) that nearly toppled the Qing and the Second Opium War (1856–1860), enabled the expansion of missionary educational facilities numerically and geographically through the primary, middle school, high school, and college levels. Western influence waxed even as China's sovereign capacities plummeted.

Chinese asserted their own agendas in the quest for western learning but initially with considerable ambivalence. The self-strengthening movement (c. 1861–1895) attempted to enact the principle of *tiyong*, retaining a core of Confucian spirit and ethics in the acquisition of western technology and sciences to develop China's military and economy. In practice, trying to preserve and act upon core Chinese values through selective adoption of foreign knowledge was difficult and highly contentious because such boundaries were impossible to demarcate and maintain. Could Chinese learn western sciences and math, so necessary to military and navigational practices, without absorbing at least some of the Enlightenment principles producing such knowledge? Was it also essential to understand western philosophies, legal and political systems, religion, and ethics to develop the kind of society and human potential that could foster science and modernity for China? To this day, Chinese remain ambivalent about the loss of core spiritual and cultural values that surely must accompany the acquisition of foreign knowledge, ideas, and practices in the name of national survival and competitiveness.

The Qing began piecemeal, starting with an informal ministry of foreign affairs (Zongli Yamen) in 1861, followed by schools to train translators in Beijing (1862), Shanghai, and Guangzhou (1864), and then at the Naval Shipyard in Fuzhou (1867) and the Jiangnan Arsenal in 1868. Shortages of suitably trained Chinese forced employment of primarily foreign instructors.[5]

The Qing also turned to sending students abroad, most famously under the leadership of the first Chinese to graduate from an American university, Yung Wing (Rong Hong) (Yale 1854, 1828–1912). Yung had studied in the Morrison Education Society School in Macao and came to America in 1848 with a missionary teacher.[6] Yung was a devout Christian *and* Chinese patriot who refused a scholarship that would have destined him for a missionary career and instead worked his way through college so that he might place his American education in the service of China. Upon graduating, Yung Wing precociously shared his vision in a letter to Yale's president regarding his goal to bring other Chinese to study in the United States so that "the rising generation of China should enjoy the same educational advantages that I had enjoyed; that through Western education China might be regenerated, become enlightened and powerful."[7]

Seventeen years after returning to China, relearning Chinese, and making his fortune as a tea merchant, and given China's dire situation at the time, Yung Wing was able to persuade the prominent reformist officials Zeng Guofan (1811–1872) and Li Hongzhang (1823–1901) that such an unprecedented venture in western learning could benefit China. Founded in 1871, the Chinese Educational Mission (CEM) pioneered a new, and untested, route into government service. Rather than intensive study of Confucian texts in preparation for the examination system that led to government service, CEM scholars would receive a total of fifteen years of education consisting first of English-language training in Shanghai. The most capable of them would then be selected for more than a decade of study in America, ultimately aiming for enrollment in West Point or the Naval Academy. Upon graduation, they were to return and undertake government service toward China's self-strengthening.

Evaluations of the CEM, the pioneer effort in Chinese study abroad, reveal the tensions between national agendas for international education and disappointment in actual outcomes, whether because students did not return or entered careers not directly related to their training in "the sciences related to army, navy, mathematics, engineering" so that "all the technological specialties of the West may be adopted in China, and the nation may begin to grow strong by its own efforts."[8] From the outset, tensions beset the program concerning the attempted melding of Chinese and American knowledge and values, and whether Chinese could learn from the west in ways that did not undermine the essence of Chinese civilization, moral ethics, and social systems. According to Y. C. Wang, Yung Wing believed that Chinese needed not only to learn "the progressive, technological culture of the West" but to acquire western viewpoints as well. Wang characterized Yung Wing as deliberately subverting the CEM. "Under his direction, a marked change developed in the boys' attitude and conduct: they played baseball, dated American girls, refused to show respect to the head of the mission, and neglected their Chinese studies to such an extent that they forgot how to speak the language. Some became Christians."[9] These signs of unwanted acculturation fueled tensions between Yung Wing and his less westernized Chinese colleagues supervising the program.

In New England, the CEM students were warmly welcomed and readily integrated into local society, in stark contrast to the hostile conditions facing their "coolie" counterparts viewed as unfair labor competition on the west coast.[10] More families than there were boys available offered to provide housing, tutoring in English, and socialization to prepare them for matriculation into college. Under such hospitable conditions, the young men, many of whom were only thirteen or fourteen at the start of their American sojourns, quickly adapted. Although they excelled academically, they also became popular socially and came to despise their lessons in Chinese language and Confucian texts at the "hellhouse" of the CEM headquarters in

Hartford, Connecticut.[11] Their very successes in adapting to western society set off alarm bells for the CEM's more conservative administrators.

In 1878, Yung Wing's colleagues reported to the Qing court that they doubted whether the students and even Yung Wing himself would prove useful to China because they had "denationalized," as illustrated by Yung Wing's Christian faith and marriage to a Euro-American woman, Mary Kellogg. As described by Emma Teng, the Qing and its successor republican administrations viewed such "international marriages" as diverting the energies of overseas students, leading them to settle abroad where they could not be of use to China. The Qing would issue an edict in 1910 forbidding such unions for students, but not for merchants or laborers, restrictions reissued by the Republican government in 1913, 1918, and 1936 but apparently to little avail.[12]

Despite these troubling signs of loss of Chineseness, however, the immediate cause of the CEM program's demise stemmed from the U.S. government's refusal to uphold stipulations in the 1868 Burlingame Treaty in denying the CEM students admission to the U.S. Naval Academy and West Point. With these ultimate targets of American public education beyond their grasp, the Chinese government withdrew from the attempt altogether and recalled the students, most of whom never attained their college degrees. Only those who could muster private funds and connections, such as Yung Wing's distant relative Yung Kwai, completed their studies in the United States.[13] A total of 8 out of 120 CEM students ended up in the United States: Yung Kwai, Li Enfou (Yan Phou Lee), and six others who managed to return after being recalled to China. Bearing out suspicions of interracial marriage, most married Euro-American women.[14] The rest made their careers in a China still deeply suspicious of westernized Chinese.

Despite uncertainties about how their American training could be useful in a Chinese setting, many of the CEM students went on to assume leading roles in establishing the foundations of modernization: railroads, mining, international trade and business, and the foreign service. In 1923, a CEM student, Wen Bingzhong (1862–1938), then Superintendent of Customs at Suzhou, summarized the attainments of his classmates: Zhong Wenyao (1861–1945) became the Chief of Customs at Hankou, a Qing Foreign Minister, and a Republican-era Minister of Communications; Liang Dunyan (1858–1924) and Tang Shaoyi (1862–1938) helped found the Customs College; Cai Tinggan (1861–1935) became an admiral and Director-General of the Water Bureau; and Zhan Tianyou (Jeme Tian Yow) (1861–1919) built the Beijing-Zhangjiakou Railroad. The many CEM graduates who served in the diplomatic corps were instrumental in building relationships and institutions making China one of the major senders of students to the United States.[15]

The Qing sponsored studies in other countries, but not in the same numbers and not with the same eventual impact. In 1875 and 1877, Fuzhou Arsenal students in smaller but more costly cohorts went to France, England, and Germany for stays of several years to acquire targeted skills in naval construction, navigation, and mining in programs that emphasized practice rather than broad intellectual training.[16] Perhaps for this reason, the CEM students had greater impact in pioneering infrastructural transformations based upon greater general knowledge, which enabled them to introduce technological and institutional innovations to China. In contrast, the Fuzhou student to attain the most prominence, Yan Fu (1854–1921), did so as a translator, a field with more limited impact. Japan became a favored destination for Chinese students after defeating China in 1894 and claiming most favored nation status alongside the European imperial powers with the Treaty of Shimonoseki in 1895, a defeat that intensified Chinese motives to study abroad.

China's continuing collapse from global treasure house to the "sick man of Asia" increased motivation and institutionalization for study abroad. In 1898, the leading minister Zhang Zhitong (1837–1909) composed the monograph "Exhortation to Learning" promoting foreign study with recommendations for optimizing outcomes. He still stressed that Chinese moral values had to rein in "Western politics and technology," but he added that Chinese international students should return to teach other Chinese in order to limit the influence of foreigners in Chinese schools, and that nearby Japan was the best place for Chinese studies abroad. The next year, the Qing government began offering provincial scholarships to encourage such foreign study, particularly in its newly powerful neighbor.[17] Japan's singularly successful modernization as an Asian nation, proximity, and lower costs made it the most popular destination for Chinese students, with numbers peaking in 1905 at around 12,000–13,000.[18] However, rising levels of Japanese xenophobia and chauvinism began discouraging Chinese from studying there, as did Japanese incursions into Manchuria. By 1910, Chinese student numbers dropped to under 4,000. Although easier access ensured a steady flow to Japan, American efforts to woo Chinese students drew many to the United States. The combination of national necessity and government initiatives fostered steady increases in the numbers of Chinese students studying abroad across the twentieth century, facilitated by American reciprocal interests in educating Chinese as a means of extending its influence in China.

The United States pioneered this form of cultural diplomacy, spurred by a confluence of events in 1905, as a means of contravening the emerging power of Japan in the western Pacific. A coalition of influential advocates, labeled the "Open Door Constituency" by Michael Hunt and including the missionary establishment, higher education administrators, and business groups such as the American Asiatic Association, lobbied the U.S. executive branch regarding the advantages of educating Chinese as a means for extending American influence over China.[19] Their agendas operated in contradiction to prevailing hostilities to Chinese workers, enshrined in the Chinese exclusion laws (1882–1943), that singled out Chinese by race as banned from citizenship by naturalization and almost entirely without entry rights into the United States. Students and merchants, however, were among the small numbers that retained rights of legal entry and residency, a legal exemption that the Open Door Constituency sought to optimize in demonstrating American friendship, if only to elite groups of Chinese. By 1905, America's "Open Door" policy, an effort to shore up Chinese sovereignty and discourage other imperial powers from a wholesale competition for spheres of influence, had failed, leaving the White House in need of a new foreign policy direction. Chinese merchants and students had organized the 1905 anti-American Boycott in major urban areas to protest the exclusion laws and their overly zealous enforcement, underscoring the importance of winning over China's intellectuals, who were viewed as the future leaders of the struggling but nonetheless substantive country. Despite the Open Door Constituency's efforts to foster friendly social experiences for educated Chinese, most Americans continued to conflate them with the despised "coolie" class and treat them accordingly, discrimination which consolidated their patriotism and intentions of returning to China. Japan's emergence as a global power also spurred American attention to educated Chinese, particularly in light of America's limited naval power in the western Pacific and the vulnerability of its new colony in the Philippines.

Such challenges led President Theodore Roosevelt to undertake an innovative solution, under the urging of missionaries such as the China expert Arthur Smith and heads of leading universities. Excess funds extracted from China in the Boxer Indemnity turned a foreign relations problem into an unexpected solution. This debilitating punishment had penalized the Qing for their support of attacks by the heterodox Righteous Harmony Society (Yihetuan), commonly known as the Boxers, against westerners, western objects, and westernized Chinese aiming to purge China of foreign contamination. After an international military alliance vanquished the Boxer Uprising (1899–1901), a coalition of eight governments imposed the Boxer Protocol that exacted heavy financial tolls amounting to more than China's total annual income. America's share of the Boxer Indemnity was US$25 million, more than double the damages it had actually incurred, taken from a nation struggling for its very survival. In 1905, Roosevelt and Congress faced the problem of accounting for these excessive demands and the embarrassment of having acted as a heartless, imperial power bullying a weaker nation.[20]

The Open Door Constituency, along with Chinese diplomats including former CEM students, campaigned for return of the excess funds, particularly in the form of scholarships to recruit students. Missionaries were particularly mindful that the Qing government had just abolished the Confucian-based examination system, leaving the door wide open for alternative educational systems and curriculum to gain ground.[21] As the main entities to have established western-style schools in China, missionaries saw an unprecedented chance to gain greater influence in the ensuing vacuum. The imminent collapse of traditional Chinese political institutions also presented great opportunity, as described by Edmund J. James, president of the University of Illinois, in a memo placed before President Roosevelt:

> China is upon the verge of a revolution. . . . The nation which succeeds in educating the young Chinese of the present generation will be the nation which for a given expenditure of effort will reap the largest possible returns in moral, intellectual, and commercial influence. If the United States had succeeded thirty-five years ago [through the CEM program] . . . and had succeeded in keeping that current large, we should to-day be controlling the development of China in that most satisfactory and subtle of all ways,—through the intellectual and spiritual domination of its leaders.[22]

The Chinese government would have preferred the money be invested in ways more directly beneficial to China's development such as railroads and modern banks. However, some American-educated Chinese advocated the benefits of western learning, as expressed by Premier Yan Huiqing (W. W. Yen) (1877–1950) in 1905:

> [W]e are to be the interpreters and expositors of America to our own people. . . . We constitute a bridge across the Pacific Ocean over which American education, American ideals, American machinery and manufactures, and all that is best of America pass to the Flowery Kingdom.[23]

The United States began returning the Boxer Indemnity in 1908 through educational programs that strengthened its relationship to China. Tsinghua College began as a prep school run "in the American way, with American personnel and an American curriculum" with all graduates through 1929 receiving full fellowships to study in the United States. The first two cohorts of Boxer Indemnity fellows were selected through highly competitive examinations and included some of the most famous of twentieth-century Chinese intellectuals, such as the linguist Zhao Yuanren (Yuen Ren Chao) (1892–1982), the literary scholar and educator Hu Shi (1891–1962), and the rocket scientist Qian Xuesen (1911–2009). Between 1912 and 1929, a total of 1,268 Boxer fellows went to the United States. Many in this generation of *liuxuesheng* returned to work in government and assumed key roles in developing the infrastructure of China's modern educational system.

The Boxer Indemnity program encouraged other Chinese to study in America, as did specialized fellowships and outreach programs funded by both Chinese and American institutions. The numbers studying in the United States increased steadily from 1900 to 1927. Y. C. Wang and Weili Ye estimate that in 1906, there were about 300 Chinese students in the United States, roughly 650 in 1911 and an estimated 1,600 by 1925 and 1926.[24]

Table 1. Chinese Students in the United States

1903	1909	1910	1911	1914	1918	1921	1943	1945
50	239	292	490	830	990	679	1,191	1,972

Source: Ministry of Education[25]

According to Bureau of Education statistics, between 1929 and 1946, 9,524 Chinese received permission to study abroad with 3,732 going to the United States and 3,483 to Japan.[26] Through their "special relationship," the United States emerged as a preferred destination for Chinese by the 1910s. For example, between 1917 and 1921, of students studying science abroad, the United States had 213 students, Japan 153, Germany 25, and England 26.[27]

The education and career of Jiang Menglin (Chiang Mon-lin) (1886–1964)—President of Peking University (1919–1927, 1930–1945), Minister of Education (1928–1930), and Chair of the Joint Committee for Rural Reconstruction—illustrate the transition from Confucian to western education and the ascendance of foreign-educated Chinese in government. Jiang began his studies traditionally in studying Confucian curriculum to prepare for the official examinations. As his family moved around to escape various outbursts of unrest, Jiang attended a hodgepodge of establishments, including the family clan school; bilingual institutions such as the Sino-Occidental School in Shaoxing—where he learned about western science, modern history, and the Japanese and English languages; and Zhejiang College in Hangzhou. In 1905, the last year they were held, he passed the lowest tier of the official exams but decided to eschew a traditional path into government service and enrolled instead in the English-language Nanyang College to prepare for study in the United States. Although he failed to win a government scholarship, his father agreed to pay for his studies abroad. In August, 1908, Jiang left for UC Berkeley where he received a BA degree in pedagogy and continued for a PhD in education at Columbia University under the mentorship of John Dewey.[28] He returned to China and pursued an illustrious career in China as a prominent educator and government official who developed modern educational institutions along American lines while contributing to stronger relations between China and the United States.

Sovereignty and Education

Entering the twentieth century, the Qing and its successor Republican administration began developing strategies and bureaucracies to impose greater structure and direction on the growing numbers of Chinese studying abroad. The Qing reestablished the CEM in 1909 to coordinate the studies of Boxer Fellows along with other Chinese students, attempting to direct their efforts by issuing regulations such as the stipulation that 80 percent of those receiving funding study practical fields such as engineering, mining, or agriculture. Of the first Boxer cohort, 43 of 47 were in scientific or technical fields; through 1929, about half of all the students studied the natural sciences, agriculture, and engineering.[29]

In 1909, the last gasp of the Qing, China had but 24 institutions of higher learning with 4,876 students who were taught by "a large number of foreign professors."[30] With the fall of the Qing in 1911, China's early experiments in republican government were unstable, with a series of weak central administrations nonetheless prioritizing expanding and modernizing China's educational infrastructure. For example, even Yuan Shikai (1859–1916) (1912–1916), China's first elected president who attempted to install himself as emperor, invested in education. Nonetheless, more students moved toward the social sciences and humanities, apparently less useful fields. Yuan's sudden death led to a decade of warlord politics, with military leaders controlling different regions and threatening China with physical fragmentation. However, Chinese political and educational leaders, including western-trained and transpacifically networked advocates, such as Hu Shi and Jiang Menglin, worked steadily to institutionalize and expand modern education systems that had become a key focus of national pride and rejuvenation in the eyes of many patriotic Chinese.

The 1919 Treaty of Versailles ignited Chinese anti-imperialist and revolutionary anger at the Chinese government's ineffectual response when foreign powers utterly ignored its sovereignty and transferred sovereignty over Shandong territories from Germany to Japan. The May Fourth movement convulsed cities and campuses throughout China, with masses of Chinese and thousands of college students, including many attending missionary schools, protesting foreign aggression and attacking the United States in particular for betraying Chinese and its own ideals of self-determinism, as voiced by President Woodrow Wilson.[31] In this broadly based movement, Chinese called for the eradication of Confucianism, now believed to have induced current national weakness, and the embrace of "Mr. Science" and "Mr. Democracy" as pathways to restore greatness. Such protests roiled the early 1920s, as university students closely monitored the actions of campus administrators and education authorities to ensure that their decisions furthered the causes of democracy and modernization for China rather than personal gain or politics.[32] In 1922, a group of U.S.-educated Chinese formed the private Federated Educational Association of China, which formulated the agenda adopted by the Ministry of Education for expanding and developing the infrastructure of modern education based on American models. This template produced rapid increases in the numbers of students and universities so that in 1925, there were 34 public and 13 private universities, mainly emphasizing the natural and social sciences.[33] In parallel, the Anti-Christian Movement and the Restore Educational Rights Campaign of 1924 led the Chinese government to impose greater restrictions on the Christian colleges in the belief that "education should have been an integral part of national sovereignty and the primary function of education was to inculcate patriotism."[34] The Christian colleges had to formally register, place more emphasis on Chinese learning, and stop requiring courses in religion. The new guidelines also recommended redirecting use of the first remission of Boxer Indemnity funds not only for fellowships for study in the United States but to foster scientific and technical training in China as well.[35]

The May Fourth upheavals led Congress to try to mend fences by voting to remit the remainder of the Boxer Indemnity funds to China.[36] American self-interest in this gesture was so transparent that it only fuelled Chinese resentments while setting the stage for the Chinese government to gain complete control over the money. Concerns that the United States retain control over the funds delayed the Congressional vote for several years in the face of growing Chinese anger. A compromise solution provided for the establishment of the China Foundation for the Promotion of Education and Culture to administer both Boxer remissions through an executive board comprised of Americans and American-educated Chinese for the purpose of "a closer cultural and educational relationship between China and America."[37] Despite objections by the Chinese government to American votes on the board, Congress insisted on this constraint. By 1929, however, Chinese had wrested away full control of the Foundation and both Boxer remissions.

Through the Northern Expedition (1927–1928), the Nationalist Party's Generalissimo Chiang Kai-shek reunified China and attained the highest level of centralized control since the fall of the Qing. Although Chiang's authority was tenuous in many regions that remained under warlord domination, his representative Hu Shi was able to force a reorganization of the China Foundation board to include members more trusted to work on behalf of Chinese agendas. Over Congressional objections, the reconstituted board then redirected use of the Boxer funds to divert resources away from study in America and toward strengthening domestic educational infrastructure. In 1929, rather than sponsoring Tsinghua graduates to study in the United States, the funds were channeled to transforming Tsinghua into a world-class university with up-to-date science and engineering facilities. By 1939, China had expanded to 41 universities, 38 colleges, and 31 professional schools with 41,922 students.

The Nationalists also gained greater control over international education. All *liuxuesheng*, whether privately or publicly funded, had to receive exit permits issued by the Ministry of Foreign Affairs in order to apply for passports, any sort of government funding or support, degree recognition, and jobs upon return. The Ministry of Education determined how many students could depart in particular fields and allocated 70 percent of government funds to those in the sciences, agriculture, engineering, and medicine with partial fellowships to encourage self-funded students to do the same.[38] In 1926, the China Foundation also established the "non-political and non-partisan" China Institute in America with the official purpose of promoting "closer cultural and economic relations" but which became the chief advocate and coordinator for Chinese students in the United States.[39]

Guo Bingwen, the first Chinese PhD graduate of Columbia University's Teacher's College was the Institute's founding director but it would be his successor, a Boxer Fellow and later graduate of Columbia, Meng Zhi (1901–1990) who turned the China Institute into the chief vehicle for attracting resources and support for Chinese students in the United States.[40] Drawing upon extensive professional and personal networks among leading politicians and educators in both countries, Meng began his long tenure as director in 1930 and remained the linchpin of its operations through 1967, during which time he consolidated and expanded the range of programs available to Chinese students, generated additional support and resources, raised American awareness and sympathy, and implemented Chinese government programs for supervision and management while negotiating for greater student rights and privileges in the United States.

Meng was uniquely suited to act as a cultural ambassador for China through a lifelong proclivity for identifying and cultivating its bicultural intersections with the United States. As a child, he studied English with a missionary at his Beijing home, and attended two institutions modeled on Philips Andover Academy: Nankai Middle School and Tsinghua College. Despite a brief imprisonment for protesting Japanese imperialism during the May Fourth Movement, Meng received a prestigious Boxer Indemnity fellowship to study in the United States in 1919. While in China, he had converted to Christianity, persuaded by the commensurable values between Confucianism and Christianity. He attended Davidson College in North Carolina as the first, and then only, Chinese for two years, an experience he cherished as his opportunity to "sinify" the college. He continued to attend Columbia's Teachers College following in the footsteps of famous westernized educators such as Hu Shi, Jiang Menglin, and Guo Bingwen.[41]

While still a student, Meng developed an extensive resumé of leadership positions in an array of Chinese student and American international education organizations such as the Chinese Student Christian Association (CSCA), the Nankai and Tsinghua alumni groups, and the YMCA-affiliated Committee for Friendly Relations among Foreign Students (CFRFS), along with stints editing the *Chinese Christian Students' Monthly* and the organization's yearbook. These roles immersed him in the world of Chinese students and facilitated substantive friendships with influential leaders of the American international education establishment such as John Mott of the YMCA's International Committee; Stephen Duggan, founding director of the Carnegie Foundation–funded Institute for International Education; and Paul Monroe of Teacher's College in Columbia, along with the most prominent of China sympathizers in the United States.

The China Institute's programs for Chinese students developed in tandem with the Institute for International Education (IIE), and Meng worked closely with its director Stephen Duggan, who had close ties to the Department of State. As did the IIE, and using the same format and section organization, the China Institute published a monthly bulletin that tracked student numbers, provided guidance regarding government regulations and practices, announced availability and procedures for scholarships, and intervened as necessary with government agencies for accommodations and changes of bureaucratic practice to facilitate international student studies. Chinese students gained greater leeway to work and train in the United States.

Perhaps most importantly, following directions from the Chinese government, the China Institute allocated fellowships and other funding resources with priority placed upon those studying the sciences and technology and those maintaining respectable academic standing. Meng undertook to bring in new resources so that more Boxer Indemnity funds could be directed to educational investments in China, while also taking over disbursement of fellowship funds and services to students in the United States when the CEM shut down in 1933. In the fiscal year ending June 30, 1938, for example, the China Institute's income of $16,735.09 included a $6,000 subsidy from the China Foundation, $2,100 from the Tsinghua University Fund, $1,015 from membership dues, $2,430 from the H. K. Lin Trust Fund, and about $1,300 each from donations and lecture fees. The China Institute disbursed a total of $87,148.66 in funds to Chinese students covering living allowances, tuition, and travel costs in both the United States and Europe.[42] Meng could also call upon the support of wealthy American supporters. For example, in 1944, upon deciding that the China Institute needed its own headquarters, he appealed to the influential publisher Henry Luce, who was born in China of a multigenerational missionary family; Luce purchased outright the townhouse at 125 East 65th Street, which still houses the organization today.

In the mid-1930s, the China Institute helped develop training programs so that Chinese engineers, technicians, scientists, and civil and military personnel could gain practical experience in leading centers for research and development in the United States, such as Northrop, Du Pont Rayon, General Electric, and Westinghouse. Based on projections of expertise and technical work mapped out by the Chinese National Resources Commission (NRC), the State Department's Bureau of Cultural Affairs and the private International Training Administration in Washington, D.C. placed Chinese trainees in field stations for the Department of Agriculture, the Tennessee Valley Authority, the Bureau of the Census, the Library of Congress, and the Division of Tax Research of the Treasury Department, and in war industries such as aircraft companies, electrical manufacturers, locomotive works, steel companies, and other engineering and scientific firms.[43] Such programs continued even during the full onset of the Sino-Japanese war as the Nationalists planned for postwar reconstruction. In 1944 and 1945, over 3,000 trainees from China arrived for both military and technical training in fields ranging from aeronautical engineering to telecommunications in over 350 U.S. companies.[44]

The contradictory coexistence of expanding services for international students alongside ongoing discrimination and segregation in America—and the powerful magnet of Chinese patriotism and its potential to modernize and save China—ensured that Chinese students remained oriented to their homeland through the late 1940s. Chinese students experienced daily discrimination and isolation, as captured in a survey of 125 Midwestern students conducted in 1932 and 1933. Tsung-kao Yieh's PhD dissertation, "The Adjustment Problems of Chinese Graduate Students in American Universities," reveals the profound nationalism binding Chinese students to their troubled homeland and their sense of alienation in the United States. High percentages complained of discrimination or the lack of meaningful interaction with Americans—with 81 percent encountering problems in "contacts with persons outside the university" and 77 percent even with "contacts with American students." The most significant problems, however, concerned financial constraints (89 percent) and the ongoing Sino-Japanese conflicts (90 percent).[45] The contrast between national purpose and national exclusion was so stark that during the mid-1930s even many American-born Chinese projected that their futures lay in China.[46]

The supremely acculturated and well-connected Meng Zhi demonstrates the fervor with which an American-educated Chinese worked on behalf of China. Meng deployed his visibility and contacts cultivated through the China Institute to encourage Americans and the United States to invest in Chinese education and students with the claim that, "Perhaps, in the history of international relations, no one nation of such magnitude as China has ever been culturally affected by another nation of a very different background to such an extent and so immediately." Using the *China Bulletin* as his platform, Meng reported constantly about educational developments in China, with particular focus on American-sponsored schools and programs such as St. John's College in Shanghai and Tsinghua College with their influential alumni cohorts. Although Meng acknowledged that it was unclear "Whether American education is entirely beneficial to Chinese students and through these students to China," he also emphasized "China's appreciation of American culture and her good will toward America."[47]

Throughout the 1930s, Meng ensured that the intensifying crisis of Japanese encroachments on China remained constantly in the American public eye through the *Bulletin*, but also radio shows, public appearances, and the 1932 publication, *China Speaks: On the Conflict between China and Japan* (MacMillan). In 1937, he detailed vividly the plight of China's approximately 50,000 university students, 8,547 of whom were enrolled in American-sponsored institutions, and the costs of schools and classrooms destroyed and the numbers of students displaced along with heroic efforts to reestablish institutions in areas remaining under Nationalist control. As the war rendered students in America destitute and homeless, Meng solicited emergency relief from American organizations such as the Rockefeller Brothers Fund, the Strong Foundation, and missionary groups. He drew upon connections to Secretary of State Cordell Hull and First Lady Eleanor Roosevelt to persuade the Department of State to allocate $500,000 in aid and was thereby able to gain a matching sum from the Chinese foreign minister, Song Ziwen.[48] Meng set up the Committee on Wartime Planning for Chinese Students in the United States in 1942 to allocate the funds, which by the end of World War II, had assisted about 4,700 Chinese students.[49]

From Students to Settlers

American knowledge of and sympathy for Chinese students, so effectively cultivated by Meng, readily evolved into willingness for them to resettle permanently in the United States when the abrupt and unanticipated outcomes of the Chinese civil war (1946–1949) concluded with the communist victory and establishing of the People's Republic of China under Mao Zedong's leadership. The original foreign relations strategy of educating Chinese in America so that they would leave to guide China in sympathy and imitation of the United States rapidly switched gears to prevent valuable human resources from falling into enemy hands. The particularly useful scientific, technical, and economic skills cultivated by this elite group of 5,000 to 12,000 Chinese students, trainees, and government representatives positioned them readily to remain and contribute to *America*'s economic, military, and cultural development, instead of China's.[50] As this group of "stranded students" lost their anticipated futures, contacts with family and friends, funds, citizenship status, and a place they could claim as a permanent home, the staff and trustees of the China Institute again took the lead in working with the Committee for Advisors of Foreign Students and the IIE to lobby "the leaders in the American Government and the State Department" concerning the immediate problems facing Chinese students cut off from funds, limited means of legal employment to support themselves, and no homes to which to return.

Beginning in March 1948, Congress acted to approve a series of legislation that provided a total of $10 million in funds, permission to remain and to seek legal employment.[51] Piecemeal refugee legislation enabled some Chinese to convert to permanent status, although this issue was not completely resolved for many until more permanent legal changes in the 1960s.[52] Many entered prestigious employment in universities and research firms, most notably the 1957 Nobel Prize winners Yang Zhenning and Li Zhengdao, the computer entrepreneur An Wang, and the architect I. M. Pei. Although others found their only options to be underemployment in restaurants and other forms of service work, they nonetheless became self-supporting and acceptable candidates for permanent residence and citizenship. In 1956, the Committee on Educational Interchange Policy issued a report assessing Congressional aid to Chinese students and described this shift in goals. "In retrospect, certainly, both humanitarian and national interests were well served." The students had completed their academic programs and many had become self-sufficient although still reporting the following problems: finding "satisfactory employment"; "the almost insoluble task of bringing their families from China"; and, above all, "a satisfactory adjustment of their immigration status is a paramount preoccupation." However, "unless Congress enacts further legislation . . . [many] may find themselves in a sort of legal limbo for years, technically subject to deportation because their student visas have long since expired, but, as long as China remains Communist, never to be forced to return."[53] Over the course of the 1950s and early 1960s, a piecemeal series of immigration reforms, focusing initially on refugee relief and culminating in the general overhaul of the 1965 Immigration Act, would enable all these highly educated and resourceful Chinese to resettle legally in America and sanction the entry of many more on the basis of employment criteria and economic needs in the United States. These legal and policy shifts regarding immigration priorities laid the foundations for the mid-1960s global crisis known as "brain drain" in which the educated elites of developing nations sought higher education in the industrialized First World, particularly the United States, where they were able to gain legal employment and choose not to return home. Although in the early twenty-first century the outcomes of "brain drain" have proven to be more circulatory rather than a zero-sum game of winners and losers in the competition for technical and scientific elites and economic development, the outcry and anxieties attending its emergence underscore the nationalist imperatives that dominate our understandings of student migrations and evaluations of their effects.

Y. C. Wang, author of the pioneering 1966 study *Chinese Intellectuals and the West*, claimed that "whatever their political affiliation, few Chinese observers believe that the movement to study abroad was a success."[54] However, Wang admitted the impossibility of the goals set for these programs: "the Chinese movement to study abroad failed primarily because of its misconceived and unattainable goal, which was no less than national rejuvenation and achievement of major-power status within the shortest possible time."[55] Wang was not alone in holding these expectations. In 1927, Y. S. Tsao, the president of Tsinghua University, questioned "Whether the Chinese student trained abroad is able to construct afterward a structure nobler and statelier [to govern China] than what he has torn down it remains to be seen."[56] If we measure the success of western educated and trained Chinese not by their failure to utterly transform China but by the degree of influence and status attained in shaping modern Chinese institutions in places like the PRC, Taiwan, Hong Kong, and Singapore, a far different understanding of international and intercultural connections emerges, in the entwining of national and institutional agendas enabled through the mobility of educated elites.

Internationally educated Chinese greatly enhanced their employability, particularly in government employment and education. In 1910, Wang tallied 82 Western-trained individuals in Beijing, with a half-dozen working as board presidents or vice presidents and others as councillors to boards, professors in government colleges, or directors of government departments. Many of the returned students ended up working in education. In 1917, of 340 returned students, 39 percent ranked education as the most important field of employment, followed by government at 32 percent.[57] According to a survey of the 1931 "Who's Who in China" by Herbert D. Lamson in an article in the *China Critic* (Feb. 16, 1933), of the 960 biographies of individuals included, 286 were educated in the United States, leading to the conclusion, "among the returned students from American colleges and universities may be found many of China's leading statesmen, her influential ambassadors and ministers to foreign countries, presidents of educational institutions, jurists and judges of international reputation, cabinet ministers, philosophers, scholars, scientists."[58]

In the Republican era, western-trained Chinese gained even more prominence. By 1939, an astonishing 71 percent of those listed in the government issued "Who's Who of China" had studied abroad, about 36 percent in the United States. This represented a sharp rise for American-educated Chinese from the 9.5 percent of 1916, but also a steep decline in the Japanese-educated from 33.7 percent in 1916 to 15.4 percent in 1939.[59] The efforts of the Republican administration to program international education and training for best advantage to economic planning coordinated through the National Resources Commission produced individuals who pursued influential careers, regardless of whether they returned to China or moved elsewhere. For example, the economic historian William Kirby conducted a case study of the first thirty-one engineers sent by the NRC in 1942 and found that these select and well-connected scientists and technicians became highly influential not only in China, but in various places of settlement. Twenty-one remained on the mainland, three in the United States, and seven went to Taiwan. Those in the PRC achieved "substantial careers in technical work" until the Cultural Revolution. Of the three taking up permanent residence in the United States, one became a shipping magnate and multimillionaire while the other two became "project engineering managers for multi-national companies." The seven that went to Taiwan in 1949 attained the most success, with one becoming a wealthy financier, three becoming presidents or chairmen of major state-run industries, and two receiving Cabinet assignments as Ministers of Economic Affairs, with one becoming Premier.[60]

*　*　*

This brief overview of the facilitated mobility and options for employment and settlement by Chinese *liuxuesheng* illuminates the very different values and outcomes associated with migration by educated elites whose internationally acknowledged credentials and adaptability render them highly advantageous assets to the nations in which they choose, or are allowed, to settle. They are further distinguished because their employment and activities are often instrumental in advancing international collaborations, such as diplomatic relations, international business, the operations of transnational projects such as missionary institutions, scientific research, technological innovation and expansion, trade and exchanges of various forms, and financial transactions. Thus, the principles of immigration controls applied to their mobility operate along a different set of rationales from that of less favored, less value-enhanced, working-class migrants that have received the bulk of attention from scholars of economics, labor, and migration. Educated migrants function as assets as demonstrated by post–World War II reforms of immigration laws in places such as Canada, Australia, and the United States, which seek to recruit for permanent resettlement such educated and professional elites.

As explored so cogently by Aihwa Ong in *Flexible Citizenship: The Cultural Logics of Transnationality*,[61] their heightened capacities for transnationality demonstrate the entwining of legal and institutional infrastructures directing migration flows with prevailing neoliberalist rationales that encourage their mobility as key agents enabling the globalization of economic and market forces. For these reasons, national prerogatives are undone particularly by the elite migrants whose mobility is most privileged by state policies. The very skills that made *liuxuesheng* so valuable in China's development also rendered them useful subjects in the United States. Even the great representative of Chinese interests, Meng Zhi, for example, found it easy to switch course once the communist victory in 1949 set China on an unacceptable path. He settled permanently in the United States where liberalizing legal and economic conditions provided greater scope for Asians, particularly those trained for technical, professional, and white-collar employment—such as the physicists Yang Zhenning and Li Zhengdao—to integrate more fully at last.[62]

From Taiwan, the Nationalist government continued to send *liuxuesheng* to the United States, but the numbers of Chinese students really took off with the thawing of relations between the United States and the PRC that began during the 1970s. Yang and Li were among the earliest visitors to return to their homeland and were instrumental in rebuilding relations through programs for educational and scientific exchange, as described in a report commissioned by the Committee on Scholarly Communications with the People's Republic of China, *Chinese Students in America: Policies, Issues, and Numbers* by Leo A. Orleans, and the anthology, *The Expanding Roles of Chinese Americans in U.S.-China Relations: Transnational Networks and Trans-Pacific Interactions*, edited by Peter Koehn and Xiaohuang Yin.[63] Yang and Li had gained transnational mobility through their education and internationally acknowledged credentials and standing as scientists, transnational capacities that they deployed in turn to promote opportunities for future generations to become educationally and economically enhanced individuals across transnational frames of operation. As assets and agents whose activities are most likely to promote globalization and international competitiveness, the mobility of educated elites such as *liuxuesheng* operate under conditions of enhanced transnationality that require us to examine not only the efforts of nation-states to limit the entry of unwanted migrants, but also to facilitate the entry and settlement of those with greater potential for advancing national interests.

NOTES

    1. Jonathan Spence, *The Search for Modern China* (New York: Norton, 1990), 122.
    2. See, for example, Wang Zuoye, "Transnational Science during the Cold War: The Case of Chinese/American Scientists," *Isis* 101 (2010): 367–377; Iris Chang, *Thread of the Silkworm* (New York: Basic Books, 1995); Y. C. Wang, *Chinese Intellectuals and the West, 1872–1949* (Chapel Hill: University of North Carolina Press, 1966); Weili Ye, *Seeking Modernity in China's Name* (Stanford: Stanford University Press, 2001); Stacey Bieler, *"Patriots" or "Traitors"? A History of*

American-Educated Chinese Students (New York: M. E. Sharpe, 2004); Liu Zhen et al., eds., *Liuxue Jiaoyu* (Taipei: Taiwan shudian, 1980); AnnaLee Saxenian, *The New Argonauts: Regional Advantage in a Global Economy* (Cambridge: Harvard University Press, 2006).

3. See Karen Sanchez-Eppler, "Copying and Conversion: An 1824 Friendship Album 'from a Chinese Youth,'" *American Quarterly* 59 (June 2007): 301–339, for a nuanced analysis of the nineteen-page friendship album produced by "Henry Martyn A'lan" in 1824.

4. Jessie Gregory Lutz, *China and the Christian Colleges, 1850–1950* (Ithaca: Cornell University Press, 1971), 27; Peter Tze-Ming Ng, *Changing Paradigms of Christian Higher Education in China, 1888–1950* (Lewiston, N.Y.: The Edwin Mellen Press, Ltd., 2002), 2.

5. Edward J. M. Rhoads, *Stepping Forth into the World: The Chinese Educational Mission to the United States, 1872–81* (Hong Kong: Hong Kong University Press, 2011), 2; Liu, *Liuxue Jiaoyu*; Wang, *Chinese Intellectuals*.

6. Zeng Laishun was actually the first Chinese to attend an American college in 1847 but did not graduate from Hamilton College in New York.

7. Yung Wing, *My Life in China and America* (New York: Henry Holt, 1909), 15.

8. Wang, *Chinese Intellectuals*, 74 [Wang's translation, Li Hongzhang, I-shu han-kao 1.19b-22a]. Also see Yung Wing's autobiography and Thomas La Fargue, *China's First One Hundred* (Pullman: State College of Washington, 1942); and Rhoads, *Stepping Forth*.

9. Wang, *Chinese Intellectuals*, 75.

10. In 1862, 1875, 1879, 1880, and 1882, Congress had passed a succession of immigration restrictions intended to severely restrict Chinese laborers from entering the United States.

11. Rhoads, *Stepping Forth*, 63.

12. Emma Teng, *Eurasian: Mixed Identities in the United States, China, and Hong Kong, 1842–1943* (Berkeley: University of California Press, 2013), 67–68. Also see Wang, *Chinese Intellectuals*, 95–97.

13. Yung Kwai married Mary Burnham and remained in the United States for the rest of his life with the status of a Chinese diplomat employed at the embassy in Washington, D.C. Four generations of the Young family have attended Yale University. Author's interview with Dana Young, November 15, 2012.

14. Rhoads, *Stepping Forth*, 222.

15. Quoted from "Reminiscences of a Pioneer Student" in Judy Yung, Gordon H. Chang, and Him Mark Lai, eds., *Chinese American Voices: From the Gold Rush to the Present* (Berkeley: University of California Press, 2006), 37. Also see Qian Ning, translated by T. K. Chu, *Chinese Students Encounter America* (Seattle: University of Washington Press, 2002), 16–17, for a more extensive list of CEM student accomplishments.

16. Wang, *Chinese Intellectuals*, 45, 48–49, 88.

17. Ibid., 52–53.

18. Bieler, *"Patriots" or "Traitors"?* 40. The absolute numbers of Chinese students in Japan remained greater than those going to the United States. Figures are somewhat sketchy, but, according to Wang, an estimated 34,081 Chinese studied in Japan between 1900 and 1937 whereas only 20,906 did so in the United States between 1854 and 1953. Wang, *Chinese Intellectuals*, 71; Liu, *Liuxue Jiaoyu*, 2636.

19. Michael H. Hunt, *The Making of a Special Relationship* (New York: Columbia University Press, 1983). Also see Delber McKee, *Chinese Exclusion versus the Open Door Policy 1900–1906: Clashes over China Policy in the Roosevelt Era* (Detroit: Wayne State University Press, 1977).

20. Akira Iriye, *Pacific Estrangement: Japanese and American Expansion, 1897–1911* (Cambridge: Harvard University Press, 1972), 122–123; Bieler, *"Patriots" or "Traitors"?* 44.

21. Liping Bu, *Making the World like Us: Education, Cultural Expansion, and the American Century* (Westport, Conn.: Praeger, 2003), 24.

22. Cited in Bieler, *"Patriots" or "Traitors"?* 41. Also see Michael C. Hunt, "The American Remission of the Boxer Indemnity: A Reappraisal," *Journal of Asian Studies* 31:3 (May 1972): 549–550.

23. W. W. Yen, "The Chinese Student's View," *Overland Monthly* (May 1911): 499, in Him Mark Lai Collection, U.C. Berkeley Ethnic Studies Library, AAS/ARC 2000/80 44:3. Yen or Yan Huiqing served as premier in several different Chinese government administrations.

24. These estimates are unreliable because neither the United States nor the Chinese government kept systematic records until the 1920s. For example, in the five volumes of *Liuxue Jiaoyu* (Overseas education) edited by Liu Zhen, of the sixteen tables in the appendixes in Volume V that provide information about numbers, majors, gender, levels, and schools of graduation in China and abroad, eight concern students in the United States alone whereas only six table document levels and types of activity in other major foreign destinations such as Japan, Germany, and England. See Volume V.

25. Liu, *Liuxue Jiaoyu* (5), 2635, Table 3.2. Other countries hosting smaller numbers of students included England, Germany, France, Italy, Australia, Canada, and Egypt. Statistics for international students during this time are highly unreliable with both American and Chinese organizations relying on self-reporting.

26. Anecdotally, students educated in Japan were associated with republican revolutionaries, Europe communists, and—in the United States—the Nationalist party.

27. Liu, *Liuxue Jiaoyu* (5), 2627, Table 2.3, which draws on Bureau of Education statistics covering 1917 through 1921.

28. Jiang Menglin (Chiang Monlin), *Tides from the West: A Chinese Autobiography* (New Haven: Yale University Press, 1947).

29. Weili Ye, *Seeking Modernity in China's Name: Chinese Students in the United States, 1900–1927* (Palo Alto: Stanford University Press, 2001), 53–55.

30. Wang, *Chinese Intellectuals*, 99.

31. Hongshan Li, *U.S.-China Educational Exchange: State, Society, and Intercultural Relations, 1905–1950* (Newark: Rutgers University Press, 2008), 78–85.

32. As an influential literary scholar and diplomat, Hu Shi was one of the leaders of the May Fourth Movement and the New Culture Movement. Together with the linguist Zhao Yuanren, who traveled around China researching various dialects and developed the first Romanized pronunciation system for Chinese, Hu advocated use of vernacular in the writing of Chinese literature.

33. "Chinese Higher Education: A Brief Report," *China Institute in America Bulletin* 4:1 (October 1939): 1.

34. Ng, *Changing Paradigms*, 6.

35. Ibid., 5.

36. Other governments, including Japan and Britain, imitated the United States in remitting their Boxer funds channeled into scholarships.

37. "China Institute Founded with Second Boxer Fund," *New York Times*, Dec. 19, 1926.

38. Li, *U.S.-China Educational Exchange*, 99–102, 110.

39. "China Institute Asks Charter in Jersey," *New York Times*, Jan. 25, 1930.

40. The Institute's other key function was to educate Americans about Chinese culture and contemporary affairs to provide some balance for the extensive exposure of Chinese to knowledge about America through missionary, trade, and study in the United States. The Institute provided lists of publications about China, maintained a roster of speakers, advised about starting libraries and Chinese studies programs, and other cultural resources about China. The Institute continues to perform many of these functions today.

41. Meng Zhi, *Chinese American Understanding: A Sixty-Year Quest* (New York: China Institute of America, 1981), 104.

42. *China Institute Bulletin*, 3 (Oct. 1938): 31.

43. Wilma Fairbank, *America's Cultural Experiment in China, 1942–1949* (Washington, D.C.: Bureau of Cultural and Educational Affairs, U.S. Department of State, 1976), 116; Committee on Foreign Relations among Foreign Students, *Unofficial Ambassadors* (1946), 7, and (1947), 6.

44. *Unofficial Ambassadors* (1945), 9–10. Almost as many trainees from Latin America arrived through this program.

45. Tsung-kao Yieh, "The Adjustment Problems of Chinese Graduate Students in American Universities," PhD Dissertation, University of Chicago Divinity School, 1934, 35.

46. See Gloria Chun's discussion of the 1936 Ging Hawk Club essay contest in *Of Orphans and Warriors: Inventing Chinese American Culture and Identity* (Newark: Rutgers University Press, 2000), 21–24.

47. Meng Zhi, "The American Returned Students of China," *Pacific Studies* 4 (Jan. 1931): 1–16.

48. Meng, *Chinese American Understanding*, 184–186. Also see Wang, *Chinese Intellectuals*, 137–138.

49. Meng, *Chinese American Understanding*, 189; *China Institute in America Bulletin* 6 (July 1942): 1.

50. Shih-shan Henry Tsai, *The Chinese Experience in America* (Bloomington: Indiana University Press, 1986), 120–121. The China Institute of America tracked the total numbers of Chinese students: 1943–1944, 706; 1944–1945, 823; 1945–1946, 1,298; 1946–1947, 1,678; 1947–1948, 2,310; 1948–1949, 3,914. Tsai, *Chinese Experience in America*, 122; Meng, *Chinese American Understanding*, 224. Although 5,000 is the number cited in most Asian American and immigration history texts, Meng estimates that by 1949, about 12,000 Chinese had "managed to escape to the United States."

51. Committee on Educational Interchange Policy, *Chinese Students in the United States, 1948–55: A Study in Government Policy* (New York: np, 1956), 7–8; Walter H. Judd Collection 72:7, Sponsored Legislation/81st Congress Aid to Chinese Students (H.R. 5495), 1949–1955; *China Institute Bulletin* (Nov. 1949), 5–6.

52. See Madeline Y. Hsu, "The Disappearance of America's Cold War Chinese Refugees," *Journal of American Ethnic History* 31 (Summer 2012): 12–33.

53. Cited in *Chinese Students in the United States, 1948–55*, 13–14.

54. Wang, *Chinese Intellectuals*, xiii. Wang systematically complained that the discrediting of Confucianism had produced an "amoral elite." See xi.

55. Wang, *Chinese Intellectuals*, xiii. Wang criticizes calls to completely abandon Chinese tradition and westernize. See 93.

56. Y. S. Tsao, the president of Tsinghua University, contributed "A Challenge to Western Learning: The Chinese Student Trained Abroad—What He Has Accomplished—His Problems" in the *News Bulletin* of the Institute of Pacific Relations (Dec. 1927), 13–16.

57. Wang found generally that most foreign-educated Chinese did not find employment in China that matched their training. For example, engineers comprised about 25 percent of the total but mostly went into education and government service. Wang identified Zhan Tianyou (Jeme Tienyou) as "the only CEM student to fulfill the goals of foreign study as set forth by the government" in becoming a railway engineer and "prototype of the technician-official that became prevalent in later decades." Wang, *Chinese Intellectuals*, 75, 79–80.

58. China Institute in America, *A Survey of Chinese Students in American Universities and Colleges in the Past One Hundred Years* (New York: China Institute in America, 1954), 21.

59. Wang, *Chinese Intellectuals*, 117.

60. William Kirby, "Continuity and Change in Modern China: Economic Planning on the Mainland and on Taiwan, 1943–1958," *Australian Journal of Chinese Affairs* 24 (July 1990): 139–141.

61. Aihwa Ong, *Flexible Citizenship: The Cultural Logics of Transnationality* (Durham: Duke University Press, 1999).

62. The 1965 Immigration Act cemented these changes in immigration conditions for Asians. See Madeline Y. Hsu, *The Good Immigrants: How the Yellow Peril Became the Model Minority* (Princeton: Princeton University Press, 2015).

63. Leo A. Orleans, *Chinese Students in America: Policies, Issues, and Numbers* (Washington, D.C.: National Academy Press, 1988) and Peter Koehn and Xiaohuang

Yin, eds., *The Expanding Roles of Chinese Americans in U.S.-China Relations: Transnational Networks and Trans-Pacific Interactions* (Armonk, N.Y.: M. E. Sharpe, 2002). According to UNESCO data, in 2012 China produced the most international students by far, with 694,400 going abroad to study, compared to only 189,500 Indians in the next most active country. The United States was the destination of choice for Chinese international students, followed by Japan, Australia, and the United Kingdom. UNESCO Institute for Statistics, Education. www.uis.unesco.org/Education/Pages/international-student-flow-viz.aspx (accessed July 15, 2015).

PART II
IMMIGRANTS AND THE
PERIODIZATION OF
TRANSNATIONALISM

CHAPTER 6

Transnationalism, States' Influence, and the Political Mobilizations of the Arab Minority in Canada

Houda Asal
Translated from the French by Sarah Abel

The Arab presence in Canada remains a topic that historians have yet to fully to explore, with still fewer having examined the history of its politicization.[1] In line with the new questions posed in this book, this chapter seeks to identify the sources of Arab political mobilizations from the 1920s through the late 1970s, paying particular attention to influence exercised by states and political controversies emanating from the region of origin. Minority political engagement has depended upon the interweaving of various factors: the heterogeneity of migrants' national and religious origins, intergenerational gaps produced by different migratory waves, the resources of collective organizations, ideological divergences and the difficulty of a unitary identification, and the political strategies favored in one period or another. In addition to these aspects—which may be qualified as internal factors, and which played an important role in the cycles of mobilizations—this chapter aims to highlight the importance of external factors, which new studies of transnationalism have set out to explore. By placing the mobilizations into their historical contexts, this chapter intends to stress the role played by states of origin in the political lives of migrants and their descendants, the influence of international relations between the Arab world and Canada in the ways in which the Canadian government perceived demands from Arab associations, and finally the impact of the representations and practices of the Canadian state toward Arab activists.

This chapter looks at how questions of politics and identity were mingled and evolved throughout the period under study. The history of political mobilization of the Arab minority[2] in Canada shows that members of this group primarily organized to reject the racial category in which they were included in the early twentieth century. Populations from the Machrek[3] were considered "Asian," which greatly restricted their admission into Canada. The strategies they then developed in order to change both the categorization that had a direct impact on their mobility and on their image in society depended not only on their ability to mobilize, but also on how they reclaimed these "racial" and "identity" categories. After 1945, identity continued to mix with politics as organizations of the Arab minority rallied in favor of a transnational "cause." The Palestinian cause became theirs because they themselves identified as Arabs. In addition to being an interesting case of loyalty that does not directly correspond to national state borders, this form of political mobilization questions the scale of transnational analyses, between the local and the global, when it comes to thinking about the roles of states in history, be it the impact of countries of origin on their diasporas, or that of countries of residence on their minorities.

Temporality, States, Nationalism, and Transnationalism

The *Century of Transnationalism* project—as with other attempts to rethink the concept of transnationalism[4]—seeks to demonstrate the impact of historical change upon practices of transnationalism by emphasizing the role of state politics and a comparative perspective in time and space. The case of the Arab minority in Canada during the twentieth century shows how historical changes in transnational activities could occur due to the changing roles of states, either through their absence or their influence, upon the political mobilizations of migrants and their descendants. An analysis of their activities has the advantage of highlighting different types of transnational links while accentuating the relationships between country of origin and country of destination over the long term.

In addition to taking a long-term perspective, ultimately the interweaving of histories, levels, and internal and external factors is indispensable to the analysis. Furthermore, the overlapping of scales can demonstrate the influence of states at the national level (Canadian politics vis-à-vis those of the Arab minority, and the actions of countries of origin regarding their diasporas); interactions, power struggles and politics between states of origin and states of settlement on an international level; and also the rivalries between different diasporas in the same country at the local level.[5]

Just as Cecilia Baeza has shown in her research on Palestinians in Latin America, this "question of scale proves to be extraordinarily revealing about the articulation of the local and the global on a complex world political scene."[6] The links between Canada, Great Britain, the United States, and the Arab world demonstrate the developments in international relations over time and the complexity of the geopolitical stakes that have influenced Canada's position in relation to its minorities on the local level. Lastly, the interest shown by countries of origin in their expatriates has likewise evolved over time and may have influenced the Arab migrants' capacity for mobilization in Canada.[7]

Therefore, relations between states have affected the capacity of immigrants and their descendants to become engaged in activities linking "here" to "there." Likewise, state relations have influenced the existence of multiple loyalties versus exclusively national loyalties. Roger Waldinger recalls that this double loyalty becomes an issue when tensions exist between migrants' countries of origin and of residence, particularly when migrants become engaged in concerted action that exceeds state borders.[8] Migrants and their descendants can build upon different visions of "community," going beyond loyalties relating to a specific place of origin or an ethnic or national "group,"[9] as in the case of the Arab minority and the Palestinian cause. It should be noted that migrants and their descendants do not feel "automatic" loyalty toward their "country of origin"; they may sometimes feel indifferent toward the latter or even reject all nationalist involvement, which gives rise to internal divisions and may explain the weakness of actions at certain periods.[10]

As Donna Gabaccia has shown in her recent book on the influence of migrants on U.S. policy (and vice versa), the international relations of migrants may sometimes extend to the public sphere in the form of political actions whose objectives are not always national. At times they aim to influence the politics of their state of residence with regards to their country of origin, or to influence immigration policies that affect the lives and trajectories of their parents/friends.[11] These two aspects constituted the major aims of the actions of Canada's Arab minority: to change Canadian immigration policy and to influence Canada's foreign policy in relation to the Arab world.

Links with the Region of Origin: The First Mobilizations of Arab Migrants in Canada (before 1950)

The "Pioneers": The Context of Arrival of the First Arab Migrants

The first Arab migrants, entering Canada at the end of the nineteenth century, came from the Ottoman Empire, in particular, that area then known as Greater Syria (now consisting of modern-day Lebanon, Syria, Palestine, and southern Turkey).[12] Their arrival occurred in the context of a broader emigration from the Ottoman Empire, converging on the Americas, in which origins in the Middle East and destinations in the Americas were tightly linked, and chain migrations, leading out from certain villages, produced a specific migration flow in each country of the Americas. In much of the western hemisphere, Maronites from Lebanon comprised the most numerous group; in Chile and Peru, however, chain migration from Palestine proved dominant.[13] By contrast, the first migrants to arrive in Canada originated in villages located in what later would become Lebanon; mainly Christians, they were of different denominations, of which the most numerous were Greek Orthodox, followed by Melchites and then Maronites. A Muslim chain migration, much smaller than the Christian inflow, began at the beginning of the twentieth century, with these migrants settling mainly in the Canadian West.[14] Arab pioneers, the majority of whom were poorly educated Christian peasants who worked as door-to-door peddlers and tradesmen upon their arrival in Canada, spread out across the whole territory. By around 1930, the Canadian Arab population numbered about 10,000–15,000 people, comprised of the first generation of pioneers and their descendants.[15] From 1908 onward, Canada multiplied its measures to restrict immigration, creating categories of "unwanted" migrants: the destitute, the sick, and criminals, but also "immigrants belonging to any race deemed unsuited to the climate or requirements of Canada."[16]

New arrivals from the Machrek, who were included in the "Asian" category in Canadian immigration statistics—a category that was particularly "unwanted" and targeted by the new laws—became progressively less and less numerous; returns to their home countries often became definitive. The Arab minority nonetheless became progressively well established and an organizational dynamic could be observed; churches and associations were consolidated, newspapers were born, and political demands multiplied.

Studies on transnationalism have focused particularly upon the links between the first generation of migrants and their countries of origin. At the turn of the twentieth century, exchanges in the form of visits to the home countries were limited, due to the length and cost of the journey, but above all due to the closure of the Canadian borders. We argue that, nonetheless, different manifestations of concern linked to the fate of the countries of origin continued over time. But, if early Arab-oriented organizations were undoubtedly composed essentially of first-wave immigrants, as indicated by their use of the Arabic language and their attachment to villages of origin, subsequent organizations and newspapers became oriented toward first-wave immigrants as well as their descendants, publishing in English in order to reach the latter and becoming more broadly interested in their region of origin. At the same time, campaigns were carried out, principally by descendants of migrants who were well acquainted with Canada's political mechanisms, in order to contest the migratory restrictions that were affecting the admission of their compatriots to Canada.

Aid via Hometown Associations

Accounts from the early period of migration confirm that individual migrants were sending money back to their family in the home countries. However, by the second decade of the twentieth century, the organization of aid became collective and formalized. The first trace of an interest shown toward countries of origin involved the development of aid organizations for the pioneers' villages of origin, such as the Brotherhood Society of Ain Hershey, founded in 1916, and the Aid Association for the People of Rashaya founded in 1926. The latter attempted to gain a national base through representatives in numerous Canadian cities as well as some in the United States. The association communicated with a committee in Rashaya in order to know exactly what the village needed, and records were kept entirely in Arabic, proof that these were first generation migrants, who still communicated in the language of their country of origin and had direct links with relatives remaining in the village.[17] Yet their descendants would have difficulty in continuing to communicate and especially to write in Arabic; few schools taught Arabic, and the association's publications appear in English from the 1930s–1940s on.

The First Mobilizations in Favor of Countries of Origin

Other forms of ties to the countries of origin, however, involving newspapers as well as political activities, began to manifest themselves with the advent of the second generation. Up until this period, the community organizations were still largely in their infancy, and the collective life of the Arab minority was mainly confined to churches. It was not until the 1930s that Arab organizations (such as the Syrian Canadian Association) and newspapers became permanent fixtures and not until the 1940s that political action became significant.

Newspapers published by the Arab minority included news from the Machrek (*The Syrian Canadian Review* or *The Syrian Lebanese Mercury*). After the Ottoman Empire was defeated in 1918 and the Empire dismantled, the successor territories were assigned to the European powers in the form of mandates of the League of Nations, with the aim of facilitating eventual transitions toward independence. However, the mandatory powers often confronted resistance on the ground. In Syria and Lebanon, the French mandatory power faced nationalist movements of different natures, some demanding an independent, Christian Mount Lebanon whereas others favored a united Syria. In Palestine, the situation was more fraught for the British mandatory power, which faced demands for Palestinian Arab independence alongside Zionist demands for a Jewish homeland in Palestine.

While the French mandatory power, in its capacity as the "protectoral" power for the Lebanese and Syrian populations, openly encouraged Lebanese nationalist organizations abroad, particularly in South America and the United States, these efforts remained extremely limited and almost invisible in Canada.[18] In 1937, discussions within the French Ministry of External Affairs raised the possibility of a consular position with responsibility for the Lebanese population across Canada, but the idea was rejected because the community was too dispersed across the country.[19] However, the reports of the French consuls in Canada suggest that another reason for rejecting the creation of such a post was due to the predominance of Greek Orthodox among the Arab community in Canada, who were less favorable to the French mandate authorities. Those reports described the Orthodox as little inclined to approach the French consulate, which had more contacts with the Catholic Lebanese, the Orthodox being closer to the Anglophone Canadians.[20] The fact that Maronites were a minority among the first Arab immigrants in Canada explains also why the reference to any Phoenician identity was almost totally absent from the archives of the period studied here.[21]

The immigrants' concern for their region of origin occasionally took the form of political action, particularly during the period of independence struggles in Syria and Lebanon from 1943 to 1945. During the Second World War, Canadian Arab organizations and churches stood alongside the French in opposition to Nazi Germany, demonstrating themselves to have taken the side of the mandatory power but also that of their country of citizenship, since migrants born in Canada were of British nationality.[22] This support, however, was not unshakable. At the end of 1943 and again in spring 1945, Canadian Arabs sent letters to the Canadian Prime Minister Mackenzie King in protest against French policy in Lebanon and Syria. This period, preceding the two countries' declarations of independence, was marked by significant clashes in Lebanon in 1943 and Syria in 1945. The signatories of letters of protest against France's violence in the two countries stated that Lebanon and Syria were the countries of their ancestors.[23] Thus, the position of Canadian Arabs became complex: in their capacity as British citizens, their allegiance was to Great Britain, but as Syrians and Lebanese, they denounced the French mandate, declaring themselves in favor of the independence of their countries of origin. During the 1940s, they at once affirmed their loyalty for a France allied to Great Britain and occupied by Germany, and yet against a France in support of Syrian and Lebanese independence, and finally against the British actions in Palestine, when those actions did not support Palestinian self-determination.

It should be noted that these extremely limited actions had no political impact whatsoever, although they demonstrate where the divergent loyalties lay of a minority that found itself at the center of complex international conflicts among several states. These actions also show the important part played by international relations in the political mobilizations of migrants and their descendants. By the time Lebanon and Syria had acquired their independence, it was their weight among the family of nations and the interest they expressed, or not, toward their diaspora that need to be taken into account in cases such as the campaign of Arab organizations against Canadian restrictive immigration laws.

Immigrants Fighting for Their Rights in Canada (1913 to 1950)

Between 1908 and 1930, various laws progressively restricted admission for new migrants arriving from Asia: one regulation demanded that all immigrants arrive in Canada without stopovers, with a ticket bought in their country of origin (a restriction that indirectly targeted immigrants from Asia because they always had to make such a stopover on their way to America); another stipulated explicitly that Asians needed to possess $200 upon their arrival in Canada. In 1930, a new ban was placed on the admission of any migrant "from any Asiatic race," except for spouses and children of Canadian citizens or residents.[24]

From 1913 onward, Arab organizations contested these measures, at the behest of members hailing from a petty bourgeoisie of businessmen and professionals, often born in Canada. The fact that they were classified as "Asians" had consequences for their reputation, prevented the eventual reuniting of families, and resulted in a negative image that negated their efforts to become assimilated and wounded their sense of loyalty to the Canadian nation.[25] Between 1913 and 1945, high-ranking officials from the Department of Immigration met with different representatives of Arab organizations in order to discuss their demands to be withdrawn from the "Asian" category. However, the fact that their actions were not well coordinated, a failure aggravated by the recession of the 1930s, may explain the weakness of their protest.[26] Besides, as stated above, the French mandatory power in Lebanon and Syria took no interest in the small community that had taken root in Canada, and perhaps hoped to avoid intervening at all in Canadian (and therefore indirectly British) affairs.[27] The absence of any intervention by the "country of origin," namely the French mandate, can thus be explained by the latter's lack of interest in its "protégés" in Canada in particular, because they were neither influential nor receptive to the defense of French interests. What was to become of such interventions when Lebanon and Syria became independent states (1943–1946)?

The campaign against anti-Asian laws was relaunched in 1946, at the initiative of the Lebanese consul in Washington (appointed in 1945). In a letter sent to Canadian authorities, the consul expressed his concern regarding the migratory controls targeting the Lebanese in Canada. This first political action of the Lebanese state in defense of its nationals abroad was taken up by the first Lebanese consul in Ottawa, newly appointed in May 1947, who described the inclusion of the Lebanese in the "Asian race" as "unfair morally and incorrect scientifically."[28]

In its response, the Canadian Immigration Bureau recognized that "Near Easterners" were indeed not of the "Asian race" but that the restrictive laws nevertheless targeted migrants originating in the Asian continent. The Lebanese consul took part once more in the campaign by joining a delegation of Arab associations that met the Minister of Immigration in March 1949.[29] Although the Lebanese consulate continued the campaign, it lacked the weight needed to pursue the issue effectively. Nonetheless, these diplomatic initiatives undertaken by the young state, which were perceived benevolently by the Canadian authorities, remain significant as indicators of the first political involvement of the Lebanese state in favor of its diaspora in Canada.[30]

Mobilizations Linked to the Palestinian Issue, a Long-standing Transnational Cause

The historiography often presents 1967 as the birth date of international mobilizations in solidarity with the Palestinian people, both in Europe and America. Undeniably, the international impact and consequences of the Six-Day War inaugurated a new period in international awareness of the demands of the Palestinian people and the fate of the Palestinian refugees. However, as some studies show, different forms of mobilizations took place before 1967, mainly in opposition to plans for a Jewish state in Palestine. In the United States, various voices had spoken out against the Zionist project after the Balfour declaration of 1917, leading to the creation of the Palestine Antizionism Society, which would later become the Palestine National League.[31] In Canada, by contrast, the archives reveal no trace of any political action taken in this respect until the mid-1940s, when publicly expressed concerns linked to the Palestinian issue emerged simultaneously with the international debates on the partition of Palestine and the creation of a Jewish state.[32] The Canadian example was specific in various respects: the history of the Arab minority in the country, Canada's geopolitical position, the roles of the countries of origin, and the power struggles at the local level between different minorities (in this case, Arab and Jewish). This case study of mobilizations in defense of the Palestinian cause in Canada, from 1945 to 1975, allows us to fill in a historiographical gap while highlighting the conditions of emergence and evolution of a collective mobilization over the long term. The actions that developed before 1967 prefigured a movement in gestation that would later be reactivated.[33]

The Emergence of the "Palestinian Cause": Internal and External Factors

An entirely new stage in international relations emerged after 1945 with the birth of the United Nations and the League of Arab States, the emergence of new independent states (Lebanon, Syria, and Iraq) in the former mandatory territories and the creation of the State of Israel in 1948. It was within this context that the first actions in solidarity with Palestine occurred in Canada, involving one association, the Canadian Arab Friendship League (CAFL), its newspaper *The Canadian Arab*, and the notable engagement of its president: Muhammad Saïd Massoud.

Formed in 1944, the CAFL took on a political objective that gave it a very particular place in the history of Arab collective action in Canada; it embodied the first series of actions and discourse concerning a cause that would become increasingly important over the following years. Up until that time, although the explosive situation in Palestine was mentioned in the Arab minority's newspapers in Canada, the centrality of the Palestinian issue was not particularly prevalent, especially given that new migrants who might bring with them the debates that were developing in their region of origin were still struggling to enter Canada. Moreover, the first mobilizations were brought about by Muhammad Massoud, an atypical figure at the heart of the minority that had taken root in Canada. A Druze Lebanese businessman, he had arrived in Montreal as an adolescent. His interest in international affairs and pan-Arabist discourse made him a trailblazer. However, as certain activists began to join him in his actions, he struggled to work as part of a team and to foster a collective dynamic around his organization.

Aside from these factors internal to the Arab population in Canada, the national context on the one hand and the international context on the other seemed equally unfavorable. Thus, neither the government nor the press paid much attention to the actions of the CAFL, proving far more responsive to the better coordinated more numerous contacts of the Jewish organizations, whose support for the partition of Palestine prevailed.[34] Research by political scientists Houchang Hassan-Yari and Janice Stein, comparing the associational scene among the Jewish and Arab populations, has noted the importance of the organizations defending Zionism on the level of Canadian politics and media as contrasted to the weakness of the "poorly organized and ineffectual" Arab camp: while a dozen publications and several associations defending Zionist demands between 1907 and 1954 increasingly benefited from significant support in Ottawa, the CAFL and its newspaper were the only source of information about the Arab point of view at that time.[35] The Canadian authorities appeared largely favorable to the solution of partitioning Palestine and therefore unreceptive to Arab demands such as those defended by the CAFL, which promoted the independence of an Arab Palestinian state.[36] This conflict thus brought two minorities face to face, each defending "its camp" and attempting to influence Canadian foreign policy on the Middle East, though on very unequal grounds. Throughout these years, the archives show no evidence of direct confrontation between the two groups, but rather their parallel lobbying attempts.

On the international level, if organizations favorable to the creation of a Jewish state in Palestine were able to make political authorities aware of their cause, it was because their demands were in accordance with Canada's desire to play a role on the international scene, by taking up a position in relation to Great Britain and the United States and by making its voice heard at the heart of the nascent UN.[37] In February 1947, after various mediation attempts in order to resolve the conflict in Palestine, the issue was put back into the hands of the UN, which commissioned the UNSCOP (United Nations Special Committee on Palestine), in the hope that it would propose an equitable solution. Canada was one of eleven state members meant to be "neutral" in the conflict. Although in 1945 Prime Minister Mackenzie King, faithful to the British standpoint, had shown himself to be skeptical with regards to the Zionist demands, Canada would eventually play a very significant role in promoting the solution of partitioning Palestine into two states and apparently played the role of architect at UNSCOP in terms of drawing the borders, considered advantageous to the Jewish side.[38] Subsequently, the efficacy of Lester B. Pearson, then Undersecretary of State for External Affairs, permitted Canada to weigh in once more upon debates regarding the elaboration of a solution that would be voted upon by the UN. Pearson managed to satisfy Zionist demands while also reconciling

Anglo-American-Soviet viewpoints concerning partition.[39] Some Zionist Canadians purportedly nicknamed Pearson "Canada's Balfour," considering that "if Balfour gave the Jews a homeland, Pearson has given them a State."[40] On November 29, 1947, the UN's General Assembly voted Resolution 181, "recommending" the partition of Palestine.

Extremely critical of the UN's stance on the matter and of Canada's role in this failure for the Palestinians and the Arab nation, from the 1950s through the 1970s Massoud pursued his political activity, focusing on the defense of Arab nationalist ideas and the right of return for Palestinian refugees. A source close to Massoud considers that he had "created an Arab embassy all by himself!"[41] On behalf of the CAFL, Massoud wrote directly to political authorities, particularly to Lester B. Pearson, Secretary of State for External Affairs (1948–1957), then Prime Minister of Canada (1963–1968), with whom he exchanged an abundant correspondence that he would later make public.[42]

The Indifference of States of Origin Regarding Canada's Biases toward Certain Activists and Certain Arab States

What became of the interventions of the home countries—the other side of the transnational equation—during the 1950s–1960s? Except for the Lebanese legations' involvement at the time of the campaign against immigration restriction in 1946–1947, the role of Lebanon (the country of origin of the largest number of Canadian Arabs) was extremely limited. Indeed, Lebanese diplomats were content with attending ceremonies, banquets, and social meetings. The World Lebanese Cultural Union (WLCU), created by the Lebanese government to promote activities for its nationals abroad, mainly organized cultural events. Aside from some charitable actions, such as a fundraiser for Palestinian refugees after the war of 1967, the embassy's political activities remained limited, perhaps because the means were lacking, the political vision was absent, and interest in Canada's Lebanese populations—far removed and few in number—was missing. Regarding the question of Palestine in particular, Lebanon was not a central actor on the international scene and did not seek to encourage mobilizations in support of the Palestinian cause, whether in Lebanon or abroad. (It must be recalled that the country harbored a significant population of Palestinian refugees, who could be a potential source of instability.)

Of course, it is imperative to point out that the nonexistence of a Palestinian state likewise explains why this pan-Arab cause could be pursued only by those states in the region with a real desire or capacity to defend this cause. Ultimately, the weak influence of Arab countries' representations in

Canada had an impact upon association dynamics. In the 1950s and the 1960s, secular associations were struggling to cope with the heterogeneity of the Arab presence in Canada, especially since they did not always have a place to gather and therefore were less visible and less established than the oriental churches built by the first Arab generations. While old associations had some difficulty in integrating recent migrants, newly emerging organizations benefited from the flow of new migrants to create a local dynamic in some cities; however, this added to the fragmentation of the Arab associations at the national Canadian level. In the early 1960s, new organizations interested in the Palestinian cause emerged, such as the Canadian Friends of the Middle East, born in 1960, replaced by the Canadian Arab Friendship Society (CAFS) in 1962. If CAFS in Toronto succeeded in linking community representatives of the older generation and newcomers, its difficulty in associating with Massoud prevented its creating a bridge between the two generations.[43] For the Arab associative world, the challenge entailed maintaining or creating links beyond informal networks and churches, between provinces, between generations, and between different organizations and their representatives. On the one hand, since they were not subordinate to the political orientation of any one state in particular, Arab mobilizations remained autonomous, which explained their margin of freedom but also their internal divisions. On the other hand, Arab associations could count on only their own resources, which proved to be limited, as states were not making funds available to support their diasporas' political activities. Thus, this pattern stands in contrast to the experience of Turks; through financing and support of associations defending Turkey's standpoints, as Sirma Bilge has shown, the Turkish embassy in Canada participated in the development of politically oriented organizations rather than cultural, charitable, or educational associations, resulting in an over-politicization of the community. In the Turkish case, this interest from the country of origin was linked to its desire to counter criticisms from other minorities in Canada, in particular the Greeks.[44]

As for Canada, the country hoped to preserve an image of equilibrium in the region, maintaining a privileged friendship with Israel while promoting stability and peace in the Middle East. As soon as these stakes were threatened, the government became closely interested in certain Arab activists. The media exposure and visibility of the CAFL in the public sphere began to interest the Ministry of External Affairs in 1954, the year in which it opened a special dossier on the organization.[45] By the time Massoud traveled to the Middle East in 1959, the Canadian authorities were interested in his activities, going so far as to monitor his appearances in the media and his meetings with Arab political authorities, for fear of "bad publicity." This trip demonstrated that Massoud was searching for support and a response to his efforts in favor of the Arab cause, activities that Canada feared would ruin its reputation in the region.[46] A reading of the Canadian government's reports regarding the CAFL demonstrates the hostility aroused by Massoud, whom they described as "stubborn": they regretted that the long correspondence he had kept up with Pearson had not diminished his determination or "the violence of his attacks and his extremist position."[47]

Pearson himself signed the internal memo on his meeting with Massoud in February 1955, an unpublished document in which he compared Massoud's position to that of another Lebanese man he met with the same day and whom he considered more reasonable, having "shown as much objectivity as any Arab could ever expect to show," while Massoud was "obviously more emotional and Arab on these problems." This perception of Massoud and of his extremism linked to his origins also provoked the hostility of the Lebanese legation in Canada; when questioned about Massoud, the Lebanese consul in Ottawa described him as a threat.[48] The Lebanese consulate seems to have served more as an informer to the Canadian government regarding the "community" than as an aid to its organization, a pattern consistent with Canada's view of Lebanon as a "moderate, relatively pro-Western state, not intransigent regarding the boycott of Israel."[49]

However, Canada was also concerned about other, albeit not too influential, Arab diplomatic groups. Thus, in 1957, the League of Arab States planned to open an information center in Ottawa. Immediately, the Israeli legation contacted the Ministry of External Affairs to voice its fears that the center would serve to promote the boycott of Israel. Canada therefore decided to monitor the center's activities, although the fact that the Arab League's envoy would be linked to the Lebanese legation reassured the authorities. Established in 1958, the Arab Information Centre's actions were actually limited to the dissemination of news and the presence of one representative, who would nevertheless be put under surveillance by Canadian authorities, to prevent him from spreading "anti-Zionist propaganda."[50] Thus, the low profile of the Arab League envoys stood in striking contrast to the role played by the Israeli diplomatic missions whose fears were taken seriously by Canada, which was also wary of the potential intelligence activity possibly undertaken by an envoy of the Arab League.[51]

Thus, international relations and the hostility inspired in the Canadian authorities by Arab demands, certain Arab states, and collective action, probably played a part in the difficulty experienced by Arab activists in

Canada in engaging in political mobilization and making themselves heard. In this respect, the opportunity structure for political transnational activity was hardly propitious for Arab activists from the 1950s up until the 1970s, when the situation would become even less favorable, as suspicions of terrorism bore down on them.

The Overlapping of International Relations and Local Issues: The Difficulties for Arab Mobilization after 1967

The Context Surrounding the Birth of the Canadian Arab Federation (CAF)

Between 1950 and 1975, the Arab community's activities developed due to the Arab population's renewal in Canada. Thanks to less restrictive immigration rules, skilled migrants, some with no ties to the previous migration chains, were admitted, which explains the diversification of countries of provenance and of migrants' socioeconomic profiles.

The composition of the new secular associations demonstrated the ongoing presence of community leaders who had been active in the 1930s–1940s and who continued to play the role of intermediaries, such as James Peters and Habeeb Salloum, who had edited Arab journals in the 1930s and participated in the activities of CAFS in the 1960s. While Muhammad Massoud occasionally participated in several group initiatives, most of his activity was done on behalf of his own association, in isolation. The question of politics seems to have united certain organizations in their modes of action and their discourse. Activists met and were inspired by one another. With regards to the Palestinian cause, they had recourse to a common rhetoric and discourse, which resembled those developed by the CAFL since 1945.

The dynamism of community activity after 1967 was also due to an increased exposure of "Arabs" in the public sphere, the media, and international political debates, because of the Six-Day War and then the Yom Kippur War (1973), the petroleum crisis, and Palestinian terrorism. In response to media attention and the positioning of Canadian foreign policy, still perceived as hostile to the Arab camp, Canadian Arab associations began to mobilize, as exemplified by the birth of the Canadian Arab Federation in 1967. The Federation sought to represent "the voices of Arabs in Canada" and would come to encompass the quasi-majority of organizations that hoped to mobilize the community on political issues and existed in the public sphere. (Throughout these years, the Federation was comprised of around fifteen member associations.) The media strategy developed by the CAF went hand in hand with its self-promotion as a political interlocutor:

the Secretary of State for External Affairs met with the Federation six times between 1967 and 1975.

Despite this unprecedented peak in mobilizations, the weak influence of countries of origin and the hostility of Canadian foreign policy toward meeting Arab demands may go a long way toward explaining the obstacles met by the Federation in this period. Official Lebanese representatives seem to have been even less active than in the preceding years, insofar as political action is concerned, with the exception of some protests when Israel made a direct attack on Lebanon. In an exceptional case in 1970, a plea from the Lebanese ambassador in Canada urged North American communities to appeal to their governments to put pressure on Israel, in order to defend "the motherland in danger," Lebanon.[52]

In general, the Arab activists in this period made note of the Lebanese diplomatic corps' lack of intervention and the limited but effective support of the Arab League's office in Ottawa. Testimonies and documents point to the limited financial resources made available in support of associations mobilizing in defense of the Palestinian cause.[53] Likewise, documentary sources suggest little presence of the Egyptian diplomatic mission even though a significant Egyptian immigration to Canada had developed by then and Egypt was considered the champion of Arab nationalism. The sole significant financial aid provided by any Arab diplomatic corps of which I have found any trace, involved the Iraqi embassy. Although few Iraqis had migrated to Canada by then, at the end of the 1970s the Iraqi embassy provided significant material aid to the Arab Community Centre of Toronto, of which 20 percent was allocated to the CAF, permitting it to buy the small building in Toronto owned today by the association, although the first meetings were carried out in the homes of members of the Federation.[54] It was not until later that organizations, including the CAF, would receive public financing from the Canadian government, thanks to general public subsidies as part of multiculturalism programs from the mid-1970s onward.

From Suspicion to Surveillance: The Specter of Terrorism

CAF met the same hurdle confronting Arab demands since 1945: a deficit in the capacity needed to influence Canadian decision making regarding geopolitical issues with which the country's foreign policy was concerned. Moreover, Israel benefited from more significant support, even though Canada attempted to present itself as a neutral state, concerned above all with international legality.[55]

Secondly, the support that the CAF had from other organizations had an effect upon the way its mobilization was perceived. Some Québécois organizations affiliated with the CAF (such as the Comité Québec Palestine and the Association Québec Palestine) became active during this period, garnering the backing of Quebec nationalists such as René Levesque, future Prime Minister of the province, and Michel Chartrand, one of Quebec's most influential trade unionists, whose well-known activism in favor of Palestine dates back to those years. However, this support was not looked upon kindly by the Canadian state, which at that time was in open confrontation with the Québécois nationalist movement, a fact that further delegitimized the Arab point of view and left them under even greater suspicion. The issue of international terrorism would later merge with the local struggle represented by the demands of Québécois separatists, who themselves were kept under surveillance and considered an internal security threat. Thus, the tolerance for what were considered to be "double loyalties" varied with the ebb and flow of international tensions, and in the case of Arab migrants in Canada, this became a matter of "triple loyalty," with international tensions connecting to struggles on a national level.[56]

During the CAF's first ten years, several incidents indicate that the police kept Arab activists under surveillance. Canada considered the Palestine Liberation Organization (PLO) to be a terrorist organization; although there is no proof to indicate any tangible links (such as financial ties) between the CAF and the PLO, the Arab activists were carefully monitored. From 1974 onward, a growing number of indicators, some ultimately confirmed, others remaining murky, suggest that CAF was under surveillance. One of the best-known cases took place during the 1976 Olympics, held in Montreal. Some activists, including the president of the CAF, were directly accused of plotting a terrorist attack on the Olympics. These "revelations" of the Canadian newspaper *The Globe and Mail*, though immediately denied by the police itself, placed the CAF in a difficult position and created a climate of suspicion around the Palestinian cause and Arab activists more generally. The media campaign sparked by this scandal is still remembered and has affected the lives of some activists who were identified as potential terrorists at the time.[57] From the early 1970s onward, as complaints multiplied about suspected police practices, accompanied by scandals broadcast in the media (linked above all to the surveillance of the Québécois separatist movements), the government decided in 1977 to establish a Commission of Inquiry.[58] The publication of the report from the Royal Commission of Inquiry into Certain Activities of the RCMP (Royal Canadian Mounted Police) in 1981 confirmed the suspicions of the Arab activists. The report described a "complainant group," presumably the CAF, which had denounced surveillance of which it believed itself to be the object. The inquiry confirmed that the

STATES' INFLUENCE AND POLITICAL MOBILIZATIONS   177

international context as well as issues on the national level had led to intensification in the surveillance of some hundred activists, linked to leftist parties, separatist movements, and "liberation organizations" suspected of "terrorism," forming "obvious" targets for the RCMP. The report concluded that there had been continuous and intensive surveillance of "this group":

> For around a decade the Security Service monitored the situation by means of communication intercepts duly authorized in respect of individuals under the appropriate sections of the Official Secrets Act. During the period 1972 to 1976 additional electronic and physical surveillance operations were conducted with a view to detecting any security threat involving the Montreal Olympics. Several members of the complainant group identified as extremists were subjected to mail openings. Close liaison and cooperation were maintained with Canadian police forces, government agencies and foreign law enforcement authorities, to monitor and report upon the international movements and contacts made by prominent activists of the group. Meetings were infiltrated and reported upon. In some cases, extensive physical surveillance was conducted in collaboration with provincial and municipal police forces. Efforts were also directed towards the recruiting and development of informants possessing the requisite language capabilities and background. A defusion programme put into effect in 1976 led to direct confrontation and interviews with group leaders.[59]

The Security Service's interpretation of who was "extremist" and suspected of "terrorism" corresponded to Canada's political position regarding the PLO and Québécois separatist organizations. At no moment does the report of the Commission of Inquiry question the "obvious link" that the RCMP had supposedly established between sympathizers of the PLO or the separatist cause and potential terrorists. Therefore, international migrants became internal foreigners, whose continuing relationships with "home" countries—much emphasized by experts on transnationalism—were precisely what brought them under suspicion. Thus, relations between states determined whether people with foreign ties were to be viewed kindly or with suspicion when they mobilized in the name of their country of origin.[60] As shown by recent studies on the impact of the repression on mobilizations, the issue of national security and the naming of an interior enemy (whether this be the Québécois extremists or foreign terrorists) allowed those in power to define protests as criminal acts, denying all legitimacy to the cause in question and to the activists.[61] Confronted by this climate of hostility, the CAF adopted a defensive strategy, which may have discouraged potential activists and put pressure on their more visible representatives. During the first ten years of the CAF, it made significant efforts to testify, denounce and fight against the surveillance and the negative media image. It was therefore difficult for it to focus on a more long-range campaign strategy. Furthermore, the CAF did not have sufficient resources and support to respond effectively. In addition, sympathy for the Palestinian cause clearly being a minority position in Canada, the anti-Israeli stance of the CAF may have been perceived as too radical. While the feeling of being attacked may have been successful in mobilizing the organization's representatives concerning the need to defend their rights, it could also have discouraged new activist vocations. The CAF chose a frontal response, pledging to affirm its support for the struggle of the Palestinian people publicly, through political lobbying and mediatization. However, this begs the question of whether, from a strategic point of view, by responding to each new attack, the group did not merely exhaust and disperse its efforts.

*   *   *

The history of the transnational politicization of the Arab minority over this long period of time demonstrates the ways in which a variety of factors affected both the capacity for mobilizations and the receptivity to the demands that these mobilizations expressed. Whether these were actions directed at the region of origin or at struggles in favor of equal rights in the country of settlement, migrants and their descendants faced external constraints that inhibited their activities and their ability to turn the balance of power in their favor. Neither the countries of origin (nonexistent, indifferent, or weak), nor international relations, nor the country of settlement seemed to constitute factors favorable to the development of the immigrants' demands. The actions in favor of the Palestinian cause present an exemplary case study, as an example of a long-distance nationalism, in which questions of scale were significant and state interests at the international level merged with national and local stakes. Nevertheless, the weak influence of countries of origin also, paradoxically, allowed the Arab minority in Canada to develop discourses and strategies unimpeded by external injunctions, since no one financed their political associations, nor attempted to orient their mobilizations. More generally, Arab collective actions were part of a continuum, but the intensity of the mobilization in each period depended on both the history of the Arab associative scene and the political context. Research on more recent Arab mobilizations remains to be done: it would show whether current political actions are sometimes part of the dynamics and structures of past struggles described in this study. Since 1975, Canada has implemented a policy of multiculturalism that has transformed the nature of the interactions between the state and minorities, particularly through grants allowed to ethnic associations. In addition, the Arab world has changed dramatically since the 1970s, from the war in Lebanon (1975–1990), which resulted in a very large wave of immigration to Canada, through both Palestinian Intifadas (in the 1980s and the 2000s), or the Israeli attack against Lebanon in 2006, which resulted in large Arab demonstrations in Canada.

NOTES

1. Brian Aboud, "Community Associations and their Relations with the State: The Case of the Arab Associative Network of Montreal," master's thesis, Université du Québec à Montréal, 1992; Aboud, "Racism, Exclusion and Resistance: The Syrian-Lebanese Challenge to 'Asiatic' Exclusion in Canada, The Early Postwar Round (1947–1949)," in Paul Tabar, *Lebanese Diaspora: History, Racism and Belonging* (Beirut: LAU, Chamas Publishing, 2005); Baha Abu-Laban, *An Olive Branch on the Family Tree: The Arabs in Canada* (Toronto: McClelland and Stewart, Multiculturalism Directorate, 1980); Abu-Laban, "Arab Canadians and the Arab-Israeli Conflict," *Arab Studies Quarterly* 10 (1988). The term *Arab* is used here to designate a population that originates from the same region and speaks the same language (Arabic). This does not rule out the heterogeneity of this group of migrants or the usage of diverse terms to label them, depending on the period. Early settlers favored the names of their towns of origin to refer to themselves, but they could also be labeled Syrians, then Lebanese, and then Middle Easterners, or known simply by their nationality of origin. The term *Arab* is used here since it was the only one to be used throughout the period by the actors themselves, be it in reference to themselves or simply to designate their origins. See Houda Asal, "Se dire 'arabe' au Canada: Un siècle de vie associative, entre constructions identitaires et mobilisations politiques (1882–1975)," doctoral thesis, École des Hautes Études en Sciences Sociales, Paris, 2011.

2. The concept of "minority" allows us to demonstrate the status of this minoritized (in the sociological sense of the term) population, while simultaneously stressing that this is a group that recognizes itself as originating from a single region (given that this is a study of collective organizations) and which is composed of migrants and descendants of migrants.

3. *Machrek*: literally the East (where the sun rises) in opposition to the *Maghreb*, which means the West. *Machrek* implies the entire Arab region surrounding Syria (Lebanon, Palestine, Jordan), the Iraqi region, and Egypt (although the latter's inclusion in the *Machrek* is sometimes disputed). The term is used to refer to this region in the past, in order to avoid any anachronism (the terms *Middle East* or *Near East* appeared later).

4. For France, among others, see Dietmar Loch, Jacques Barou, and Marie-Antoinette Hily, eds., "Migrations, transnationalisme et diaspora: théorie et études de cas," in a special issue of *Revue Européenne des Migrations Internationales* 28 (2012).

5. Asal, "Se dire 'arabe' au Canada."

6. Cecilia Baeza, "Les Palestiniens d'Amérique latine et la cause palestinienne," doctoral thesis, Institut d'études politiques, Paris, 2010.

7. See Nancy L. Green and François Weil, eds., *Citoyenneté et émigration. Les politiques du départ* (Paris: Éditions de l'EHESS, 2006); Stéphane Dufoix, Carine Guerassimoff, and Anne Tinguy, eds., *Loin des yeux, près du cœur? Les États et leurs expatriés* (Paris: Presses de Sciences Po, 2010); Pauline Peretz, "Une influence méconnue de l'État hébreu sur sa diaspora," *Hypothèses* 1 (2004): 179–188; Sirma Bilge, "Communalisations ethniques post-migratoires: le cas des 'Turcs' de Montréal," doctoral thesis, Institut du monde anglophone (études canadiennes), Université Paris III-Sorbonne Nouvelle, 2002.

8. Roger Waldinger, "'Transnationalisme' des immigrants et présence du passé," trans. Jean-Luc Pinel, *Revue Européenne des Migrations Internationales* 22 (2006): 23–41.

9. Roger Waldinger and David FitzGerald, "Transnationalism in Question," *American Journal of Sociology* 109 (March 2004): 1177–1195.

10. Asal, "Se dire 'arabe' au Canada"; Baeza, "Les Palestiniens d'Amérique latine et la cause palestinienne."

11. Donna R. Gabaccia, *Foreign Relations: American Immigration in Global Perspective* (Princeton: Princeton University Press, 2012).

12. Greater Syria: *Bilad el Cham* in Arab. This explains why, at the beginning of the period in question, migrants called themselves "Syrians" (never "Turks," even though Canadian statistics recorded them as the latter on their arrival). However, the forerunners often defined themselves according to their attachment to a village of origin, with self-denominations then becoming more complex. See Asal, "Se dire 'arabe' au Canada."

13. Denys Cuche, "Un siècle d'immigration palestinienne au Pérou. La construction d'une ethnicité spécifique," *Revue Européenne des Migrations Internationales* 17, 3 (2001): 87–118; Oswaldo Truzzi, "Libanais et Syriens au Brésil (1880–1950)," *Revue Européenne des Migrations Internationales* 18, 1 (2001); Gildas Bregain, *Syriens et Libanais d'Amérique du Sud (1918–1945)* (Paris: L'Harmattan, 2008).

14. The Greek Orthodox Church was the most important church among migrants who settled in Canada and established their first church in Montreal in 1905. Various Eastern Catholic denominations existed, mainly Melchites of Byzantine rite who established the very first oriental Christian mission in Canada in 1892 in Montreal and Maronite Christians belonging to a Catholic Church of Eastern rite with a significant Roman influence. The Melchites, of which there were many in Syria, were more numerous in Canada than the Maronites, who nonetheless constitute the leading Christian church of modern-day Lebanon. Finally, Sunnite Muslims came to reside in some towns in the West, such as Lac Labiche or Edmonton, which in 1938 would become home to Canada's first mosque. On religious life throughout the whole period, see Asal, "Se dire 'arabe' au Canada," 88–95, 113–116, and 271–286.

15. The census and other statistics on immigration do not permit us to know the exact number of admissions and the profile of the Arab population residing in Canada for this period. Categories differed from one year to another and the data

accounting practices often changed during the century. See Houda Asal, "Discours et stratégies identitaires face aux catégorisations étatiques. La minorité arabe au Canada," *Migrations Société* 22, 128 (2010): 147–158.

16. Valérie Knowles, *Strangers at Our Gates. Canadian Immigration and Immigration Policy*, 1540–1997 (Toronto: Dundurn Press, 1997), 49–50, 84–86.

17. See Brian Aboud, "Min Zamaan/depuis longtemps. La communauté syrienne-libanaise à Montréal de 1882 à 1940," *Bulletin du Centre d'Histoire de Montréal*, 44 (2nd trimester 2003); book of official records and minutes from meetings of the *Aid Association for the People of Rashaya*, 1926. Archives from the Syrian Canadian Association, Montreal.

18. France attempted to encourage those migrants known to be sympathetic to its cause by financing pro-mandate newspapers and offering honorary prizes to France's allies, yet it failed to use sufficient means to allow its propaganda to become widely circulated. Bregain, *Syriens et Libanais d'Amérique du Sud*, 214–218. The French embassy in Canada suggested giving financial support to the American journal *Al Hoda* and encouraging Lebanese groups in favor of the French mandate. For a detailed study of this newspaper and its founders, see Michael Suleiman, "The Mokarzels' contributions to the Arabic-speaking community in the United States," *Arab Studies Quarterly* 21 (1999): 71–88.

19. Archives of the French Ministry of Foreign Affairs, Nantes. August 21, 1943, French embassy. AMAE-N, Syrie Liban, "Colonies syro-libanaises à l'étranger 1941–1948," box 786 (inv.7).

20. Archives of the French Ministry of Foreign Affairs, Nantes. April 1, 1937, French consulate in Montreal. AMAE-N, box 67, 1928–1944.

21. The Phoenician reference has been used more recently. For example, in 2009, the city of Montreal commemorated the arrival of the first Lebanese there, over 125 years ago, with a work of art representing the letters of the Phoenician alphabet (Daleth). Systematically describing all of the Arab-speaking immigrants as Lebanese and using the term Phoenician, which was never used in the period under study, appears both anachronistic and ideological. See Asher Kaufman, *Reviving Phoenicia: The Search for Identity in Lebanon* (London: I. B. Tauris, 2004); Aboud, "Community Associations and Their Relations," 65–66.

22. June 20, 1941, from Raoul Aglion to the French information service in Canada. AMAE-N, Ottawa Embassy, box 177, 1945–1951, file 728, "colonies syriennes au Canada."

23. See Anne-Lucie Chaigne-Oudin, *La France et les rivalités occidentales au Levant: Syrie-Liban, 1918–1939* (Paris: L'Harmattan, 2006), 93–122; November 30, 1943, Petition to the Prime Minister; December 18, 1943, letter signed by four associations to the Prime Minister. RG25, v. 3248, file 5934-40. June 18, 1945, A memorandum that relates that during the months of May and June, the Department received letters from "6 Canadian residents of Lebanese and Syrian origin" and "6 Syrian and Lebanese organizations in Canada." RG25, v. 3248, file 5934-40.

24. Ninette Kelley and Michael Trebilcock, *The Making of the Mosaic. A History of Canadian Immigration Policy* (Toronto: University of Toronto Press, 1998), 149.

HOUDA ASAL

Aboud, "Racism, Exclusion and Resistance," 2005.

26. April 18, 1927, Elias Karam to the Minister of Immigration, Microfilm C10617, RG76, v. 522, file 801591, part 1-2-3, 1908–1945, National Archives of Canada, Ottawa.

27. The archives consulted in Nantes make no allusion to Canadian immigration policies. However, in his research on South America, Gildas Brégain has demonstrated the French authorities' concern regarding the potential tightening of immigration laws against the Lebanese in Argentina. Brégain, *Syriens et Libanais d'Amérique du Sud*, 113.

28. May 7, 1947, Lebanese consul at Ottawa to the Secretary of State for External Affairs, RG26, v. 123, file 3-33-2, part 1; October 2, 1946, Charles Malik (Lebanese consul at Washington) to Lester B. Pearson, microfilm C10617, Lester B. Pearson was ambassador of Canada in the United States until September 1946, when he became Undersecretary of State for External Affairs, and then Secretary of State for External Affairs from 1948 to 1957.

29. February 22, 1949, Elias Karam to the Minister of Immigration. RG26, v. 123, file 3-33-2, part 1.

30. For a detailed analysis of the campaign against restrictive migration laws, see Aboud, "Racism, Exclusion and Resistance," and Asal, "Discours et stratégies identitaires."

31. Lawrence Davidson, "Debating Palestine: Arab-American Challenges to Zionism, 1917–1932," in Michael Suleiman, *Arabs in America: Building a New Future* (Philadelphia: Temple University Press, 1999), 227–240.

32. Houda Asal, "Les premières mobilisations d'immigrants arabes au Canada, à travers l'exemple du journal *The Canadian Arab*, 1945–1948," *Journal of International Migration and Integration* 9 (2008): 1–19.

33. Verta Taylor, "Social Movement Continuity: The Women's Movement in Abeyance," *American Sociological Review* 54 (1989): 761–775.

34. Eliezer Tauber, "Jewish and Arab Lobbies in Canada and the UN Partition of Palestine," *Israel Affairs* 5 (1999): 236–242.

35. Houchang Hassan-Yari, *Le Canada et le conflit israélo-arabe depuis 1947* (Paris: L'Harmattan, 1997); Janice Stein, "Canadian Policy in the Middle East," in *De Mackenzie King à Pierre Trudeau: quarante ans de diplomatie canadienne*, ed. Paul Painchaud (Québec: Les Presses de l'Université Laval, 1989), 379–384.

36. Tauber, "Jewish and Arab Lobbies in Canada," 229–44; David Dewitt and John Kirton, *Canada as a Principal Power: A Study in Foreign Policy and International Relations* (Toronto: John Wiley, 1983), 370.

37. Hassan-Yari, *Le Canada et le conflit israélo-arabe.*

38. Ali Dessouki, *Canadian Foreign Policy and the Palestine Problem* (Ottawa: Middle East Research Centre, 1969): 2–3.

39. Hassan-Yari, *Le Canada et le conflit israélo-arabe*, 32–33; Eliezer Tauber, "Elizabeth P. MacCallum and the Arab-Israeli Conflict," *Journal of Israeli History* 19 (1998): 93–107.

40. Robert Spencer, *Canada in World Affairs from UN to NATO, 1946–1949* (Toronto: Oxford University Press, 1959): 145–147.

41. Interview, May 6, 2009, Montreal, with a former member of the *Canadian Arab Friendship League.*

42. Massoud published his letters to Pearson and some of the responses he received from him. Muhammad Massoud, *I Fought as I Believed. An Arab Canadian Speaks Out on the Arab-Israeli Conflict* (Montreal: AT Ateliers des sourds, 1976), 424–450.

43. For details on Arab associational life at that time, see Asal, "Se dire 'arabe' au Canada," 297–304.

44. Bilge, "Communalisations ethniques post-migratoires."

45. September 8, 1954, Ministry of External Affairs, RG25, v. 6669, part 1, file 12158-40, Arab Friendship League, 1954–1963.

46. June 4, 1959, Undersecretary of External Affairs to the Canadian Embassy in Cairo; June 5, 1959, Canadian Embassy in Beirut to the Undersecretary of External Affairs, RG25, v. 6669, part 1, file 12158-40.

47. February 21 and 23, 1955, RG25, v. 6669, part 1, file 12158-40.

48. September 1954, Memorandum "The CAFL." RG25, v. 6669, part 1, file 12158-40.

49. October 8, 1957, Canadian Legation in Beirut to the Middle Eastern Division in Ottawa; November 7, 1957, memorandum, Undersecretary of State for External Affairs, RG25, v. 7061, file 7631-B-1-40.

50. October 30, 1957, Undersecretary of State for External Affairs, RG25, v. 7061, file 7631-B-1-40.

51. A significant correspondence from the Middle Eastern division shows that the Arab League envoys requested diplomatic visas; they were refused while at the same time the envoys were under surveillance. RG25, series G-2, v. 7061, file 7631-B-40, and RG25, series G-2, v. 7061, file 7631-B-40.

52. *Canadian Arab World Review* 1 (March 4, 1970), "Appel à tous les Libanais du Canada"; *Canadian Middle East Journal,* February-March 1972, 1–2, and May 1972, 1.

53. *The Arab Case, Documents and Testimonies, 1968–1969; Arab-Canada* (1969–1970); *Arab Canada Newsletter* then *Arab Review* in 1976, Arab Information Centre, Ottawa. National Archives of Canada, Ottawa.

54. Interview with a former active member of the *Comité Québec Palestine,* May 3, 2009. Interviews with activists from the *Arab Community Centre* November 5 and 7, 2007, and with a former president of the FCA, November 7, 2007, Toronto.

55. Hassan-Yari, *Le Canada et le conflit israélo-arabe,* 50–58.

56. Waldinger, "'Transnationalisme' des immigrants"; Waldinger and FitzGerald, "Transnationalism in Question."

57. The *Globe and Mail* provided the description of 14 suspects, without giving their names, but the biographical details in the article allowed identification of several people, mostly known activists of the CAF. Arnold Bruner and Peter Moon, "RCMP probes plot to supporting terrorists at Olympics," *Globe and Mail,* October 27, 1975.

58. The Commission's report discusses mainly the abusive surveillance of Québécois nationalist groups, but article 34 of the third volume indicates that numerous Arab activists were the targets of strict surveillance based upon a body of information linked to their origins and political opinions. Third Report: Certain RCMP Activities and the Question of Governmental Knowledge (Ottawa: Supply and Services Canada, 1981), 337–339.

59. Ibid., 337–339.

60. Waldinger, "'Transnationalisme' des immigrants"; Waldinger and FitzGerald, "Transnationalism in Question."

61. Hélène Combes and Olivier Fillieule, "De la répression considérée dans ses rapports à l'activité protestataire. Modèles structuraux et interactions stratégiques," *Revue française de science politique* 61 (2011), 1047–1072.

CHAPTER 7

TOWARD A HISTORY OF AMERICAN JEWS AND THE RUSSIAN REVOLUTIONARY MOVEMENT

Tony Michels

The migration of some two million Jews from the Russia Empire to the United States between the 1880s and 1920s led to myriad interactions between the world's two largest Jewish communities. In the realm of politics, socialists affiliated with various parties on both sides of the Atlantic cultivated ties through exchanges of ideas, publications, money, and other materials.[1] This paper delineates transnational connections between socialists during the four-decade era of mass Jewish immigration from Russia to the United States. It focuses on New York City, where a unique confluence of social and demographic factors gave rise to the world's largest Jewish workers' movement before World War I. The city's extraordinarily large number of Jews (1.75 million by the 1920s), their dense geographic concentration (540,000 on the Lower East Side alone as of 1914), their rapid proletarianization in the garment industry, and, finally, the absence of traditional structures of communal authority enabled immigrants to build labor institutions, articulate ideologies, and invent forms of culture in the Yiddish language that, in many instances, had few antecedents in "the old country."[2] Consequently, a popular Jewish labor movement arose in the United States almost ten years before the birth of its counterpart in Russia and fifteen years before the Russian Jewish workers' movement grew into a significant force. Even with the burst of Jewish political activity in and around the 1905 revolution, no city in Russia matched New York's Jewish labor movement, in terms of size and scope of activity, until the downfall of the Tsar in 1917. Furthermore, New Yorkers influenced developments on the other side of the Atlantic and even played a formative role in the Jewish workers' movement in Russia's Pale of Settlement. New York thus stood as the capital of Jewish socialism from the 1880s to the 1920s.

Recognition of New York's centrality in the evolution of Jewish socialism suggests the need to revise the standard core-periphery conception of Russian Jewish immigration. According to that view, New York represented little more than an outpost, albeit an exceptionally large one, of Russian Jewry wherein immigrants transplanted established forms of politics and culture before adapting them to American society. This unidirectional conceptualization reflects, in large measure, U.S. immigration historiography's traditional emphasis on processes of Americanization within local and national contexts. To be sure, Jewish immigrants must be situated in the localities where the vast majority of them settled.[3] Transnationality did not transcend place or undermine the national, despite claims to the contrary by some historians.[4] Still, analysis that focuses exclusively on the local level fails to capture reciprocal relationships across the Atlantic; the local, national, and transnational operated as three interrelated planes.

For the purpose of understanding transnational Jewish politics, the era of mass immigration may be divided into three time periods. The first, dating from 1880 to 1900, witnessed the arrival of roughly 800,000 Russian and other eastern European Jews in the United States. Very few of those immigrants—perhaps a couple of thousand, mostly intellectuals—had participated in or sympathized with the Russian revolutionary movement before coming to the United States. Most immigrants in the first period originally encountered socialist ideologies and organizations in New York or other American cities. However, in the first decade of the twentieth century, the complexion of Russian Jewish immigration became manifestly political. This change reflected the rapid rise of Jewish parties in Russia in the years leading up to and through the 1905 revolution. These parties differed sharply from one another, but all sought to synthesize some kind of revolutionary socialism with forms of Jewish nationalism. As of 1906, their combined estimated membership totaled somewhere between 60,000–70,000, an estimate that does not include those swept up by the unrest without formally joining a party.[5] Exactly how many Jewish revolutionaries immigrated to the United States between 1900 and 1914 remains unclear, but their numbers certainly ran into the thousands amid an overall Jewish immigration of some 1.2 million. These newcomers injected a spirit of militancy into the immigrant Jewish community and contributed greatly to the rise of powerful unions in the garment industry and the ascendency of socialism in New York politics. They also introduced Jewish nationalist programs (autonomism, territorialism, and Zionism) hitherto little known in the United States. Hence, the years between 1900 and 1914 constituted the second period of transnational Jewish socialism. The third and final period began in 1919, following the end of World War I, and continued until Congress drastically restricted immigration from Europe in 1924. Although brief, this postwar boom totaled more than 280,000 individuals. Few historians have treated these arrivals as a distinct subset within the overall immigration of Jews to the United States, but there is good reason to do so. Like the 1905 generation, a significant minority of postwar immigrants belonged to revolutionary parties or their youth auxiliaries. Yet six years of war, revolution, and pogroms—cataclysmic events that devastated Russian Jewry—radicalized them to a greater extent than did the 1905 revolution earlier immigrants. Many postwar immigrants, including those unaffiliated with a political party, fervently believed in the Bolshevik regime and, after settling in the United States, gravitated toward the Communist Party. This leftward surge reoriented Jewish politics once again and played an important role in the establishment of Communism in American society.

In short, Jewish immigration assumed a progressively radical character over a forty-year period. A relatively tiny number of immigrants in the late nineteenth century brought any socialist "baggage" with them, whereas many who arrived after 1900 came as experienced revolutionaries. The First World War and the Russian revolution sent many Communists and Communist sympathizers to the United States at the very moment when the country decided it no longer wanted immigrants, "Reds" least of all. As the latter point implies, the ramifications of transnational ties shifted over time. Prior to the 1917 revolution, immigrant Jews in the United States suffered no known repercussions for their efforts on behalf of Russian revolutionaries. After 1917, pro-Soviet sentiment among immigrant Jews and the disproportionate role of Jews in the Communist movement amid the postwar Red Scare resulted in accusations of disloyalty, subversion, and conspiracy that continued into the Cold War era.

If the character of immigration changed over time, so too did the kinds of aid provided by Jews in the United States to the Russian revolutionary movement. During the 1880s and 1890s, their most noteworthy contributions were Yiddish publications for use by the fledgling Jewish workers' movement in the Pale of Settlement, whose members could not produce their own materials, mainly because of censorship. After 1900, American Jewish socialists continued to export Yiddish publications, but, more importantly, they donated large sums of money to various political parties to cover costs of propaganda, strikes, self-defense groups, aid to pogrom victims, and other expenditures. Furthermore, whereas aid in the late nineteenth century went mainly to Jewish workers' organizations, in the 1900s, it went to Jewish and non-Jewish parties alike (although not to all parties equally). After 1917, the nature of interactions changed once again. Until then, immigrant Jews supported revolutionary parties against the tsarist regime. After the Bolsheviks' rise to power, however, the immigrant Jewish labor movement became divided between supporters of the Soviet government and opponents. The near universal support for Soviet Russia within the Jewish labor movement during the early years of the revolution gave way to polarization between Communists, on the one hand, and anarchists and democratic socialists, on the other.

The divide between Communists and anti-Communists within the immigrant Jewish labor movement mirrored the schism that occurred within the American left (in fact, the socialist movement worldwide), but the divide was especially pronounced among Jews. Connected to Russia by bonds of family, kinship, and politics, immigrant Jews felt a strong stake in the revolution. Developments there directly affected families, friends, and comrades. Furthermore, as longtime supporters of the revolutionary movement, immigrant Jews wanted nothing more than to see socialism realized in Russia. Given their overall left-wing orientation and personal connections to Russia, immigrant Jews could not help but react to Bolshevik policies with the strongest emotions. Few issues proved more divisive among Jews than the "Russian Question." Yet debates among immigrant Jews amounted to more than an internal communal affair, for the simple reason that immigrant Jews, with their mass-membership unions, fraternal orders, and powerful Yiddish press, overlapped with the American left to a considerable extent in the interwar period. To trace the evolving, complicated relationship of immigrant Jews to Russia is to willy-nilly tell much of the history of the American left during the first half of the twentieth century.

Publications, Money, and Weapons for Russian Revolutionaries

The American Jewish labor movement came into existence in 1885–1886 amid the national strike wave known as The Great Upheaval. During that two-year period, left-wing intellectuals established the first labor unions, Yiddish newspapers, and political clubs catering to Jewish workers, all of which led to more numerous and larger organizations in the following decade. Demonstrations, parades, rallies, strikes, and street-corner soapboxers became regular features of immigrant Jewish neighborhoods in the 1890s. Socialists were still ten to fifteen years away from leading stable, mass-membership organizations and winning elections, but they succeeded in shaping the public life and opinion of Yiddish-speaking New York at an early point. In Russia, by contrast, Jewish revolutionaries lagged behind. They did not decide to create an autonomous Jewish workers' organization until late 1893 and, even then, they operated surreptitiously on a small scale because of state repression. Furthermore, the founders of the first Russian Jewish socialist organization, known as the Vilna Social Democrats, did not know Yiddish well—in certain cases not at all—and they possessed little in the way of propaganda materials. Members of the Vilna group often relied on handwritten Yiddish translations of Russian booklets, but those texts, produced in 10–15 copies at a time, were in such short supply that propagandists had to translate them on the spot during meetings. Their translations left much to be desired and sometimes amounted to mere "gibberish," according to one activist. Although Vilna Social Democrats made some progress toward producing their own Yiddish materials during the 1890s, they never achieved self-sufficiency. From the outset, they looked to New York and, to a lesser extent, London for assistance. In fact, the sheer abundance of socialist literature in the west encouraged the Vilna group to adopt Yiddish in the first place. As Julius Martov, a leading Vilna Social Democrat, noted retrospectively, he and his comrades turned to Yiddish on the presumption that they could "make use of the socialist Yiddish literature coming out in London and New York."[6] The historian Jonathan Frankel has elaborated Martov's recollection in his landmark study of Russian Jewish politics: "The ability of [immigrant Jews] in London—and much more spectacularly in New York—to create a self-supporting Yiddish press and Yiddish-speaking trade-union movement inspired growing respect. Nothing succeeds like success, and in the years 1891–5 socialists throughout eastern Europe sought to repeat what had been achieved in the East End and the Lower East Side."[7] Frankel's point is important for understanding the influence of New York and London. Jewish socialists in those cities not only enabled Russian Jews to disseminate socialism, but also helped to legitimate the very idea of using Yiddish as an instrument of socialist agitation. The creation of the Jewish workers' movement in Lithuania, according to Frankel, "can largely be explained in terms of the overseas example."[8]

During the 1880s and 1890s, New Yorkers shipped thousands of copies of Yiddish newspapers, journals, and pamphlets for use in Russia. In at least one instance, a group was established for the sole purpose of exporting pamphlets. Named the Jewish Socialist Post from America to Poland, this group published two Yiddish pamphlets in runs of 3,000 copies each for use by the Polish Socialist Party.[9] More than a dozen titles published in

New York were utilized by Russian Jewish revolutionaries. In Bialystok, for instance, *Der alef-beys fun anarkhizmus* (The ABC of Anarchism) by the journalist Shoel Yanovsky was well-received by the city's textile workers. (The following decade, a return migrant to Bialystok helped establish the city's first illegal anarchist printing press.[10]) In addition to pamphlets, Yiddish newspapers and newspaper clippings also circulated widely. The first socialist Yiddish newspaper to reach Russia was the *Di nyu-yorker yidishe folkstsaytung* (New York Jewish People's Newspaper) in 1886. The person responsible was Shmuel Rabinovitsh, a revolutionary from Warsaw then living in Paris, who discovered the New York weekly and London's *Arbeter fraynd* (Worker's Friend) in a friend's apartment. Rabinovitsh ordered ten copies each of *Di nyu-yorker yidishe folkstsaytung* and *Arbeter fraynd*, which he shipped to a comrade in Warsaw, who, in turn, dispatched them to Bialystok, Brisk, Minsk, and Vilna. It is not known how many individuals saw the newspapers or how they responded, but the government censor in St. Petersburg made his reaction clear. He promptly banned *Di nyu-yorker yidishe folkstsaytung* (*Arbeter fraynd* seems to have eluded authorities at that point) for its "very harmful" criticism of the czar and praise for Russian revolutionaries. Nonetheless, Yiddish newspapers continued to make their way into Russia. They were especially valued as sources of protest poetry, which revolutionaries set to music and used as "singing agitation" at meetings and gatherings. In a very different vein, "scientific" journals were used in workers' study circles run by intellectuals for the purpose of developing a second tier of revolutionary activists. The key publication used for workers' education was the monthly *Di tsukunft*, published by the Yiddish-speaking sections of the Socialist Labor Party, the main Marxist party in the United States in the late nineteenth century. *Di tsukunft* provided something akin to a general education to those who had no secular schooling or access to languages other than Yiddish. According to the recollection of an "underground militant" in Minsk (the Russian Jewish labor movement's second city after Vilna), comrades treated each new issue of *Di tsukunft* as a "true holiday." A group from Warsaw reported, in 1896, that its members distributed "the entire American socialist Yiddish literature, especially *Di tsukunft*."

Without the thousands of pamphlets, newspapers, and journals exported from New York (and London), Russian Jewish revolutionaries could not have functioned effectively. They needed Yiddish publications from abroad in order to propagate socialism and spread secular knowledge. As an activist recalled in 1912, "The first pioneers of the Jewish workers' movement in Russia, not having their own literature or a very significant one, had to depend on the American Yiddish revolutionary literature for help in their educational work." That revolutionaries risked long prison sentences by smuggling and disseminating Yiddish contraband may be taken as a measure of its importance.[11]

New York's influence on the Russian Jewish workers' movement seems to have been strongest during its infancy in the 1890s. With the establishment of the Bund (Jewish Workers' Alliance of Russia, Poland, and Lithuania) in October 1897, followed by the party's rapid growth in the early 1900s (reaching a peak estimated membership of 33,000), the emergence of other Jewish revolutionary parties, and the easing of censorship after the 1905 revolution, Russian Jews succeeded in producing their own ramified party literatures. To be sure, publications from New York continued to flow into Russia, perhaps in even larger quantities than before. All of the Bund's major branches regularly received copies of *Di tsukunft*, for instance, between 1907 and 1914. Nonetheless, after 1905, the role of New York seems to have been supplemental—filling in gaps in the overall body of Yiddish literature produced in Russia—rather than crucial.

If influence traveled from west to east during the early period of Jewish socialism, this trend was reversed in and around the 1905 revolution. Members of the Bund and Jewish parties with a Zionist or territorialist orientation came to the United States by the thousands and profoundly altered the ideological character of Jewish politics.

The founders of New York's Jewish labor movement considered themselves strict "internationalists" who utilized Yiddish for purely practical reasons. They thought of the language as a tool needed to reach Jewish workers but did not seek to maintain Jewish group identity, pursue Jewish communal goals, or develop Jewish culture, let alone religion. The 1905-era immigrants, however, affirmed both working-class and Jewish "national" solidarities. The Bund's program combined Marxism with an insistence on the right of the Russian Jewish nation, defined as a Yiddish-speaking cultural entity, to govern their cultural and educational affairs ("national cultural autonomy"). Socialist-Zionists agreed with Bundists that Russian Jewry constituted an oppressed nation but believed the problems of anti-Jewish violence, discrimination, and poverty could be solved only through the creation of a Jewish homeland in Palestine. Other Jewish socialist parties wanted to establish a Jewish homeland wherever feasible, not necessarily in Palestine, and/or full-fledged Jewish communal autonomy in Russia, not just in the realm of culture and education (as the Bund would have it) but in all communal affairs.

At the same time, some newcomers rejected independent Jewish politics in the name of internationalism. Before coming to the United States, they opted for all-Russian parties (the Russian Social Democratic Workers' Party, for instance) that advanced no specifically Jewish goals and subsumed the problem of anti-Semitism under the larger struggle against capitalism and autocracy. Such internationalists (a label that should be used advisedly because many Bundists and socialist-Zionists also professed commitment to internationalism, as they understood the term) argued that the removal of legal restrictions on Jews within a framework of equal rights for all Russian citizens would put an end to anti-Semitism, therefore obviating the need for independent Jewish parties.[12] Whatever their differences, members of the new parties, including those with no special interest in Jewish politics, swelled the ranks of the American Jewish labor movement and introduced new ideas that affected both the Jewish community and the general American labor movement (in the field of labor education, for instance[13]), all the while reinforcing political connections across the Atlantic.

Immigrants formalized transnational ties by creating American affiliates of Russian parties. These affiliates organized speaking tours for party emissaries, coordinated fund-raising campaigns, and publicized their causes to the Jewish community and the wider American public. Supporters of the Russian Social Democratic Workers' Party established the Russian Social Democratic Society, which published a Russian-language newspaper and raised money for the Menshevik wing of Russian Social Democracy. The Bund's sympathizers (as distinct from party members) established Friends of the Bund, led by the labor lawyer and future Socialist Party congressman Meyer London.[14] Bundists who came from the same city, town, or region in the Russian Empire established *landsmanshaftn*: mutual aid societies based on both geographic and political identities. In 1903, these and other Bundist groups established the Central Union of Bundist Organizations and, three years later, the organization reported 3,000 members in fifty-eight locals.[15] Another party with a vigorous presence among immigrant Jews was the Socialist Revolutionaries. Although a peasant-based party, the Socialist Revolutionaries counted a number of Jews in its leadership, some of whom also participated actively in Jewish politics. The key figure in this regard was Chaim Zhitlovsky, a founder of the Socialist Revolutionaries and the chief theoretician of Yiddish cultural nationalism, from which the Bund drew its program of "national cultural autonomy."[16] In New York, Socialist Revolutionaries found strongest support among Jewish anarchists, who established the New York Group of Socialist Revolutionaries on the Lower East Side. Anarchists formed a different organization for the purpose of aiding political prisoners in Russia. In 1908, Jacob Katzenelenbogen and Harry Weinstein, themselves former prisoners from Bialystok, established the Anarchist Red Cross in New York City to much fanfare. Local branches soon emerged in Chicago, Philadelphia, Detroit, and Baltimore. The Chicago branch, which numbered 300 members at its peak, raised considerable funds through its annual Peasant Ball and other events. By 1915, the Anarchist Red Cross nationwide collected $5,167.[17]

Supporters of Russian Social Democracy, the Bund, the Socialist Revolutionaries, and other parties conducted active, almost continuous, fundraising efforts between 1903 and 1907. The Bund sent no less than six representatives to the United States who raised some $50,000 while the Central Union of Bundist Organizations raised another $11,500. A report to the Bund's annual convention in 1906 estimated that monies donated by American Jews covered as much as half the expenses of local party organizations in Russia.[18] The Socialist Revolutionaries were equally successful. The party sent Zhitlovsky and Katerina Breshkovskaia, the acclaimed "grandmother" of the Russian revolution, on a speaking tour of the United States in the fall of 1904. Within five months the two raised $10,000 and purchased a large quantity of weapons shipped from San Francisco. Nikolai Tshaikovsky, the legendary Grigori Gershuny (rumored to have escaped Siberian captivity in a barrel of cabbage), and Ivan Narodny followed. Narodny's mission yielded a "sizable purchase of grenades."[19]

The high point of Socialist Revolutionary activity occurred in late 1905 and reflected the fervent emotions of the period. In November, the New York Group of Socialist Revolutionaries issued an appeal to all "Jewish federations, unions, societies, and lodges" to attend an emergency meeting to discuss ways to organize a "mighty protest" in reaction to the pogroms that had broken out in the previous month. Those in attendance selected a committee, which, in turn, established the Jewish Defense Association. Its purpose was to create a special fund to purchase weapons for Jewish self-defense groups in Russia. "The Jewish people is arming itself," the association's manifesto declared. "We must create the means." The planned protest took place on December 4th in the form of a day of mourning. The Jewish Defense Association called on all Jewish-owned businesses to close their doors for a mass march. Some 125,000 men and women, dressed in black and wearing armbands, proceeded solemnly from the heart of the Lower East Side to Union Square, while another hundred thousand lined the streets. As the procession passed along Broadway and 10th Street, Grace Cathedral rang its church bell in a display of sympathy. Mourners, no longer able to restrain their grief, began sobbing. "Before their eyes," the head of the Jewish Defense Association recollected, "the entire horror, misfortune, and disaster of Jewish history arose and demanded an answer for the rivers of bloodshed." According to the *New York Times*, "Men and women burst into tears, some moved by their losses, others by the dramatic intensity of sound and scene."[20] Within three months, the Jewish Defense Association raised $26,500, which it distributed to the Socialist Revolutionaries and the Marxist-Zionist Poale Tsion party. Commenting on the plethora of benefits held between 1905 and 1906, one Yiddish journalist observed wryly:

> Never has one danced as much in the Russian colony in New York as during this last year. One danced for the Bund; one danced for the free-thinking Socialist Revolutionaries; and one even danced for the scientific Social Democrats. One danced for the Jewish widows and orphans of Odessa; for the revolutionary sailors of Sebastopol; for the Latvian socialists and the Polish socialists. . . . The more they went on strike and went hungry in Europe, the more one danced in New York. The more shooting there, the more quadrilles danced over here.[21]

A decade later, the Jewish labor movement's official historian, Herts Burgin, described the symbiotic relationship between "Russia" and "America" in the years around 1905: "Russia gave America fire, life, and revolutionary forces; America thus paid her with thousands of dollars for literature, conferences, strikes, demonstrations, weapons, self-defense groups, and the like. Never had the workers' movements in both countries lived with such common interests as they did in the first half of the 1900s."[22]

The aid provided by emigrated Jews to revolutionary organizations dismayed Russian authorities, who were increasingly regarding Jews as threats to the tsarist regime.[23] According to one source, the Russian government began monitoring, sometimes through paid informants, revolutionary activity in New York as early as the 1890s. This claim was made in 1910 by Vladimir Bourtzeff, a Socialist Revolutionary famous in Europe for ferreting spies out of the revolutionary movement. Bourtzeff came to New York with the intention of investigating Alexander Evalenko, a Yiddish book publisher and prominent figure in the Russian Social Democratic Society. According to Bourtzeff, Evalenko had intermittently served as a police agent since he had settled in New York in 1894. In at least one instance, Bourtzeff charged, Evalenko provided information to Russian authorities that resulted in the execution of a Socialist Revolutionary. After Bourtzeff accused him publicly, Evalenko requested a hearing by a committee comprised of Socialist Revolutionaries, Social Democrats, and the editor of the socialist daily *Forverts*, Abraham Cahan. Based on police records and other documents presented by Bourtzeff, the tribunal unanimously found Evalenko guilty. In response, he filed a libel suit of $100,000 against Bourtzeff but dropped it after a Russian officer testified against Evalenko in federal court and Bourtzeff's defense attorney produced an incriminating photograph of Evalenko. Having committed no crime against U.S. law, Evalenko went unpunished, but the scandal ruined his standing in the immigrant Jewish community. The Evalenko affair suggests the need for more research into the extent and nature of Russian police activity in New York. Bourtzeff estimated a dozen spies had operated in New York over the previous two decades.[24]

American authorities, unlike the Russian government, did not seem to object to Jewish assistance to Russian revolutionaries. Public opinion in the United States was generally hostile to the Tsar and sympathetic to Russian Jews, especially after the notorious Kishinev pogrom of 1903. In 1906, in response to renewed outbreaks of mob violence against Jews, both houses of Congress unanimously passed a resolution, endorsed by Theodore Roosevelt, stating "That the people of the United States are horrified by reports of the massacre of Hebrews in Russia, on account of their race and religion."[25] The prevailing opinion regarded Russia as a backward autocracy in need of a democratic revolution, even though Americans knew little of Russian politics and few could distinguish between a Socialist Revolutionary and a Social Democrat. Furthermore, efforts to aid Russian revolutionaries carried no risk because they did not threaten America's national security. If anything, ties to Russia served something of an integrative function, at least among American intellectuals, who sought out Jewish expertise about Russia, especially after the outbreak of the Russo-Japanese war and the 1905 revolution. As the historian Christine Stansell writes in her study of Greenwich Village, American intellectuals came to regard their Jewish counterparts with a "new seriousness" in the early years of the twentieth century.[26] Through lectures, articles, scholarly books, and translations of Russian authors, Jewish intellectuals served as interpreters of Russian politics, society, and culture.[27]

The Bolshevik Revolution

The Bolshevik revolution marked a major turning point in the relationship of immigrant Jews to Russia. Prior to 1917, immigrant Jewry was united in its hostility toward the Tsar, and all celebrated his downfall. The Bolshevik ascent to power, however, gave rise to a more complicated relationship with Russia. It began with widespread enthusiastic support for the Soviet government, which was expressed, in part, through the established practice of fund-raising. A small number of immigrants were not content merely to support Soviet Russia and joined the American Communist Party with the goal of sparking a workers' revolution in the United States. The early Communists viewed themselves not as an independent revolutionary group but the American section of the Communist International dedicated to following the lead of Soviet Russia. This orientation marked a dramatic departure in the history of the American left, as well as Jewish politics. Never before had socialists or Jews pledged loyalty to a foreign government, a dangerous position in the wake of World War I and the subsequent suppression of civil liberties. In the postwar xenophobic climate, immigrant Jews came under suspicion as a disloyal, subversive population. Political ties to Russia now worked against them.

During the early years of the revolution, from 1917 to the early 1920s, most Jewish socialists praised the Bolsheviks for both Jewish-ethnic and socialist-ideological reasons. They applauded efforts to build the first work-ers' state in adverse circumstances caused by war and foreign intervention. At the same time, they hailed the Soviet government's policies toward Jews. The Bolsheviks banned expressions of anti-Semitism, halted the mass slaugh-ter of Jews in the Ukraine, and granted national rights to Jews, something which the Bund and other parties had advocated for almost two decades, but which the Bolsheviks had adamantly rejected until they found them-selves ruling over Russia's large Yiddish-speaking population. For all these reasons, Jewish socialists overwhelmingly supported Lenin and his party. "It seems to me," wrote Abraham Cahan, the editor of the *Forverts* (with a national circulation approaching 200,000), in 1918, "that even the most bitter anti-Bolshevik, if he is a socialist, must forget everything and become filled with love for them when he imagines the statue of Karl Marx standing in the Kremlin. We have criticized them. Some of their utterances often ir-ritate us; but who can help rejoicing in their triumph? Who can help going into ecstasy over the socialist spirit with which they have enthroned the country, which they now rule?" The president of the International Ladies' Garment Workers' Union (ILGWU), Benjamin Schlesinger, upon his return from a visit to Soviet Russia in the fall of 1920, similarly explained that he supported Bolshevism. "One thing is certain," Schlesinger told the editor of the ILGWU's newspaper, "the greatest experiment ever attempted in this world is being made in Russia today. It is three years already since a coun-try, owned by workers, is existing in this world. Understand me, a country where there is no exploitation, where capitalism has been wiped out, where the workmen are the leaders of the land. No matter what the outcome of this experiment is, the fact in itself is of immense historical importance."[28] The overthrow of Lenin's regime, he added, would result in "the greatest massacre of Jews." Amalgamated Clothing Workers of America (ACWA) president Sidney Hillman (a former Bundist) expressed a similar opinion. "The Bolshevik group," Hillman commented after returning from Russia in the fall of 1921, "is the only group with force enough and vigor enough to govern Russia. Any change in the workers' form of government would lead to chaos and disorder."[29] The following year Hillman established the Russian-American Industrial Corporation (RAIC) for the purpose of reconstructing Russia's clothing industry. By 1924, the RAIC invested two million dollars toward the modernization of 34 factories that employed 17,500 workers.[30] Immigrant Jews, during the 1920s and 1930s, donated millions of dollars to aid Soviet Jewish colonization projects (most famously, the establishment of the Jewish Autonomous Region in Birobidjan), provide technical training for Russian Jews, and offer other forms of relief. Beyond the ranks of the Jewish labor movement, the American Jewish Joint Distribution Committee (JDC), the largest and most ambitious relief organization to operate in Soviet Russia, established an agricultural colonization project that, by 1928, built 217 Jewish farm colonies with a total population of 100,000 men and women. This project, which entailed negotiations with Soviet officials years before the United States recognized Moscow, demonstrated the commitment of American Jews to the revolution's success and the well-being of Soviet Jewry, understood by many as inextricably connected.[31]

Amid the enthusiasm, a minority of immigrant Jews went so far as to join the newborn U.S. Communist Party in 1919. Many Jewish Communists were former Bundists and socialist-Zionists, who had immigrated to the United States in the decade prior to the First World War or in the years immediately afterward. The postwar arrivals felt intense admiration for the Bolsheviks and hungered for a militant esprit de corps they found lacking in the established Jewish labor organizations and the Socialist Party. Even those who did not consider themselves died-in-the-wool Leninists gravitated to the Communist Party because it provided a sense of belonging and purpose, not to mention a direct connection to the Soviet experiment. Communists and their sympathizers formed a strong current in the labor movement known as *Di linke* (the Left). Most of those associated with *Di linke* never joined the Communist Party, but they participated in organizations closely tied to the party and controlled by party members. *Linkistn* (or Leftists) built a network of summer camps, schools, cultural societies, theater groups, Yiddish publications, and, eventually, a housing cooperative in the Bronx that, all told, encompassed tens of thousands of Communist Party members, sympathizers, and their families. Communists also won a strong following among Jewish workers in the needle trades and even came close to capturing control of the ILGWU between 1923 and 1926. To be sure, Jewish Communists were in the minority, but they were far from isolated and had reason to believe they represented the vanguard of Jewish labor.

A small, albeit unknown, number of Communists returned to Russia during the 1920s for the purpose of building socialism. (According to an incomplete survey of American Communist party records from 1924–1925, at least thirty-two men and women applied for permission to move to Soviet Russia.[32]) Certain returnees even assumed positions of responsibility in the Soviet government. Two such individuals were Shachno Epshteyn and Max Goldfarb, former Bundists who returned to Russia in 1917. Epshteyn, who first settled in the United States in 1909, was a well-known Yiddish lecturer, journalist (for a time, he edited the ILGWU's Yiddish-language newspaper), and activist in the Socialist Party's Yiddish-speaking section. Epshteyn originally opposed the Bolsheviks but changed sides during the Red Army's occupation of Odessa. He assumed the editorship of the government's Yiddish daily, *Der emes* (The Truth), served as director of the state Yiddish publishing house, and sat on the Central Committee of the Communist Party's Jewish section. "We are living here with all our senses," Epshteyn wrote to a colleague in New York; "every day is for us a piece of history."[33] In the summer of 1921, the Communist International sent Epshteyn to New York to launch a Yiddish daily and conduct "party work" among American Jews.[34] Over the following years, Epshteyn traveled back and forth between the United States and Soviet Russia. He might have played a role in the disappearance of Juliet Poyntz, an erstwhile Communist and educational director of the ILGWU, who was last seen with Epshteyn.[35] (Poyntz's case remains unsolved to this day.) During World War II, he served as secretary of the Soviet Union's Jewish Anti-Facist Committee, which played an active role in mobilizing American Jewish support for the war effort. (One of the Jewish Anti-Fascist Committee's allied organizations in the United States, the Jewish Council for Russian War Relief, raised ten million dollars for the Soviet war effort between 1943 and 1945.[36]) He died of natural causes in 1945.

Max Goldfarb, who immigrated to the United States in 1912 and worked as labor editor of the *Forverts*, returned to Russia in 1917. He served as mayor of Berdichev in 1918 and head of its Jewish communal body. In January 1919, Goldfarb survived the first openly planned and coordinated attack on Jews during the civil war. Shortly thereafter, he moved to Moscow and, at some point during the year, joined the Communist Party. By 1920, Goldfarb had changed his last name to Petrovsky and was appointed director of all officer training schools for the Red Army. Later in the decade, the Communist International sent him to England as an agent, using the last name Bennett. He was later appointed head of the Comintern's Anglo-American Secretariat and, in that capacity, oversaw the formulation of the

Communist Party's policy on the "Negro Question." Goldfarb and his wife were arrested and executed by Soviet authorities on charges of Trotskyism during the late 1930s.[37]

Epshteyn and Goldfarb were not part of a large migration to Russia. Immigrant Jews had among the lowest rate of return migration of all European immigrants, save the Irish. Nonetheless, some observers feared immigrant Jews playing an inordinate role in the Russian revolutions. According to Samuel Gompers's American Alliance for Labor and Democracy, New Yorkers, such as Epshteyn and Goldfarb, "contributed in no small share to the present chaotic state of affairs in Russia."[38] Gompers, a Jew himself, did not indulge in anti-Semitism, but the nefarious association of Jews with Communism became a staple of anti-Semitic discourse. In his testimony to a Senate subcommittee in 1919, Reverend George Simons, the former Superintendent of the Methodist Episcopal Church in Russia and Finland, stated, "the present chaotic conditions in Russia are due in large part to the activities of Yiddish agitators from the East Side of New York City, who went to Russia immediately following the downfall of the Czar." "These Yiddish agitators from the New York East Side," Simons continued, "followed in the trail of Trotzky, who was himself on the East Side at the time of the Czar's overthrow. I have met hundreds of these East-Siders. I have seen them on Nevsky Prospect, and some of them called on me at my home in Petrograd. Let me make it plain that these men are apostate Jews."[39] An Army captain in New York went so far as to request the formation of a special machine gun battalion to put down any possible Jewish-led insurrection.[40] Such fears were, of course, wildly exaggerated. Individual Jews did participate in the revolution, but they surely did not contribute in any significant way to the overall "chaotic conditions" in Russia, just as New York Jews posed no threat to the stability of the U.S. government. It was true, however, that many immigrant Jews sympathized with Soviet Russia and a small number of them, including Epshteyn and Goldfarb, moved there. The large presence of Jews in the Bolshevik party and Soviet state apparatus aided misperceptions of those who could not distinguish between a Russia dominated by the Jews and one inclusive of them.

Transnational Anti-Communism

Most Jewish socialists in New York were pro-Soviet during the first several years of the revolution, but the consensus broke down in the mid-1920s. Political repression in Russia was the key factor. During the revolution's early years, the "Red Terror" elicited little criticism. Arrests, executions, and suppression of free speech and assembly were considered unfortunate but necessary measures needed to defeat counterrevolutionary armies and restore order. However, as the Bolsheviks consolidated power, repression became increasingly difficult to ignore or justify. Immigrant Jews, because of their large numbers on the left, close knowledge of and connections to Russian parties, and organizational clout through the ILGWU and *Forverts* (economic powerhouses both), *The New Leader*, and the Socialist Party's Yiddish-speaking section played the leading role in creating an anti-Soviet alliance on the political left.

Anarchists were among the earliest and most outspoken anti-Communists. Although relatively small in number, anarchists nonetheless had a real presence on the American left, especially among immigrant Jews. They occupied important positions in major labor organizations, including the ILGWU, whose president at the time, Morris Zigman, was an anarchist. The most famous Jewish anarchists, however, no longer lived in the United States as of 1920. They were Alexander Berkman and Emma Goldman, who were deported to Russia in December 1919. Although opposed philosophically to Marxism, Berkman and Goldman had endorsed the Bolshevik seizure of power at the outset and were generally hopeful about the revolution's prospects when they landed in Russia. Their optimism eventually soured, however, and came to a decisive end with the Kronstadt Rebellion of March 1921. Angered by the Red Army's suppression of the uprising, Berkman and Goldman left the country at the end of the year. They were never permitted to return to the United States, but they nonetheless played an important role in the early development of American anti-Communism. They published numerous articles and several books—most famously, Goldman's *My Disillusionment with Russia* (1923)—that served to dampen enthusiasm for Soviet Russia among radicals and liberals. In addition, Berkman initiated a campaign on behalf of political prisoners that brought the subject of political repression to the fore.

The campaign began in 1924. Berkman, then based in Berlin, organized a committee of émigrés to document the plight of Soviet political prisoners. Named the Joint Committee for the Defense of Revolutionists Imprisoned in Russia, the group enlisted the help of Berkman's friend in New York, Henry Alsberg, *The Nation* magazine's former Moscow correspondent. Alsberg asked Roger Baldwin, director of the American Civil Liberties Union, to send a representative to Russia on a fact-finding mission, the results of which would lead to the formation of a committee to raise awareness of their plight. Baldwin expressed interest in Berkman's proposal but moved cautiously. He considered himself a friend of Soviet Russia and wanted to avoid anything that might give ammunition to its enemies. Baldwin did not accept Berkman's total condemnation of Soviet Russia but ultimately agreed to send Henry Ward, a prominent Unitarian minister sympathetic to the Bolsheviks, to gather information. Ward's report to Baldwin, couched in apologetics and reliant on official Soviet sources, angered Berkman. As far as he was concerned, Ward typified naive and misinformed liberals who, as Berkman put it to the ACLU director, "persistently ignore . . . the fact that the prisons and concentration camps of Russia are filled with politicals." Despite deficiencies in Ward's report, it included enough evidence to convince Baldwin of the need for action. In December 1924, Baldwin established the International Committee to Protect Political Prisoners (ICPP), which brought together prominent liberals and a small number of socialists for the gently stated purpose of making "an appeal to those portions of the general public interested in the Russian situation." Toward that end, the ICPP staged a large Town Hall meeting in the spring of 1925 and published, later in the year, a remarkable collection of documents entitled *Letters from Russian Prisons*, compiled and translated by Berkman and his group of researchers in Berlin.

At the same moment that Berkman and Baldwin were making plans to establish the ICPP, the Socialist Party's Yiddish section, known as the Jewish Socialist Farband, was planning its own action on behalf of Soviet political prisoners. Funded by the *Forverts*, whose editors had turned against Soviet Russia during the early 1920s, and housed in its building, the Jewish Socialist Farband was led by three men with close ties to Russian parties. The Farband's national secretary was a veteran of the Bund named Nokhum Khanin, a man familiar with the inside of Russian prisons; its national organizer was Sol Levitas, a Menshevik émigré and former vice mayor of Vladivostok; and the editor of the Farband's Yiddish weekly was David Shub, another former Menshevik who would later author a popular biography of Vladimir Lenin.

The trio decided, in the fall of 1924, to organize a speaking tour for Raphael Abramovitch, a leading Bundist and Menshevik, then living in Berlin. During the first several years of the revolution, Abramovitch was a member of the Moscow Soviet, but after several arrests, he concluded he had no future in Russia. In Berlin, Abramovitch served as an ambassador for the Menshevik organization in exile and joined the Socialist and Labor International's Executive Committee. Under the latter's auspices, Abramovitch authored a report entitled *The Terror against the Socialist Parties of Russia and Georgia*, republished in the United States by the ICPP and in a Yiddish translation by the Jewish Socialist Farband.

As it turned out, Abramovitch's visit resulted in controversy. In January 1925, the Communist International sent a cable to the American Communist Party's Secretariat warning that Abramovitch planned to launch a "propaganda" campaign against Soviet Russia. The Comintern outlined a countercampaign to discredit Abramovitch, and the Communist Party pledged to "carry on an intensive agitation" against him "in [the] press, thru mass meetings, pamphlets, and leaflets."

The Communist Party made good on its promise. At Abramovitch's first public appearance in New York City, Communists brought his speech to a halt by causing a scene of sheer "bedlam," according to one press account, in which no less than a dozen fistfights broke out. A week later, Abramovitch arrived at a speaking engagement in Philadelphia under police protection. Again, Communists tried to disrupt his speech, leading to 43 arrests on charges of incitement to riot. In cities across the country, Communists attempted to shout him down and party newspapers in English, Russian, and Yiddish vilified Abramovitch in terms extreme even by Communist standards of invective. Roger Baldwin who, as the director of the ACLU, had defended the First Amendment rights of Communists and whose board included the Communist Party leader William Z. Foster, beseeched the party to cease disrupting Abramovitch's lectures. The Communist Party refused to comply, but Abramovitch nonetheless raised $14,000 from immigrant Jews during his tour of the United States.

Abramovitch's lectures and articles provided detailed, authoritative information about the Bolshevik dictatorship and galvanized opposition to Soviet Russia. They did so not for the purpose of restoring the Romanovs to the throne—Abramovitch, in fact, favored diplomatic recognition of Soviet Russia—but for the sake of realizing the Russian revolution's democratic promise. In subsequent decades, American Jewish labor organizations continued to assist Mensheviks and other left-wing anti-Communists in Europe. In 1940, the Jewish Labor Committee, an organization established by the ILGWU and the *Forverts* for the purpose of rescuing socialists, Jews and gentiles alike, endangered by the Nazis, brought the Mensheviks' foreign delegation from Paris to the United States. The émigré Mensheviks, Abramovitch among them, gained prominence in the United States primarily as scholars and political commentators. They dominated the foreign affairs desk at *The New Leader*, which, after World War II, came to be regarded as one of the most authoritative sources of information on Russian politics. ("*The New Leader*," as one writer quipped, "became the only place the Mensheviks ever won a revolution.") Through their contacts abroad, the magazine's editors, with Sol Levitas at the helm, published articles by such Eastern European dissident intellectuals as Milovan Djilas and Leszek Kolakowski, whose writings had circulated underground in eastern Europe before *The New Leader* brought them to an American readership. As for Abramovitch, he contributed frequently to *The New Leader* and the *For-*

verts and served as director of the AFL's American Labor Conference on International Affairs, which, between 1943 and 1950, conducted research on American foreign policy and published a journal of international politics, *The Modern Review*, which featured a distinguished assortment of socialist and liberal intellectuals.[41]

The émigré Mensheviks, although few in number (the foreign delegation consisted of just ten members), reflected the widening influence of Jewish labor anti-Communists after World War II. No longer confined to the immigrant Jewish community or the Socialist Party, Jewish labor organizations began to operate in larger arenas. Probably no person represents this development more than the former Communist Party leader Jay Lovestone. Born in Russia but raised in New York, Lovestone was expelled from the party in 1929 for promoting the theory that capitalism in the United States, unlike in Europe, was robust enough to withstand crises in the foreseeable future and that American Communists should formulate strategy accordingly. After his expulsion from the Party, Lovestone and his followers formed an alternative organization that had no real influence anywhere except in the ILGWU, where the "Lovestoneites" controlled one of the largest locals and occupied important positions in the union bureaucracy. By the outbreak of World War II, Lovestone renounced Communism altogether and dedicated the rest of his life to combating it overseas. In 1943, the ILGWU president, David Dubinsky, appointed Lovestone director of the ILGWU's International Affairs Department. He later directed the AFL's American Institute for Free Labor Development, which worked in cooperation with the CIA to organize anti-Communist labor unions in Europe and Latin America. Over the following three decades, Lovestone served as executive secretary of the International Confederation of Free Trade Unions and as director of the AFL-CIO's International Affairs Department, which covertly channeled millions of dollars from the CIA to anti-Communist activities internationally, particularly in Latin America. Lovestone held that position until 1974, when the AFL-CIO expelled him upon discovery of his long-standing CIA connections.[42]

* * *

Starting in the late nineteenth century, immigrant Jewish labor in the United States developed ties to Russian revolutionary parties that often involved donations of large quantities of illegal Yiddish publications and money. This aid was of crucial importance during the early years of the Russian revolutionary movement, when socialists there faced severe political repression. During the early 1900s, however, Russian Jews themselves became rapidly politicized, and the migration of thousands of revolutionaries to New York City and other immigrant centers reversed the direction of influence now from East to West. These immigrants altered American Jewish politics by introducing Jewish nationalist ideologies and injecting a militant spirit carried over from the 1905 Russian revolution. At the same time, immigrant Jews in the United States broadened their contacts to include not only Jewish parties, such as the Bund, but also all-Russian parties, such as the Socialist Revolutionaries in Russia.

Prior to the Bolshevik ascent to power in 1917, relations with the Russian revolutionary movement brought few, if any, negative consequences to immigrant Jews in the United States, although they aroused suspicions among Russian officials, who, in at least one instance and quite possibly more, hired informers to monitor revolutionary activity in New York. After 1917, however, widespread Soviet sympathies among immigrant Jews and the visible presence of Jews in the Communist movement in the United States and Russia aroused suspicion in the United States. At the same time, the pro-Soviet consensus among immigrant Jews did not last beyond the early 1920s, as the question of political repression in the Soviet Union moved to the forefront of immigrant Jewish public life and produced a deep, permanent rift among former supporters.

The division of immigrant Jews, and the American left generally, into Communist and anti-Communist camps continued into the post–World War II era. The relative strength of each camp shifted over time, reflecting recurring cycles of enchantment and disenchantment with Soviet Russia. To those who directly or indirectly lived through the catastrophic events of the First World War and the Civil War, the Russian revolution offered salvation to the Jews. The intensity of their identification with Soviet Russia reflected the belief that Communism had solved the previously intractable "Jewish Question" during a dire period. Likewise, at later points, Jews viewed the Soviet Union as their protectors. During the 1940s, many Jews lauded Russia for its role in defeating Nazi Germany and providing crucial diplomatic and military support (this from Communist Czechoslovakia with Soviet approval) to the newborn state of Israel. And yet, in other instances—such as the German-Soviet nonaggression pact of 1939, the dismantling of Yiddish cultural institutions, and the party's anti-Semitic campaigns in the late Stalin period—the Soviet Union appeared as enemies of the Jewish people.

Such extremely varied policies toward Jews created a highly emotional, often anguished, relationship between American Jews and Communism, in which any given time, Jews ranked among Communism's most devoted followers and its most formidable opponents. No political issue between the 1920s and 1950s proved more divisive, capable of dividing comrades, friends, and families, than the "Russian Question." In the late nineteenth century, American Jewish ties to the Russian revolutionary movement were little noticed outside the immigrant community, but, over time, they served to bring Jews into the public eye. In and around 1905, Jewish connections to Russia helped bring them into contact with Americans increasingly interested in events in that faraway country. After 1917, Jewish sympathies for the Bolsheviks were met with anti-Semitic reactions. The turn toward anti-Communism by democratic socialists and anarchists, on the other hand, paved the way for the Jewish labor movement's accommodation with American institutions during the Cold War.

NOTES

1. For recent transnational approaches to American Jewish history, see Rebecca Kobrin, *Jewish Bialystok and Its Diaspora* (Bloomington: Indiana University Press, 2010), 1–18; Adam Mendelsohn, "Tongue Ties: The Emergence of the Anglophone Jewish Diaspora in the Mid-Nineteenth Century," *American Jewish History* 93 (June 2007): 177–209; Daniel Soyer, "Transnationalism and Mutual Influence: American and East European Jewries in the 1920s and 1930s," in *Rethinking European Jewish History*, ed. Jeremy Cohen and Moshe Rosman (Oxford: The Littman Library, 2009), 201–220. On the role of Jews in trans-Atlantic business networks, see Sarah Abrevaya Stein, *Plumes: Ostrich Feathers, Jews, and a Lost World of Global Commerce* (New Haven: Yale University Press, 2008), 1–27.

2. Eli Lederhendler, *Jewish Immigrants and American Capitalism, 1880–1920: From Caste to Class* (New York: Cambridge University Press, 2009), 38–84; Tony Michels, *A Fire in Their Hearts: Yiddish Socialists in New York* (Cambridge: Harvard University Press, 2005), 7–16.

3. Jews had the lowest rate of return (4.3 percent for men) of all European immigrant groups of the period. Thomas J. Archdeacon, *Becoming American: An Ethnic History* (New York: The Free Press, 1983), 139.

4. See, for instance, David Thelan, "The Nation and Beyond: Transnational Perspectives on United States History," *Journal of American History* 86 (Dec. 1999): 967. On the debate over immigrants and transnationalism, see David G. Gutierrez and Pierrette Hondagneu-Sotelo, "Nations and Migration," *American Quarterly* 60 (Sept. 2008): 503–521.

5. Jack Jacobs, *On Socialists and "The Jewish Question" after Marx* (New York: New York University Press, 1992), 118–124.

6. Iuli Martov, *Zapiski sotsial-demokrata* (Berlin: Gržebin, 1922), 227. I thank David McDonald for this translation from the Russian. For a Yiddish translation of Martov's account, see L. Martov, "Di yidishe arbeter-bavegung in Rusland farn Bund," *Der veker*, May 12, 1922, 16.

7. Jonathan Frankel, *Prophecy and Politics: Socialism, Nationalism, and the Russian Jews, 1862–1917* (Cambridge: Cambridge University Press, 1981), 176.

8. Ibid., 194.

9. Joshua D. Zimmerman, *Poles, Jews, and the Politics of Nationality* (Madison: University of Wisconsin Press, 2004), 30–31.

10. Kenyon Zimmer, *Immigrants against the State: Yiddish and Italian Anarchism in America* (Urbana: University of Illinois Press, 2015), 115–116.

11. Tony Michels, "Exporting Yiddish Socialism: New York's Role in the Russian Jewish Workers' Movement," *Jewish Social Studies* 16 (Fall 2009): 1–26.

12. Frankel, *Prophecy and Politics*, 90–364, 453–560; Ezra Mendelsohn, *On Modern Jewish Politics* (New York: Oxford University Press), 3–36; Michels, *Fire in Their Hearts*, 125–178; Enzo Traverso, *The Marxists and the Jewish Question: The History of a Debate, 1843–1943*, trans. Bernard Gibbons (Atlantic Highlands, N.J.: Humanities, 1994).

13. Dan Katz, *All Together Different: Yiddish Socialists, Garment Workers, and the Labor Roots of Multiculturalism* (New York: New York University Press, 2011), 72–163.

14. Herts Burgin, *Di geshikhte fun der yidisher arbeter bavegung* (New York: United Hebrew Trades, 1915), 672.

15. Most Bundist groups eventually merged into preexisting Jewish labor and socialist organizations, such as the Arbeter Ring (Workmen's Circle) fraternal order and Yiddish-language branches of the Socialist Party, thereby indicating the intention of their members to remain in the United States despite deeply felt connections to the Bund and their places of origin. Y. Sh. Herts, *50 yor Arbeter-ring in yidishn lebn* (New York: Arbeter Ring, 1950), 65–69; M. Invenski, "Di role fun bundistishe landsmanshaftn in dem oyfboy fun Arbeter-ring," in *Zamlbukh aroysgegebn tsum finf-un-tsvantsikstn yorfest fun dem Dvinsker bundistisher brentsh 75 Arbeter-ring*, ed. S. Volos (New York: np, 1929), 74–76; Workmen's Circle Bund Archives, folder 101; Daniel Soyer, *Jewish Immigrant Associations and American Identity in New York, 1880–1939* (Cambridge: Harvard University Press, 1997), 66–70.

16. Michels, *Fire in Their Hearts*, 125–154.

17. "Fun di aroysgeber" in M. Berezin, *Fun keytn tsu frayhayt* (New York: Anarkhistisher royter krayts, 1915), 5–6; B. Yelensky, *In the Struggle for Equality: The Story of the Anarchist Red Cross* (Chicago: A. Berkman Aid Fund, 1958), 21–32. On Jews in the Russian anarchist movement, see Paul Avrich, *The Russian Anarchists* (Princeton: Princeton University Press, 1967), 40–49.

18. G. Aronson et al., *Geshikhte fun Bund*, vol. 2 (New York: Unzer Tsayt Farlag, 1962), 421; Herts, *50 yor Arbeter-ring*, 67; Yehezkel Lifshits, "Avraham Lesin: Kavim li-demuto le-fi mikhtavov, zikhronotav, ve-khen zikhronot benei doro," *Measef* 6 (Mar. 1974): 23.

19. Arthur W. Thompson, "The Reception of Russian Revolutionary Leaders in America, 1904–1906," *American Quarterly* 18 (Autumn 1966), 452–476. Also see A. Bullard, "The St. Petersburg Massacre and the Russian East Side," *Independent*,

Feb. 2, 1905, 252–256. "Throng Cheers the Hero of the Barrel Escape," *New York Times*, Dec. 15, 1906, 2; "Arms to Free Russia, Tchaykoffsky's Appeal," *New York Times*, Mar. 30, 1906, 9.

20. "Jews, in Huge Parade, Mourn Dead in Russia," *New York Times*, Dec. 4, 1905; Frankel, *Prophecy and Politics*, 487–493; Y. Kopelov, *Amol un shpeter* (Vilna: Farlag Altnay, 1932), 98.

21. Quoted in Frankel, *Prophecy and Politics*, 492.

22. Burgin, *Di geshikhte fun der yidisher arbeter bavegung*, 669.

23. Hans Rogger, *Jewish Policies and Right-Wing Politics in Imperial Russia* (Berkeley: University of California Press, 1986), 56–112.

24. *New York Times*, Jan. 7, 1910; Jan. 20, 1910; Apr. 26, 1910; Oct. 13, 1910; Nov. 8, 1912. For a retrospective account of the affair, see Abraham Cahan, *Bleter fun mayn lebn* (New York: Forverts Association, 1926), 4: 581–588.

25. Quoted in Eli Lederhendler, "Democracy and Assimilation: The Jews, America, and the Russian Crisis from Kishinev to the End of World War I," in *The Revolution of 1905 and Russia's Jews*, ed. Stefani Hoffman and Ezra Mendelsohn (Philadelphia: University of Pennsylvania Press, 2008), 251. Also, see Cyrus Adler, ed., *The Voice of America on Kishineff* (Philadelphia: Jewish Publication Society, 1904); David S. Foglesong, *The American Mission and the "Evil Empire": The Crusade of a "Free Russia" since 1881* (New York: Cambridge University Press, 2007), 7–45; Jane E. Good, "America and the Russian Revolutionary Movement, 1888–1905," *Russian Review* 41 (July 1982): 273–287; David Hecht, *Russian Radicals Look to America, 1825–1894* (Cambridge: Harvard University Press, 1947).

26. Christine Stansell, *American Moderns: Bohemian New York and the Creation of a New Century* (New York: Metropolitan Books, 2000), 64.

27. Steven Cassedy, *To the Other Shore: The Russian Jewish Intellectuals Who Came to America* (Princeton: Princeton University Press, 1997), 105–127; Charles W. Meister, "Chekhov's Reception in England and America," *American Slavic and East European Review* 12 (Feb. 1953): 109–121; Tony Michels, "The Lower East Side Meets Greenwich Village: Immigrant Jews and the New York Intellectual Scene," in *Choosing Yiddish: New Frontiers of Language and Culture*, ed. Shiri Goren, Hannah Pressman, and Lara Rabinovitch (Detroit: Wayne State University Press, 2012), 69–85; Ernest Poole, "Maxim Gorki in New York," *Slavonic and East European Review. American Series* 3 (May, 1944): 77.

28. S. Yanofsky, "An Interview on Russia with Pres. Schlesinger," *Justice*, Nov. 19, 1920, 5.

29. "Amalgamated Leader Gets Warm Greeting," *Advance*, Nov. 11, 1921, 2.

30. Steven Fraser, "The 'New Unionism' and the 'New Economic Policy,'" in *Work, Community, and Power: The Experience of Labor in Europe and America, 1900–1925*, ed. James E. Cronin and Carmen Sirianni (Philadelphia: Temple University Press, 1983), 173–196.

31. John L. Dekel-Chen, *Farming the Red Land: Jewish Agricultural Colonization and Local Soviet Power, 1924–1941* (New Haven: Yale University Press, 2005),

34–95; Henry Srehnik, "Diaspora, Ethnicity and Dreams of Nationhood: American Jewish Communists and the Birobidzhan Project," in *Yiddish and the Left*, ed. Gennady Estraikh and Mikhail Krutikov (Oxford: Legenda, 2001), 80–108.

32. Information on some Communist Party members who emigrated to Soviet Russia or requested permission to emigrate there can be found in Reels 32–34 of the Records of the Communist Party of the United States in the Comintern Archives (Fond 515), microfilm edition compiled by the Library of Congress and the Russian State Archive of Social and Political History (Tamiment Library copy).

33. Zvi Gitelman, *Jewish Nationality and Soviet Politics: The Jewish Sections of the CPSU, 1917–1930* (Princeton, N.J., 1972), 261–262, 278, 130; Epshteyn to Liessin, Sept. 27, 1920 (Abraham Liessin Collection, folder 387, YIVO Institute).

34. Michels, *Fire in Their Hearts*, 228.

35. Herbert Solow, "Missing a Year! Where Is Julia Poyntz?" *New Leader*, July 2, 1938, 3, 7; Carlo Tresca, "Where Is Julia Stuart Poyntz?" *Modern Monthly* (March 1938): 12–13; Irina Vodonos, "Juliet Stuart Poyntz: Suffragist, Feminist, Spy," Barnard College Archives. www.barnard.edu/archives/history/notable/poyntz (accessed Dec. 23, 2015).

36. Shimon Redlich, *Propaganda and Nationalism in Wartime Russia: The Jewish Antifascist Committee in the USSR* (Luxembourg: Harwood Academic Publishers, 1995), 103–104.

37. Gitelman, *Jewish Nationality and Soviet Politics*, 84, 226, 324; Mark Solomon, *The Cry Was Unity: Communists and African Americans, 1917–1936* (Jackson: University of Mississippi Press, 1998), 68–91.

38. *New York Times*, Nov. 30, 1917, 3. In fact, neither Goldfarb nor Epshteyn were Communists at this early point.

39. Quoted in "Jews from America in the Bolshevik Oligarchy," *Literary Digest* 60, Mar. 1, 1919, 32. Also, see Elias Tabenkin, "Russians Who Once Lived Here Now Abuse Us," *New York Times*, Jan. 20, 1918.

40. Joseph W. Bendersky, *The "Jewish Threat": Anti-Semitic Politics of the U.S. Army* (New York: Basic Books, 2000), xi–xii.

41. Daniel Bell, "*The Modern Review*: An Introduction and Appraisal," *Labor History* 9 (Fall 1968): 380–383; Myron Kolatch, "Introduction," *New Leader* (Jan./April 2006): 5–8; Andre Liebich, "Mensheviks Wage the Cold War," *Journal of Contemporary History* 30 (April 1995): 247–264; Hugh Wilford, "Playing the CIA's Tune? The *New Leader* and the Cultural Cold War," *Diplomatic History* 27 (Jan. 2003): 15–34.

42. Ted Morgan, *A Covert Life: Jay Lovestone, Communist, Anti-Communist, and Spymaster* (New York: Random House, 1999); John P. Windmuller, "Foreign Affairs and the AFL-CIO," *Industrial and Labor Relations Review* 9, "The AFL-CIO Merger" (Apr. 1956): 419–432.

CHAPTER 8

PERIODIZING INDIAN ORGANIZATIONAL TRANSNATIONALISM IN THE UNITED KINGDOM

Thomas Lacroix

Immigrant associations have, for long, been mostly analyzed with regards to their role in integration processes. However, as pointed out by an old body of research, migrant organizations endorse a large array of transnational functions: they are vectors of information from the sending country, loci of mobilization for overseas causes, or development actors in sending areas.[1] And yet, systematic research on these aspects has been rare until recently. A growing body of research has highlighted their importance in the maintaining of cross-border connections,[2] not only with the country of origin, but also with other countries of settlement. Associations are not isolated units; rather, through their activities and partnerships, they form networks of organizations that condition the practices and access to resources of their members. Migrant associations therefore weave together "organizational fields."

First coined in France by Abdelmalek Sayad, the concept of "champ associatif" (associational field) differs from and complements the concept of "transnational social field." Whereas the latter primarily focuses on interpersonal cross-border networks, the concept of associational field, as defined by Sayad, entails networks of interrelated organizations whose position and meaning depend on the relations that they maintain with one another.[3] Drawing on Sayad's work, I seek to adapt this notion for the study of cross-border voluntary organizations. Such an approach provides the possibility to analyze an array of forces affecting the constitution and evolution of organizational fields. Indeed, voluntary activities intersect with the social background of organizations' members, the structure of civil societies, and the wider political context in which the organizations are embedded.

This chapter depicts and explains the long-term evolution of the Indian organizational field in the United Kingdom and its transnational extensions.

The field of Indian organizations is of a rare complexity. It is the product of a stratification of different generations of organizations, which appeared at different moments in the settlement of the Indian community. Likewise, the form and orientations of transnational connections evolved and became increasingly complex.

This chapter is based on a three-year research project supported by the Volkswagen Foundation.[4] A listing of 1,210 Indian organizations was compiled by combining different sources: the charity commission directory and the directory on religious organizations put together by Derby University.[5] The database includes information about the name, the year of creation, the location of its headquarters, the main activity, and the transnational orientation of each association.[6] Complementary investigations were carried out through internet and telephone interviews among a sample of twenty organizations engaged in cross-border activities. Field visits and interviews with key informants and local authorities were undertaken in four of the main places of settlement of the Indian community in the UK: Birmingham, Slough, Southall, and Coventry. The final step involved a case study of two key associations: the Birmingham branch of the Indian Workers' Association, which was the largest Indian association until the eighties, and the Sikh Human Rights Group, based in London, an influential Sikh organization created during the Indo-Punjab conflict.

It should be kept in mind that the methodology introduces two biases. In the first place, the listing is not comprehensive as it includes only registered associations. But while it does not provide accurate figures regarding the number of existing associations, the database reveals key trends in the structuration of the organizational field. The second bias stems from the primary focus on Sikh organizations, once again due to the time and resource constraints of the project. But Sikh Punjabis still represent the largest Indian ethnic grouping in the UK and their historical precedence still holds a strong sway over the structuration of the contemporary Indian organizational field. To balance this account, the chapter also discusses new emerging fields among Hindu groups.

This chapter distinguishes four main periods. The first one, from 1947 (year of India's independence) until the early sixties is the age of pioneer migrants, characterized by the informality of migrant organizations, except for a handful of large political associations supporting the fight for independence in the origin country. The second period is the one of the structuration of the organizational field at the local and national levels. It started with the mass arrivals of labor migrants. The third period, during the eighties, is a period of transition marked by political unrest that affected Punjab between

1984 and 1992 and the surge of the Khalistani movement (a movement supportive of Punjab independence during the Indo-Punjab conflict in the late nineties). During the second half of the eighties, the UK-based Indian voluntary sector reconfigured. The fourth and last period started with the end of the conflict in Punjab and the outbreak of the financial crisis in India, which led the Indian government to adopt a new behavior toward its diaspora. From the early nineties onward, the Indian organizational field in the UK crystallized into its contemporary features. It reflects the sheer socioeconomic, religious, generational, ethnic, and political diversity of this community (and, indeed, the extreme diversity of India itself). Likewise, the transnational connections of Indian organizations evolved a great deal. If they were initially mostly of a political nature and oriented toward India, they have undergone a complex reorientation toward homeland development, on the one hand, and toward a diasporization of organizational networks on the other.

Throughout this historical account, the intent is to elicit the factors that underpin the evolution of migrant organizational fields. This chapter links the main periods of the organizational life not only to the features of the Indian community, but also to its national and international context. Particular attention will be paid to the following factors: composition and orientation of immigrant flows, the class and ethnic characteristics of the Indian population and their evolution over time, the social movements and conflicts in the host and origin settings, and the policies implemented by sending and receiving states.

Migrant Organizations among Working-class Indians (1947–1984)

1947–1962: Labor Migration after Indian Independence

After India's independence in 1947, the Indian migratory system underwent a complete transformation. From the 1950s onward, the United Kingdom, the United States, and Canada attracted a low-skilled workforce from South Asia. After the Second World War, the United Kingdom implemented a laissez-faire immigration policy by granting freedom of circulation and settlement to Commonwealth citizens. However, once independent, the Indian government endorsed an opposite stance. The national authorities adopted a development strategy oriented toward self-sustainability with a view to making a break with its past as a colonized country. In this context, emigration was a reality that did not fit with the overall narrative of an independent nation-building process. It was perceived as an individual choice with which the state should not interfere (and certainly not encourage), and people outside the national territory were outside the sphere of competence and responsibility of the state.[7] Emigrants were widely viewed negatively, as deserters or as contributing to brain drain.[8] Emigration was discouraged and passports were sparingly delivered.

However, the Punjab was treated differently. Having heavily suffered from the partition of British India into the separate countries of India and Pakistan, the region's economic and social situation was in ruins. Indian authorities turned a blind eye to the circulation of illegal departure permits and the multiplication of migration brokers. In addition, the region enjoyed long-standing migration networks that had supplied, until 1947, a large number of workers, administrators, and policemen to the British Empire. The Punjabis, coming for the most part from the districts of Jullundur and Hoshiarpur, constituted the bulk of the postwar unskilled immigration. Indian communities sprang up in industrial areas of London (Southall), the Midlands, and the Northern districts (Manchester, Liverpool, Bradford). The population was relatively homogenous in terms of class and ethnic background, with the majority comprised of Sikh Jats, a caste of small landowners.

During this period, the UK Indian organizational field emerged around two distinct layers. The first layer involved the "hometown networks" maintained by migrants and their place of origin. They played a key role in maintaining migration routes and were conducive to the clustering of people in the same neighborhoods. Hometown organizations framed the formation of a primary social field of kith and kin at the place of arrival. They remained informal, loosely structured groups of people whose primary function was to provide support and conviviality to their members. Circulating information coming from the village of origin, hometown groups could also occasionally mobilize to provide support to the village community. The first development initiatives of hometown groups, such as the building of a school or the restoration of Panchayat[9] buildings, began from the early sixties onward, illustrating their growing capacity for action.[10]

The second layer of the organizational field was comprised of self-help and religious organizations founded to cater to the needs of local Indian communities. They gave shape to a community social field beyond the primary ties of relatives. Most of them were Gurudwaras, Sikh places of worship, but early on there were mosques (the Indian Muslim Welfare Society created in 1957 by southern Gujarati in Batley) as well as Jain[11] temples (the Jain Ashram of Birmingham in 1960). However, this organizational field was characterized by its low level of formality. Places of worship and other associations' premises were located in the homes of their members and only a handful of organizations maintained a level of outreach beyond their local communities.

The Indian Workers' Association (IWA) was the main exception to this pattern. During the postwar period, the IWA was not a proper "national organization," but rather a federation of local branches that had their own agendas. A first branch opened in 1953 in Coventry, and then other groups were created in Wolverhampton and Southall in 1956 and Birmingham in 1959. Branches were opened in the Midlands, East and West London, Northern England, and Scotland. In some areas, the organization was reported to enlist half of the male Indians working there.[12] While the vast majority of the members were Sikh Punjabis, the IWA was not a Sikh association and was open to any person regardless of political, religious, and ethnic background. Likewise, the IWA had no official political affiliation, although communist activists controlled the largest number of branches. The organization was (and still is) primarily a working-class association following an internationalist political line that objects to "communalist" inclinations. And yet for decades it has kept a strong sway over the British Sikh community by mixing cultural and political activities. The IWA was one of the few UK-based Indian organizations engaging with both Indian and British public authorities and entrepreneurs. For instance, Prime Minister Nehru received IWA representatives during his official visit in the UK in 1957. During the meeting, they addressed the problem of forged passports (widespread among the Indian immigrants) that interfered with the possibility of formalizing their situation in the UK. The activities of the organizations were mostly directed toward the welfare and rights of the Indian workers in Britain. However, transnational connections with Indian far-left groups were established during the same period. A number of IWA leaders were linked to politically active families in India, connections that in turn underpinned the long-standing relationships between IWA and its main overseas partner, the Desh Baghat Yadgar Hall in Jullundur (central Punjab). The Gadr party, originally created in 1913 in San Francisco, was the first party advocating for the independence of India. During the First World War, it attempted to spur an armed rebellion in Punjab, but failed. The members were jailed by the British authorities and released after independence, in 1947. In 1959, it was decided to build a conference hall and documentation center in Punjab to commemorate the memory of the Gadr party, the Desh Baghat Yadgar Hall. The initiative received extensive backing from IWA members who organized several public meetings in support of the initiative and engaged in considerable fund-raising. The Hall remains the main overseas partner of the IWA.

The other main Indian group enjoying a national presence across Britain was the Indian Overseas Congress. Partly founded by former members of the India League, a pro-independence movement active during the interwar period, the IOC was not a mass organization like the IWA but instead a network that recruited among Indian professionals and students close to the Congress party. Because of its poor outreach in the immigrant population, and because the question of the diaspora was not high on the Congress's agenda, the association maintained a low profile until its registration as an official organization, in 1969.

1962–1980: The Age of Mass Settlement

This period was marked by a rapid increase in the number of associations. Local organizations mushroomed to provide local communities with a space for socializing. Two events explain this rapid surge. First, the restrictive immigration policy implemented in the UK after 1962 stopped the temporary migration of unskilled laborers that had prevailed until then. The closure of borders accelerated the arrival of wives and children through family reunification and favored the formation of immigrant communities.[13] In parallel, the government implemented a new integration policy endorsing a multiculturalist approach. The new policy took shape through a succession of laws adopted in 1965, 1968, and 1981, which sought to promote the collective insertion of community groups at the local level. Municipalities became the implementation authorities in charge of designing integration strategies.

The growth of the population and policy demand were the two main factors responsible for the subsequent development of the organizational field. This process was conducive to a diversification of the services offered to local migrant communities: religious services, schooling, and so forth. A third factor accounting for this surge was the arrival of Indians expelled from Africa by newly independent states (mostly Tanzania, Kenya, and Uganda). The deportation of East African Indians led cohorts of Gujaratis and Ramgharias to the UK,[14] a migration that accelerated the slow but noticeable ethnic and religious diversification of the Indian population. This led to the emergence of new forms of organizations.

Until the late sixties, hometown organizations were the main form of "primary ties" organization, but caste associations, such as the Ramgharia Sikh organization created in 1967, the Kutch Madhapar Karyalaya formed in 1968, and the Shree Sorathia Prajapati established in 1969, then became widespread. But this new immigration also imported new ideological strands. Shakas, branches of the Rashtriya Swayamsevak Sangh (RSS), the largest

Hindu nationalist organization, were transplanted to the UK by Hindu newcomers.[15] In 1966, these Shakas were federated into the Hindu Swayam Sangh (HSS) with the goal of adapting the rules and practices of the Shakas to the Western context.

The ethno-religious diversification of the Indian community fueled a dynamic of fragmentation of the primary (interkinship) and secondary (intracommunity) layers of the organizational field. This led to the multiplication of local communities pooled around a caste/faction oriented place of worship, which itself hosted a community center where after-school classes were organized for youngsters, where women and elderly people could meet and find support. Beyond their religious function, places of worship provided a space around which community life became organized, including in its political aspects. This characteristic of the Indian organizational field accounted for a strong entanglement between the welfare, political, and religious spheres at the local level.

This grassroots diversity contrasted with the homogeneity of the organizational field at the national level. In the sixties and seventies, the IWA was the largest and almost only organization occupying the third level of the field, the level of community relationships beyond the local scale. Some estimate that there were 200,000 affiliates in 1965, three quarters of whom might have been Punjabis.[16] The federative form of the IWA enabled the association to engage with British and Indian state and nonstate actors at the national level while keeping strong sway over local communities. At the local level, the IWA, along with other major political organizations such as the Overseas Congress (after 1969) and the Akali Dal,[17] was competing to control the main UK Gurudwaras.[18] At the national level, the IWA became increasingly enmeshed in the British civil rights movement. The constitution of an overarching immigrant Black Minority Ethnic civil rights movement was its prevailing political objective. The organization played a leading role in various organizational platforms, such as the CARD (Campaign against Racism and Discrimination) launched in the midsixties, the CARF (Campaign against Racism and Fascism, between 1977 and 1979), and the CND (Campaign for Nuclear Disarmament). However, this quasi monopoly over the political voice of the Indian community was challenged by a series of conflicts and splits among the different branches of the association. The first one occurred in 1967 between the UK-wide organization (based in Birmingham) and its largest branch in Southall. A second split happened in 1983 when the Wolverhampton branch pulled out from the federation. The splits themselves were caused by a mix of political and personal rivalries, occurring in the aftermath of the split of the Indian communist party (between pro-Soviet and pro-Chinese wings),[19] and affected by divergent views regarding relations with public authorities and religious communities.

With the mushrooming of the UK-based Indian civil society, one could have expected a densification of transnational relationships with the homeland, but this did not happen. There is no evidence of a sustained transnational embedding of grassroots organizations until the Punjab civil war. Religious organizations were primarily oriented toward the local community and most cross-border organizational activities were "translocal," sustained by ethnic-based organizations, such as hometown and caste organizations, and linked toward specific places of origin in India. But these associations were mostly informal and endowed with limited resources, and their role was limited to the circulation of information or to the facilitation of migration and settlement. The same can be said of IWA activities. At the international level, the contributions of IWA members to political activities were limited to occasional support to the Punjabi communist party and the Desh Baghat Yadgar Hall. There were, however, no official linkages between the Indian-based communist parties and the IWA. The IWA also published occasional statements supporting international causes such as the creation of an independent Palestinian state, the condemnation of apartheid in South Africa, and an Irish solution to the Irish problem. Outside India, the IWA maintained relations with other leftist organizations such as IPANA (Indian People's Association in North America) in Canada. Individual visits of members were frequent on both sides of the Atlantic. These two organizations collaborated occasionally on common political issues, information exchanges about respective campaigns, and literature exchanges, and they also coorganized international tours of Punjabi political leaders and poets. By and large, this type of cross-border contact was more the exception than the rule: maintaining only loose relationships with a wider Indian leftist transnational organizational field, the IWA's activities were almost exclusively oriented toward local communities in Britain.[20]

The reasons for this relative scarcity of transnational relations are unclear. The existing multifarious transnational organizational linkages show that there was no structural impediment to their deployment (the relations with the IPANA are a case in point). It can be assumed the problems faced by the Indian population in the settlement country were absorbing the bulk of their energy. But it should also be kept in mind that the international context was not favorable to cross-border extensions of associative activities. Indian authorities sought to discourage any political activism among the expatriates. As shown above, this policy was, in the wake of the country's independence, a consequence of the negative prejudices attached to migration. From the

sixties onward, this line was reinforced by the foreign policy of nonalign-
ment. As the first large independent country, India was seen as spearhead-
ing the anticolonial struggles, and it maintained privileged relationships
with Southern countries. To preserve this role within the nonaligned bloc,
India sought to maintain good relationships with Southern states hosting a
sizable Indian population and therefore avoided bringing attention to the
thorny question of the rights and problems of Indians abroad.[21] After the
mid-eighties, the voluntary blindness of state authorities on migration issues
became gradually unsustainable.

1984–2012: The Changing Patterns of Organizational Transnationalism

The 1980s set the stage for a profound reconfiguration of the Indian organizational field. This decade is marked by the rise of new ethno-nationalist
movements: the consolidation of the Hindu nationalist constellation and
the emergence of the Sikh nationalist movement, the so-called Khalistani
movement, in the wake of the civil conflict in Punjab. The latter is examined
in greater detail insofar as it is directly responsible for the end of the Indian
Workers' Association.

1975 to the Early Eighties: Structuring of the Sangh Parivar

The evolution of the Hindu nationalist organizational field was originally
linked to the wave of discontent that shook India in the mid-seventies. Facing the so-called "new social movement" throughout the whole country,
Indira Gandhi imposed a state of emergency (a suspension of civic freedoms)
between 1975 and 1977. The government temporarily banned the Hindu
nationalist organization, the RSS. This episode led RSS leaders to radically
transform its strategy. In particular, they reoriented its focus of activity
toward the diaspora, its unique source of funding and communication as
a means to circumvent censorship during the emergency state. The general
architecture of the "Sangh Parivar" (Sangh Family), that is to say, the set
of organizations linked to the RSS, was replicated in the main settlement
countries of Hindu immigrants. In the UK, an assembly of representatives
of Shakas (connected to a religious association, the VHP-UK) was created
in 1972; a student Union, a women's association, a branch of the Bharatiya
Janata Party (BJP, the RSS political party) in 1976; and a relief organization, Sewa International, in 1978. Directly under the control of the India-
based hierarchy, the UK organizations received their general instructions,
along with trainers, itinerant preachers, and volunteers from India.[22] The

particularity of the British Hindutva is that it was strongly influenced by a Hindu sect that was imported from Eastern Africa, the Swaminarayan, dominated by a caste of Gujarati farmers, the Patel. Created in 1959, the Swaminarayan Hindu Mission established around 30 branches, mostly in the London area, the Midlands, Bradford, and the South of England. Its British headquarters were set up in 1995 in Neasden.[23]

Power Shift among the Sikhs: The Khalistani Movement

The upheavals that shook Punjab between 1984 and 1992 durably affected the configuration of the diasporic organizational field as well as the attitude of the Indian state toward its expatriates. Of course, the Punjabi crisis was primarily a domestic affair, inscribed in a history of riots and upheavals that affected India since the 1960s: the Naxalite movement in West Bengal in 1965, the Other Backward Class (OBC) movement,[24] the so called "new social movement,"[25] and so forth. This long series of events was symptomatic of the erosion of the legitimacy of the Congress party, the political economic tensions generated by the disjuncture between the rigidity of the caste system, and the social transformations induced by the economic development of the country. The violent conflict that flared up in Punjab in 1984 is yet another event to be added to this list.

As shown earlier, after the independence of the country, migration permitted the Punjab economy to keep afloat despite the aftermath of the partition. In 1965, in the wake of a series of severe famines, Prime Minister Indira Gandhi launched the Green Revolution that turned Punjab into the "granary" of India. Thanks to the mechanization of farming, the use of new seeds and chemical inputs, the country achieved food self-sustainability. But the policy also deeply affected the social structures of Punjab, traditionally based on small landowners. The rise of radical Sikh movements stemmed from the disruption of community structures, the growing indebtedness of small farmers and the increasing gap between rich and poor induced by land concentration and the industrialization of agriculture.[26] In 1984, a radical group occupied the Golden Temple, the holiest shrine of the Sikh religion, triggering the intervention of the army in Operation Blue Star, an event that spurred widespread protest among the Sikhs of India and abroad. In October of the same year, two Sikh bodyguards assassinated Indira Gandhi, leading to countrywide riots and lynching against Sikh people. Upon the assassination of the head of the Akali Dal by Khalistani[27] (pro-independence) activists, Punjab dived into civil war a year later, a conflict that caused around 25,000 casualties. The war lasted for six years, ending with the holding of elections that gave the direction of Punjab to Akali Dal.[28]

Distinctive with respect to its violence and duration, as well as by the echo it received abroad in the diaspora, the conflict radically transformed the UK-based Indian civil society. Although the Sikh autonomist movement had been active outside Punjab since the beginning of the twentieth century, it enjoyed only a limited audience until 1984, after which time the ethno-national movement gained support among all strata of the community abroad. The very first demonstrations were spontaneously called by Gurudwaras; a wide range of separatist organizations then rapidly sprang up to organize the movement in every major country of settlement, with the Council of Khalistan, the International Sikh Youth Organization, Babbar Khalsa, and Dal Khalsa comprising the most important organizations in the UK.[29] By contrast, the previously dominant associations, the Indian Overseas Congress and the Indian Workers' Association, which both opposed the separatist movement, rapidly lost their support within the community. Hence, in the span of just a few years, the movement led to a complete reshaping of the Sikh organizational field.

In fact, the rise of the Khalistan movement revealed and amplified trends that were already at play within the immigrant population. The economic downturn in the seventies and the eighties accelerated the mutation of Indians' employment structure in the UK. Employment in the industrial sector steadily decreased, while the emergence of a business sector was conducive to the formation of Indian commercial centers in the main areas of settlement, such as Handsworth in Birmingham or Southall in Ealing. Families' investment in the education of their children resulted in the emergence of a new elite of doctors and engineers.[30] From the mid-eighties onward, a highly skilled migration of engineers, students, or doctors arrived in Europe and North America, further diversifying the profile of the Indian diaspora, which in turn undermined the working-class identity that had prevailed during the previous decades. The IWA, committed to a Marxist line of thinking, refused to open its ranks to the younger generation of new, higher skilled workers, thereby disrupting the delicate balance between the association's ethnic and political identifications. Moreover, in this decade of economic crisis, ethnic and family linkages served as a source of social capital, enabling entrepreneurs to create their own businesses and provide jobs to the community. This "ethnicization" of the immigrant economy subsequently opened a way out of the industrial sector, thus undermining the membership basis of the IWA. Unable to adapt to the new realities of the immigrant population, it lost its sway over the Indian population.

The "Randy affair" in the early eighties illustrates this tension between class politics and ethnicity. Prominent entrepreneurs in Birmingham, the

Randys, were also sweatshop owners employing Punjabi women under harsh conditions and low wages. The IWA took issue in favor of the employees and supported a series of strikes, but the event divided members between those who gave primacy to the workers' situation over ethnic allegiances and those supporting an opposite stance.

The reconfiguration of the Indian organizational field in the UK was the outcome of both major geopolitical events occurring in India (the emergency state in the seventies, the Punjabi conflict in the eighties) and of the long-term evolution of the Indian population in the UK. The instant reactivity of the community in the wake of the events in Punjab revealed that constant contacts were maintained with the country of origin; sustained by informal family and hometown networks, but also by interpersonal contacts between members of religious and welfare organizations, these ties conveyed information about the political and social life of India. In turn, the mobilizations triggered by the Punjabi conflict proved conducive to a formalization of the organizational relationships with the country of origin. Whereas up until this time, all the associations created in the UK had primarily focused on the local community, the then newly created Khalistani and Sangh Parivar organizations had India as their main focus of interest. Not only did these associations establish ties with other Indian partners, they also connected with their counterparts in other countries of settlement, such as the United States, Canada, or Eastern Africa. In other words, this period set the stage not only for a transnationalization but also for a diasporization of organizational networks. Despite the resolution of the conflict, this trend continued, as the following section shows.

The Political Background in India and the UK: The Evolution of Integration and Diasporic Policies

The previous section focused attention on the societal factors in the UK and India that transformed organizational linkages. But the changing political background induced by evolving policies toward Indian expatriates must also be taken into account. The financial and political support that diasporic groups provided to radical movements motivated the Indian government to pay greater attention to the diasporic organizational field. Hence, it was in the early eighties that legislation dating from 1922 (prior to independence) was modified to set up the contemporary legal framework. The 1983 Emigration Act created the Protector General of Emigrants (PGE) to ensure the protection of vulnerable categories of nationals abroad.[31] During the second part of the eighties, Rajiv Gandhi, who was elected Prime Minister after the death of his mother Indira, broke with the disinterest of his predecessors regarding the diaspora.[32] This change was motivated by the necessity to exert a tighter control over diaspora organizations and therefore to create new links with overseas associations. The policy implemented until the early nineties was, however, focused on security. Using the weapon of diplomacy, India convinced host governments to classify the Khalistani associations as terrorist organizations, thereby reducing their legitimacy and capacity to exercise influence at the international level. India similarly persuaded the main countries of settlement to limit their acceptance of political refugees from the Punjab. In addition to these moves focused on security aspects, Rajiv Gandhi also attempted to develop a new approach, seeking out contacts with prominent entrepreneurs and intellectuals abroad. While this policy fell short, insofar as it never went beyond a series of informal contacts, it nonetheless announced the reform of the diasporic policy that would take place from the 1990s onward.

In the UK, although the British authorities were quick to disqualify Khalistani organizations, a gradual evolution occurred in the multicultural policy that had supported the ethnicization of volunteerism. Indeed, with the arrival of the Tory party to state affairs in the UK, the definition of ethnic identities shifted from cultural/linguistic considerations to religious ones.[33] Religious associations became recognized as spokespersons for the various strands of the Indian population. This, in particular, legitimized the implantation of the Hindu nationalist movement in the country. Government officials (including Margaret Thatcher) and MPs attended major events organized by the HSS or related organizations. Among the patrons of Sewa International, the main Sangh Parivar charity, there are four Lords of Indian origin. The Hindu nationalist movement has created an official lobby at the national level, the Hindu Forum UK, existing since 2003. The paradigmatic shift of the multicultural policy has, more recently, served the interest of the post-Khalistani movement. They obtained the creation of the category of "Sikh" in the 2001 UK census, distinct from "Indian."[34]

Diasporization and Diversification of the Indian Organizational Field

The recent period has been characterized by a strong internationalization of the Indian organizational field, one observed at all levels and extending from grassroots organizations to large umbrella organizations. Two such trends can be distinguished. The first involves a diasporization of organizational linkages, that is to say a formalization of partnerships and activities among organizations in different countries of settlement.

The second entails a strengthening of the relationships with the country of origin, mostly through the multiplication of development projects and other philanthropic initiatives. We will see that this internationalization occurred against the backdrop of a deep reform of the diasporic policy of the Indian state, and, more broadly, of the implementation of a neoliberal socioeconomic agenda favoring the substitution of state engagements by private actors.

Ethnicization and Development: The Two Sides of the Diasporization of the Indian Organizational Field

The internationalization of the organizational field mostly regards organizations primarily based on kinship/caste relations (the first layer of the organizational field, mentioned earlier) and those that are concerned with the Indian community above the local level (the third layer). But, a closer examination reveals that these two processes do not necessarily follow the same logic.

The diasporic ramifying of third-level organizations is linked to a broader trend of politicization of ethnicity. This trend was initiated by the emergence of the Khalistani movement during the eighties. This movement was largely dismantled after the conflict ended in the early nineties, but it has been reconfigured into what some call the post-Khalistani movement. The International Sikh Youth Federation, the Sikh Federation, United Sikhs, and the Sikh Human Rights Groups are among the main organizations promoting the rights of Sikhs in India and around the world. After the mid-nineties, the Khalistani activists reoriented their activities toward the Sikh community inside and outside Punjab at large and not specifically toward the creation of an independent state (a still hotly debated issue, as a number of associations have questioned the legitimacy of an independent Punjab). The Sikh Human Rights Group is a case in point. The organization was created during the civil war with the view to denounce human rights abuses in Punjab and to support refugee groups in the UK. Since the end of the civil war in 1991, it has evolved toward the promotion of rights for Sikh minorities throughout the diaspora. For example, it provides legal support to a youngster in France who is suing the French government in the wake of the adoption of the law banning religious signs in public schools.[35]

Beyond the Sikh movement, the second case in point is the strengthening of the Sangh Parivar movement abroad. The radical Hinduist networks benefited from the surge of a new class of engineers, professionals, and entrepreneurs that form the basis of the movement both in India and abroad.

Hindutva organizations attracted a large number of new members from the late eighties onward. The UK Sangh Parivar, for example, benefited from the anti-Muslim sentiments triggered by Muslim mobilizations such as the Salman Rushdie affair[36] and the Hizb Ut Tahrir campaign. Likewise, in India, the Ayodhia affair, named after a city in which a mosque was said to be built over a temple of the Rama divinity, attracted strong support to the RSS in the diaspora. Finally, this growing success is linked to a strategy of normalization of the movement. The electoral success of the BJP, *Bharatiya Janata Party*, a radical Hinduist party and political facade of the Sangh Parivar, in the 1998 general elections, but also the symbolic support provided by local and national politicians in the UK, contributed to neutralizing the image of the extremist movement among the overseas middle class. However, in 2004, the "stop funding hate" campaign,[37] led by a coalition of NGOs, revealed that, through a network of charities (including Sewa International), the RSS had managed to draw financial support from the diaspora. In particular, under the pretense of carrying out philanthropic actions, a large part of the money served to finance Hindutva schools in Gujarat. The report led to the dismantling of a number of associations.

The transnational reorientation of kinship organizations has followed neither the same logic nor the same scale. We have seen that the politicization of ethnic identifications has been conducive to the creation of organizational linkages at the diasporic scale. In contrast, grassroots groups tend to strengthen their relations with the country of origin through depoliticized activities and more specifically through their commitment to development projects. Collective philanthropy is certainly the most widespread form of transnational engagement of immigrant organizations. A plethora of development projects such as the building of schools, hospitals, sport centers, and places of worship have sprung up since the nineties in the main areas of departure. A wide array of associations carries out regular or occasional development projects in India. Hometown and caste organizations, although initially created to facilitate the coming and settlement of fellow villagers in the host setting, have found in development activities a motivation to renew their activities (e.g., the Pakowal Village Association, the Bilga General Hospital Charitable Trust, Dhilwan International Development Society, and so forth). As shown elsewhere,[38] this surge of philanthropic activity is primarily motivated by the process of integration of the Punjabi population into British society. The formation of an elite group comprised of professionals, entrepreneurs, engineers, and others explains the multiplication of community leaders who use their resources to reactivate hometown networks around homeland development projects. In recent years, this phenomenon has spread beyond the grassroots level to touch

local community organizations. Numerous professional or religious organizations spend a part of their time and resources on overseas development. For
example, Guru Nanak Nishkam Sewa Jatha in Birmingham has carried out
several renovation projects of Sikh shrines since the early nineties, mostly in
Punjab but also in Kenya. Finally, the surge of such activities has given birth
to a lively sector of migrant NGOs. Indian-led migrant organizations for
development based in the UK were key members listed in Connection for
Development, a platform of migrant NGOs active between 2003 and 2009.
The same has been observed in the United States.[39]

It is worth mentioning that the cross-border reorientation of grassroots
associations does not only proceed from a greater engagement with development. Caste groups have created international federations in various parts
of the world in order to organize matrimonial arrangements around the
globe. These federations are the outcome of the recomposition of traditional
biraderi[40] groups at a global level. However, this trend is certainly stronger
in the United States than it is in the UK where caste associations are of less
importance demographically.

The Neoliberal Underpinnings of Indian Diasporic Policy

Although the mutation of the Indian organizational field is linked to social
and political dynamics at play within host societies, it is also the result of
the evolution of homeland politics. First, during the economic crisis of the
early nineties, the government revised its position and started to perceive
emigrants as an economic asset to be tapped. Until the nineties, the Indian
diaspora was regarded as a political burden unfit for nation-building narratives and international policies. In the space of a few years, those who
were once portrayed as betrayers became "angels" of development.[41] The
Indian authorities adopted measures to enhance migrant remittances to
India. Today, India is the first beneficiary of immigrant remittances before
China and Mexico. Their amount nearly trebled during the last decade,
increasing from $15.8 billion in 2001 to $55 billion in 2010.[42] 44 percent
come from North America, 24 percent from Gulf countries and 13 percent
from Europe.[43] Contrary to financial remittances, Foreign Direct Investment from the diaspora has remained notoriously weak: $2,470 million in
2003 compared to $52,740 million for China.[44] The limited flows of FDI
reflect the barriers to investment imposed by the Indian planned economy
and the resistance from Indian industrial cartels.[45] A second step occurred
after the BJP's electoral victory in 1998, at which time the development of
diaspora policy was motivated not simply by the goal of capturing economic
resources found in the diaspora but also by that of reinforcing the influence
of nationalist networks among wealthy Western-born Indians working in

the private sector abroad.[46] The internationalization of the Sangh Parivar movement abroad is the direct outcome of this strategy to strengthen a political stronghold within the diaspora. Part of this strategy was the necessity to reform the political and institutional framework of the relationships between the Indian state and expatriates. A high-level committee was convened to this end in 2000 to study the possibility of establishing new legislation. The outcomes of the Singhvi report are numerous. Beside the status of Non-Resident Indian (NRI), the status of OCI (Overseas Citizens of India) included a new title with the view to formalizing a legal bond with persons having lost their Indian nationality, the "Person of Indian Origin" (PIO). The Pravasi Bharatiya Divas (PBD) is the flagship event of the new Indian diasporic policy. Every year it gathers diaspora representatives and Indian officials. The PBD 2009 was attended by over 1,500 persons, mostly from the private sector. This political orientation was maintained by the Singh government, when the Congress party won back the parliamentary majority in 2003. In 2005, a Ministry of Overseas Indian Affairs (MOIA) was constituted to implement the new policy. Its missions fall under three categories: framing the departure flows, providing protection to overseas Indians, and enhancing the development impacts of the diaspora.

The migration and development strategy of the Indian government is part of a wider neoliberal policy aiming to substitute private sector investment for that of the state. From 1991 on, the economic crisis led the government to adopt a World Bank and IMF-designed structural adjustment plan, which broke with 45 years of staunch protectionism and state intervention. In this context, the government enforced a wide array of measures meant to deregulate and open the economy to foreign investments. This paralleled lesser state involvement in economic affairs and a decrease of public investment. This withdrawal was partly offset by the enforcement of decentralization measures increasing the power of local authorities and the recognition of civil society (73d and 74th amendments to the constitution). The financial and political withdrawal of the administration from the local scene left a void filled by local and diasporic voluntary organizations. A survey in 477 villages of the Punjab shows that NRI transfer payments for religious and social development projects there amounted to $4.5 million.[47] This scenario is not specific to India and explains the general surge of collective remittances throughout the world.[48]

The Cross-border Extensions of the UK-based Indian Organizational Field Today

The analysis of the database of Indian organizations in the UK opens a window onto past tendencies and contemporary trends of Indian organizational activism. Graph 1 presents the evolution of the types of UK-based Indian associations created each year since 1954. It gives a bird's-eye view of half a century of Indian voluntarism in the UK: the prevalence of religious and other community-oriented organizations until the nineties, the surge of political organizations during the second half of the eighties, and the growing number of overseas development organizations created since the mid-nineties. Now, service to the local community remains the main focus of interest (see Graph 2), although the large majority of organizations (73 percent) are not in fact linked to India or a third country. The structuration that emerged in the sixties, characterized by a constellation of associations more or less connected to local places of worship is still in place. 55 percent of registered Indian associations are religious organizations (see Graph 3). The organizational field has been largely modeled by British multicultural policy, which promoted the insertion of local migrant communities within their urban context. Local authorities in charge of implementing multicultural policy used associations as the privileged representatives of immigrant communities.

A focus on the 27 percent of organizations maintaining cross-border relations reveals a variety of situations. Today, the UK-based Punjabi community displays highly diversified occupational, cultural, and ethnic profiles, yielding, in turn, a composite organizational landscape and varied overseas connections. These relations can be translocal (in particular in the case of small development projects), trans-state or even global: one of the specificities of the Indian diaspora is to maintain ties not only with the country of origin but also among Indian communities in the main receiving countries (United States, Canada, Australia, Kenya, and so forth). By and large, three broad types of organizations can be distinguished.

The first category is mostly composed of host country associations, which are occasionally committed to a specific project abroad, mainly working in partnership with other organizations (such as local NGOs or local places of worship), without maintaining formal structures abroad. Once the project is completed, the association reverts to its prior condition of a purely local organization based abroad, and the relationship with partners in India is not institutionalized. This category can include first-level organizations such as hometown associations, which are occasionally engaged in a development project for the benefit of the village of origin as well as second- and third-level organizations working within local communities and beyond, but engaged in occasional development initiatives or international political campaigns. This type of connection is not new, since, as noted earlier, the Indian Workers' Association has regularly supported the projects of the Desh Baghat Yadgar Hall, dedicated to the memory of the Gadr Party, since the 1950s.

The second group involves associations that principally seek to deliver services to the UK-based community but maintain affiliations with transnational networks. These associations do not engage in any form of activity/project/campaign abroad. Through their partnerships, however, the members participate in international meetings and activities, mainly through political and religious organizations, which have formed cross-border organizational networks, sometimes under the overarching structure of a federative body. This is the case for religious organizations that are linked to a central institution in India, such as the Arya Samaj or the Sikh Shiromani Parbandhak Committee. Similar cases include religious or Yoga organizations based in India but which count a number of branches all over the diaspora, like the Shiromani Akali Dal.

Transnational organizations created specifically with a view to developing activities abroad form the third group. They mostly are political (Sikh Human Rights Group) and development organizations, created by hometown groups (Bilga General Hospital Charitable Trust) or by professionals active in international development projects (Alternative India Development). These organizations often have branches, defined as "mother" or "sister" organizations abroad. An important number of organizations that fall under this category are hometown groups that have created their own association in order to carry out a development project for the benefit of their place of origin. Some have woven linkages among the main places of settlement of their expatriate community. These links are not necessarily formalized but are mobilized when needed. For example, in order to build a hospital in Rurka Kalan (district of Jalandhar), the head of the hometown organization in Birmingham collected money not only in the various cities of the UK but also from fellow hometown organizations in the United States and Canada.

*   *   *

This chapter takes a bird's eye view of the past evolution and current trends of Indian voluntary associations in the UK, analyzing the gradual transformation of the organizational field over four distinct periods. After the Second World War, the needs of the immigrant population were mostly taken care of by informal kinship networks. It is only when the population reached a critical mass, from the sixties onward, that the organizational field coalesced into local communities at the neighborhood or city level. This trend was largely encouraged by the UK multicultural policy that delegated to local authorities the duty to manage intercommunity relations. At the time, the Indian Workers' Association had a quasi monopoly regarding the voice and representation of the Indian population at the national level.

This period is characterized by the informality of cross-border relations, mostly carried out through informal relations maintained by grassroots organizations and interpersonal contacts. The correlate of this low level of transnational dynamism can be seen in the political disinterest in diasporic and homeland affairs displayed both by the IWA and the Indian state.

However, these linkages were only dormant, ready to be reactivated by homeland turbulence. The attack on the Golden Temple in 1984 turned out to be an event whose ripple effects were transmitted by informal but dense cross-border channels. The eighties appear to be a transitional period during which the organizational field went through a radical transformation. This watershed marked the entry of the UK-Indian diaspora into a new age, characterized simultaneously by embeddedness in its local as well as global environment. The rise of the Khalistani movement, bridging identity and diaspora politics, announced the contemporary trends in transnational organizing. Indeed, one sees today a general diasporization of organizational linkages spearheaded by ethno-political movements such as the post-Khalistani and Sangh Parivar movement. But this last period is also marked by a renewal of kinship organizations that have discovered in homeland development a way of renewing their raison d'être. This internationalization, which was primarily propelled by first- and third-level organizations, is increasingly affecting local community associations: it is not rare to see local temples or civic associations dedicating a part of their funding and resources to occasional overseas projects.

This long-term analysis highlights a number of factors that drive the emergence of organizational fields. First, it shows that the gradual transformation of the organizational field has paralleled the evolution of both migration and migrant populations. Since the Second World War, new generations of organizations have appeared to cater to the needs of an emergent community. More recently, the social and class diversification of the population has led to the demise of working-class organizations. Second, the evolution of the organizational field in the immigrant context and the transformation of the society of origin seem to have occurred in parallel, as illustrated by two developments highlighted in this chapter: the conflict in Punjab in the eighties and the social and economic implications of the neoliberal adjustment policy in the nineties. Both developments triggered a reaction within the diaspora that has durably affected the face of its organizational field. Third, the organizational field has been affected by the respective policies implemented by *both* the origin *and* the receiving states. The multicultural policy of the UK appears to have bolstered the structuration of the organizational field into a web of local communities. While this influence remains visible today, it appears to be of lesser importance, as the relative economic and social achievement of the Indian population has rendered it less sensitive to integration policies. Conversely, India's own diasporic policy has become increasingly geared toward members of the successful elite abroad.

The current face of the Indian organizational field is marked by an apparent contradiction. Immigrant voluntary activity is firmly embedded in the arrival society, with transnational connections characterizing only a small minority of the organizations (a quarter, according to our census). Yet where it exists, transnational embedding is not confined to a minority of a cosmopolitan elite but instead involves all the layers of the population, albeit in various ways. Beyond the variety of actors and practices, two key features characterize contemporary trends: a growing interconnection of migrant associations established in different parts of the world, and the massive commitment to long distance development activities. One can wonder whether this apparent paradox is specific to the Indian population and its settlement history in the UK, or if it is a trait shared by other immigrant groups. Whereas the developmentalist feature of immigrant voluntary activity is shared by a large number of migrant groups around the world—including Latin Americans in the United States,[49] North Africans in France,[50] and West Africans in Europe,[51] among others—there has been less research dedicated to the diasporization and ethnicization of organizational fields.[52] These common trends pointed out in the academic literature raise the question of the internal dynamics of organizational fields. The Indian case in the UK is typical of a postcolonial migrant group whose migration is linked to the postwar labor force needs of the European countries. The arrival of mostly unskilled men, followed by their kin after the restriction of entry regulations, and the reorientation of migration flows toward high-skilled migrants in the nineties are some of the aspects shared by this type of group. Likewise, the postcolonial economic strategies of sending states, affected by a series of economic downturns in the eighties and the nineties, and the ensuing adoption of structural adjustment policies and opening of borders to international capital and goods flows are historical trends shared by a large number of major sending states. The identification of these parallel tendencies opens the possibility of grounding a periodization of organizational transnationalism at the global level and exploring the relevance of the approach taken here for other migrant groups, whether varying by national origin or type (such as high-skilled or refugee migrations).

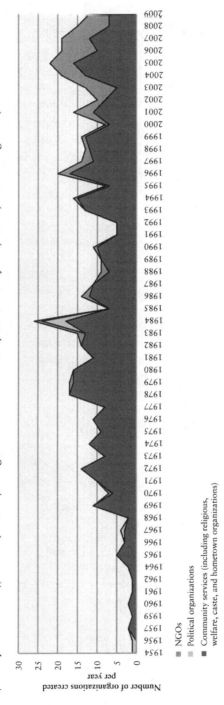

Graph 1: UK-based Indian Organizations, According to Their Date of Creation and Category (1954–2009). Source: UK Register of Charities (Charity Commission), P. Weller, ed. 2007. *Religions in the UK: A Multi-faith Directory 2007–2010*, web investigations, 2010.

Graph 2: Patterns of Cross-border Engagement among UK-based Indian Organizations (2010). Source: UK Register of Charities (Charity Commission), P. Weller, ed. 2007. *Religions in the UK: A Multi-faith Directory 2007–2010*, web investigations, 2010.

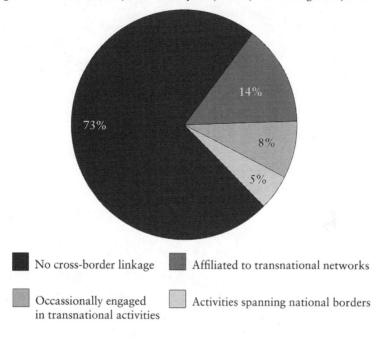

■ No cross-border linkage   ■ Affiliated to transnational networks

■ Occassionally engaged   ☐ Activities spanning national borders
  in transnational activities

Graph 3: Indian Organizations in the UK According to Type of Activity (2010). Source: UK Register of Charities (Charity Commission), P. Weller, ed. 2007. *Religions in the UK: A Multi-faith Directory 2007–2010*, web investigations, 2010.

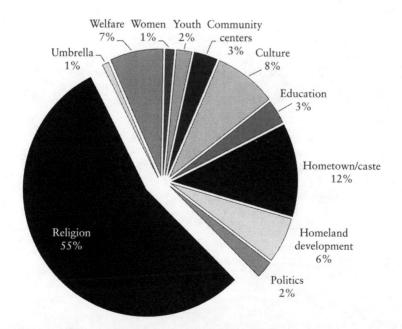

NOTES

1. José C. Moya, "Immigrants and Associations: A Global and Historical Perspective," *Journal of Ethnic and Migration Studies* 31, 5 (2005): 833–864; Ben Gidley, "Diasporic Memory and the Call to Identity: Yiddish Migrants in Early Twentieth Century East London," *Journal of Intercultural Studies* 34, 6 (2013): 650–664.

2. Laura Morales and Laia Jorba, "The Transnational Links and Practices of Migrants' Organisations in Spain," in *Diaspora and Transnationalism: Concepts, Theories and Methods*, ed. Rainer Bauböck and Thomas Faist (Amsterdam: Amsterdam University Press, 2010); Alejandro Portes, Cristina Escobar, and Renelinda Arana, "Bridging the Gap: Transnational and Ethnic Organizations in the Political Incorporation of Immigrants in the United States," *Ethnic and Racial Studies* 31 (2008): 1056–1090; Ludger Pries and Zeynep Sezgin, *Cross-Border Migrant Organizations in Comparative Perspective* (Basingstoke: Palgrave Macmillan, 2012).

3. Abdelmalek Sayad, *La Double Absence* (Paris: Seuil, 1999), 141.

4. This study was carried out in the framework of the international research program "Diffusion and Contexts of Transnational Migrants' Organizations in Europe" (TRAMO). www.ruhr-uni-bochum.de/tramo/en/index.shtml (accessed Dec. 21, 2015). TRAMO has been funded by the Volkswagen Foundation. It started in October 2007 and has been supervised by Ludger Pries at Ruhr-University Bochum, Department of Sociology / Organization, Migration. Beside the German team, the research consortium consists of researchers from Oxford University, the University of Granada, and the University of Warsaw.

5. Paul Weller, *Religions in the UK: A Multi-faith Directory 2007–2010* (Derby: The Multi-faith Centre, University of Derby in association with the Faculty of Education, Health and Social Sciences, 2007).

6. The listing is likely to be slightly biased. Associations that do not rely on external funding tend to remain informal and therefore more difficult to track. Conversely, a number of organizations can be registered under different statuses, databases, and names. Despite the difficulties, the database obtained is the most comprehensive listing that is possible to compile for a limited research team.

7. Marie Lall, "Mother India's Forgotten Children," in *International Migration and Sending Countries*, ed. Eva Ostergaard Nielsen (Basingstoke: Palgrave Macmillan, 2003), 121–139.

8. Binod Khadria, "India: Skilled Migration to Developed Countries, Labour Migration to the Gulf," in *Migration and Development. Perspectives from the South*, ed. Stephen Castles and Raul Delgado Wise (Geneva: IOM, 2008), 79–112, 98.

9. *The Panchayat* is the name given to the municipal authorities in India.

10. Thomas Lacroix, "Collective Remittances and Integration: North African and North Indian Comparative Perspectives," *Journal for Ethnic and Migration Studies* 39 (2013): 1019–1035.

11. *Jainism* is a religion from India that is said to be one of the oldest existing religions of the world.

12. John De Witte, *Indian Workers' Association in Britain* (Oxford: Oxford University Press, 1969), 47.

13. Roger Ballard, "The South Asian Presence in Britain and Its Transnational Connections," in *Culture and Economy in the Indian Diaspora*, ed. Bhikhu C. Parekh, Gurharpal Singh, and Steven Vertovec (London: Routledge, 2003), 197–222; Judith M. Brown, *Global South Asians. Introducing a Modern Diaspora* (Cambridge: Cambridge University Press, 2006); Ceri Peach, "South Asian Migration and Settlement in Great Britain, 1951–2006," *Contemporary South Asia* 15 (2006): 133–146.

14. Parminder Bhachu, *Twice Migrants. East African Sikh Settlers in Britain* (London: Tavistock, 1985).

15. Christophe Jaffrelot, *Hindu Nationalism. A Reader* (Princeton: Princeton University Press, 2007).

16. John King, *Three Asian Associations in Britain*, Monographs in Ethnic Relations (Coventry: Centre for Research in Ethnic Relations, 1994), VII 67.

17. The Akali Dal is the main Sikh political party. It is the political branch of the Shiromani Gurudwara Parandhak Committee (SGPC), the mainstream organization in charge of the administration of the Sikh religion.

18. Darshan Singh Tatla, *The Sikh Diaspora. The Search for Statehood* (London: UCL Press, 1999).

19. In 1966, during the Sino Indian war, the British communist party, in allegiance to the Moscow politburo, took a position against the Chinese military action against India. In reaction, a large number of IWA Maoist leaders, backing Beijing against the Indian government, resigned from the CPUK and participated in the creation of the Association of Indian communists. A second split occurred in 1967, mirroring the split of the India communist party between the CPI Marxist (CPI-M) and the CPI Marxist-Leninist (CPI M-L) branches. The division occurred in the wake of the rise of the Maoist "Naxalite" movement in Bengal, the CPI-M supporting the movement while the CPI-ML was opposed to it.

20. This was not true before the Second World War. A number of organizations, such as the India League founded in 1929 in London or the first Indian Workers' Association created in 1938 in Coventry, were active in support of pro-independence movements in India. But this anticolonial activism faded after 1947.

21. Lall, "Mother India's Forgotten Children."

22. Christophe Jaffrelot and Ingrid Therwath, "The Sangh Parivar and the Hindu Diaspora in the West: What Kind of 'Long-Distance Nationalism'?" *International Political Sociology* 1 (2007), 278–295.

23. Christophe Jaffrelot and Ingrid Therwath, "Le Sangh Parivar et la diaspora hindoue en occident: Royaume-Uni, États-Unis et Canada," *Questions de recherche* 22 (2007): 72.

24. *OBC* (Other Backward Castes) is a category gathering the castes that are not regarded as scheduled (untouchables) but have nevertheless limited access to state resources and public administration jobs. Those are small entrepreneurs, craftsmen, and peasant small landowners.

25. Christophe Jaffrelot, ed., *L'Inde contemporaine de 1950 à nos jours* (Paris: Fayard, CERI, 2006).

26. Pritam Singh, *Federalism, Nationalism and Development* (Oxford: Routledge, 2009); Tatla, *Sikh Diaspora*.

27. *Khalistan* is the name given by radical groups to an independent Punjab. In turn, pro-independence organizations are known as "Khalistani" organizations.

28. Anne Vaugier-Chatterjee, *Histoire politique du Penjab de 1947 à nos jours* (Paris: L'Harmattan, 2001).

29. Tatla, *Sikh Diaspora*.

30. Peach, "South Asian Migration."

31. Binod Khadria, "Tracing the Genesis of Brain Drain in India through State Policy and Civil Society," in *Citizenship and Those Who Leave: The Politics of Emigration and Expatriation*, ed. Nancy L. Green and François Weil (Urbana: University of Illinois Press, 2007), 265–279.

32. Khadria, "India: Skilled Migration."

33. Mary Searle-Chatterjee, "'World Religions' and 'Ethnic Groups': Do These Paradigms Lend Themselves to the Cause of Hindu Nationalism?" *Ethnic and Racial Studies* 23 (2000): 497–515.

34. Gurhapal Singh and Darshan Singh Tatla, *Sikhs in Britain. The Making of a Community* (London: Zed Books, 2006), 119.

35. Thomas Lacroix, *Indian and Polish Immigrant Organisations in the UK*, Final Report of the Transnational Migrant Organisations (TRAMO) Project (Oxford: International Migration Institute, 2011), 86. www.imi.ox.ac.uk (accessed Dec. 21, 2015).

36. Pnina Werbner, *Imagined Diasporas among Manchester Muslims: The Public Performance of Pakistani Transnational Identity Politics* (Oxford: James Currey, 2002).

37. www.stopfundinghate.org/ (accessed Mar. 1, 2013). The campaign was launched in 2002 in the wake of anti-Muslim pogroms in Gujarat. It involved an awareness campaign in major settlement countries and the writing of a report on Hindutva funding networks in the diaspora.

38. Lacroix, "Collective Remittances and Integration."

39. Devesh Kapur, "Indian Diasporic Philanthropy: Some Observations," ed. by Global Equity Initiative, 2003, 24. www.fas.harvard.edu/~acgei/PDFs/Philanthropy PDFs/Phil_Indian_Diasporic.pdf (accessed Apr. 1, 2013).

40. A *biraderi* is the portion of the caste within which youngsters can marry.

41. Khadria, "India: Skilled Migration."

42. World-Bank, *Migration and Remittances Factbook 2011* (Washington, D.C.: The World Bank), 275. www.siteresources.worldbank.org/INTLAC/Resources/Factbook 2011-Ebook.pdf (accessed Feb. 25, 2013).

43. Muzaffar Chishti, "The Rise in Remittances to India: A Closer Look," *Migration Information Source*, Feb. 1, 2007, 9. www.migrationinformation.org/Feature/display .cfm?id=577 (accessed Dec. 21, 2015).

44. Jayanta Roy and Pritam Banerjee, "Attracting FDI from the Indian Diaspora: The Way Forward," 2007, 36, 3. Confederation of Indian Industry.

45. Lall, "Mother India's Forgotten Children," 132.

46. Ingrid Therwath, "Les 'journées des Indiens à l'étranger.' Le Gouvernement face à la diaspora," in *Loin des yeux, près du coeur. Les Etats et leurs expatriés*, ed. Stéphane Dufoix, Carine Guerassimoff, and Anne De Tinguy (Paris: Presses de Sciences Po, 2010), 205–220, 216.

47. Satnam Chana, "NRI Investment in Social Development Projects. Findings from Two Sample Surveys in Doaba, Punjab," in *Sikh Diaspora Philanthropy in Punjab*, ed. Verne A. Dusenbery and Darshan Singh Tatla (New Delhi: Oxford University Press, 2009), 107–119, 131.

48. Thomas Lacroix, *Les Réseaux marocains du développement: Géographie du transnational et politique du territorial* (Paris: Presses de Sciences Po, 2005); L. Goldring, "The Mexican State and Transmigrant Organizations: Negotiating the Boundaries of Membership and Participation," *Latin American Research Review* 37 (2002): 55–99.

49. Carol Zabin and Luis Escala Radaban, *Mexican Hometown Associations and Mexican Immigrant Political Empowerment in Los Angeles*, Non-profit Sector Research Fund Working Paper Series (Los Angeles: The Aspen Institute, 1998), 41; Manuel Orozco, *Hometown Associations and Their Present and Future Partnerships: New Development Opportunities?* (Washington, D.C.: U.S. Agency for International Development, Interamerican Dialogue, September 2003), 58; Jonathan Fox, "Mapping Mexican Migrant Civil Society," 2005, 43.

50. Lacroix, *Les Réseaux marocains du développement*.

51. Claire Mercer, Ben Page, and Martin Evans, *Development and the African Diaspora. Place and the Politics of Home* (London: Zed, 2008); Christophe Daum, *Les associations de Maliens en France. Migrations, développement et citoyenneté* (Paris: Karthala, 1998); Valentina Mazzucato, "The Double Engagement: Transnationalism and Integration. Ghanaian Migrants' Lives between Ghana and the Netherlands," *Journal of Ethnic and Migration Studies* 34 (2008): 199–216.

52. Karsten Paerregaard, "Interrogating Diaspora: Power and Conflict in Peruvian Migration," in Bauböck and Faist, *Diaspora and Transnationalism*, 91–108.

CHAPTER 9

Transnationalism and Migration in the Colonial and Postcolonial Context

Emigrants from the Souf Area (Algeria) to Nanterre (France) (1950–2000)

Marie-Claude Blanc-Chaléard
Translated from the French by Melanie Moore

After World War II, the end of the colonial empires was accompanied by great waves of economic migrations to the former colonial powers in Europe. The migrants' position as former colonized subjects and the unique relationships between host states and their one-time colonies are specific variables that need to be analyzed when thinking about transnationalism. That is our purpose here in looking at the history of a chain migration between Algeria and France during the great migration cycle of the 30-year postwar boom.

Algerians accounted for the largest migration originating in the French colonies, with numbers residing in France rising from 22,000 in 1946 to 711,000 in 1975.[1] Algeria occupied a unique position within France's nineteenth-century empire. First to be conquered in 1830, it was divided into three French-style departments.[2] It was also the empire's only settlement colony, and one where the European colonists, who made up one-tenth of the population, dominated the remaining nine-tenths comprised of the so-called "natives." Lastly, Algeria's decolonization process was the most painful, with a war of independence lasting nearly eight years from November 1954 to March 1962, followed by the immediate exodus of the colonists.

Immigration by Algerians, that is to say, the population classified as "natives" at the time of colonization, began at the start of the twentieth century, but it evolved into mass immigration only after 1945. Until 1962, that migration took place within a colonial context. After independence, however, the now "foreign" migrants continued to be treated in a very specific fashion. Because the French state devised all sorts of public policies to manage and control this flow, these policies have gained extensive research attention.[3] For sociologist Abdelmayek Sayad, "to think about immigration is to think about the state," and migration reproduces the colonial relationship of domination (what we will call here "postcolonial" treatment).[4]

In this respect, immigrants have largely been seen only as political objects. The transnational perspective entails reversing this point of view and analyzing the lived experience of the immigrants and their capacity for initiative, which represents a challenge within the specific context we are about to discuss. Moreover, since it targets not just the immigrants themselves but their movement between two countries, the transnational approach opens up complex questions about their position between the country of origin and the host country within a history that moves from a colonial situation in which the two countries were a single unit to a situation in which two states confront one another in order to manage the colonial past.[5]

I explore this approach by using the findings of a recent collective oral history project that enabled us to reconstitute the history of an Algeria-France chain migration that began in the 1950s and stretched from a small oasis enclave on the edge of Algeria's Eastern Sahara, the area of Oued Souf to the town of Nanterre, an industrial suburb to the west of Paris. The survey was conducted in both France (Nanterre) and Algeria (Guemar and El Oued, the two main localities in the Souf), between 2010 and 2013, among some 40 migrants and their children. This cooperative project, carried out by the audiovisual team at the Bibliothèque de Documentation Internationale Contemporaine (BDIC) in Nanterre and historians at Paris Ouest Nanterre La Défense University, had a double objective, both historical and memorial.[6] It focused on memories of the slums of Nanterre, which, in the 1950s–1970s were largely occupied by Algerian migrants, including an area known as Les Pâquerettes where the Souafas congregated.[7]

The project did not focus on the networks and movement associated with transnationalism, but its findings can be usefully mined as they furnished much relevant material. In this chapter, I follow the migration cycle of the Souafas of Nanterre chronologically, examining the transnational perspective at each stage. The bulk of migration occurred between 1950 and the end of the twentieth century. During that time, the general context of migrations to Europe changed from a period of weak border controls during 30 years of economic growth (1945–1973), to border closures in 1974 when the economy went into recession. The Souafas' story can be told in three parts: first an extended first stage lasting until 1962, which was still a story of colonized people, and then tracking changes that occurred in the following two periods (1962–1970, 1974–2000).

The Beginnings of Migration to Nanterre: Colonization and the War of Independence (1945–1962)

Prehistory: The Souafas and Tunisia

As the resources of the Souf area oasis were often unreliable, small farm holders had long engaged in migration in order to find ways of complementing the unpredictable and, moreover, extremely arduous, cultivation of date palms. They went to eastern Algeria where they took jobs as seasonal agricultural workers, merchants, heavy laborers, and dockers. Neighboring Tunisia, the other destination, became the main focus of Algerian emigration once Tunisia was incorporated into the French Empire as a protectorate in 1881. Along with traditional nomadic movements and smuggling,[8] the opening of phosphate mines in Gafsa (in southern Tunisia) and the development of the city of Tunis generated an intense male migration between the two colonies in keeping with changes brought about by the colonizer. As families also settled and reproduced in emigration, people from the Souf area came to make up the largest Algerian group in Tunis.[9] A good many of them would later find themselves in Nanterre. "Our 'bidonville' is like a mini-state. We are all from the same place. Most of us are from Tunisia and lived there for many years."[10]

This prehistory shows how the Souafas' social migration field, based on a tradition of short-distance migration, was strengthened by colonization, which offered as many opportunities (new horizons that were seized upon by the peasants) as restrictions (more or less authorized travel, depending on the period). Furthermore, the diversity of statuses did not cancel out national differences within the Maghreb: the Algerians were "French subjects" from a colony subject to French administrative practices; the Tunisians, "French protected persons," had a more favorable situation. In Tunis, the Souafas were regarded as "immigrants" and assigned the least attractive tasks, such as garbage collection. At the same time, cross-border smuggling continued.[11]

Post 1947: The Origins of the Souf-to-Nanterre Chain Migration

With the exception of a few men who were mobilized during World War I, the Souafas had no experience of France before the end of the Second World War.[12] Previously, there had been numerous restrictions on the immigration of Algeria's "French subjects" to France, reaching a ceiling of about 100,000 laborers, nearly all them ethnic Kabyles.[13] As part of a new colonial policy after World War II, France granted full citizenship to Algeria's Muslims in 1947, a significant turning point that pointed Algerians toward the metropole. Citizenship gave them a freedom of movement that put them in a privileged position compared to foreigners who had to obtain a work contract from the National Immigration Office (ONI). The growth of "Algerian" migration was, therefore, the result of changes in colonial policy, pursued by France. While postwar reconstruction in France needed labor, the immense population pressure in Algeria had to be reduced (there was also serious famine in the Souf area at the end of the 1940s); above all, the nationalist agitation that was developing across North Africa had to be curbed. Mass emigration to France took place against a background of decolonization and conflict. In 1954, the first attacks occurred in Algeria; in 1956, Morocco and Tunisia gained independence.

According to some of our sources, the French authorities encouraged departures from the Souf area after the start of the independence uprising in an attempt to keep young men out of the resistance. Above all, it is important to note that when Tunisia gained its independence in 1956, the French Consulate organized emigration, paying for families to leave for Marseille. In addition, the new policy corresponded to the desire for change of a whole generation, whether actively nationalist or not. The young men of the "second age" of migration according to Abdelmalek Sayad's typology,[14] those born at the end of the 1930s, rejected the hard labor of palm cultivation, as they did the weight of tradition in an area of puritanical Islam (a "desire to live my life," "not wanting to shovel sand all my life," to "go somewhere young people can let their hair down"[15]). They also had plenty of illusions about working and living in France, as they would soon discover.[16]

Several networks linked the Souf area with France. One connected El-Oued to Strasbourg, but the main path led to the Parisian region, where Nanterre rapidly acquired mythic status. More than 5,000 Algerians were living there in 1954, with 3,000 of them in the slums. Certainly, upon arrival, the slum of Les Pâquerettes, on the very edge of the commune, offered a rude awakening, with its piles of shacks in the wasteland, the mud, and the fires.[17] But some felt at home there. "When I got there, I realized I knew everyone" (Mohamed O., arrived 1959). "Unmarried" laborers and families lived separately, the former at 7, rue Déquéant, the latter at 102, rue des Pâquerettes. Large numbers of families began to arrive as of 1959, fleeing the war or joining fathers who had gone ahead as scouts. Part of the migration project proved successful: work was easy to find, recruitment networks connected people to certain employers (such as Aspapa—a company that tarred roads and pavements—the City of Paris, and refuse collectors), and salaries were regarded as high. Young men were happy to send most of their pay back to their fathers. In this way, the slum became community territory, the far end of a chain migration that had begun in the Algerian desert.

Slum, War, and Nation

The small community of Souafas did not only have to battle a decrepit physical environment. It also had to settle into a daily routine of exclusion and violence. The immigrants experienced almost total social exclusion, living in slums that constituted the forgotten spaces of the city. The Algerian immigrants did not seem part of society, and less than fully French. Nor were they fully French officially, since they were legally categorized as French Muslims of Algeria (FMA), with "diminished citizen" status, overseen by a special police force, and subject to different treatment.[18] Furthermore, as of 1958, the policy of surveillance became one of repression as the war of independence spread to France itself. From 1955 on, the National Liberation Front (FLN), which was leading the struggle in Algeria, tried to take the battle to the metropole, where it sought to organize the émigrés and collect funds that would support the armed conflict. In a merciless factional fight, FLN also sought to eliminate another movement, that of Messali Hadj's supporters (the Mouvement national algérien, MNA), which, until then, had enjoyed greater émigré support.[19] Hadj's movement was practically eradicated in the Paris region by 1958.

> I arrived in August 1958. On arrival, I discovered the conflicts between the Massalists and the FLN. Five days after I arrived, I saw with my very own eyes two men whose throats had been cut. I had never seen anything like it before. I was so shocked I wanted to leave. Then I got used to it. (Abdelmajid M., El Oued, March 2012)

For their part, the Parisian police cracked down on the places where immigrants lived, undertaking commando operations designed to flush out individual militants and engaging in large-scale repression, of which the bloody suppression of a demonstration on October 17, 1961, is the most infamous example.[20] The French state also stepped in, however, to manage its migrants in the guise of welfare assistance, launching a slum clearance policy and engaging a specialist construction firm—Sonacotral—to build and administer workers' hostels.[21] In actual fact, this "social policy" only exacerbated state intrusion via the brutal demolition of parts of the slums, accompanied by the suppression of any attempt to improve the shacks.

Rehousing was sudden and authoritarian: the men were put into hostels and families put into transit camps where men, women, and children were most often kept apart.

The fact that the chain migration began in this dual context of colonization and the fight for independence challenges the classic understanding of transnationalism. As suggested by Roger Waldinger and Nancy Green in the Introduction to this volume, a distinction must be made between state and nation. The Souafas of 1947 moved within an administratively unified territory and were French citizens. In France, they insisted on their right to equal treatment and to state protection, most notably their right to the newly constructed social housing (Habitation à Loyer Modéré, HLM).[22] The contradiction inherent in colonial policy remained, however. In practice, the FMAs were treated as second-class citizens, excluded from French society (for instance, the companies that built the housing projects into which the working class moved during these years wanted nothing to do with them). The war only strengthened this colonial split, of two nations within one state, one of which was fighting for its independence. In that fight, moreover, the combatants discovered a certain number of very specific resources within the émigré community. As elsewhere in the history of decolonization, support for the anticolonial cause came also from Algerians living within the metropole itself.

For one thing, pro-independence nationalism for Algeria developed initially in the metropole between the wars, thanks to Messali Hadj. At the same time, many fighters who wanted to join the fight in Algeria opted to emigrate to the metropole instead, as was recounted to us by certain Mujahideen (former revolutionary fighters) from the Souf area (which was not in fact a very militant region). The émigré community would be central in funding the national liberation movement by transferring vast amounts of money with the help of French citizens.

The bulk of émigrés from the 1950s were, nevertheless, in a peculiar situation. The FLN battle was under way in Algeria itself and its support bases were in North Africa rather than in France. The establishment of the FLN within the émigré community seemed like a victory. Its activities relied on a growing number of militants. In the Pâquerettes slum, several Souafas acted as go-betweens, helping particularly in collecting funds, and no one there doubted the justice of the national cause: the behavior and excesses of the hated Harkis, Algerian soldiers loyal to the French, made the imperative of independence clearer every day. After independence in 1962, no one would retain their French nationality. Brahim Y., for example, who worked at the Nanterre mayor's office, said he would rather have lost his job with the local authorities than remain French, although he was nonetheless kept on, albeit in a less-skilled job.

However, from several informants' statements it seems that the FLN was more feared than loved: "we paid the tax like everyone else"; "on October 17, everyone had to turn up, there was no choice." The FLN's rules were uncompromising and sought to control migrants suspected of indiscipline: drinkers, like those who refused to pay the tax, were executed in cold blood.

If independence made it possible to end any ambiguity about the political border dividing the two groups, it only raised tensions for migrants over identity issues. On the one hand, emigrants would become an object of lasting suspicion to the Algerian state, where, once in power, the FLN would barely acknowledge the role that the émigré community had played in the "National Revolution." On the other hand, allegiance to the ex-colonial power through naturalization seemed impossible.

Local Identity

Even so, the statements of Souafa migrants in Nanterre show that their lived experience extended beyond the single issue of citizenship. They speak of the community, strengthened in these difficult years by the usual practices of solidarity and certain resources specific to the district of Nanterre. As in Tunis, the previous destination of migration, community life was organized on the basis of family connections, the lynchpin of solidarity in this society of extended families, where siblings often lived together. Newcomers were made welcome and were helped to become familiar with the local environment: the "Quatre Chemins" food market was where the men congregated, the health center was for the women, and school for the children. In this world of ex-colonized unskilled labor, identity merged with employee status ("I'm proud I worked all my life and my boss thought well of me"). Self-employment seemed out of the question, and the few who were self-employed (butchers, grocers) never went outside the slum. With community resources so weak, it was hard to manage without local assistance. Christian organizations looked after the children. The mayor of Nanterre, a communist and therefore opposed to the Gaullist authorities who were waging war in Algeria and engaged in repression in France, was viewed as a friend.

> He did everything he could for the immigrants. He would let us know when there was going to be a police raid. He let families eat free in the canteens when they couldn't afford to pay, etc. (Azzedine R., arrived in the slum at age 11)

As a result of becoming part of local life in this way, a feeling of having found another "home" emerged, conveyed in our interviews through lively memories, heard particularly from those whose childhood was spent in the slums. Independence led to a wave of return migration, especially of militant single men, a few of whom would re-emigrate some years later. The majority, however, remained in Nanterre where the community continued to grow.

"A Social Field between the Place of Origin and the Place of Settlement"? Between the Souf Area and Nanterre (1962–1970)

This period seemed to favor the flourishing of an autonomous migration field to which the classic advocates of "transnationalism" have drawn attention.[23] Peace had been restored and the economic boom increased demand for immigrant labor in France, with full employment and rising wages. The Souafas already occupied a busy area within the most dynamic part of the country, the Paris region. Even so, they had to reconcile themselves to the new relationship between Algeria, of which they were citizens and which stood for the dignity of independence, and France, where they were henceforth aliens. However, the colonial past, which weighed upon both states and societies, now curtailed the migrants' room for maneuver.

Postcolonial Times: Between Two States

The Evian Agreements, which set the terms for independence in March 1962, retained freedom of movement between Algeria and France. Algerian immigrants thereby maintained their privileged position of unconditional access to French territory and its workers' social rights.[24] Though independence triggered a sizable influx, restrictions set in early. The first, occurring in 1964, took the form of agreements between France and the new state of Algeria, which set quotas for the number of workers to arrive each year and sought to curb the arrival of families by increasing restrictions on housing.[25] Other measures were to follow, such as the 10-year resident card introduced in 1968—which was a step backward for the Algerians, who had not needed a resident card before.[26] While the number of migrants subsequently varied, there was henceforth a marked decrease in the number of families arriving. The last Souafa families in our survey arrived in Nanterre in 1964.

Neither of the two states actually wanted massive migration. On the French side, losing the war had increased the authorities' rejection of Algerians: already little accepted when they were French citizens, they were now undesirables, who, it was feared, would become a fixture. While steps were taken to encourage the arrival of other foreigners, notably the

Portuguese and Moroccans, an overwhelming majority of administrative archival documents attest to a discourse clearly marking rejection of Algerians.[27] The colonial past was also a heavy burden for the new Algerian state, jealous of its prerogatives and suspicious of the emigrants. On the one hand, it had to assert its authority in the face of the former colonial power. On the other, it sought to monitor the émigrés, for whom presence on French soil could mean greater freedom. Looking unkindly on the emigrants when they decided to settle in France after independence had been secured, the FLN authorities took part in the restrictive policy sought by France on the condition that the new Algerian state could monitor departures (through the Office National Algérien de la Main-d'œuvre, ONAMO). Similarly, Algeria agreed to restrict family emigration, preferring instead single workers who would send money back to Algeria and who, ideally, would return themselves. In France, Algeria charged the consulates and a migrants' organization, which it totally controlled—the Amicale des Algériens en Europe—with keeping an eye on the migrants. Our informants said little about this organization but it is notable that no independent community organizations were created. To be sure, French legislation prior to 1981 made it difficult for foreigners to set up their own legal organizations (police permission was required), but it is unlikely that the initiative would have been encouraged by the ruling FLN. For the Souafas, this led to an increasingly larger gap between their attachment to the Algerian nation and their disappointment with the Algerian state whose policies did not match their expectations. During this time of full employment and relative freedom of movement, the lives of families and workers were focused on the bipolar territory between the Souf area and Nanterre.

Two Models of Migration

In general, two models of traveling to and from the Souf area coexisted.

Temporary Migration. Temporary male workers were the most numerous. Mostly married, they left their families behind, living in the hostels set up by Sonacotral during the Algerian war (see earlier discussion). Rebaptized as Sonacotra, these hostels were found all over France, where they were open to immigrant workers of all types and became the standard accommodation for temporary immigrants. Sociologists in the 1970s condemned them as emblematic of capitalist exploitation and neocolonialist domination. The hostel managers were usually ex-military personnel who had served in Algeria.[28] While some of the former migrants whom we interviewed felt lost and uprooted during their years of residence in these hostels (Abdelaziz H., born in 1931, single, no returns between 1957 and 1972), the surprise finding of the survey was that for many people this way of life was a conscious choice. Laïche R. (born in 1937) initially spent five years in the slum between 1959 and 1963. From his second stay onward, which began in 1964, he lived in hostels in Gennevilliers and then in Colombes (two poor Paris suburbs near Nanterre). He married in 1967, but left his wife behind in Algeria, returning yearly for one- to two-month visits there. He ran a butcher's shop with his cousin rather than working as a bricklayer, which allowed him to buy a car in 1970 that he used to drive to El Oued. As of 1993–1994, Laïche R. started work on extending his parents' home there, and ever since retiring in 2003, after several years of unemployment in France, he has been living in El Oued with his wife and the family of one of his sons.

These men present a 1960s Algerian version of the migrant who lives a double life, a figure that has existed as long as mass migration has existed. Its originality was that they did so by fitting themselves into the mold of the "temporary migrant worker" needed by the host country. Employers agreed to lengthy stays in the home country in return for greater flexibility and lack of promotion. No doubt embellished through memory, this life, divided between the family in the Souf area and the hostel in the Paris suburb, appears to have satisfied contradictory desires: the desire to "live my own life" (the interviewees talked fairly freely about going out, alcohol, and women) while observing traditional strictures: "Children raised in France don't respect their parents any more"; "I didn't bring my family over because I was afraid I wouldn't be able to control them." It was a man's choice, adapted to the cultural habits still prevalent in the Souf region, where men and women lead separate lives. The women were scarcely given the opportunity to express their views but it would appear that not all of them wanted to emigrate.[29]

Families at the Center of the Settlement Process. The history of the families is reminiscent of the classical first stage of settlement, in which there is a dream of return even as the process of putting down roots appears to be becoming inevitable. The desert and domes of the Souf area lived on as the migrants' imagined community, although they began investing in their life in France, in and around Nanterre. This is the story told by Brahim Benaïcha in the book and later movie, *Vivre au paradis.*[30] Many of the families we met had links to the Benaïcha family and shared a similar experience: a common past in Tunisia, a lengthy time in a slum in Paris, and a sojourn just as long in a transit camp (many in the Port District camp in Gennevilliers)[31] before becoming comparatively spread out in French housing projects from the 1970s onward. The Nanterre pole was always centered on the slum. Clearance took some time, but the Souafas' territory already spread outward to the nearby working-class suburbs that were home to the main Sonacotra hostels and transit camps where many families lived after the clearance (Gennevilliers, Colombes, Argenteuil).

Mohamed L. O. (born in 1932) arrived at 7, rue Dequeant, in 1956. He stayed for periods of six months until 1963. Then he came back with his wife, whom he had married in 1956, and had his first son. They lived in the slum until 1968. They were rehoused, first in the Port District camp in Gennevilliers, then in an HLM in Nanterre in 1971. In 1963, he found work with Aérospatiale, where he drove lifting equipment, and stayed there until he retired—he is extremely proud of that fact. His wife died in 1977 while giving birth to twin daughters, leaving him with five children. He got married again very quickly to a woman who came to Nanterre and with whom he went on to have five more children, though the marriage was unhappy and the couple divorced. As of the interview, Mohamed L. O. owned his own apartment in Nanterre, where one of his sons lives. Mohamed L. O. himself had returned to the Souf shortly after retiring in 1995.

Connections with the Souf region conformed to the type of migratory pattern linking the two poles, home and host, of a chain, with social relations and identities extending from and shared by place of destination and origin: temporary accommodation for workers and relatives in France, remittances sent home (although the amount was limited by having to meet the needs of very large families in France), and holiday visits to the Souf region for those who could afford them. At the local level, the group was bound together by helpful support networks (fetching water, helping one another with the children, and so forth) and by celebrations (circumcision, Eid festivities). Acculturation in France merged with putting down roots "among themselves" in Nanterre. The men lived their own lives between their sometimes distant places of work and the cafés. The women's horizons were more open (even though not all girls were allowed to stay on at school if it meant traveling too far). Dressed "à la française" (this was the time of the miniskirt), some of these women were changing. At the time, there was a great desire for migrants from Algeria to appropriate the host society's cultural codes, which were disseminated on the televisions that had penetrated into the shacks in the slum. Husbands were observed buying their wives fashionable clothes, although this was obviously far removed from the fundamentalism that continued to dominate in the Souf area ("the full veil for married women, with just a little gap to see through," recounts Zohra M.).[32]

Nevertheless, these changes did not entail genuine entry into the surrounding society. The establishment of these families ran counter to France's vision, which wanted them to return home. As a result, despite an enduring illusion regarding the benevolence of the Nanterre municipality, the latter arranged things so as to avoid permanently rehousing the Algerians. The transit camps where they awaited social housing turned into ghettos. Within the school system, even the best students were systematically channeled into vocational subjects, which many resented as discrimination. Their fathers' working lives were punctuated by unacknowledged workplace accidents and, however long their employment, they remained stuck with lower status and lower pay.[33] What was at play here was the status of the excluded and the dominated that affects former colonized people. The history of migration was still young, however (only 15 years or so), and hope remained as long as full employment persisted.

At the same time, relations with the oasis of origin were complex. Geographical distance meant that visits were few. Within Algeria, the Souf area remained neglected, scarcely affected by change and gripped by a serious agricultural crisis linked to variations in the water table. The migrants seemed far removed from this situation, giving the impression of having been separated from their point of departure. Although religious brotherhoods were prevalent in the Souf area, they did not give rise to any particular religious organization among the immigrants. The weight of tradition might have been crushing, but it was transmitted within families.

> I didn't know Guemar, but Guemar was very present in my life. My uncles used to write to my father: "You must stop making Zohra study. Nothing good comes of girls studying." (Zohra, now a sociology graduate, Nanterre, Feb. 20, 2012)

At this time, perhaps the best period for Nanterre's Souf area migrants, the workers and their families felt they had great freedom of choice, and their incomes had improved. Their status as former colonized but legal foreigners in France offered some advantages in the 1960s, particularly access to family allowances, health care, and education, of which many illegal aliens were deprived. Even if the Algerian state offered more restrictions than support, its existence had priceless symbolic significance for these formerly colonized individuals. Émigré life was able to be organized between the two poles of their existence, and one can conclude that a sort of optimal resource management enabled a genuine migration success story. Thus the immigrants' struggle to free themselves of state constraints yielded positive results. Nonetheless, they did not belong to either of the two societies upon which they were dependent. This was particularly true of families. Subject to growing difficulties if they wished to remain in France and acquire decent housing, the immigrants continued to live apart although they had long been genuine residents of the suburbs. The authorities persistently rejected their housing demands, arguing the anti-Arab racism of a portion of the French population. Keeping a low profile, our informants frequently denied that anti-Arab racism existed at the time. Yet that sentiment exploded in 1970 in a wave of attacks that killed several Algerians. The antiracist movement only grew from that period on, with immigrants becoming a public issue, focusing on Algerians in particular. The Algerian state protested and decided to suspend emigration in September 1973. In reality, it was afraid of the Mouvement des Travailleurs Arabes, a protest movement led by Maghreb students close to the French far left.[34]

As long as growth continued, workers in hostels or in families continued their careers, negotiating disadvantages as best they could and hoping for better days. The closure of the borders put an end to their illusions.

Border Closure: Transnational Transit Undermined (1974–2000)

The Shock of Altered Circumstances

Like most of its European neighbors, France suspended immigration in 1974 immediately after the first oil crisis. This change of circumstance affected all of Europe's immigrants. They would have to face a future marked by the end of full employment and ever more radical border closures. For everyone, it was time to ask the question that had been put off during previous decades: that of the end of migration, of return to the country of origin, or of settling down for good, or even applying for citizenship. The European immigration states endeavored to establish policies of return. In France, this was an opportunity for new measures that discriminated against the Algerians, who were the target of a program of forced returns. The plan, which was originally envisaged in 1977 and negotiated with Algeria,[35] led nowhere but fed into the climate of rising xenophobia in France at the time. Anti-Arab racism forced its way into public opinion in the 1980s with the rise of the Front National.[36]

To the Algerians, these developments came as a wakeup call. The issue of permanent settlement had arisen at the very moment that Algerian migrants realized just how rejected they were. The Souf area survey of people who had returned to Algeria was very enlightening on this point. Little by little, racism and unemployment transformed the way the migrant workers perceived France, making the 1980s and 1990s the decades in which their life stories appeared to unravel. The men, proud of their identity as immigrant workers, were plunged into another life, its story marked by periods of joblessness, precarious employment, reluctant employers, and growing resentment. Refusals to hire were seen as discrimination.[37] These experiences were all made worse by family breakdown. Access to HLM social housing as a long-awaited achievement often coincided with personal tragedy: divorce or children who turned to crime or died of AIDS. Mohamed O.'s upward mobility broke down when he fell out with his second wife who divorced him, with the result that he was forced to leave his HLM flat and live for a while in a hostel. Several of our informants went back to Algeria after a similar family breakup.[38]

Returns and Ruptures

These deteriorating circumstances led to a significant wave of spontaneous returns in the 1980s and 1990s: 25 people, i.e., more than half of our respondents, left France in those decades. Pensioners excepted, these returns sound like ruptures. Even pensioners, who would draw pensions that offered better terms, were forced to return early because of the context of unemployment. According to our interviews, returns took several patterns. Like Mohamed O., just described above, some men left France after a family breakup. Some married again, had more children, and tried to set up a business in Algeria. Other re-emigrants were young adults, like El Hadj Mohamed L., who came to France in 1958 at the age of seven. "Put off by the rejection [he] felt and the difficulty of working," he surrendered his resident card in 1977. Some of the people in this group said they had felt discriminated against since their schooldays. Some families also returned to Algeria, like Mansoura and her husband, because "they were afraid for their children." But two of their daughters ran away. Today, all of their children are in France and Mansoura must endure the cloistered life of a widow in the Souf area.

Many people found going back difficult. Immigration had created a divide between the host society and the homeland. The gap was deepened at the cultural level with the rise of Islamism in Algeria and the civil war period of the 1990s, known there as "the black decade." El Oued was one of the first hotbeds of Islamist agitation and saw an increase in fundamentalism, which was already widespread. This development owed nothing to emigration and showed the extent to which the emigrants were not part of the processes of change in the region. Shortly afterward, the region underwent economic modernization as a result of internal factors unrelated to the emigrants themselves. Only in the private sphere did their personal practices bring about some change (such as when former emigrants installed French-style lavatories in their homes). For women used to living in France, the norms of this society have been hard to bear—and for a good many men as well—with regard to alcohol abstinence or religious observance, for example. In this way, the Nanterre returnees living in El Oued form a group apart.

Some of the group, moreover, suffered from the breakdown of chain migration since travel was seriously impeded. In France and subsequently in the European Schengen space, the policy of border closure policies intensified. After the Islamist attacks of 1985–1986, visas became mandatory. From then on, the route to France was closed for all those without the minimum social capital needed to overcome these constraints. For former migrants, opportunities to travel freely remained but they had to have a resident permit, a pensioner's I.D. card (since 1998) or dual nationality. The material conditions for transnationality were severely curtailed, a context that nonetheless privileged pensioners, as we shall now see.[39]

The "Chibanis," Retirees in France and Algeria

Most of the retirees whom we interviewed in the Souf Valley area spend part of the year in France. Some stay with children who sometimes live in their parents' old flat, which they have either bought or rent. Many have a room in their old hostel. French law has gradually if belatedly taken the situation of these pensioners into account. Here too, Algerians would appear to be favored. In October 1980, France and Algeria signed an agreement covering pensions and enabling Algerians to draw their pensions in Algeria. In order to travel, they could just use their retiree I.D. card, which has required no visa since the 1998 Chevènement law.[40] In reality, of course, things are not so simple. Red tape and ill will from the banks and the authorities in Algeria mean that pensions are drawn in France. To do so, one must have a resident card, and to have a resident card, one must spend half the year in France. Recently, administrative pressure has been growing and tolerance waning, as the price of renting rooms rises and tension over resident cards has increased. Very many retirees also have long-term illnesses, however, which justify treatment in France. A great deal has been written about the punishing life of these Chibanis,[41] condemned to travel back and forth or abandoned in hostels. In reality, these men, shaped by their movement as migrants, need this breathing space:

"Why not stay in Guemar for good?
    "You never know what might happen. You have to keep the connection, the papers. And then, I've spent nearly all my life over there." (Mahmoud G.)

Meeting up with friends, returning to the atmosphere of Nanterre and the hostel, allows migrants to escape the pressures of local life in Algeria and a political "incompetence" many of them find irritating. Many have a comfortable income for the Souf area. Ahmed A.'s monthly pension is the equivalent of the salary of a university lecturer of 12 years' standing.[42] The "immigrants" are both despised and envied. They show their commitment to the wave of piety gripping the region (many welcomed us wearing their traditional costume, breaking off the meeting to go and pray). Their identity may be in Algeria, but the way they manage their pensions could well be called "transnational."

Nanterre-Guemar: Binational Identity

What about those living in Nanterre? There has long been something shameful about having French citizenship. Children born in France after 1962 (and there were many of them, as we have seen) automatically had French nationality by double jus soli.[43] For many, the question of which country's citizenship they held was obscure. They did not really know whether they were French or not, and applying for citizenship was a problem, resolved only during the unrest of Algeria's "black decade" of the 1990s. "Afterwards, everyone applied for citizenship" (Hakim H. became a French citizen in 1998). The uncertain future of the "longed-for" homeland and the cost of travel (the number of French visas halved in the 1990s) brought home to the Souafa residents of Nanterre that their place was in France. Postcolonial history was turning a page.

It was within this circle of people who had spent their childhood in the slums of Nanterre that a new dimension of social territory emerged, that of memory. This is a specific group that is well integrated locally (several hold local office or teach) and encountered a favorable environment while growing up. The memory of the migrations has played an important role in France since the end of the 1980s, particularly in local life. The takeoff of interest in memory was, in particular, the 1992 publication of Brahim Benaïcha's book, *Vivre au Paradis. D'une oasis à un bidonville*. In it, the author, now an accountant, tells the story of growing up in the slum of Les Pâquerettes. The book was followed by a film in 1999 (Bourlem Guerjou, *Vivre au Paradis*). Subsequently, Nanterre's local government, in association with the author and his friends, raised the idea of creating a partnership with the Souf area. In 2003, the mayor of Nanterre (who had gone to school in Les Pâquerettes) went to Guemar to open a fountain in the commune's main street. The very same fountain had supplied water in the French slum and was donated by the Nanterre history society. Since the 2000s, the slums and Algerian immigration have been the focus of intense commemorative activity in the community, spearheaded by a movement that also operates at a national level.[44] Collaboration on certain (environmental) projects was meant to follow, taken to Guemar by a group of officials close to the former Nanterre mayor who was Brahim Benaïcha's cousin. The Nanterre-Guemar Association was subsequently set up on the French side, which is where our oral history project got its start. In this way, the history of the Souafas in Nanterre acquired an emblematic dimension.

This is reminiscent of the process of Italian immigration described in François Cavanna's book, *Les Ritals*, about his childhood in rue Sainte-Anne and the life of the Val Nure Italian community in Nogent.[45] The book gave rise to a TV film and led to favorable political statements by local authorities and also to historical research. Ultimately, the Nogent community space became a symbol of Italian immigration. The local identities that are the issue in both cases recall the similarities of the migrant experience within chain migration. In the Italians' case, this *renaissance identitaire* was accompanied by an intense renewal of contacts between the valley they left behind and Nogent.

Difficulties specific to Algerian history complicate the memorial endeavor, however. In the Souf area, our survey was very popular among ex-migrants, but the authorities were split over its merits. Our joint work was suddenly called off by Guemar's new mayor, and interest waned at El Oued University. Emigration is not a subject of research in Algeria and history is taught exclusively in Arabic. This partial failure could be interpreted as the lack of a "transnational" social space capable of giving physical consistency to the emotional ties of those in "the memory business." In addition to the lack of political will in Algeria, we think, given our informants' accounts, that visits there by Nanterre Souafas are less frequent than in the past, particularly due to shifts in gendered practices. Women, whether openly breaking away, like one woman named Djema (renamed Laure), do not go to visit, claiming a lack of interest. "My wife doesn't have family any more. She doesn't know what she'd be doing over there," Hakim H. explained. He went on to say that he had never taken his daughters to Guemar in order to avoid having to face the pressure of multiple marriage requests (one of the rare ways Algerians emigrate today).

We should add that there is a difference between emigrating to Nanterre and running a business back home. Migrants' money, classically, went into building or renovating houses in Algeria, opening a small local business, and, above all, sustaining large families there. In France, many emigrants' children worked as civil servants, social workers, local government employees, and teachers. The Souafas, meanwhile, were renowned for their success in retail. When we were in Algeria, we met heads of businesses who testified to that. They spoke perfect French and moved unhindered within their international networks. They had never truly re-emigrated.

New Mobilities

Even if no one can imagine the future of the connections forged between places and families, it seems that the story of the Souafas in Nanterre is now a thing of the past. Emigration to France is slowing down, occurring only in a few rare marriages. Other forms of migration are taking its place and things are changing in the field of migration from the Maghreb. Algerian writers are producing abundant research into "the new migrations." Émigrés from today's Algeria are young urban graduates, including many women, whose emigration is accepted even in working-class communities.[46] The profile of the new migrants, common to all of Africa, seems like a break with the past. They fall roughly into three groups. The minority, who receive the most attention, are those with real commitment to countries in need of bright minds and skills. Our informants told us that young people emigrating from the Souf area today no longer go to France but to "completely different places." Research in Algiers suggests that these destinations are the United States, Canada, and the United Kingdom. This is quite new, because previously Algerian emigration—unlike that of the Moroccans—had headed only to France. Emigration by the other two groups—students and those who try their luck as illegal migrants, the *harragas*, who set out from Annaba to cross the Mediterranean—is less stable. Their plans, which are just as much constrained by border closures as they are actively chosen, are both personal and transnational: now present in Spain and Italy, these migrants incorporate the concept of traveling and re-emigrating without a preselected destination. There is no denying that new patterns are at work.

*   *   *

At the end of this journey in the company of the Souf area migrants, it appears that the interpretative framework of transnationalism applies only in part. If we question "the processes by which immigrants build social fields that link together their country of origin and their country of settlement,"[47] we may draw two conclusions. The first is that the Souafas do have a genuine independent social field. It took shape between the Souf area and Tunisia in the context of colonization, was reorganized in Nanterre against a backdrop of the war of decolonization, continued in the better days of the first decades of independence, and endured at the level of emotions and memory once the migration cycle ended. At the bilocal level, this social field stretches between the Souf area and Nanterre and displays a continuity at variance with a succession of short-term shocks. From this point of view, our research shows that the migrants' scant initiative, which had been developing against a background of freedom of movement and full employment, was

254 MARIE-CLAUDE BLANC-CHALÉARD

undermined for the foreseeable future by the suspension of labor immigration in 1974 and the end of economic growth.

Even so, we do not think this partly independent social field can be qualified as purely transnational, if we consider our project's partial findings. The "transmigrant" as initially theorized is someone whose position between two or more states permits freedom from the constraints that weigh upon ordinary nationals. The transmigrant's action is typified by an ability to invest in the country of departure, supported by strong community organization in the host country. We found nothing of this kind in the Souafas' case. On the contrary, their case shows how a back-and-forth movement that could be called "transnationalism" is, in fact, constantly constrained. The first phase of migration in the colonial period negated any transnational space in the state sense of the term. Rather, it launched a unique framework of state pressure that continued in the postcolonial period. As in colonial times, it generated a combination of control and assistance. Discrimination similarly continued, limiting the opportunities for empowerment through the creation of businesses and organizations. The birth of the independent Algerian state exacerbated the situation as it introduced controls of its own and promoted a climate of suspicion toward the émigrés.

We have remarked on the Souafas' poor ability to invest in their region of origin and their difficulties in resettling upon their return. Only one form of transnationality is practiced: that of single workers, who subsequently became pensioners, and who, at the cost of a fragmented family life at both ends of the migration chain, were able to adapt to both societies to some extent. This poor man's transnationalism, far from freeing itself from what states wanted, instead conformed to a model desired by the host as much as the home state.

No doubt colonial history does not provide all the answers as to why the Algerians' transnational activities were thus inhibited, but the unique nature of this case raises questions. In this volume, Thomas Lacroix shows that things were very different for Indians in the United Kingdom. The most telling example is that of the Moroccans: formerly colonized by the French, they came to France later than the Algerians although their numbers are now almost the same. They were, however, encouraged by their home state, and constituted a community network with diasporic ramifications as they had long been emigrating to other countries (Belgium, Germany, and more recently, the Mediterranean space and across the globe). In other work, where Thomas Lacroix also compares community projects in the departure villages of migrants of three origins—Indian (Punjabis), Moroccan (Chleuhs), and Algerian (Kabyles)—the limited nature of Kabyle investment stands out in comparison to the activism of the others.[48] Something specifically Algerian is demonstrated by the Souafas' experience. That particularity is vanishing today within the framework of new Algerian mobilities which, by putting an end to the exclusive relationship with France, mark a departure from the postcolonial era.

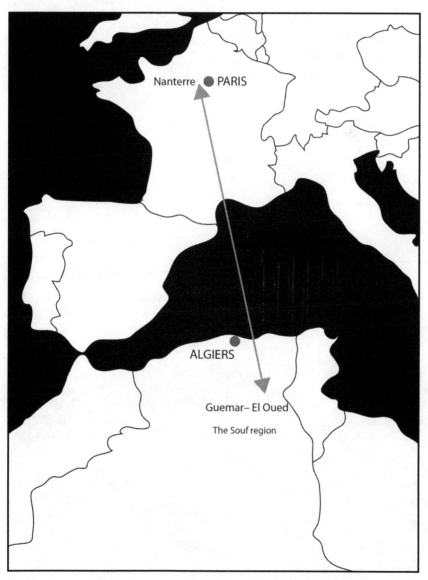

Map 1. The Nanterre/Souf area migration circuit.

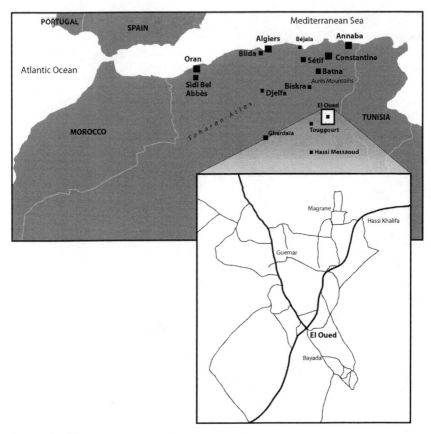

Map 2. Souf Area

NOTES

1. Algerians make up the second largest foreign population in France today. The 2007 census put their number at 475,000 in 2007, following 490,000 Portuguese, and ahead of 450,000 Morrocans.

2. This was called "administrative assimilation" in that the inhabitants of Algeria were under French administrative rule. However, the distinction between "indigènes" and "Européens" meant that social assimilation was impossible.

3. Cf. Works by P. Weil, V. Viet, A. Spire, L. Pitti, C. Hmed, S. Laurens, F. de Barros, and E. Blanchard. Cf. the author's (unpublished) habilitation thesis on "The Policy of Slum Clearance in the Paris Region" (Paris 1, 2008), and Muriel Cohen's thesis on "Algerian Families in France in the 1950s–1980s" (Paris 1, 2013). See also the recent publication of Amelia Lyons's thesis, *The Civilizing Mission in the Metropole. Algerian Families and the French Welfare State during Decolonization* (Stanford: Stanford University Press, 2013).

4. Abdelmalek Sayad, "Immigration et 'pensée d'Etat,'" *Actes de la recherche en sciences sociales*, 129 (Sept. 1999): 5–14.

5. We encountered difficulties with sources for Algeria as its archives are hard to access.

6. The project was supported by the municipality of Nanterre, the "Nanterre-Guemar" Migrants' Association, and the University of El Oued in Algeria. We put together a filmed oral record. The interviews were carried out by a team of historians, sociologists, and film students. They took place in both French and Arabic. The informants were chosen by word of mouth in Nanterre, through the Guemar tourist board, and via the El Oued Mujahideen Association (war veterans from the war of independence). First-generation migrants accounted for two-thirds of the corpus. There were only five women, four of them from the second generation. The life stories we gathered were concentrated on the slum experience.

7. People from the Souf area are called "Souafas" ("Soufi" in the singular, not to be confused with the Muslim sect). Most of our informants are from Guemar and call themselves "Guemaris."

8. According to demographer Kamel Kateb, who first stressed its significance, the early Algerian migrations to Tunisia, Morocco, and Syria were a kind of resistance to French occupation and a rejection of non-Muslim authorities. He does not mention ulterior economic incentives, although these were decisive. Kamel Kateb, *Européens, "indigènes" et Juifs en Algérie (1830–1962)* (Paris: INED, cahier 45, 2001).

9. Jamel Haggui, "Les Algériens originaires du Sud dans la ville de Tunis à l'époque coloniale (1881–1956): Mozabites, Souafas et Ouarglias," diplôme d'études avancés, 2004, Université de Manouba, Tunis; Claude Bataillon, *Le Souf, étude de géographie humaine*, DES, Université d'Alger, Institut de recherches sahariennes, 1953, chapter IX, "L'émigration."

10. Brahim Benaïcha, *Vivre au Paradis. D'une oasis à un bidonville* (Paris: Editions du Sable d'or, 2005), 39 (1st ed. Brussels: Desclée de Brouwer, 1992), note 17.

11. El Oued, the capital, only became the seat of the military administration in 1930.

12. This is clear both from our research and from the rare studies that discuss the history of mobility in the El Oued region—a remote, underadministered area that was more often in contact with Tunisia than with Algiers or metropolitan France. We have found no information concerning conscription in that area during the First World War, but it is clear that there was no migration flow from that region to the metropole in the interwar years.

13. "Kabyles" are the inhabitants of Kabylie, located in the North-East of the country. They are ethnically Berbères, and they were preferred by the colonizers as against the Arabs who populate the rest of Algeria. See Neil MacMaster, *Colonial Migrants and Racism: Algerians in France, 1900–62* (Basingstone: Palgrave Macmillan, 1997).

14. In a classic article, the sociologist Abdelmayek Sayad distinguished between three "ages" of migration. The first, before World War II, was comprised of single

men, who were very mobile, and whose focus remained on their home villages. After the war, a second age consisted of once again mostly male emigrants, but this time they stayed longer periods in France. The third age is that in which entire families migrated, stabilizing the immigrants in France. This typology is more nuanced today. A. Sayad, "Les trois âges de l'immigration algérienne," *Actes de la recherche en sciences sociales*, June 1977/1, vol. 15, 59–79.

15. These quotes come from interviews with retirees in Guemar and El Oued.

16. A. Sayad also noted this among the Kabyles: "People talk only of France," "Les trois âges," reprinted in A. Sayad, *La double absence: Des illusions de l'émigré aux souffrances de l'immigré* (Paris: Seuil, 1999), 31.

17. Brahim Benaïcha, who was born in Guemar in the Souf area, arrived in Nanterre at the age of nine. He told the story of his childhood in the Pâquerettes slum in his important book *Vivre au Paradis*.

18. Emmanuel Blanchard, *La police parisienne et les Algériens, 1944–1962* (Paris: Nouveau Monde, 2011).

19. MNA = Algerian National Movement. The story of the Algerian war in France has generated an abundant literature. Cf. Mohammed Harbi and Benjamin Stora, eds. *La guerre d'Algérie 1954–2004: La fin de l'amnésie* (Paris: R. Lafont, 2004).

20. In protest against a curfew imposed on Algerians by the Paris police department, the FLN organized a large, pacifist demonstration on October 17, 1961, that included large numbers of women and children. The police responded with a violent attack that led to a fierce gun battle, men being thrown into the Seine, and mass arrests. For many years, the administration refused to admit the extent of the violence, but today the event is commemorated as a symbol of colonial repression against immigrants. Jim House and Neil MacMaster, *Paris 1961—Algerians, State Terror, and Memory* (Oxford: Oxford University Press, 2009).

21. *Sonacotral* = Société nationale de construction pour les travailleurs algériens (National Construction Company for Algerian Workers). It came into being in December 1956, under the aegis of the Interior Ministry, to improve immigrants' housing while keeping them under surveillance.

22. In France at that time, a substantial amount of collective social housing, the HLMs (Habitations à loyer modéré or low-rent housing), was built. Given the vast housing crisis, they were reserved for the French. FMA families were entitled to live there in theory. Now, these HLMs have been abandoned by the French and are largely populated by immigrant families.

23. Nina Glick Schiller, Linda Basch, Cristina Blanc-Szanton, "Transnationalism: A New Analytic Framework for Understanding Migration," in Steven Vertovec and Robin Cohen, eds., *Migration, Diaspora and Transnationalism* (Aldershot: Edward Elgar, 1999), 26–49.

24. The ambiguous status of Algerian immigrants in France in the years following independence have been well analyzed by Amelia H. Lyons, "French or Foreign? The Algerian Migrants' Status at the End of Empire (1962–1968)," *Journal of Modern European History* 12:1 (2014): 126–145. See also Todd Shepard, *The Invention of*

Decolonization: The Algerian War and the Remaking of France (Ithaca: Cornell University Press, 2006).

25. The Nekkache-Granval Agreements: a housing certificate, required by the mayor, was necessary to apply for family reunification (a measure reinforced in 1967).

26. A 10-year residence card for privileged immigrants had existed since 1945, but when it was applied to Algerians in 1968, it represented a limitation on their status, since they had previously been exempt from needing a resident card altogether.

27. In this volume, see Victor Pereira, "Portuguese Migrants and Portugal."

28. The company still exists under the name ADOMA. It still manages workers' hostels as well as accommodations for the disadvantaged.

29. The wife of Laïche R. went to France once for a month: "she didn't like it."

30. Benaïcha, *Vivre au Paradis*.

31. Transit camps (*cités de transit*) offered temporary accommodations to families leaving the slums. They presented little in the way of comfort and performed an educational function: families were supposed to spend two years there to "learn how to live." Some families stayed for 30 years!

32. Interview in Nanterre, Nov. 2012.

33. Cf. Laure Pitti, "Renault, la forteresse ouvrière à l'épreuve de la guerre d'Algérie," *Vingtième siècle*, 83, 2004; Émile Temime and Jacqueline Costa-Lascoux *Les Hommes de Renault-Billancourt, Mémoire ouvrière de l'île Seguin 1930–1992* (Paris: Éd. "Autrement," 2004).

34. It also wanted to portray itself as a champion of anticolonialism: the non-aligned countries had just held their conference in Algiers (Sept. 5–9, the suspension of emigration was announced on Sept. 19). Patrick Weil, *La France et ses étrangers* (Paris: Gallimard Folio, 2004), 101 (1st ed. Calmann-Lévy, 1991).

35. Cf. Weil, *La France et ses étrangers*.

36. The Front National (National Front) is the name of the xenophobic party that appeared on the French political scene in 1983. Led at the time by Jean-Marie Le Pen and now by his daughter, Marine, it has played a major role in disseminating a xenophobic and subsequently islamophobia mindset in France. Although it has recently won some municipal elections, it has a generally poor parliamentary showing.

37. Mohamed L. claimed that in 1977 a job center advisor at the national employment agency (ANPE) showed him a memorandum saying that people from the Maghreb should not be hired.

38. We felt there might be some significance to the number of family breakups and their concentration in time. However, from research done among Italian immigrants, it is clear that other immigrant communities also suffered from family conflicts and tragedies.

39. The director of the Guemar Museum, who was invited to take part in a one-day workshop on June 24, 2013, that was to release the findings of the survey in which he had been very much involved, was unable to acquire a visa in time to go to Nanterre.

40. The Chevènement Law, voted during the socialist government of Lioniel Jospin, eased the rules concerning immigration and notably the possibility for retirees to move back and forth. This is compulsory for the basic old-age pension and for social insurance. A. Math, "L'accès des vieux migrants aux droits sociaux: un chemin semé d'embûches," Catred website (www.catred.org), March 2009 (accessed Aug. 30, 2013).

41. The name given to retired workers from the Maghreb, living in hostels.

42. According to the university colleague who conducted the interview with me.

43. Born in France of parents who were themselves born in France (or, to be precise, in French Algeria up until 1962).

44. Particularly since the 50th anniversary of the War of Independence. A "Boulevard du 17 octobre" was opened in Nanterre in October 2012.

45. François Cavanna, *Les Ritals* (Paris: P. Belfond, 1978); cf. Pierre Milza et Marie-Claude Blanc-Chaléard, *Le Nogent des Italiens* (Paris: Éd. "Autrement," 1995).

46. Kadri Aïssa, "Générations migratoires: des paysans déracinés aux intellectuels 'diasporiques'" *NAQD* 26–27 (Autumn-Winter 2009): 127–157; Labdelaoui Hocine, "L'Algérie face à l'évolution de son émigration en France et dans le monde," *Hommes et Migrations* 1:298 (July-Aug. 2012), 23–37. See also *Hommes et Migrations*, 1:300 (Nov.-Dec. 2012), "Les nouveaux modèles migratoires en Méditerranée."

47. Glick Schiller, Basch, and Blanc-Szanton, "Transnationalism," 26.

48. Thomas Lacroix, "Transnationalisme villageois et développement: Kabyles algériens, Chleuhs marocains en France, Panjabis indiens en Grande-Bretagne," *Revue Européenne des Migrations Internationales* 28 (2012): 71–84.

CONTRIBUTORS

Houda Asal, sociologist and historian, is a postdoctoral fellow at McGill University, Montreal, and a research associate at the Maurice Halbwachs Center, École Normale Supérieure, Paris. Her doctoral thesis entitled "Se dire *arabe* au Canada. Un siècle de vie associative, entre constructions identitaires et mobilisations politiques" (École des Hautes Études en Sciences Sociales, 2011) is forthcoming. She has published several articles on migrant associations, identity construction and the political mobilization of the Arab minority in Canada, as well as on Canadian immigration policy. Her current research is on islamophobia and political mobilization around the question of Islam in France and Canada. She has participated in the E-Diasporas Atlas and is currently part of the international EODIPAR (Experience of discrimination, participation, and representation) project studying several cities.

Marie-Claude Blanc-Chaléard, historian, is emeritus professor at the Université de Paris Ouest Nanterre La Défense. She is a specialist in the relations between migrants and the city in France, and she has published extensively on the integration of Italians in the Paris region (1880–1960) and on the clearing of the slums (1950–1970), including: *Les Italiens dans l'Est parisien. Une histoire d'intégration (années 1880–1960)* (Rome: École française de Rome, 2000); *Histoire de l'immigration* (Paris: La Découverte, 2001); "Old and New Migrants in France: Italians, and Algerians," in *Paths of Integration. Migrants in Western Europe (1880–2004)*, ed. L. Lucassen, D. Feldman, and J. Oltmer (Amsterdam: Amsterdam University Press, 2006), 46–63; *Les Petites Italies dans le monde* (coed. with A. Bechelloni, B. Deschamps, M. Dreyfus, and E. Vial) (Rennes: PUR, 2007); *En finir avec les bidonvilles. Immigration et politiques du logement dans la France des trente glorieuses* (Paris: Publications de la Sorbonne, 2016).

Caroline Douki, historian, is associate professor at the University Paris-8. She also belongs to a research unit of the CNRS (National Center for Scientific Research): Institutions et Dynamiques Historiques de l'Économie et de la Société (IDHES). She was a member of the École Française de Rome (Italy) from 1993 to 1996. She specializes in the social history of modern international migrations in the Mediterranean and trans-Atlantic areas, and in the history of migration policies in the nineteenth and twentieth centuries.

David Scott FitzGerald is Theodore E. Gildred Chair in U.S.-Mexican Relations, professor of sociology, and codirector of the Center for Comparative Immigration Studies at the University of California, San Diego. He is coauthor of *Culling the Masses: The Democratic Roots of Racist Immigration Policy in the Americas* (Cambridge: Harvard University Press, 2014); author of *A Nation of Emigrants: How Mexico Manages Its Migration* (Berkeley: University of California Press, 2009), and coeditor of six books on Mexico-U.S. migration. FitzGerald's work on the politics of international migration, transnationalism, and research methodology has been published in the *American Journal of Sociology, International Migration Review, Comparative Studies in Society and History, Ethnic and Racial Studies, Qualitative Sociology, New York University Law Review, Journal of Interdisciplinary History*, and *Journal of Ethnic and Migration Studies*. His current project examines asylum policies in comparative perspective.

Nancy L. Green is professor (*directrice d'études*) of history at the École des Hautes Études en Sciences Sociales in Paris, where she is a member of the Centre de Recherches Historiques. A specialist of migration history, comparative methods, and French and American social history, her major publications include: *Ready-to-Wear and Ready-to-Work: A Century of Industry and Immigrants in Paris and New York* (Durham: Duke University Press, 1997); *Repenser les migrations* (Paris: Presses Universitaires de France, 2002); (with François Weil, eds.), *Citizenship and Those Who Leave* (Urbana: University of Illinois, 2007); (with Marie Poinsot, eds.), *Histoire de l'immigration et question coloniale en France* (Paris: La Documentation Française, 2008); and *The Other Americans in Paris: Businessmen, Countesses, Wayward Youth, 1880–1941* (Chicago: University of Chicago Press, 2014).

Madeline Y. Hsu served as the director of the Center for Asian American Studies (2006–2014) and is presently professor of history at the University of Texas at Austin. She wrote *Dreaming of Gold, Dreaming of Home: Transnationalism and Migration between the United States and South China,*

1882–1943 (Stanford: Stanford University Press, 2000), which received the 2002 Association for Asian American Studies History Book Award. She is editor of *Chinese American Transnational Politics* (Urbana: University of Illinois Press, 2010) and coeditor with Sucheng Chan of *Chinese Americans and the Politics of Culture* (Philadelphia: Temple University Press, 2008). Her second monograph, *The Good Immigrants: How the Yellow Peril Became a Model Minority* (Princeton: Princeton University Press, 2015) explores intersections between American foreign policy goals, immigration laws and practices, and shifting racial ideologies through the migration of Chinese intellectuals.

Thomas Lacroix, geographer, is CNRS (Centre national de recherche scientifique) research fellow and associate director of the research institute Migrinter at the University of Poitiers. He works on immigrant transnationalism, development, and integration with a specific focus on North Africans in France. Lacroix published *Les Réseaux Marocains du Développement* in 2005 (Paris: Presses de Sciences Po) and *Hometown Transnationalism: Long Distance Villageness among Indian Punjabis and North African Berbers* (Palgrave) in 2015.

Tony Michels is the George L. Mosse Professor of American Jewish History at the University of Wisconsin, Madison. He is the author of *A Fire in Their Hearts: Yiddish Socialists in New York* (Cambridge: Harvard University Press, 2005) and editor of *Jewish Radicals: A Documentary History* (New York: New York University Press, 2012). He is coeditor of the journal *Jewish Social Studies*.

Victor Pereira, historian, is associate professor (*maître de conférences*) at the Université de Pau et des Pays de l'Adour. His research focuses on Portuguese emigration and twentieth-century Portuguese history. He published *La Dictature de Salazar face à l'émigration. L'État portugais et ses migrants en France (1957–1974)* in 2012 (Paris: Presses de Sciences Po).

Mônica Raisa Schpun is a historian at the Centre de recherches sur le Brésil colonial et contemporain of the École des Hautes Études en Sciences Sociales in Paris, where she is the editor of the journal *Brésil(s). Sciences humaines et sociales*. She has notably published: *Justa. Aracy de Carvalho e o resgate de judeus: trocando a Alemanha nazista pelo Brasil* (Rio de Janeiro: Civilização Brasileira, 2011); a special issue of *Brésil(s)* concerning "*Tsiganes*" (ed. with M. Bordigoni), n. 2 (Nov. 2012); "Les premiers migrants juifs d'Afrique du Nord dans la France de l'après-guerre: une découverte pour les services sociaux," (*Archives juives* 45/1, 2012); *Migrações e dinâmicas* *urbanas: Brasil-França, séculos XIX–XXI* and *Migrações e dinâmicas urbanas: folclorização dos espaços, exotização das populações* (both ed. with L. Wittner; São Paulo: Alameda, forthcoming).

Roger Waldinger is distinguished professor of sociology at UCLA. He has published seven books, including *The Cross-border Connection: Immigrants, Emigrants, and their Homelands* (Cambridge: Harvard University Press, 2015) and *How the Other Half Works: Immigration and the Social Organization of Labor* (Oakland: University of California Press, 2003). Waldinger is also the author of many articles and book chapters, including "The Politics of Cross-border Engagement: Mexican Emigrants and the Mexican State," *Theory and Society* (2014); "Crossing Borders: International Migration in the New Century," *Contemporary Sociology* (2013); "Inheriting the Homeland? Intergenerational Transmission of Cross-border Ties in Migrant Families," (with Thomas Soehl), *American Journal of Sociology* (2012). A 2008 Guggenheim Fellow, Waldinger received the 2012 Distinguished Career Award from the International Migration Section of the American Sociological Association.

INDEX

historians, 1, 3, 4, 5, 28, 57, 64; critique of transnationalism, 6; on goals of Italian emigration policy, 39; on Italian return migration, 48; on transatlantic shipping prices, 36
historiography, 2, 5, 36; of Palestinian cause, 168–169; of return migration, 50–51; on U.S. immigration, 186
Hizb Ut Tahrir campaign, 223
Hobsbawm, Eric, 24, 25
Holy Ghost festivals, 71
home states. *See* sending states
hometown associations, 6, 13; Arabs in Canada, 165; development projects of, 212, 227; Indians in UK, 212, 214, 216, 223, 226–227; Mexicans in the United States, 106, 115, 119, 120; of Swedes in the United States, 106
hometown networks, 212, 220, 223
Hong Kong, 151
Honolulu, 63
housing, 137, 240, 244; conditions, 63, 247; cooperative, 197; demands, 248; French policy, 245, 247; hostels 241; restrictions, 243; social, 241, 247, 249, 258n22
Hsu, Madeline, 23, 24, 27
Huerta, Victoriano, 110, 113
Hull, Cordell, 149
Hunt, Michael, 140
Hu Shi, 142, 143, 145, 146

Iberian Peninsula, 70
Illinois, 209
imagined community: *italianità*, 38; Portuguese, 73
immigrants, definition of, 1; emigrants as, 10; incorporation of, 25; as newcomers, 17; radicals, 16; voluntary associations of, 28
immigration: Algerians in France, 236–260; Arabs in Canada, 161–184; Brazilian policy, 84–86, 92; burial in country of, 72; Canadian policies, 163, 167, 168, 174; countries of, 39, 47, 61, 62, 64, 69, 98; Egyptians in Canada, 175; in France, 77, 236, 238, 239, 251, 252; France as "unwitting country of," 64; French policy, 248; Indians in UK, 209–235; Japanese in Brazil, 86–88, 98–100; Mexicans in the United States, 106–131;

new Indian to UK, 214; in Portugal, 60; role of in Brazil, 84; Russian Jews in the United States, 185–208; supervised, 90, 101; United Kingdom policy, 211, 214; unskilled Indian, 212; U.S. policies, 107, 125, 150, 163; U.S. services, 35. *See also* family migration
immigration laws: Australian, 152; Canadian, 152, 164, 167–168, 171
immigration laws, U.S., 152; Chinese Exclusion Laws, 140; Immigration Reform and Control Act (IRCA), 112; 1965, 150; restrictions, 154n10, 187
India, 8, 12, 22, 23, 28, 69, 133, 134, 221; Ayodhia affair in, 223; communist party of, 215; development projects in, 223; development strategy of, 225; discontent in, 217, 218; emigration policy, 211, 217, 220–221, 222, 225, 229; financial crisis, 211; focus of organizations on, 220; geopolitical events, 220; immigrants' place of origin, 216; independence, 210, 211; Overseas Citizens (OCI), 225; partition, 212; politically active families, 213; Punjab as granary, 218; radical Hindu nationalists controlled from, 217; radical Hindu network, 222; remittances to, 224; Sikhs, 218, 222; ties of Indian Workers' Association outside of, 216
India League, 214; organizations linked to, 226; religious organizations in, 227
Indian diasporic policy. *See* India, emigration policy
Indian immigrants: in Brazil, 91; elite of, 219; migration history of, 211–212, 214; origins of in India, 210, 212; in UK, 13, 24
Indian organizational field, 209–235
Indian Overseas Congress, 219
Indian People's Association in North America, 217
Indians: in Brazil, 91; in the UK, 209–235
Indian Workers' Association (IWA), 16, 210, 213–214, 216, 217, 226, 228; conflict with ethnic entrepreneurs, 219–220; loss of influence, 219, 226
Institute for International Education (IIE), 146, 149
Institute for Mexicans Abroad (IME), 120

Tanzania, 214
Tarrow, Sidney, 16
tea, 134, 136
technocratic elites: China, 134; Mexico,
123, 124, 125. *See also* elite migration
technology: Brazilian need of, 100; China's
desire for western, 133, 134, 136, 139,
147; as explanation of transnationalism,
4, 6, 27, 107, 115, 125
temporary migration, 44, 47, 49, 57, 76, 85,
90, 214, 244–245, 246; seasonal, 114,
238
Teng, Emma, 138
territorialists (Jewish), 186
terrorists, suspicion of, 22, 174, 175–178
Texas, 109, 110, 113, 114
textile: industry, 100; workers, 190. *See also*
garment industry
Thatcher, Margaret, 221
Thierry, Augustin, 64
Thistlethwaite, Frank, 5
Toronto, 172, 175
Trans-Atlantic: crossing, 6, 21, 36, 44, 45,
50, 59, 61, 62, 216; isles, 65; market for
crossing, 36, 44, 45, 46; migration movements, 50; perspective, vii; relationships,
69, 70, 186, 192; space, 76; transfer of
money, 21; visits by Indian activists, 216
transborder politics (Mexican), 106–131
translator, 135, 136, 139
translocal: organizational activities, 216;
ties, 13
transnational: communities, 15; connections
with far left groups, 213; dynamism, 228;
functions, 209; identity, 27; networks,
227; orientation of associations, 210,
211; perspective, 1, 2, 24; practices, 50,
58, 59, 68, 69, 71, 74, 76, 77, 78; relationships with homeland, 216; reorientation of kinship groups, 223; scope of
Italian belonging, 38; situations of Italian
migrants, 41; social field, 209; territories,
36; ties, 8, 28, 88, 210, 229; "way of
life," 73
transnationalism, 1, 4, 73, 102, 106, 108,
133, 134, 152, 153, 162, 209, 237, 241,
243, 253; from above, 58, 59–64; amid
violence, 84–105; from below, 58, 69–76,

106–107; blockages, 248, 250; causes,
102, 168–171; and Chinese modernity,
133; circuits, 106; communities, 106;
conflating history and historiography, 2;
connections, 185; continuities, 5; defined,
2–3; and formerly colonized subjects,
236, 237; global level, 229; in historical
perspective, 20; and home countries, 171,
177, 187; Indian organizational in UK,
210–235; influence of sending states on,
19–20; limits of, 253–254; links, 162,
164, 192, 210, 211; literature on, 10,
17, 56–57; and the local, 186; mobility,
153; and the national, 186; networks,
153, 237; not as reduced to discourse,
69; novelty of, 4–6, 124–125; orientation
of hometown associations, 210; political
mobilization, 124, 161, 174, 178, 186;
"poor man's," 25, 254; practices of, 162,
237, 251, 254; produced by the transnational, 2–3; questioned, 102; religious,
71–73; return migration as aspect of,
27, 50; social field, 209, 252; sporting,
73–75; study abroad, 132; technologically driven theories of, 27, 107; temporal boundaries, 6
Tres por Uno, 120
Trotsky, 199
Tsao, Y. S., 151
Tshaikovsky, Nikolai, 193
Tsinghua: College, 141, 145, 146, 148;
University, 147, 151
Tsung-kao Yieh, 148
Tunis, 238, 242
Tunisia, 239; Souafas in, 238, 245, 253
Turkey, 163
Turks in Canada, 172

Uganda, 214
Ukraine, 196
United Farm Works of America, 113
United Kingdom, 13, 26; Algerian emigra-
tion to, 253; and Arab world, 162, 166;
immigration restriction by, 214; Indian
immigrants in, 209–235; multicultural
policy of, 214, 221, 226, 227
United Nations, 169, 170, 171; Special
Committee on Palestine (UNSCOP), 170

STUDIES OF WORLD MIGRATIONS

The University of Illinois Press
is a founding member of the
Association of American University Presses.

University of Illinois Press
1325 South Oak Street
Champaign, IL 61820-6903
www.press.uillinois.edu